# THE
# SCHOOL
# MATHEMATICS
# PROJECT

REVISED
ADVANCED
MATHEMATICS

BOOK 3

CAMBRIDGE UNIVERSITY PRESS

CAMBRIDGE

LONDON   NEW YORK   MELBOURNE

Published by the Syndics of the Cambridge University Press
The Pitt Building, Trumpington Street, Cambridge CB2 1RP
Bentley House, 200 Euston Road, London NW1 2DB
32 East 57th Street, New York, NY 10022, USA
296 Beaconsfield Parade, Middle Park, Melbourne 3206, Australia

© Cambridge University Press 1968, 1970, 1978

SMP *Advanced Mathematics Books 3* and *4* first published 1968
Reprinted 1970 (metricated)
Revised and combined as SMP *Revised Advanced Mathematics Book 3* 1978

Printed in Great Britain at the University Press, Cambridge

ISBN 0 521 22012 2
(ISBN 0 521 08107 6 SMP *Advanced Mathematics Book 3*)
(ISBN 0 521 08108 4 SMP *Advanced Mathematics Book 4*)

# THE
# SCHOOL MATHEMATICS PROJECT

When the SMP was founded in 1961, its main objective was to devise radically new secondary-school mathematics courses (and corresponding GCE and CSE syllabuses) to reflect, more adequately than did the traditional syllabuses, the up-to-date nature and usages of mathematics.

This objective has now been realized. SMP *Books 1–5* form a five-year course to the O-level examination 'SMP Mathematics'. *Books 3T, 4* and *5* give a three-year course to the same O-level examination (the earlier *Books T* and *T4* being now regarded as obsolete). *Revised Advanced Mathematics Books 1, 2* and *3* cover the syllabus for the A-level examination 'SMP Mathematics', replacing *Advanced Mathematics Books 1–4*. Five shorter texts cover the material of the various sections of the A-level examination 'SMP Further Mathematics'. There are two books for 'SMP Additional Mathematics' at O-level. All the SMP GCE examinations are available to schools through any of the Examining Boards.

*Books A–H*, originally designed for non-GCE streams, cover broadly the same development of mathematics as do the first few books of the O-level series. Most CSE Boards offer appropriate examinations. In practice, this series is being used very widely across all streams of comprehensive schools, and its first seven books, followed by *Books X, Y* and *Z*, provide a course leading to the SMP O-level examination. SMP *Cards I* and *II* provide an alternative treatment of the mathematics in *Books A–D* in card form. SMP *7–13*, designed for children within that age range, began publication in 1977 with *Units 1* and *2* for the younger age groups concerned. The remaining four units are in preparation, and publication will be complete in 1980.

Teachers' Guides accompany all these series of books.

The SMP has produced many other texts, and teachers are encouraged to obtain each year from the Cambridge University Press, Bentley House, 200 Euston Road, London NW1 2DB the full list of SMP books currently available. In the same way, help and advice may always be sought by teachers from the Executive Director at the SMP Office, Westfield College, Hampstead, London NW3 7ST, from which may also be obtained the annual Reports, details of forthcoming in-service training courses and so on.

The SMP will continue to develop its research into the mathematical curriculum. The team of SMP writers, numbering some one hundred school and university mathematicians, is continually evaluating old work and preparing for new. But at the same time, the effectiveness of the SMP's future work will depend, as it always has done, on obtaining reactions from a wide variety of teachers— and also from pupils— actively concerned in the class-room. Readers of the texts can therefore send their comments to the SMP in the knowledge that they will be warmly welcomed.

The authors of the original books on whose contributions this edition is broadly based, are named in *The School Mathematics Project: the first ten years*, published by Cambridge University Press.

The *Revised Advanced Mathematics Book 3* has been produced by a team consisting of

| | | |
|---|---|---|
| W. M. Aitken | C. C. Goldsmith | P. V. Moody |
| P. G. Bowie | D. Knighton | A. T. Rogerson |
| E. A. Door | M. J. Leach | R. Webb |
| L. E. Ellis | P. G. T. Lewis | |

and edited by P. V. Moody.

Many others have helped with advice and criticism, particularly the teachers and pupils who have tested the material in draft form.

# CONTENTS

# PREFACE

This volume completes the revised SMP A-level course. It follows on directly from *Revised Advanced Mathematics Books 1* and *2*, and the general remarks made in the Prefaces to those books apply here also.

As the final book in the series, it attempts to draw together the strands of development and extend the range of applications.

Now that electronic calculators are in common use in sixth-forms and sanctioned in examinations, the burden of numerical calculations at A-level has been considerably eased and we have taken advantage of this wherever it seemed appropriate.

Once again, calculus provides much of the back-bone of the book. In Chapter 29 the logarithmic function is developed from a gap left in previous work— the need to integrate the reciprocal function. The exponential function is seen first as the inverse of the logarithmic function and then as the basis for models of growth and decay. These models provide a first introduction to differential equations which are then developed numerically in Chapter 33 and analytically in Chapter 38. Both chapters stress the applications of differential equations in a wide variety of contexts. Chapter 31 collects together the work on integration and extends the ideas to further geometrical and physical applications.

The development of probability also forms a major part of the book. Chapter 30 extends ideas of independence and repeated trials to develop the binomial probability model. Chapter 35 first introduces the ideas of expected value and standard deviation of probability models in a discrete context. Probability models for continuous variables are then discussed and the definitions of expected value and standard deviation are extended. In Chapter 39 one particular continuous probability distribution, the Normal, is studied in detail, both as a model to fit a wide variety of statistical situations with continuous variables, and as an approximation to the discrete binomial model for a large number of trials. The probability and statistics of the course is rounded off by a brief discussion of hypothesis testing.

Chapters 34 and 36 complete the mechanics of the course, covering momentum, impulse, work and energy. As before, the treatment is vectorial, and solution by drawing vector diagrams to scale is encouraged.

The need for complex numbers was seen much earlier, in Chapter 19. In Chapter 32 we extend the previous work on polynomial equations to include complex roots. We also look at the geometry of complex numbers and point out isomorphisms with vectors and transformations. Chapter 37, on electricity, as well as setting up a model for direct-current networks (giving an application of simultaneous linear equations), provides an immediate practical example of the use of complex numbers in alternating-current circuits, and links together previous work on waves with both vectors and complex numbers.

Finally, Chapter 40 introduces $3 \times 3$ determinants and uses them to link previous interpretations of three linear equations in three unknowns (as a set of planes in Chapter 21 and as a transformation in three-dimensional space in Chapter 26). The material of this chapter is not in the A-level syllabus.

The needs of pupils preparing for A-level examinations are provided for by two extended sets of revision exercises at the back of the book, as well as the usual revision exercises to each chapter. One set consists of five revision papers with ten short questions in each, on a balanced range of topics; the other has a series of longer questions arranged under broad topic headings.

Finally there are project exercises which, like the miscellaneous exercises at the end of each chapter, are designed to stimulate those who have absorbed the main ideas of the course quickly. Their themes, like those in the previous books, are on the fringe of the syllabus, and they provide the opportunity for more open-ended work.

Once again we record our thanks to the editorial staff and printers of the Cambridge University Press for the speed and efficiency with which this book has been published.

We also thank the Oxford and Cambridge Schools Examination Board for permission to reproduce questions set in the SMP A-level examinations. (These questions are marked (OC).)

# GLOSSARY OF SYMBOLS

Additional to those in earlier books

## CALCULUS

| | |
|---|---|
| $\ln a$ | Natural logarithm of $a$; $\displaystyle\int_1^a \frac{1}{x}\,dx$ |
| $e$ | Base of natural logarithms |
| $\exp x$ | Alternative notation for $e^x$ |

## ALGEBRA

| | |
|---|---|
| $z$ | Complex number $z = x + jy$ <br> $\qquad = r(\cos\theta + j\sin\theta)$ <br> $\qquad = [r, \theta]$ |
| $z^*$ | Conjugate of $z$: $z^* = x - jy$ <br> $\qquad = [r, -\theta]$ |
| $\|z\|$ | Modulus of $z$: $\|z\| = r = \sqrt{(x^2 + y^2)}$ |
| $\arg z$ | Argument of $z$: the angle $\theta$ in $z = [r, \theta]$ |
| $\begin{vmatrix} a & b \\ c & d \end{vmatrix}$ | Determinant of matrix $\begin{pmatrix} a & b \\ c & d \end{pmatrix} = ad - bc$ |
| $\det \mathbf{A}$ | Determinant of matrix $\mathbf{A}$ |

## SETS

| | |
|---|---|
| $\mathbb{C}$ | The set of complex numbers |

## PROBABILITY

| | |
|---|---|
| $\dbinom{n}{i}$ | Binomial coefficient $= \dfrac{n!}{i!(n-i)!}$ <br> also the number of subsets size $i$ contained in a set of $n$ elements |
| $p_i$ | Probability of $i$ successes in a sequence of trials (also written $p(i)$) |
| $p(x_i)$ | Probability of the outcome $x_i$ |
| $\phi(x)$ | Probability density function; $p(a \leq x \leq b) = \displaystyle\int_a^b \phi(x)\,dx$ |
| $\Phi(X)$ | Cumulative probability $p(x \leq X) = \displaystyle\int_{-\infty}^X \phi(x)\,dx$ |

*Parameters of probability models*

|  |  | Discrete model | Continuous model |
|---|---|---|---|
| $\mu$ | Mean (expected value) | $\sum x_i p(x_i)$ | $\int x \phi(x)\, dx$ |
| $\sigma^2$ | Variance | $\sum x_i^2 p(x_i) - \mu^2$ | $\int x^2 \phi(x)\, dx - \mu^2$ |

## MECHANICS

| | |
|---|---|
| **I** | Impulse |
| $e$ | Coefficient of restitution |
| $W$ | Work |
| $P$ | Power |
| $\longrightarrow$ | Momentum or impulse |

## ELECTRICITY

| | |
|---|---|
| d.c. | Direct current |
| a.c. | Alternating current |
| p.d. | Potential difference |
| $Q$ | Charge |
| $V$ or $v$ | Voltage |
| $I$ or $i$ | Current |
| ⊢ | Battery, positive terminal to the left |
| ~ | A.c. source |
| $R$ | Resistor with resistance $R$ |
| $C$ | Capacitor with capacitance $C$ |
| $L$ | Inductor with inductance $L$ |

## UNITS

| | |
|---|---|
| Ns | Newton seconds |
| J | Joules |
| W | Watts |
| A | Amperes (current) |
| C | Coulombs (charge) |
| V | Volts |
| $\Omega$ | Ohms (resistance) |
| F | Farads (capacitance) |
| H | Henries (inductance) |

# 29

# LOGARITHMIC AND EXPONENTIAL FUNCTIONS

## 1. INTRODUCTION

**1.1 The gap in the pattern.** The regularity of mathematical patterns often helps us to predict new results and to show how they relate to existing ones.

Sometimes, though, patterns can mislead us; equally, they may contain surprising irregularities.

Consider the following table of derivatives:

| $f(x)$ | $f'(x)$ |
|--------|---------|
| $x^3$ | $3x^2$ |
| $x^2$ | $2x^1$ |
| $x^1$ | $1x^0$ |
| $x^0$ | $0$ |
| $x^{-1}$ | $-1x^{-2}$ |
| $x^{-2}$ | $-2x^{-3}$ |

The left-hand column consists of descending integer powers of $x$, but the right-hand column has a surprising gap:

$$x^{-1} \text{ is missing.}$$

In fact no function we have yet met has $x^{-1}$ as its derivative, or, to put it another way, we cannot yet integrate the innocent-looking function

$$f: x \to \frac{1}{x}.$$

**1.2 The area under the graph of $y = \dfrac{1}{x}$.** We first met integration in the context of evaluating the area under a graph (Chapter 10). The area under the graph of $y = f(x)$ from $x = a$ to $x = b$ is written as

$$\int_a^b f(x)\, dx = \left[ F(x) \right]_a^b$$

where $F$ is a primitive of $f$, i.e. $F' = f$.

We shall investigate the nature of the primitive $F$ for $f(x) = \dfrac{1}{x}$ by looking at areas under its graph numerically.

### *Exercise A*

**1.** (*a*) Estimate a lower bound for $\displaystyle\int_1^3 \frac{1}{x}\,dx$ by finding the area of the four shaded rectangles beneath the curve in Figure 1.

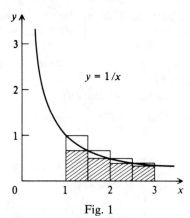

Fig. 1

(*b*) Estimate an upper bound for $\displaystyle\int_1^3 \frac{1}{x}\,dx$ by using four rectangles enclosing the curve (also shown in Figure 1).

(*c*) Calculate the mean of your answers to (*a*) and (*b*).

**2.** Repeat Question 1 for $\displaystyle\int_1^2 \frac{1}{x}\,dx$ using the two rectangles enclosing the curve and the two beneath it, as shown in Figure 1.

**3.** Use rectangles of width $0 \cdot 5$ to estimate:

(*a*) $\displaystyle\int_1^6 \frac{1}{x}\,dx$;   (*b*) $\displaystyle\int_2^4 \frac{1}{x}\,dx$;   (*c*) $\displaystyle\int_2^6 \frac{1}{x}\,dx$;   (*d*) $\displaystyle\int_1^4 \frac{1}{x}\,dx$.

In each case find the mean of the areas enclosed by and enclosing the curve.

**4.** (*a*) Do your answers to Questions 1, 2 and 3 suggest a simple relation between the values of $\displaystyle\int_1^6 \frac{1}{x}\,dx$, $\displaystyle\int_1^3 \frac{1}{x}\,dx$ and $\displaystyle\int_1^2 \frac{1}{x}\,dx$? If so, what is it?

(*b*) How do $\displaystyle\int_1^2 \frac{1}{x}\,dx$ and $\displaystyle\int_2^4 \frac{1}{x}\,dx$ seem to be related?

(*c*) How do $\displaystyle\int_1^3 \frac{1}{x}\,dx$ and $\displaystyle\int_2^6 \frac{1}{x}\,dx$ seem to be related?

(d) What about $\int_1^2 \frac{1}{x}\,dx$ and $\int_1^4 \frac{1}{x}\,dx$?

**5.** (a) Write a flow chart to repeat the process of Question 1, but with rectangles of width $h$.

(b) If you have a pocket calculator, find new estimates for $\int_1^2 \frac{1}{x}\,dx$, $\int_1^3 \frac{1}{x}\,dx$, $\int_1^4 \frac{1}{x}\,dx$ and $\int_1^6 \frac{1}{x}\,dx$ by taking $h = 0\cdot1$. Check that your conjectures in answer to Question 4 are confirmed.

(c) If you have access to a computer, translate your flow chart into a program to carry out the calculations of (b) using even thinner rectangles with $h = 0\cdot01$.

**6.** Simpson's rule for just two intervals is $A \approx \frac{1}{3}h(y_0 + 4y_1 + y_2)$ (see Figure 2).

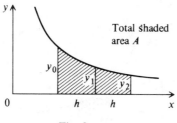

Fig. 2

(a) Use this rule to estimate: (i) $\int_1^3 \frac{1}{x}\,dx$; (ii) $\int_2^6 \frac{1}{x}\,dx$. What do you find?

(b) Use this rule to estimate $\int_1^2 \frac{1}{x}\,dx$. Deduce an estimate for $\int_1^6 \frac{1}{x}\,dx$.

**7.** Using Simpson's rule with four intervals, or a computer or calculator with the program or flow chart from Question 5, find an estimate for $\int_1^5 \frac{1}{x}\,dx$. Use it, together with your previous values, to estimate:

(a) $\int_1^{10} \frac{1}{x}\,dx$;  (b) $\int_2^{10} \frac{1}{x}\,dx$;  (c) $\int_1^{20} \frac{1}{x}\,dx$;  (d) $\int_{10}^{20} \frac{1}{x}\,dx$.

Check your answers by calculating these areas directly.

**8.** Use your flow chart or program from Question 5 to estimate the value of $a$ for which $\int_1^a \frac{1}{x}\,dx = 1$.

739

## 2. THE AREA FUNCTION

A number of interesting results emerge from our calculations in Exercise A. To study them in detail it is useful to set out a table of results correct to 3 decimal places for the area

$$F(a) = \int_1^a \frac{1}{x}\, dx$$

for integral values of $a$.

| $a$ | 1 | 2 | 3 | 4 | 5 | 6 | 7 | 8 | 9 | 10 |
|------|---|---|---|---|---|---|---|---|---|----|
| $F(a)$ | 0 | 0·693 | 1·099 | 1·386 | 1·609 | 1·792 | 1·946 | 2·079 | 2·197 | 2·303 |

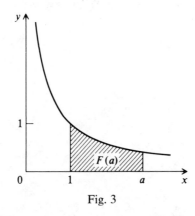

Fig. 3

Use this table to check that to 3 significant figures the following are true:

$$F(6) = F(2) + F(3);$$

$$F(8) = F(2) + F(4);$$

$$F(10) = F(2) + F(5).$$

It would seem then that in general it may be true that

$$F(ab) = F(a) + F(b).$$

Similarly check that

$$F(4) = 2F(2);$$

$$F(8) = 3F(2);$$

$$F(9) = 2F(3).$$

740

What generalization can you suggest for $F(a^n)$?

What function have you met with these properties?

If we plot the values $(a, F(a))$ from the table and join them with a smooth curve, we obtain the graph of Figure 4.

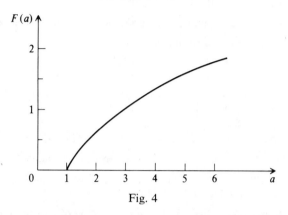

Fig. 4

**2.1 The natural logarithm.** Now, $F(ab) = F(a) + F(b)$ is the fundamental combination law of logarithms (see Chapter 8, pp. 166–8), so it seems that $F$ behaves like a logarithmic function. (This is investigated more fully in Exercise B and Section 3.1.)

You should also recognize Figure 4 as having the same shape as part of the graph of a logarithmic function (see Chapter 8, p. 165).

$\int_1^a \dfrac{1}{x}\, dx$ is called the *natural logarithm* of the number $a$ and is normally written as $\ln a$.

We shall assume for the moment that

$$\ln ab = \ln a + \ln b.$$

(The proof is given in Section 3.)

**2.2 Tables.** Values of the natural logarithm have been tabulated (see SMP *Advanced Tables, Third Edition*, p. 44). In tables, it is usual to give values of $\ln x$ only over the interval $1 \leqslant x < 10$, together with logarithms of powers of 10; natural logarithms of other numbers can be found using

$$\ln ab = \ln a + \ln b.$$

For example,                    $\ln 13 = \ln 10 + \ln 1 \cdot 3$

$$= 2 \cdot 3026 + 0 \cdot 2624$$

$$= 2 \cdot 565.$$

### Exercise B

**1.** Use the table of values of $F(a)$ in Section 2, together with the combination law of logarithms, to estimate values of:

(a) $\ln 12$;    (b) $\ln 20$;    (c) $\ln 100$;    (d) $\ln 64$;    (e) $\ln 2 \cdot 5$.

Use tables of natural logarithms and/or a calculator to check your answers.

**2.** Use tables of natural logarithms to evaluate:

(a) $\displaystyle\int_1^{2\cdot5} \frac{1}{x}\,dx$;    (b) $\displaystyle\int_1^{15} \frac{1}{x}\,dx$;    (c) $\displaystyle\int_1^{200} \frac{1}{x}\,dx$;    (d) $\displaystyle\int_3^7 \frac{1}{x}\,dx$;

(e) $\displaystyle\int_1^{0\cdot5} \frac{1}{x}\,dx$;    (f) $\displaystyle\int_1^{2\cdot5} \frac{1}{t}\,dt$;    (g) $\displaystyle\int_1^{15} \frac{1}{u}\,du$.

**3.** Verify numerically that $\ln \frac{6}{2} = \ln 6 - \ln 2$ and show in general that
$$\ln \frac{c}{a} = \ln c - \ln a \text{ can be deduced from } \ln ab = \ln a + \ln b.$$

**4.** By writing $0 \cdot 05$ as $\frac{5}{100}$, use the result of Question 3 and tables of natural logarithms to find $\ln 0 \cdot 05$. Find also (a) $\ln 0 \cdot 75$, (b) $\ln 0 \cdot 0039$.

**5.** Assuming that $\ln ab = \ln a + \ln b$, use the method of induction to prove that $\ln a^n = n \ln a$ for any natural number $n$.

**6.** Interpret $\ln 0 \cdot 6$ in terms of an area under the graph of $y = \dfrac{1}{x}$. Find its value approximately. Explain why (a) $\ln 1 = 0$, (b) $\displaystyle\int_1^b \frac{1}{x}\,dx$ is negative for $0 < b < 1$.

**7.** Assuming that $\ln ab = \ln a + \ln b$, show that $\ln \dfrac{1}{a} = -\ln a$. Use the table in Section 2 to write down values of $\ln \frac{1}{2}$, $\ln \frac{1}{4}$, $\ln \frac{1}{10}$. Copy the graph of Figure 4 and plot the three new points corresponding to these values. Sketch the graph of the function $x \to \ln x$ for $x > 0$.

**8.** (a) Apply the two-way stretch described by the matrix $\begin{pmatrix} 2 & 0 \\ 0 & \frac{1}{2} \end{pmatrix}$ to the shaded region under $y = \dfrac{1}{x}$ shown in Figure 5. (Consider the images of the four vertices and at least one other point on the curve, e.g. $(\frac{5}{3}, \frac{3}{5})$.) What is the area scale factor of this transformation?

(b) Use your result in part (a) to explain why
$$\int_1^2 \frac{1}{x}\,dx = \int_2^4 \frac{1}{x}\,dx.$$

(c) Show further that $\displaystyle\int_1^2 \frac{1}{x}\,dx = \int_4^8 \frac{1}{x}\,dx = \int_8^{16} \frac{1}{x}\,dx = \ldots$.

**9.** Use the matrix for the two-way stretch (scale factors 2 parallel to the $x$-axis and $\frac{1}{2}$ parallel to the $y$-axis) given in Question 8 to show that
$$\int_1^3 \frac{1}{x}\,dx = \int_2^6 \frac{1}{x}\,dx,$$

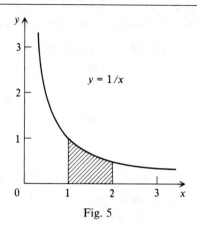

Fig. 5

and hence show that

$$\int_1^6 \frac{1}{x}\,dx = \int_1^2 \frac{1}{x}\,dx + \int_1^3 \frac{1}{x}\,dx.$$

**10.** Use a similar method to that of Questions 8 and 9 to show that

$$\int_1^{12} \frac{1}{x}\,dx = \int_1^3 \frac{1}{x}\,dx + \int_1^4 \frac{1}{x}\,dx.$$

**11.** By substituting $x = 2u$ (see Chapter 13, p. 312), show that

$$\int_2^6 \frac{1}{x}\,dx = \int_1^3 \frac{1}{u}\,du.$$

**12.** By a suitable substitution (see Question 11), show that

$$\int_3^{12} \frac{1}{x}\,dx = \int_1^4 \frac{1}{u}\,du,$$

and hence prove that

$$\int_1^{12} \frac{1}{x}\,dx = \int_1^3 \frac{1}{x}\,dx + \int_1^4 \frac{1}{x}\,dx.$$

$$\left( \text{Note that } \int_1^4 \frac{1}{x}\,dx = \int_1^4 \frac{1}{u}\,du \text{; see footnote on p. 746.} \right)$$

**13.** (a) Use a sketch graph of $y = \dfrac{1}{x}$ to show that $\ln 2 > \frac{1}{2}$.

(b) Show further that $\ln 2^n > \frac{1}{2}n$ for all natural numbers $n$ (use the result of Question 5).

(c) Deduce that $\ln 2^{-n} < -\frac{1}{2}n$ (use Question 7).

**14.** Suggest the appropriate domain for the function $x \to \ln x$. Explain why the function:

(a) is increasing;

(b) is continuous;

743

(c) tends to infinity as $x$ tends to infinity [Hint: use the results of Question 13];

(d) tends to minus infinity as $x$ tends to zero from above.

**15.** Prove that $\ln a^n = n \ln a$ for all rational $n$ by substituting $x = u^n$ in the integral

$$\int_1^{a^n} \frac{1}{x}\, dx.$$

# 3. THE NATURAL LOGARITHM

**3.1 Proof of $\ln ab = \ln a + \ln b$.** The numerical work we have done so far suggests that the natural logarithm as defined in Section 2.1 obeys the combination law of logarithms, and we have demonstrated this for special cases in Exercise B.

Our general proof here follows the lead suggested by Question 9 of that exercise. The proof is in terms of areas: we need to show

$$\int_1^{ab} \frac{1}{x}\, dx = \int_1^{a} \frac{1}{x}\, dx + \int_1^{b} \frac{1}{x}\, dx.$$

By the additive property of areas,

$$\int_1^{ab} \frac{1}{x}\, dx = \int_1^{a} \frac{1}{x}\, dx + \int_a^{ab} \frac{1}{x}\, dx,$$

so we have to show that

$$\int_1^{b} \frac{1}{x}\, dx = \int_a^{ab} \frac{1}{x}\, dx.$$

Assume for the moment that $a$ and $b$ are both greater than one: what happens if we apply the linear transformation $T$ whose matrix is $\begin{pmatrix} a & 0 \\ 0 & 1/a \end{pmatrix}$ to the region shaded in Figure 6(a)?

This transformation is the combination of a stretch with scale factor $a$ parallel to the $x$-axis and a stretch with scale factor $1/a$ parallel to the $y$-axis.

A general point $(t, 1/t)$ on the curve $y = \dfrac{1}{x}$ is mapped by $T$ onto the point $\left(at, \dfrac{1}{at}\right)$ which is also on the curve. In particular the boundary point $P\,(1, 1)$ maps to $P'\,(a, 1/a)$, and $Q\,(b, 1/b)$ maps to $Q'\,(ab, 1/ab)$.

744

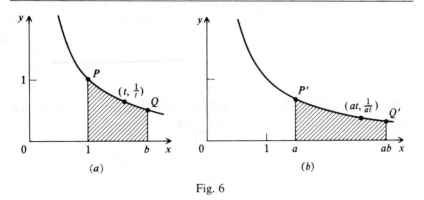

Fig. 6

Also, $(1, 0) \overset{T}{\to} (a, 0)$ and $(b, 0) \overset{T}{\to} (ab, 0)$ so that our shaded region in Figure 6($a$) with area $\int_1^b \frac{1}{x} \, dx$ is transformed by $T$ into the region shown in Figure 6($b$) with area $\int_a^{ab} \frac{1}{x} \, dx$.

But the transformation $T$ leaves areas unaltered since the area scale factor of $T$, given by the determinant of $\begin{pmatrix} a & 0 \\ 0 & 1/a \end{pmatrix}$, is $a \times \frac{1}{a} = 1$, so

$$\int_1^b \frac{1}{x} \, dx = \int_a^{ab} \frac{1}{x} \, dx.$$

**3.2** If $0 < b < 1$, the proof of the preceding section will need modification, though the result is still true. Questions 11 and 12 of Exercise B suggest an equivalent method of proof using a formal substitution in the integral rather than the explicit transformation; in fact such a method avoids the problem of $b < 1$.

## 4. THE LOGARITHMIC FUNCTION

So far we have been mainly interested in the arithmetic of areas under $y = \frac{1}{x}$. Now we look more closely at the area function itself. It has been defined as $F(a) = \ln a = \int_1^a \frac{1}{x} \, dx$. This is not a convenient notation since we normally like to write $F(x)$.

To say $\ln x = \int_1^x \frac{1}{x} \, dx$ would be confusing because we should be using the same symbol as a limit and within the integral. So we use areas under

745

$y = \dfrac{1}{t}$ instead and define

$$\ln x = \int_1^x \frac{1}{t}\, dt \quad \text{for } x > 0.†$$

The function $x \to \ln x$ so defined is a continuous mapping of the positive real numbers on to the real numbers. The graph of $y = \ln x$ is shown in Figure 7.

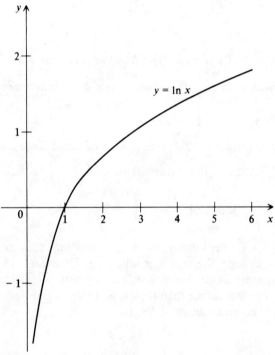

Fig. 7

**4.1  The derivative of ln x.** The fundamental theorem of analysis (Chapter 10, p. 219) tells us that integration is the inverse process of

† The symbol $x$ for the variable of integration in $\displaystyle\int_a^b f(x)\, dx$ is a 'dummy' symbol: the value of the definite integral of a given $f$ is a number depending on $a$ and $b$ alone; $\displaystyle\int_a^b f(t)\, dt$ and $\displaystyle\int_a^b f(u)\, du$ will have the same value.

differentiation. Having found that $f: x \to \dfrac{1}{x}$ has the integral function $F: x \to \ln x$, we can at once say that $x \to \ln x$ has the derived function $x \to \dfrac{1}{x}$. That is, for $x > 0$,

if $$\ln x = \int_1^x \frac{1}{t} \, dt \quad \text{then} \quad \frac{d}{dx}(\ln x) = \frac{1}{x}.$$

## 4.2 Composite functions.

The basic rules of logarithms can often be used to make differentiation of composite logarithmic functions more straightforward.

*Example* 1

Differentiate $\ln 3x$.

$$\ln 3x = \ln 3 + \ln x \implies \frac{d}{dx}(\ln 3x) = 0 + \frac{1}{x}$$

(since $\ln 3$ is a constant).

*Example* 2

Differentiate $\ln x^2$.

$$\ln x^2 = 2 \ln x \implies \frac{d}{dx}(\ln x^2) = 2 \times \frac{1}{x} = \frac{2}{x}.$$

The chain rule for differentiating composite functions can of course be used as an alternative method in these simple examples; if we put $u = x^2$ in Example 2, $\dfrac{d}{dx}(\ln x^2) = \dfrac{d}{du}(\ln u) \times \dfrac{du}{dx} = \dfrac{1}{u} \times 2x = \dfrac{1}{x^2} \times 2x = \dfrac{2}{x}$ as before.

Sometimes the chain rule is the *only* method.

*Example* 3

Differentiate $y = \ln (3x^2 + 5)$.

Putting $y = \ln u$, where $u = 3x^2 + 5$,

then $$\frac{dy}{du} = \frac{1}{u} \quad \text{and} \quad \frac{du}{dx} = 6x.$$

The chain rule states that $\dfrac{dy}{dx} = \dfrac{dy}{du} \times \dfrac{du}{dx}$

so here
$$\frac{dy}{dx} = \frac{1}{u} \times 6x = \frac{6x}{3x^2 + 5}.$$

**4.3** $\int \frac{1}{x}\,dx$ **for** $x < 0$. Since there is little difference in appearance between

$$\int_3^5 \frac{1}{x}\,dx \quad \text{and} \quad \int_{-5}^{-3} \frac{1}{x}\,dx$$

it might be thought that we could find a value for the second as easily as for the first. But we soon find that we need a different approach for the second integral. For if we say $\int_{-5}^{-3} \frac{1}{x}\,dx = \Big[\ln x\Big]_{-5}^{-3}$ we can proceed no further, since $\ln x$ is not defined for $x < 0$.

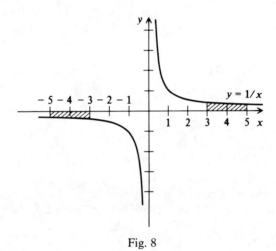

Fig. 8

Using the symmetry of the graph about the origin (see Figure 8) we can correctly write

$$\int_{-5}^{-3} \frac{1}{x}\,dx = -\int_3^5 \frac{1}{x}\,dx$$
$$= -(\ln 5 - \ln 3)$$
$$= \ln 3 - \ln 5$$
$$= \ln \tfrac{3}{5}.$$

Notice that this is $\Big[\ln |x|\Big]_{-5}^{-3}$.

748

In general we have

$$\int_a^b \frac{1}{x}\,dx = \left[\ln|x|\right]_a^b = \ln|b| - \ln|a|$$

for $a$, $b \neq 0$ *and* both positive or both negative. Figure 9 shows that any integral where $a$ and $b$ have opposite signs, like $\int_{-1}^2 \frac{1}{x}\,dx$, cannot be evaluated because it consists of two parts, both infinite in area (see Exercise B, Question 14). It is essential to sketch such integrals before attempting to evaluate them, to make sure that no attempts are made to integrate through discontinuities.

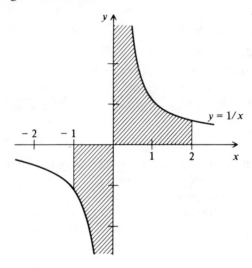

Fig. 9

For indefinite integrals, we have $\int \frac{1}{x}\,dx = \ln x + k$ if $x > 0$, $\ln(-x) + k$ if $x < 0$. That is, $\int \frac{1}{x}\,dx = \ln|x| + k$.

### Exercise C

**1.** Rewrite the following, using the basic rules of logarithms where possible, and then differentiate.

(a) $\ln 5x$;     (b) $\ln kx$;     (c) $\ln x^3$;

(d) $\ln \dfrac{1}{x}$;     (e) $\ln 5x^3$;     (f) $\ln \sqrt{x}$.

Check each part by differentiating using the chain rule.

**2.** Differentiate:

(a) $\ln(1+x^2)$;  (b) $\ln\left(\dfrac{x+1}{x}\right)$;  (c) $(\ln x)^2$;  (d) $\ln\cos x$.

**3.** Use the product or quotient rules to differentiate:

(a) $x\ln x$;  (b) $\dfrac{\ln x}{x}$;  (c) $x^2\ln 3x$;

(d) $x\ln\sin x$;  (e) $x\ln x - x$.

**4.** With the same axes, sketch the graphs of $y = \ln x$ and $y = \ln 3x$, and use them to explain why $\dfrac{d}{dx}(\ln x) = \dfrac{d}{dx}(\ln 3x)$. State two different transformations, each of which maps the first graph onto the second.

**5.** Differentiate:

(a) $\ln(1+x)$;  (b) $\ln(1+2x)$;  (c) $\ln(3+x^2)$;

(d) $\ln(4-x^3)$;  (e) $\ln\sin x$.

Use the results to write down the following integrals:

(f) $\displaystyle\int\dfrac{1}{1+x}\,dx$;  (g) $\displaystyle\int\dfrac{1}{1+2x}\,dx$;  (h) $\displaystyle\int\dfrac{2x}{3+x^2}\,dx$;

(i) $\displaystyle\int\dfrac{x^2}{4-x^3}\,dx$;  (j) $\displaystyle\int\cot x\,dx$.

**6.** Write down the derivative with respect to $x$ of $\ln|f(x)|$. Use the answer to explain your method of integration in Question 5.

**7.** Draw a quick sketch of the region whose area is represented by each of the following integrals and hence write down approximate values for them. Confirm by integration.

(a) $\displaystyle\int_4^5\dfrac{1}{x}\,dx$;  (b) $\displaystyle\int_{\frac{1}{2}}^1\dfrac{1}{x}\,dx$;  (c) $\displaystyle\int_0^5\dfrac{1}{1+x}\,dx$;

(d) $\displaystyle\int_4^6\dfrac{1}{x-2}\,dx$;  (e) $\displaystyle\int_1^4\dfrac{1}{x-6}\,dx$;  (f) $\displaystyle\int_1^3\dfrac{1}{4-x}\,dx$.

## 5. THE EXPONENTIAL FUNCTION

**5.1  The number $e$.** We have seen in Sections 2 and 3 that the natural logarithm can be used as a logarithm in that it possesses the logarithmic property $\ln a + \ln b = \ln ab$.

But is the natural logarithm, defined by the integral, a logarithm in the sense of Chapter 8? What number is the *base* of natural logarithms? Is there a function $x \to q^x$ which is the inverse of the function $x \to \ln x$?

If such a base number $q$ exists, we can find its value using the common property of logarithms that the logarithm of the base is one:

$$\log_q q = 1.$$

For the natural logarithm function this number $q$ is denoted by the letter $e$, so we need to find $e$ to satisfy

$$\log_e e = 1 \quad \text{or} \quad \ln e = 1.$$

The table in Section 2 (p. 740) shows that $e$ must be just less than 3. It is in fact an irrational number whose value to 4 significant figures is 2·718. We shall see in Section 8 of this chapter how $e$ may be calculated to any desired accuracy.

**5.2  The inverse of the natural logarithm function.** We have seen (Exercise B, Questions 5 and 15) that for rational values of $n$

$$\ln a^n = n \ln a.$$

Taking $a = e$, we have

$$\ln e^n = n \ln e = n.$$

This means that the natural logarithm is the function which maps the number $e^n$ onto $n$. It is therefore the inverse of the 'exponential function' which maps $n$ on to $e^n$. That is,

$$y = \ln x \iff x = e^y$$

which is, in the notation of our definition from Chapter 8,

$$y = \log_e x \iff x = e^y.$$

Thus natural logarithms are the same as logarithms to base $e$.

**\*5.3**  We could not include *irrational* values of $n$ in our discussion because $e^n$ has as yet no meaning if $n$ is irrational. We use the equivalence

$$y = e^x \iff x = \ln y$$

to define $e^x$ for *all* real $x$. Since the function $x \to \ln x$ defined as an integral takes every real value just once as $x$ increases from zero (it is continuous and strictly increasing), its inverse will map all the reals on to the positive reals.

So, for instance, since $y = e^\pi \iff \ln y = \pi$, we interpret $e^\pi$ as 'the number whose natural logarithm is $\pi$'.

**5.4**  The function $x \to e^x$ is called *the* exponential function. An alternative notation to $e^x$ is exp $x$.

The graph of $y = e^x$ is obtained from that of $y = \ln x$ by reflection in $y = x$. The two graphs are shown in Figure 10.

751

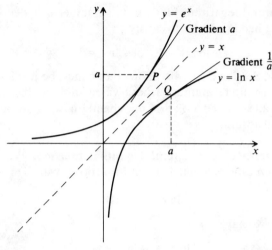

Fig. 10

**5.5 The derivative of exp $x$.** Certain characteristics of the derived function of $x \rightarrow e^x$ are obvious from the graph in Figure 10: it is positive and strictly increasing.

The value of the derivative at any point on $y = e^x$ is also easy to obtain from Figure 10. Since the graphs are reflection images of each other in the line $x = y$, the point $Q$ on $y = \ln x$, where $x = a$ and the gradient is $\dfrac{1}{a}$, reflects to the point $P$ on $y = e^x$, where $y = a$ and the gradient is $a$. So at each point on $y = e^x$, the gradient is equal to the value of $y$.

In general,

$$y = e^x \;\Rightarrow\; \frac{dy}{dx} = y = e^x.$$

Composite exponential functions can be differentiated using the chain rule.

*Example 4*

Differentiate $y = \exp x^2$.

$y = \exp x^2$ can be written $y = \exp u$ where $u = x^2$. Then

$$\frac{dy}{du} = \exp u \quad \text{and} \quad \frac{du}{dx} = 2x.$$

The chain rule states that

$$\frac{dy}{dx} = \frac{dy}{du} \times \frac{du}{dx},$$

so here
$$\frac{dy}{dx} = \exp(u) \times 2x = 2x \exp x^2.$$

## 5.6 Integrating exp x.

Using the result above that
$$\frac{d}{dx}(e^x) = e^x,$$

it clearly follows that
$$\int e^x \, dx = e^x + k.$$

*Example 5*

Evaluate $\displaystyle\int_0^1 e^{2x} \, dx.$

Now, $\dfrac{d}{dx}(e^{2x}) = 2e^{2x}$, so $\displaystyle\int_0^1 e^{2x} \, dx = \left[\tfrac{1}{2}e^{2x}\right]_0^1 = \tfrac{1}{2}(e^2 - 1).$

## 5.7 Composite exponential and logarithmic functions.

The inter-relation between $e^x$ and $\ln x$ as inverses needs examination in greater detail, as does their relationship to other exponential and logarithmic functions. Some examples will illustrate the techniques.

*Example 6*

Find the values of $x$ which satisfy $\exp(-x^2) = 0\cdot 1$.
   A flow diagram for $x \to \exp(-x^2)$ and its inverse can be a useful aid:

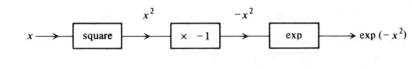

It is frequently important to be able to rewrite other exponential functions in terms of $e^x$.

*Example 7*

Express $10^x$ in the form $e^{kx}$.

Since
$$a = e^b \iff \ln a = b,$$
$$10^x = e^{kx} \implies \ln 10^x = kx.$$

But $\qquad\qquad$ $\ln 10^x = x \ln 10,$

so $\qquad\qquad$ $k = \ln 10$

and $\qquad\qquad$ $10^x = e^{x \ln 10} \approx e^{2 \cdot 3x}.$

This example illustrates one of the two important results arising from the inverse relationship

$$y = \ln x \iff x = e^y.$$

Substitution gives $\qquad x = e^{\ln x}$ (for $x > 0$)

and $\qquad\qquad$ $y = \ln e^y$ (for all $y$).

### Exercise D

**1.** Sketch the graph of $y = e^{-x}$. On the same diagram sketch the graph of its inverse function. Write down the equation of this inverse and state its domain and range.

**2.** Sketch $y = e^x$, $y = e^{2x}$ and $y = 2e^x$ on the same diagram. Write down the inverses of the functions $x \to e^x$, $x \to e^{2x}$ and $x \to 2e^x$, and their derived functions.

**3.** Use tables to find: (a) $e^2$; (b) $e^{-1}$; (c) $e^{10}$; (d) $e^{0 \cdot 1}$; (e) $e^{-5}$.

**4.** Differentiate: (a) $e^{3x}$; (b) $e^{-x}$; (c) $\exp(x^3)$; (d) $x e^x$; (e) $e^x \sin x$; (f) $e^x/x$; (g) $e^{\sin x}$.

**5.** Find:

(a) $\displaystyle\int e^{-x}\, dx$; $\quad$ (b) $\displaystyle\int x \exp(x^2)\, dx$; $\quad$ (c) $\displaystyle\int e^{x+1}\, dx$; $\quad$ (d) $\displaystyle\int \frac{dx}{e^{x/2}}$.

**6.** Evaluate:

(a) $\displaystyle\int_0^2 e^{x/2}\, dx$; $\quad$ (b) $\displaystyle\int_{-1}^1 x \exp(-x^2)\, dx$; $\quad$ (c) $\displaystyle\int_0^4 (1 - e^{-x})\, dx$.

**7.** (i) Write down the derivatives of: (a) $y = e^x$; (b) $y = 2e^x$; (c) $y = 5e^x$. In each case express your answers as functions of $y$.

(ii) Sketch the graphs of the three functions on the same diagram and explain your results.

(iii) State *two* simple transformations, each of which maps $y = e^x$ onto $y = 5e^x$ and say which transformation is used in your explanation in (ii).

**8.** (i) Find $\dfrac{dy}{dx}$ for: (a) $y = e^{3x}$; (b) $y = 7e^{3x}$; (c) $y = 20e^{3x}$. In each case express your answer as a function of $y$.

(ii) Find $\dfrac{dy}{dx}$ for: (a) $y = e^{-2x}$; (b) $y = Ae^{-2x}$. In each case, express your answer in terms of $y$.

(iii) Write down $\dfrac{dy}{dx}$ in terms of $y$ for $y = Ae^{kx}$. Check your answer by direct differentiation.

754

**9.** If $y = xe^{-x}$, find $\dfrac{dy}{dx}$ and $\dfrac{d^2y}{dx^2}$. Hence find the coordinates of the maximum point and the point of inflexion of the graph of $y = xe^{-x}$. Discuss the behaviour of this function as $x$ tends to infinity and sketch the graph.

**10.** Find $\displaystyle\int_0^a xe^{-x}\,dx$ and its limit (if any) as $a$ tends to infinity.

**11.** Evaluate $\dfrac{d}{dx}(\exp(-x^2/2))$ and hence find the inflexions on the graph of $y = \exp(-x^2/2)$. Sketch the graph.

**12.** Find the solution sets of:

(a) $e^x = 10$;      (b) $e^{3x} = 20$;      (c) $\exp(-x^2/2) = 0.05$;

(d) $e^{x+5} = 50$;      (e) $\ln x^2 = 4$;      (f) $e^x > 10^6$;      (g) $e^{-x/2} < 0.01$.

**13.** Simplify where possible:

(a) $\ln e^2$;      (b) $\ln 1/e$;      (c) $e^{\ln x^2}$;      (d) $e^{3\ln x}$;

(e) $\ln(2 + e^x)$;      (f) $\ln(e^x . e^y)$;      (g) $e^{1+\ln x}$.

**14.** Make $x$ the subject of the following formulae (flow diagrams can be helpful):

(a) $y = 2e^{3x}$;      (b) $y = 5 + e^{x-2}$;      (c) $y = 7 + 5\ln x$;

(d) $\ln y = 2 + \ln x$.

**15.** Express the following in the form $Ae^{kx}$:

(a) $2^x$;      (b) $1000(4.5)^x$;      (c) $20e^{x+5}$;      (d) $1.02^{12x}$.

## 6. EXPONENTIAL GROWTH AND DECAY

**6.1** When a sum of money is invested at compound interest, the interest in a particular year is a given fraction of the amount at the beginning of the year; and therefore the total sum invested is multiplied by a fixed proportion each year. For example, if the rate of interest is 4%, the increase in the capital is $0.04$ times its value at the beginning of the year, so that the capital at the end of the year is $1.04$ times as much as at the beginning. It follows that after $t$ years the capital is multiplied by $1.04^t$. We say that it increases exponentially, because the number of years appears in the exponent, or index, in the formula.

In this example the actual addition of interest is made just once a year; the capital does not grow continuously right through the year. There are, however, examples (particularly from science) where a quantity increases continuously—or so nearly continuously that we cannot distinguish the difference—at a rate which is proportional to its value at the time. Now this is a property which we can express mathematically by a *differential equation*. If $x$ is a measure of the quantity at time $t$, its rate of increase is $dx/dt$; the fact that this is proportional to $x$ is written

$$\frac{dx}{dt} = cx$$

where $c$ is a constant of proportionality (the 'growth factor').

We now know that such a differential equation is satisfied by an exponential function. In Exercise D, Question 8, we saw that

$$y = Ae^{kx} \implies \frac{dy}{dx} = ky$$

because $\frac{dy}{dx} = k \cdot Ae^{kx}$. So here

$$\frac{dx}{dt} = cx \quad \text{has} \quad x = Ae^{ct} \quad \text{as a solution.}$$

When $c$ is negative, the amount of $x$ is decreasing or *decaying* with time at a rate proportional to its value.

We shall look more closely at the formulation of differential equations in Chapter 38.

### Exercise E

**1.** Show that $x = e^{7t}$, $x = 3e^{7t}$ and $x = Ae^{7t}$ all satisfy $\dfrac{dx}{dt} = 7x$.

**2.** Show that $x = e^{-t}$, $x = 5e^{-t}$ and $x = Ae^{-t}$ all satisfy $\dfrac{dx}{dt} = -x$.

**3.** Show that $x = Ae^{5t}$ satisfies $\dfrac{dx}{dt} = 5x$ and find $A$ if $x = 33$ when $t = 0 \cdot 1$.

**4.** A bacteriologist finds that the rate of growth of a culture of a certain type of bacteria is described by the differential equation

$$\frac{dm}{dt} = 0 \cdot 4m$$

where $m$ grams is the total mass of the culture at time $t$ hours after observations began.

(a) Show that $m = m_0 \exp(0 \cdot 4t)$ (where $m_0$ is a constant) satisfies the differential equation.

(b) Find $m_0$ if $m = 10$ when $t = 0$.

(c) With this value of $m_0$ find the mass at (i) $t = 1$, (ii) $t = 2$.

(d) Find the percentage increase in the mass during (i) the first hour, (ii) the second hour.

**5.** The mass $m$ kg of radioactive lead remaining in a sample $t$ hours after observations began is given by $m = 2 \exp(-0 \cdot 2t)$.

(a) Find the mass left after 12 hours.

(b) Find how long it takes for the mass to fall to half its value at $t = 0$ (the *half-life*).

(c) Find how long it takes for the mass to fall to (i) one-quarter, (ii) one-eighth of its value at $t = 0$.

(d) Express the rate of decay as a function of $m$.

**6.** A car tyre is inflated to a pressure of 30 units. Eight hours later it is found to have deflated to 10 units. If the pressure $P$ at time $t$ is given by $P = P_0 \exp(-\lambda t)$, find the constants $P_0$ and $\lambda$ and calculate the initial rate of loss of pressure.

**7.** The population of a small island has increased since 1945 at a rate (measured in people per year) equal to 2% of the number of people alive at that instant. Write down the differential equation which expresses this information, and show that $P = 1000 \exp(0 \cdot 02t)$ satisfies it. If this is the function which gives the population of the island $t$ years after 1945, what was the population in 1945? Calculate the population (a) in 1960, (b) in 1970. In what year is the population twice what it was in 1945?

**\*8.** The way in which compound interest, say on £1000 at 4% per annum, is calculated varies in different commercial applications.

(a) Interest of 4% on the previous capital may be added on at the end of each year.

(b) Interest of 2% on the previous capital may be added on at the end of each half-year.

(c) Interest of 1% on the previous capital may be added on at the end of each quarter.

(d) The interest may be supposed to be added on 'continuously', so that the rate at which the capital grows in £ per year is 4% of the instantaneous value of the capital.

Calculate, for each of these ways, the total sum invested at various times over a five-year period; express the results in formulae, and draw the corresponding graphs.

Generalize this problem by considering a sum of money invested at $100r\%$ per annum, the interest being added on either $n$ times a year or continuously. Deduce that, when $n$ is large,

$$\left[1 + \frac{r}{n}\right]^n \approx e^r.$$

# 7. INTEGRATION USING LOGARITHMS

**7.1   The chain rule reversed.** We saw in Exercise C, Question 6, that when the chain rule was used to differentiate composite logarithmic functions, the result was a rational function of the form $Q'(x)/Q(x)$.

For instance,       $$\frac{d}{dx} \ln(4 - x^3) = \frac{-3x^2}{4 - x^3}.$$

Reversing this procedure gives a method of integration for a wide range of rational functions.

*Example* 8

Find $\dfrac{d}{dx}\ln(3x^2+1)$ and use your answer to find $\displaystyle\int \dfrac{x}{3x^2+1}\,dx$.

Using the chain rule,

$$\frac{d}{dx}\ln(3x^2+1)=\frac{1}{3x^2+1}\cdot 6x=\frac{6x}{3x^2+1}.$$

To carry out the integration, we have to put $\displaystyle\int \dfrac{x}{3x^2+1}\,dx$ in the form

$\displaystyle\int \dfrac{Q'(x)}{Q(x)}\,dx$. That is,

$$\int \frac{x}{3x^2+1}\,dx=\frac{1}{6}\int \frac{6x}{3x^2+1}\,dx$$

$$=\frac{1}{6}\ln|3x^2+1|+k.$$

In general,        $\dfrac{d}{dx}\ln f(x)=\dfrac{f'(x)}{f(x)}.$

So        $\displaystyle\int \dfrac{f'(x)}{f(x)}\,dx=\ln|f(x)|+k.$

The basis of the method is to recognize, if faced with an algebraic fraction to integrate, when the top of the fraction is a constant multiple of the derived function of the bottom.

**7.2   Division.** One or more steps of division may be needed to obtain the form $f'(x)/f(x)$.

*Example* 9

$$\int \frac{4x}{2x+5}\,dx=\int \left(2-\frac{10}{2x+5}\right)dx$$

$$=2x-5\ln|2x+5|+k.$$

**7.3   Partial fractions.** In Chapter 4 we saw that the rules for manipulating algebraic fractions are identical to those for arithmetical fractions. In particular, when adding or subtracting we find the L.C.M. of the denominators and express each fraction in an equivalent form with this L.C.M. as denominator.

758

*Example* 10

Express $\dfrac{3}{x+1} - \dfrac{1}{2x-1}$ as a single fraction.

$$\frac{3}{x+1} - \frac{1}{2x-1} = \frac{3(2x-1)}{(x+1)(2x-1)} - \frac{(x+1)}{(2x-1)(x+1)}$$

$$= \frac{3(2x-1)-(x+1)}{(x+1)(2x-1)}$$

$$= \frac{5x-4}{(x+1)(2x-1)}$$

$$= \frac{5x-4}{2x^2+x-1}.$$

There are a number of situations in which it is essential to be able to reverse this process, i.e. to take an algebraic fraction like $\dfrac{5x-4}{2x^2+x-1}$ and re-express it as the sum or difference of several *partial fractions*, in this case $\dfrac{3}{x+1}$ and $\dfrac{1}{2x-1}$.

We are concerned in this chapter with the separation into partial fractions of simple algebraic fractions which contain only unrepeated linear factors in the denominator. For these we can quickly establish a procedure which is little more than the reversal of the working in Example 10.

*Example* 11

Express $\dfrac{7x+5}{x^2+x-2}$ in partial fractions.

First factorize the denominator: $\dfrac{7x+5}{x^2+x-2} = \dfrac{7x+5}{(x-1)(x+2)}$. Now we need to find rational numbers $A$, $B$ so that

$$\frac{7x+5}{(x-1)(x+2)} \equiv \frac{A}{(x-1)} + \frac{B}{(x+2)},$$

where the symbol $\equiv$ means 'is identically equal to' and signifies that the two expressions are equal for all allowable values of $x$. Recombining the right-hand side we have

$$\frac{7x+5}{(x-1)(x+2)} \equiv \frac{A(x+2)+B(x-1)}{(x-1)(x+2)}$$

which means that
$$7x + 5 \equiv A(x + 2) + B(x - 1). \tag{1}$$

To find $A$ and $B$, we may equate coefficients of powers of $x$ on the two sides of (1), giving
$$7 = A + B$$
and
$$5 = 2A - B$$
and solving these equations gives $A = 4$, $B = 3$. Alternatively, since the two sides of (1) must have the same value for *all* $x$, we may replace $x$ by any number we please. It is convenient to choose the values which make $(x - 1)$ or $(x + 2)$ zero.

Putting $x = 1$ we obtain $\quad 12 = 3A \Rightarrow A = 4$,

and $\quad x = -2$ gives $\quad -9 = -3B \Rightarrow B = 3$.

Finally,
$$\frac{7x + 5}{(x - 1)(x + 2)} \equiv \frac{4}{x - 1} + \frac{3}{x + 2}.$$

*Example* 12

Express $\dfrac{3x^2 - x}{x^2 - 1}$ in partial fractions and hence find $\displaystyle\int \left(\dfrac{3x^2 - x}{x^2 - 1}\right) dx$.

This example illustrates an important preliminary to the partial fraction process. When the degree of the numerator is equal to or greater than that of the denominator, it is necessary to divide out until (as in Example 11 above) the degree of the numerator is less than that of the denominator:

$$
\begin{array}{r}
3 \phantom{xxxxx} \\
x^2 - 1 \overline{)\, 3x^2 - x} \\
3x^2 - 3 \phantom{x} \\
\hline
3 - x
\end{array}
$$

So
$$\frac{3x^2 - x}{x^2 - 1} \equiv 3 + \frac{(3 - x)}{x^2 - 1}.$$

Then
$$\frac{3 - x}{x^2 - 1} \equiv \frac{A}{x - 1} + \frac{B}{x + 1} = \frac{A(x + 1) + B(x - 1)}{(x - 1)(x + 1)}$$

$$\Rightarrow 3 - x \equiv A(x + 1) + B(x - 1).$$

Put $x = 1$ to give $A = 1$, and $x = -1$ to give $B = -2$. So finally
$$\frac{3x^2 - x}{x^2 - 1} \equiv 3 + \left(\frac{1}{x - 1} + \frac{-2}{x + 1}\right)$$

$$= 3 + \frac{1}{x - 1} - \frac{2}{x + 1},$$

and
$$\int \left(\frac{3x^2-x}{x^2-1}\right) dx = \int \left(3+\frac{1}{x-1}-\frac{2}{x+1}\right) dx$$
$$= 3x + \ln |x-1| - 2 \ln |x+1| + k.$$

**7.4   A standard integral.** Since $\int \dfrac{dx}{x^2-a^2}$ is quite a common example of a logarithmic integral involving partial fractions, the result is to be found in tables of standard integrals. Show for yourself that

$$\int \frac{dx}{x^2-a^2} = \frac{1}{2a} \ln \left|\frac{x-a}{x+a}\right| + k.$$

### Exercise F

**1.** Find:

(a) $\displaystyle\int \frac{1}{4x+7} dx;$   (b) $\displaystyle\int \frac{x-2}{x^2-4x+11} dx;$   (c) $\displaystyle\int \frac{x^2-x}{x^2-3x+3} dx;$

(d) $\displaystyle\int \tan x \, dx$ (express in terms of $\sin x$ and $\cos x$);

(e) $\displaystyle\int \frac{\sin x + \cos x}{\sin x - \cos x} dx.$

**2.** (a) Differentiate $\ln (\sec x + \tan x)$ with respect to $x$ and recast your answer in the form of an indefinite integral.

(b) Find $\displaystyle\int \csc x \, dx$ by a similar method.

**3.** Show that $\dfrac{d}{dx} (\ln \tan \tfrac{1}{2}x) = \csc x$. Demonstrate the equivalence of the two apparently different results for $\displaystyle\int \csc x \, dx$ given in this question and in Question 2(b).

**4.** (a) Find $A$ and $B$ when $\dfrac{3x+1}{(x-2)(x+5)} \equiv \dfrac{A}{x-2}+\dfrac{B}{x+5}.$

(b) Find $A$, $B$ and $C$ when $\dfrac{4x+2}{x(x-1)(x+2)} \equiv \dfrac{A}{x}+\dfrac{B}{x-1}+\dfrac{C}{x+2}.$

**5.** Use the method of partial fractions to find:

(a) $\displaystyle\int \frac{9x+1}{(x-3)(x+1)} dx;$   (b) $\displaystyle\int \frac{8}{x^2-16} dx;$   (c) $\displaystyle\int \frac{x^2+10x-33}{x^2-5x+6} dx;$

(d) $\displaystyle\int \frac{1}{x^2+3x-4} dx;$   (e) $\displaystyle\int \frac{x+9}{x^2-9} dx.$

**6.** (a) Express $\dfrac{6}{(x-4)(x-1)}$ in partial fractions. Use your result to find $\dfrac{dy}{dx}$ if $y = \dfrac{6}{(x-4)(x-1)}$ and hence find the maximum value of $y$. Sketch the graph.

761

(b) Find $\displaystyle\int_{-1}^{0} \frac{6}{(x-4)(x-1)}\,dx$ and $\displaystyle\int_{5}^{6} \frac{6}{(x-4)(x-1)}\,dx$

and explain with the aid of a graph why they are equal.

**7.** Sketch the curve $y = \dfrac{10}{(x+2)(x-5)}$. Find the area between the curve, the lines $x = 1$ and $x = 2$, and the $x$-axis.

**8.** Evaluate:

(a) $\displaystyle\int_{3}^{5} \frac{x-3}{x(x-2)}\,dx;$ (b) $\displaystyle\int_{6}^{8} \frac{x-6}{(x-3)(x-5)}\,dx.$

Sketch the graphs of $y = \dfrac{x-3}{x(x-2)}$ and $y = \dfrac{x-6}{(x-3)(x-5)}$ and comment on your answers to (a) and (b).

**9.** Find:

(a) $\displaystyle\int \frac{1}{x^2-1}\,dx;$ (b) $\displaystyle\int \frac{x}{x^2-4}\,dx;$ (c) $\displaystyle\int \frac{1}{x(x+1)}\,dx;$

(d) $\displaystyle\int \frac{2x+3}{x^2+3x-4}\,dx;$ (e) $\displaystyle\int \frac{x+1}{x^2-3x+2}\,dx.$

**10.** Find the following indefinite integrals. (Be wary, some have nothing to do with this chapter at all!)

(a) $\displaystyle\int \frac{x^2}{x^2-9}\,dx;$ (b) $\displaystyle\int \frac{1}{(x+1)^2}\,dx;$ (c) $\displaystyle\int \frac{4x}{x^2-4}\,dx;$

(d) $\displaystyle\int \frac{1}{x^2-16}\,dx;$ (e) $\displaystyle\int \frac{3x^2}{x^2-5x+4}\,dx;$ (f) $\displaystyle\int \frac{1}{x^2+4}\,dx;$

(g) $\displaystyle\int \tan 2x\,dx.$

**\*11.** Try to find $A$ and $B$ so that $\dfrac{5+x}{(x-2)(x+1)^2} \equiv \dfrac{A}{(x-2)} + \dfrac{B}{(x+1)^2}$. Use the method of equating coefficients of $x$. What goes wrong? Explain how using $\dfrac{Bx+C}{(x+1)^2}$ instead of $\dfrac{B}{(x+1)^2}$ leads to a possible set of partial fractions. Finally complete the process by finding $A$, $D$ and $E$ so that

$$\frac{5+x}{(x-2)(x+1)^2} \equiv \frac{A}{(x-2)} + \frac{D}{(x+1)} + \frac{E}{(x+1)^2}.$$

**\*12.** (a) Express $\dfrac{8x-72}{(x+1)(x-3)^2}$ in the form $\dfrac{A}{(x+1)} + \dfrac{B}{(x-3)} + \dfrac{C}{(x-3)^2}.$

(b) Express $\dfrac{1}{(x+1)(x-1)^2}$ in partial fractions and hence find $\displaystyle\int \frac{dx}{(x+1)(x-1)^2}.$

(c) Evaluate $\displaystyle\int_{2}^{3} \frac{x}{(x+1)(x-1)^2}\,dx.$

**\*13.** (*a*) Find constants $A$, $B$ and $C$ so that

$$\frac{x^2+2x+7}{(x-1)(x^2+4)}\equiv\frac{A}{x-1}+\frac{Bx+C}{x^2+4}.$$

(*b*) Find constants $A$, $B$ and $C$ so that

$$\frac{1}{x^3-1}\equiv\frac{A}{x-1}+\frac{Bx+C}{x^2+x+1}.$$

## 8. POLYNOMIAL APPROXIMATIONS

**8.1**   The method of local approximation by polynomials described in Chapter 22 can be applied to the logarithmic and exponential functions and provides a useful means of computing values of these functions.

We shall apply the general form for such Taylor approximations (see Summary, p. 564)

$$f(a+h)\approx f(a)+hf'(a)+\frac{h^2}{2!}f''(a)+\ldots+\frac{h^n}{n!}f^{(n)}(a)$$

where $h$ is small. This fits a polynomial of degree $n$ to the function at $x=a$.

**8.2   A polynomial approximation for exp $x$.** First we find the Taylor approximation to $e^x$ near $x=0$:

$$f(x)=e^x, \qquad f(0)=1$$
$$f'(x)=e^x, \qquad f'(0)=1$$
$$f''(x)=e^x, \qquad f''(0)=1 \text{ etc.}$$

Putting $a=0$ in the equation for Taylor's approximation,

$$f(0+h)\approx f(0)+hf'(0)+\frac{h^2}{2!}f''(0)+\frac{h^3}{3!}f'''(0)+\ldots+\frac{h^n}{n!}f^{(n)}(0).$$

So here

$$e^h\approx 1+h+\frac{h^2}{2!}+\frac{h^3}{3!}+\ldots+\frac{h^n}{n!}.$$

Because the denominators in the successive terms ($2!$, $3!$ etc.) increase very rapidly, this turns out to be a very effective approximation even for comparatively large values of $h$. A particularly important result is obtained by taking $h=1$, giving

$$e\approx 1+\frac{1}{1!}+\frac{1}{2!}+\frac{1}{3!}+\ldots+\frac{1}{n!}.$$

This expression enables us to calculate the value of $e$ to any desired accuracy.

**8.3   A polynomial approximation for ln $(1+x)$.** The most convenient point at which to fit a polynomial approximation for the logarithmic function is $x = 1$. (See Figure 11. Why is $x = 0$ not suitable?)

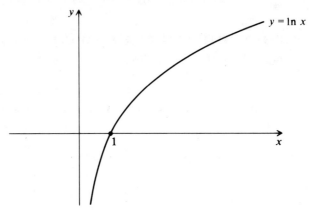

Fig. 11

$$f(x) = \ln x, \qquad\qquad f(1) = 0$$

$$f'(x) = \frac{1}{x}, \qquad\qquad f'(1) = 1$$

$$f''(x) = \frac{-1}{x^2}, \qquad\qquad f''(1) = -1$$

$$f'''(x) = \frac{2}{x^3}, \qquad\qquad f'''(1) = 2$$

$$f^{(4)}(x) = \frac{-3!}{x^4}, \qquad\qquad f^{(4)}(1) = -3!$$

$$f^{(5)}(x) = \frac{4!}{x^5}, \qquad\qquad f^{(5)}(1) = 4! \quad \text{etc.}$$

The pattern that emerges after the first few derivatives is that for the $r$th derivative the denominator is $x^r$. The numerator is $(r-1)!$ if $r$ is odd and $-(r-1)!$ if $r$ is even; we can express all this by saying that the $r$th derivative is

$$\frac{(-1)^{r-1}(r-1)!}{x^r}.$$

764

Taylor's approximation near $x = 1$ is given by

$$f(1+h) \approx f(1) + hf'(1) + \frac{h^2}{2!}f''(1) + \frac{h^3}{3!}f'''(1) + \frac{h^4}{4!}f^{(4)}(1) + \ldots + \frac{h^n}{n!}f^{(n)}. \quad (1)$$

So for $f(x) = \ln x$ we have

$$\ln(1+h) \approx 0 + h - \frac{h^2}{2!} + \frac{2!h^3}{3!} - \frac{3!h^4}{4!} + \ldots + (-1)^{n-1}\frac{(n-1)!h^n}{n!}$$

$$= h - \frac{h^2}{2} + \frac{h^3}{3} - \frac{h^4}{4} + \ldots + \frac{(-1)^{n-1}h^n}{n}.$$

Notice that there are no factorials in the denominators; successive terms only decrease rapidly if $h$ is small.

Figure 12 shows a comparison between the graph of $y = \ln(1+x)$ and the graph of its fifth-degree polynomial approximation over the interval $-1 < x < 1.5$. It is important to notice the divergence from the logarithmic curve of the approximating polynomial graph for values of $x$ beyond 1, a divergence which will indeed be *more* accentuated as more terms are taken. This means that, if we want to compute values of the natural logarithm, the polynomial approximation furnishes quite an efficient method for values of $h$ which are comfortably within the interval $-1 < h < 1$; but it will give quite misleading results outside this interval.

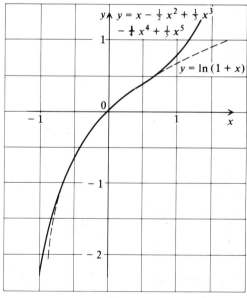

Fig. 12

765

*Example* 13

Find ln 1·3.
    The fourth-degree polynomial approximation with $h = 0·3$ gives

$$\ln 1·3 \approx 0·3 - \frac{0·3^2}{2} + \frac{0·3^3}{3} - \frac{0·3^4}{4}$$

$$= 0·3 - 0·045 + 0·009 - 0·002\ 025$$

$$= 0·261\ 975.$$

The size of the last term suggests that the answer should be rounded to 0·262. For more accuracy we need to take more terms, or to use an alternative polynomial like the one we develop in the next section.

**8.4  Calculating values of natural logarithms.** Clearly, the Taylor approximation we have derived in Section 8.3 is of very limited use. It cannot be used directly to calculate values of ln $(1 + h)$ outside the range $-1 < h \leqslant 1$ and, for values of $h$ approaching unity, a very large number of terms would be needed for reasonable accuracy. How then can we calculate logarithms of larger numbers?
    The answer is found by a more indirect approach. We have

$$\ln (1 + h) \approx h - \frac{h^2}{2} + \frac{h^3}{3} - \frac{h^4}{4} + \dots$$

Substituting $-h$ for $h$ we obtain

$$\ln (1 - h) \approx -h - \frac{h^2}{2} - \frac{h^3}{3} - \frac{h^4}{4} - \dots$$

and subtracting we have

$$\ln (1 + h) - \ln(1 - h) = \ln \left(\frac{1+h}{1-h}\right) \approx 2 \left(h + \frac{h^3}{3} + \frac{h^5}{5} + \dots\right).$$

This approximation too will be valid for $-1 < h < 1$. The next example illustrates its usefulness.

*Example* 14

Find ln 3.
    If $\dfrac{1+h}{1-h} = 3$, then $h = 0·5$ and

$$\ln 3 \approx 2\left(0·5 + \frac{(0·5)^3}{3} + \frac{(0·5)^5}{5} + \frac{(0·5)^7}{7} + \frac{(0·5)^9}{9} + \dots\right)$$

$$= 1 + 0·083\ 333 + 0·012\ 500 + 0·002\ 232 + 0·000\ 434$$

$$= 1·098\ 499.$$

766

The size of the last term suggests that $\ln 3 = 1 \cdot 099$ to 4 significant figures. It can be seen that, even with $h$ as large as $0 \cdot 5$, successive terms decrease reasonably quickly.

### Exercise G

**1.** Work out the value of $e$ to 5 decimal places in the way suggested in Section 8.2. (Consider carefully how to avoid tiresome calculation by finding the simple relationship between successive terms.)

**2.** Evaluate $\sqrt{e}$ and $1/\sqrt{e}$ to 4 decimal places using the Taylor approximation for $e^x$. Check by multiplying your answers together.

**3.** Draw graphs of $y = 1 + x$, $y = 1 + x + \dfrac{x^2}{2!}$, $y = 1 + x + \dfrac{x^2}{2!} + \dfrac{x^3}{3!}$ and $y = e^x$ over the interval $-2 \leqslant x \leqslant 2$.

**4.** Use the Taylor approximation for $\ln(1 + x)$ to evaluate to 4 decimal places: $(a)$ $\ln 1 \cdot 1$; $(b)$ $\ln 0 \cdot 8$; $(c)$ $\ln 1 \cdot 44$. Use four-figure tables to check your answers.

**5.** Show that the square of $1 + x + \dfrac{x^2}{2!} + \dfrac{x^3}{3!}$ agrees with $1 + 2x + \dfrac{(2x)^2}{2!} + \dfrac{(2x)^3}{3!}$ as far as the term in $x^3$. What is the significance of this result?

**6.** Write down the cubic approximations for $e^h$ and $e^{-h}$ for small $h$ and multiply them together. Explain the result.

**7.** Write a flow chart to compute the value of $e^{0 \cdot 85}$ to 6 decimal places.

**8.** Write a flow chart to compute and print out a table of natural logarithms over the interval $1 \leqslant x \leqslant 1 \cdot 2$, by steps of $0 \cdot 01$, to 4 decimal places.

**9.** Use the Taylor approximation for $\ln(1 + x)$ to find $\ln 1 \cdot 5$ and $\ln 0 \cdot 5$ to 3 decimal places. Deduce values for: $(a)$ $\ln 3$; $(b)$ $\ln 0 \cdot 75$; $(c)$ $\ln 2$.

**10.** Find a fourth-degree polynomial approximation for $\exp(x^2)$ near $x = 0$. Use it to find an approximate value for $\displaystyle\int_0^1 \exp(x^2)\,dx$.

**11.** $(a)$ Discuss what degree polynomial approximation to $\ln(1 + h)$ would be needed to evaluate $\ln 2$ to 4 significant figures by substituting $h = 1$.
$(b)$ Find $\ln 2$ to 4 significant figures using the method of Section 8.4.
$(c)$ Deduce a value for: (i) $\ln 4$; (ii) $\ln 8$.

**12.** Use the Taylor approximation to $\ln\left(\dfrac{1 + x}{1 - x}\right)$ to find $\ln 5$ and $\ln \frac{8}{5}$ to 3 decimal places. Deduce a value for $\ln 8$. Compare it with the value you obtained in Question 11.

### Miscellaneous Exercise

**1.** Find the turning points on the graph of $y = e^{-x}\sin x$ and sketch the graph. Write down the equation of the exponential curves on which $(a)$ all the maxima fall; $(b)$ all the minima fall.

**2.** (*a*) If $I = \int e^x \sin x \, dx$, show by twice using the method of integration by parts that

$$I = -e^x \cos x + e^x \sin x - I.$$

Hence find $I$. Check by differentiation.

(*b*) Use a similar method to find $\int e^{2x} \cos x \, dx$. Check by differentiation.

**3.** By writing $\int \ln x \, dx = \int (\ln x) \times 1 \, dx$ and integrating by parts, find $\int \ln x \, dx$ $\left( \text{take } u = \ln x \text{ and } \dfrac{dv}{dx} = 1 \text{ in the formula } \int u \dfrac{dv}{dx} \, dx = uv - \int v \dfrac{du}{dx} \, dx \right)$. Check by differentiation.

**4.** (*a*) Differentiate $\ln [x + \sqrt{(x^2 - 1)}]$ with respect to $x$ and recast your answer in the form of an indefinite integral.

(*b*) Find $\int \dfrac{1}{\sqrt{(x^2 + 1)}} \, dx$ by a similar method.

**5.** What is the connection between $\ln x$ and $\log_{10} x$? Draw graphs of the two functions on the same diagram and explain how one can be transformed into the other.

**6.** Find $\dfrac{dy}{dx}$ for (*a*) $y = \log_{10} x$ and (*b*) $y = 10^x$.

**7.** Simplify and differentiate $\ln (x^n e^{-x})$ where $n \geq 1$ and $x \geq 0$. Find the turning point on the graph of $y = \ln (x^n e^{-x})$ and sketch the graph. Explain informally why $x^n e^{-x} \to 0$ as $x \to \infty$.

**8.** If $u$, $v$ and $y$ are differentiable functions of $x$ such that

$$\ln y = \ln u + \ln v,$$

obtain an equation connecting their derivatives by differentiating this relation implicitly with respect to $x$ (see Chapter 20). Deduce the product rule given in Chapter 16.

**9.** For $y = \dfrac{x}{(x-1)(x-4)}$, show that $\ln y = \ln x - \ln (x-1) - \ln (x-4)$. By differentiating this relation implicitly with respect to $x$, find the turning values of $y = \dfrac{x}{(x-1)(x-4)}$ and sketch the graph.

**10.** Use the method of Question 9 to differentiate:

(*a*) $y = \dfrac{(1+x)^2}{1-x}$; (*b*) $y = \dfrac{\cos^2 x}{(1+x)^2}$.

**11.** For $y = x^x$, show that $\dfrac{dy}{dx} = (1 + \ln x)x^x$. Find the minimum point on the graph $y = x^x$ and sketch the graph, with domain the positive real numbers.

768

**12.** Differentiate $\exp\left(-\tfrac{1}{2}x^2\right)$.

You are given that, if $f(x) = \dfrac{1}{\sqrt{(2\pi)}} \exp\left(-\tfrac{1}{2}x^2\right)$, then $\displaystyle\int_{-\infty}^{\infty} f(x)\, dx = 1$.

Deduce that
$$\int_{-\infty}^{\infty} x f(x)\, dx = 0, \qquad \int_{-\infty}^{\infty} x^2 f(x)\, dx = 1,$$
$$\int_{-\infty}^{\infty} x^3 f(x)\, dx = 0, \qquad \int_{-\infty}^{\infty} x^4 f(x)\, dx = 3.$$

**13.** Find the maximum point on the graph of $y = \dfrac{\ln x}{x}$ and sketch the graph.

Deduce that there is only one pair of different positive integers $a, b$ such that $a^b = b^a$.

**14.** In a model of an economic situation, the cost of living index is assumed to increase continuously at a rate proportional to its value at the time. The expression for the rate of increase is $0 \cdot 04C$ points per year, where $C$ is the current index. If the index is chosen to have the value 100 at a particular date, what will it be $t$ years later? By what percentage will it have increased: ($a$) at the end of a year; ($b$) at the end of 10 years?

In the same model the wage rate index is assumed to increase at a rate of $0 \cdot 06W$ points per year, where $W$ is the current index. An index of 'real purchasing power' is defined by the expression $W/C$. Obtain a differential equation describing how this third index varies with time.

**15.** Evaluate $\displaystyle\int_4^6 \left(ax + b - \frac{1}{x}\right)^2 dx$.

It is desired to make this integral as small as possible by choosing appropriate values of $a$ and $b$. Write down two equations which $a$ and $b$ must satisfy to achieve this, and solve them. Explain why you might expect the function $x \to ax + b$, with these values of $a$ and $b$, to give the 'best' linear approximation to the reciprocal function $x \to 1/x$ over the interval $4 < x \le 6$.

**16.** A function $f$ has the property that $f(x) + f(u) = f(xu)$ for all $x$ and $u$ in its domain. By differentiating this relation with respect to $u$ for a particular value of $x$, and then making the substitution $u = 1$, prove that $f$ must be a primitive of a function of the form $p/x$. Prove also, from the original relation, that $f(1) = 0$. Deduce that
$$f(a) = \int_1^a \frac{p}{x}\, dx.$$

**17.** Let $p$ be any positive number, and write
$$L(a) = \int_1^a \frac{p}{x}\, dx.$$

($a$) Prove that $L(a) + L(b) = L(ab)$.
($b$) Prove the existence of a number $q$ such that $L(q) = 1$.
($c$) Prove that $L(x)$ is the same as $\log_q x$.
($d$) If $q', p'$ are related to each other in the same way as $q, p$, prove that
$$\log_q a = \frac{p}{p'} \log_{q'} a, \quad \text{and} \quad \frac{p}{p'} = \log_q q'.$$

**18.** Express $\dfrac{1}{i(i+1)}$ in partial fractions. Use your answer to rewrite

$$S_n = \sum_1^n \frac{1}{i(i+1)}$$

as the difference of two series. Calculate $S_{10}$ and $S_n$.

## SUMMARY

$$\ln a = \int_1^a \frac{1}{x}\,dx \quad \text{for } a>0.$$

$\ln a = \log_e a$, the natural logarithm of $a$.

$\ln ab = \ln a + \ln b$.

$\ln a^n = n \ln a$.

$$y = \ln x \iff x = e^y \quad \text{or} \quad \exp y.$$

$$\frac{d}{dx}(\ln x) = \frac{1}{x}.$$

$$\frac{d}{dx}(e^x) = e^x.$$

$$\int \frac{1}{x}\,dx = \ln |x| + k.$$

$$\int e^x\,dx = e^x + k.$$

$$\int \frac{f'(x)}{f(x)}\,dx = \ln |f(x)| + k.$$

$$\int \frac{dx}{x^2 - a^2} = \frac{1}{2a} \ln \left| \frac{x-a}{x+a} \right| + k.$$

$$\frac{dx}{dt} = cx \iff x = Ae^{ct}.$$

*Taylor approximations*

$$e^h \approx 1 + h + \frac{h^2}{2!} + \frac{h^3}{3!} + \ldots + \frac{h^n}{n!} \quad \text{for small } h.$$

$$\ln(1+h) \approx h - \frac{h^2}{2} + \frac{h^3}{3} - \ldots + (-1)^{n-1}\frac{h^n}{n} \quad \text{for small } h.$$

770

# 30

## BINOMIAL MODELS

### 1. INTRODUCTION

Enquiries show that one in five of the pupils at a large school is left-handed. How many left-handers would you expect to find in a class of 30? There *might* be none, there might be as many as 30, or any number in between. What probabilities can we associate with these numbers?

To find a way to answer this, we shall take a smaller group of pupils first. What is the probability that, out of four pupils selected at random, three are left-handed? We saw in Chapter 15 that a tree diagram is the most useful way to illustrate questions like this.

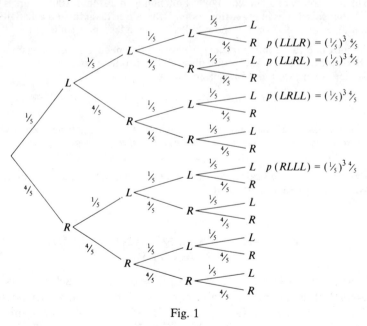

Fig. 1

In Figure 1, $L$ stands for left-handed, $R$ for right-handed, and we have assumed statistical independence (i.e. whether one person asked is left- or right-handed makes no difference to the next). Out of the sixteen possible routes through the diagram, four give us the result we want: three left-handed pupils and one right-handed. We can list these routes

771

as *LLLR*, *LLRL*, *LRLL* and *RLLL*. Notice that each has the same probability, $(\frac{1}{5})^3 \times \frac{4}{5}$, and so, in total,

$$p(3 \text{ out of } 4) = p(LLLR \text{ or } LLRL \text{ or } LRLL \text{ or } RLLL)$$

$$= p(LLLR) + p(LLRL) + p(LRLL) + p(RLLL)$$

$$= 4 \times (\tfrac{1}{5})^3 \times \tfrac{4}{5}$$

$$\approx 0 \cdot 0256.$$

How many routes through the tree diagram correspond to two left-handed and two right-handed in our sample of four people? What is the probability of obtaining that result? Calculate also $p(0 \text{ out of } 4)$, $p(1 \text{ out of } 4)$ and $p(4 \text{ out of } 4)$ and check that the five probabilities have a sum of 1.

### Exercise A

**1.** The probability of a Gloworm light bulb failing in less than 1000 hours is $0 \cdot 3$. I have four such bulbs in my sitting room. Draw a tree diagram and calculate the probabilities of 0, 1, 2 or 3 of these bulbs failing in less than 1000 hours.

**2.** 5% of Circe cars coming off the production line need a minor adjustment to the boot lock. What is the probability that two out of four cars tested by a consumer organization need this adjustment?

**3.** Find the probabilities of obtaining 0, 1, 2, 3, or 4 heads in four tosses of a fair coin.

**4.** Check from a tree diagram that the *number of ways* of getting three sixes in five throws of a die is the same as the *number of ways* of getting two sixes in five throws. Calculate the corresponding probabilities.

**5.** Extend Figure 1 and calculate the probability that (*a*) two, and (*b*) three out of five people asked are left-handed.

## 2. BINOMIAL SYSTEMS AND PASCAL'S TRIANGLE

All the questions in Exercise A are of the same kind. Each consists of a sequence of independent trials in which there are just two possible outcomes: left or right, fail or not fail, head or tail. We can symbolize these outcomes as success or failure, *S* or *F*. Further, the probability of success or failure at each trial remains the same.

Such sequences of trials are called *binomial systems* (or sometimes *Bernouillian systems* after Jacob Bernouilli (1654–1705)).

In any of the calculations of Exercise A we need to know the number of routes through the tree diagram giving the required overall result.

For example (see Figure 2), there are ten routes which give two successes out of five trials.

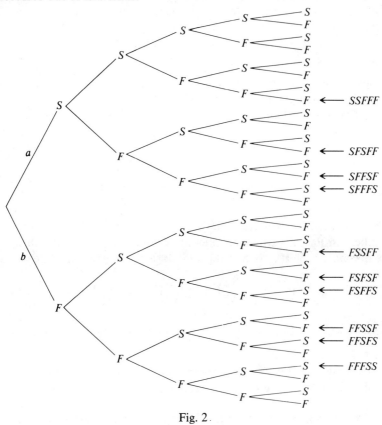

Fig. 2.

The table below summarizes our results so far, showing the number of routes for two, three, and four trials:

| Number of trials | Number of routes with | | | | | |
|---|---|---|---|---|---|---|
| | 0 S | 1 S | 2 S | 3 S | 4 S | 5 S |
| 2 | 1 | 2 | 1 | | | |
| 3 | 1 | 3 | 3 | 1 | | |
| 4 | 1 | 4 | 6 | 4 | 1 | |
| 5 | ? | ? | 10 | ? | ? | ? |

Copy the table and use Figure 2 to work out the missing numbers in the last row. Where have you seen this number pattern before?

**2.1  Pascal's triangle.** You may have recognized the table above as part of *Pascal's triangle*, a number pattern which crops up in a great number of contexts. Its properties were investigated by Blaise Pascal (1623–62), although it had been in use for many years before.

Each line is formed by adding consecutive pairs of numbers from the previous line.

For example, the line        1   4   6   4   1
gives rise to the next line    1   5   10   10   5   1
according to the scheme

$$1 \quad 4 \quad 6 \quad 4 \quad 1$$

$$1 \quad 1+4 \quad 4+6 \quad 6+4 \quad 4+1 \quad 1$$
$$=5 \quad =10 \quad =10 \quad =5$$

**2.2  Binomial coefficients.** It helps to have a name and notation for the numbers in Pascal's triangle. They are called *binomial coefficients*, and the numbers 1, 5, 10, 10, 5, 1 relevant to samples of size five are written

$$\binom{5}{0}, \binom{5}{1}, \binom{5}{2}, \binom{5}{3}, \binom{5}{4} \quad \text{and} \quad \binom{5}{5}.$$

Thus $\binom{5}{2}$ stands for the number of ways of obtaining two successes in five trials, which is 10.

The values of the binomial coefficients for samples of up to 20 are tabulated on p. 61 of the SMP *Advanced Tables, Third Edition*.

**2.3**  Why do numbers of routes through the tree diagram add like the numbers in Pascal's triangle? We can see by taking an example:

$$\binom{5}{2} = \binom{4}{1} + \binom{4}{2},$$

or the number of ways of achieving two successes out of five is the sum of the number of ways for one success out of four and two successes out of four.

Figure 3 shows that when the first trial gives success (the upper part of the diagram), there are then $\binom{4}{1}$ ways of obtaining a further success in the next four trials, while after a failure in the first trial (lower part of the diagram) we require two successes from the other four trials and there are $\binom{4}{2} = 6$ ways of obtaining this.

774

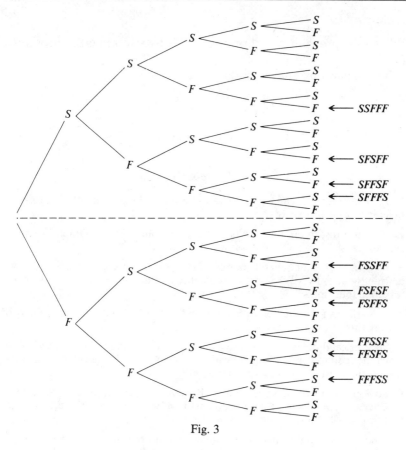

Fig. 3

An argument along similar lines justifies the more general relation

$$\binom{k+1}{i} = \binom{k}{i-1} + \binom{k}{i}.$$

**2.4   The binomial probability model.** If the probability of success for each trial in Figure 3 is $a$ and the probability of failure is $b$, then the probability of each of the ways of obtaining two successes and three failures is $a^2b^3$. So the total probability of two successes and three failures is $\binom{5}{2}a^2b^3$ or $10a^2b^3$.

In general, for a sequence of $n$ independent trials where the probabilities of success and failure in each are $a$ and $b$ respectively, the probability of $i$ successes and $(n-i)$ failures is

$$p_i = \binom{n}{i}a^ib^{n-i}.$$

## Example 1

What is the probability of throwing exactly two sixes in eight throws of a fair die?

If we count throwing a six as a success,

$$a = \tfrac{1}{6}, b = \tfrac{5}{6}$$

and

$$p_2 = \binom{8}{2}(\tfrac{1}{6})^2(\tfrac{5}{6})^6 = 28(\tfrac{1}{6})^2(\tfrac{5}{6})^6 \approx 0 \cdot 26.$$

### Exercise B

**1.** Four people each cut a pack of cards. What is the probability that three of them will get picture cards?

**2.** A coin is tossed ten times. What is the probability that it will fall five heads and five tails?

**3.** Over a period of several months, my baby son wakes me up early two mornings out of five. What is the probability that in the next seven days he will wake me four times?

**4.** A marksman hits the bull with a probability of $0 \cdot 8$. What is the probability of scoring three or more bulls with five rounds?

**5.** 30% of candidates offered places on a certain course are expected to fail to reach the required entrance qualifications. In a batch of five selected candidates, what is the most likely number of failures?

**6.** 80% of the plants from a batch of Brompton stocks seeds are expected to produce double flowers. I have six plants in a bed. What are the probabilities that 0, 1, 2 will fail to produce double flowers?

**7.** Find the probability that when I plant ten marrow seeds at least eight will germinate if the probability of each germinating is $0 \cdot 85$.

**8.** Find the probability that there will be more than one underweight cereal packet in a random sample of ten packets taken from the output of a filling machine from which 95% of the packets are greater than or equal to the stated weight.

**9.** The probability that a student will do a certain kind of calculation correctly is $0 \cdot 4$. With the help of a calculator, find the probability that he will get more than half the calculations right on a test of eight questions.

**\*10.** Explain why the numbers $\binom{n}{2}$ in the third column of Pascal's triangle are the triangle numbers. Find a formula for $\binom{n}{2}$ in terms of $n$.

**\*11.** (a) Show that $\binom{7}{3} = \binom{2}{2} + \binom{3}{2} + \binom{4}{2} + \binom{5}{2} + \binom{6}{2}$ and that

$$\binom{9}{4} = \binom{3}{3} + \binom{4}{3} + \binom{5}{3} + \binom{6}{3} + \binom{7}{3} + \binom{8}{3}.$$

776

(b) Generalize the results of (a) and explain them in terms of the inductive rule for Pascal's triangle: $\binom{k+1}{i} = \binom{k}{i-1} + \binom{k}{i}$.

*12. (a) Find $\sum_{2}^{6} \frac{1}{2}i(i-1)$ and $\sum_{2}^{n-1} \frac{1}{2}i(i-1)$ using the results of Chapter 9, and interpret your answers by reference to Questions 10 and 11.

(b) Use the answer to (a) and a similar method to show that

$$\binom{n}{4} = \frac{1}{24}n(n-1)(n-2)(n-3).$$

**13.** Explain the symmetry of each row of Pascal's triangle through consideration of the numbers of 'words' made from suitable combinations of the letters $S$ and $F$.

## 3. COMBINATORIAL METHOD

Pascal's triangle provides a convenient method of finding $\binom{n}{i}$ when $n$ is a small number; but to use it to find $\binom{30}{10}$, say, would involve a great deal of labour. It is an advantage to have a formula that enables us to calculate binomial coefficients directly.

Such a formula can be obtained by a closer look at the tree diagrams.

**3.1 A formula for $\binom{n}{2}$.** Referring again to Figure 3, which shows all the outcomes for a series of five trials, we can see that every route through the diagram consists of five stages (call them $A, B, C, D, E$). At each stage, the tree may branch up or down, corresponding to success or failure. So we can represent any route using the abbreviated diagram shown in Figure 4. For instance, Figure 5 shows a success on the first

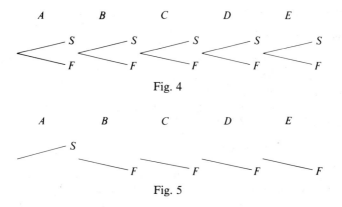

Fig. 4

Fig. 5

trial followed by four failures. Now to find $\binom{5}{1}$ we want to know how many routes there are altogether with one $S$ and four $F$s. Clearly the $S$ could be at any of the five stages, so $\binom{5}{1} = 5$.

How do we find $\binom{5}{2}$? This time we want the total number of routes through the diagram with two $S$s and three $F$s. We can work this out systematically by saying that we could choose any of the five stages for one of the $S$s and for each choice we can take any of the remaining four for the second $S$, making $5 \times 4 = 20$ selections in all.

But the tables give $\binom{5}{2} = 10$. What has gone wrong? Listing the 20 selections in full shows us that we have counted each route twice. If we denote a success at stage $A$ and a success at stage $B$ (and the rest failures) by $AB$ and so on, the 20 selections referred to can be listed

|    |    | $AB$ | $AC$ | $AD$ | $AE$ |
|----|----|------|------|------|------|
| $BA$ |    |      | $BC$ | $BD$ | $BE$ |
| $CA$ | $CB$ |      |      | $CD$ | $CE$ |
| $DA$ | $DB$ | $DC$ |      |      | $DE$ |
| $EA$ | $EB$ | $EC$ | $ED$ |      |      |

So we can see for instance that a success at $B$ and at $D$ has been counted as *BD and DB.*

Thus $\binom{5}{2} = \dfrac{5 \times 4}{2}$.

The argument is easily extended to show that $\binom{n}{2} = \dfrac{n(n-1)}{2}$.

### 3.2 A general formula for $\binom{n}{i}$.

How do we calculate $\binom{5}{3}$, the number of routes through a five-stage tree giving three successes? Adopting an argument similar to that for our calculation of $\binom{5}{2}$, we can choose one success at any of five stages, the next at any of four, the third at any of three, giving $5 \times 4 \times 3 = 60$ selections in all.

How many repetitions are there in this case? Take for example the route with successes at $A$, $B$ and $C$. We shall have counted it as $ABC$, $ACB$, $BAC$, $BCA$, $CAB$, $CBA$. Similarly, every other route will have been counted six times, giving $\binom{5}{3} = \dfrac{5 \times 4 \times 3}{6}$.

Notice that the number of repetitions can be found by a similar argument to that already used. For the example above, with successes at

778

$A$, $B$ and $C$, it is the number of ways of arranging the letters $A$, $B$, $C$: there are three choices for which letter comes first, two for second place and the last letter is then decided, making $3 \times 2 \times 1$ ways in all.

So finally $\dbinom{5}{3} = \dfrac{5 \times 4 \times 3}{3 \times 2 \times 1}$.

Using similar arguments, write down expressions for $\dbinom{10}{3}$, $\dbinom{12}{3}$ and $\dbinom{7}{4}$. Evaluate your answers and check with the values given in the table on p. 61 of the SMP *Advanced Tables, Third Edition*.

The derivation of a general formula for $\dbinom{n}{i}$ proceeds along similar lines. We now have $n$ stages with $i$ $S$s. The first $S$ can be placed in any of the $n$ stages, the second in $(n-1)$ and so on. When the final $S$ is about to be placed, $(i-1)$ stages have been used so there are $n-(i-1)$ or $n-i+1$ stages left. We therefore have $n(n-1)(n-2)\ldots(n-i+1)$ selections *including* repetitions. The number of repetitions, by an extension of the argument used for three $S$s, is $i(i-1)(i-2)\ldots 1$ for each route. So finally we have

$$\binom{n}{i} = \frac{n(n-1)(n-2)\ldots(n-i+1)}{i(i-1)(i-2)\ldots 1}.$$

Thus
$$\binom{10}{6} = \frac{10 \times 9 \times 8 \times 7 \times 6 \times 5}{6 \times 5 \times 4 \times 3 \times 2 \times 1} = 210.$$

Note that in the extended form there are the same number of factors in the numerator and the denominator.

**3.3  Factorial form for $\dbinom{n}{i}$.** The formula just derived can be recast in terms of the factorial function.

For example, in the expression for $\dbinom{10}{6}$ above, the denominator can be abbreviated to $6!$, the product of the first six natural numbers. The numerator $10 \times 9 \times 8 \times 7 \times 6 \times 5$ can be converted into the form

$$\frac{10 \times 9 \times 8 \times 7 \times 6 \times 5 \times 4 \times 3 \times 2 \times 1}{4 \times 3 \times 2 \times 1}$$

which is $\dfrac{10!}{4!}$. It follows that $\dbinom{10}{6} = \dfrac{10!}{6!4!}$.

779

The same method leads to the general result

$$\binom{n}{i} = \frac{n!}{i!(n-i)!}.$$

**3.4   Calculating $\binom{n}{i}$ for large $n$.** When $n \leqslant 20$ we can use the table for $\binom{n}{i}$ already referred to. For larger values of $n$ we use the expanded form derived in Section 3.2 (which can be worked out quite easily as a chain calculation on a calculator).

An alternative is to use the tables of $\log_{10} x!$ and find approximate values using the factorial expression in Section 3.3.

**3.5   Application to probability.** We can now give the general formula for binomial probability.

In a sequence of $n$ independent trials such that the probabilities of success and failure in each are $a$, $b$ respectively, the probability of $i$ successes is

$$p_i = \binom{n}{i} a^i b^{n-i} = \frac{n!}{i!(n-i)!} a^i b^{n-i}.$$

*Example* 2

If three-quarters of the housewives in a small town buy their groceries at Madbury's Supermarket, what is the probability that exactly 20 out of a random sample of 25 housewives interviewed will shop at Madbury's?

Here $n = 25$, $a = \frac{3}{4}$, $b = \frac{1}{4}$, and $i = 20$. So

$$p_{20} = \binom{25}{20}\left(\frac{3}{4}\right)^{20}\left(\frac{1}{4}\right)^5 = \frac{25!}{20!5!}\left(\frac{3}{4}\right)^{20}\left(\frac{1}{4}\right)^5 = \frac{25!}{20!5!} \times \frac{3^{20}}{4^{25}}.$$

| $x$ | $\log_{10} x$ | $x$ | $\log_{10} x$ |
|---|---|---|---|
| $3^{20}$ | $9{\cdot}5420 (= 20 \times 0{\cdot}4771)$ | $4^{25}$ | $15{\cdot}0525 (= 25 \times 0{\cdot}6021)$ |
| $25!$ | $25{\cdot}1906$ | $20!$ | $18{\cdot}3861$ |
|  | $34{\cdot}7326$ | $5!$ | $2{\cdot}0792$ |
|  | $35{\cdot}5178$ |  | $35{\cdot}5178$ |
| $0{\cdot}164$ | $\bar{1}{\cdot}2148$ |  |  |

So   $p_{20} \approx 0{\cdot}164$.

780

### Exercise C

**1.** (a) Write $\binom{12}{7}$ in factorial form and calculate its value. Check by reference to Pascal's triangle.

    (b) Calculate $\binom{30}{6}$, $\binom{50}{47}$, $\binom{25}{2}$, $\binom{10}{5}$.

**2.** How can you tell without knowing the formula that $\binom{30}{6} = \binom{30}{24}$? Write down a similar result for $\binom{n}{i}$.

**3.** From your tables write down the values of:

    (a) $\binom{14}{5}$;    (b) $\binom{20}{8}$;    (c) $\binom{16}{9}$;

    (d) $\binom{19}{14}$;    (e) $\binom{15}{13}$;    (f) $\binom{20}{15}$.

**4.** Use the table of $\log x!$ to calculate approximately:

    (a) $20!$;    (b) $76!$;    (c) $\binom{80}{25}$;    (d) $\binom{100}{60}$;

    (e) $\binom{44}{22}$;    (f) $\binom{30}{10}(0\cdot3)^{10}(0\cdot7)^{20}$;    (g) $\binom{25}{15}(0\cdot6)^{15}(0\cdot4)^{10}$.

**5.** Use tables to show that $59! \approx (35!)^2$.

**6.** (a) Express $\binom{60}{20} \div \binom{60}{19}$ as a fraction in its simplest form.

    (b) *Without* using tables, show that $\binom{48}{15} > \binom{48}{34}$.

**7.** According to a motoring organization, one car in ten has defective brakes. Calculate the probability that, in a sample of 20 cars at a roadside check, exactly five have defective brakes.

**8.** A wholesale fruit merchant has found that, on average, one pear in 60 is bruised. Find the probabilities that in a particular box of 100 pears he finds (a) none, (b) one, (c) two bruised pears.

    Discuss the assumptions made in using a binomial model for this situation. How are the pears in a box likely to become bruised? Will successive trials be independent?

**9.** The probability that a match chosen at random from a box will not light is $0\cdot02$. Find the probabilities of finding (a) exactly two defective matches, (b) more than two defective matches in a box of 40.

**10.** Calculate the probabilities of an exact half-and-half split between heads and tails if a coin is tossed (a) 10 times, (b) 100 times, (c) 1000 times. Account briefly in non-technical terms for the trend of your answers.

781

**11.** One-quarter of the population is thought to have watched the Cup Final on television. On this assumption, calculate the probabilities that a random sample of 100 people will contain (*a*) 25, (*b*) 20, (*c*) 30 people who watched the programme.

**12.** Samples from a production line producing a small plastic moulding are taken at random. It is known that on average 5% of the mouldings will be defective. If the sample size is 20, find the probabilities that (*a*) exactly one will be defective, (*b*) one or more will be defective.

**13.** In a certain large school, the probability of a pupil chosen at random being left-handed is $\frac{1}{5}$. Calculate the probabilities that in a class of 30 there will be (*a*) five, (*b*) six, (*c*) seven left-handed pupils.

**14.** For a binomial model with $n = 8$, $a = 0 \cdot 3$, $b = 0 \cdot 7$, show that the probability of two successes is

$$p_2 = \frac{8 \times 7}{2 \times 1} \times (0 \cdot 3)^2 \times (0 \cdot 7)^6.$$

Write down $p_3$ in the same form. Show that

$$p_3 = p_2 \times \frac{6}{3} \times \frac{0 \cdot 3}{0 \cdot 7}.$$

Obtain similar relations between (*a*) $p_4$ and $p_3$, (*b*) $p_5$ and $p_4$.

## 4. RELATION BETWEEN SUCCESSIVE BINOMIAL PROBABILITIES

**4.1** We can now return to the example of left-handed and right-handed pupils with which we began the chapter. It would be possible, using the formula of Section 3.5, to calculate each of the probabilities of finding 0, 1, 2, 3, ..., 30 left-handed pupils in a class of 30, and to use the results to answer questions like 'calculate the probability of finding less than five left-handed pupils in a class of 30'.

However, you will have realized from the examples in Exercise C that calculating several probabilities for the same binomial model, using the formula, is a very tedious business. How can we shorten the work? We look at the ratio of successive probabilities.

Now for $n = 30$, $a = 0 \cdot 2$, $b = 0 \cdot 8$,

$$p_5 = \binom{30}{5}(0 \cdot 2)^5(0 \cdot 8)^{25}$$

$$= \frac{30 \times 29 \times 28 \times 27 \times 26}{5 \times 4 \times 3 \times 2 \times 1}(0 \cdot 2)^5(0 \cdot 8)^{25},$$

and

$$p_6 = \frac{30 \times 29 \times 28 \times 27 \times 26 \times 25}{6 \times 5 \times 4 \times 3 \times 2 \times 1}(0 \cdot 2)^6(0 \cdot 8)^{24}.$$

The second expression contains most of the factors of the previous one; there is an extra '25' in the numerator and a '6' in the denominator, one more '0·2' and one fewer '0·8'.

In other words, $p_6 = p_5 \times \dfrac{25}{6} \times \dfrac{0·2}{0·8} = p_5 \times \dfrac{25}{6} \times \dfrac{1}{4}$.

In the same way, show that

$$p_7 = p_6 \times \frac{24}{7} \times \frac{1}{4},$$

and

$$p_8 = p_7 \times \frac{23}{8} \times \frac{1}{4}.$$

There is a clear pattern, and once we have calculated one of these probabilities (by the hard way), we can quickly work out all the others using these ratios.

Given that $p_0 = 0·001\ 238$, check the following, which are rounded to 3 decimal places:

| $i$   | 0     | 1     | 2     | 3     | 4     | 5     | 6     |
|-------|-------|-------|-------|-------|-------|-------|-------|
| $p_i$ | 0·001 | 0·009 | 0·034 | 0·079 | 0·133 | 0·172 | 0·179 |

| $i$   | 7     | 8     | 9     | 10    | 11    | 12    | 13    |
|-------|-------|-------|-------|-------|-------|-------|-------|
| $p_i$ | 0·154 | 0·111 | 0·068 | 0·035 | 0·016 | 0·006 | 0·002 |

All the subsequent probabilities are smaller than 0·001.

**4.2 Probability histograms.** The way these probabilities increase and then diminish is shown in the bar chart of Figure 6.

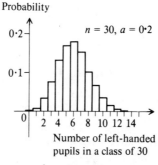

Fig. 6

Is the shape of this picture roughly what you would have anticipated? At the beginning, without calculating any probabilities, we could have said that if the probability of *one* person being left-handed is $\frac{1}{5}$, then about $\frac{1}{5} \times 30 = 6$ people in 30 would be left-handed. It turns out that 6 is indeed the most likely outcome.

We apply the word *histogram* to Figure 6 because in it *areas* represent probabilities. In fact the vertical axis should be labelled *probability density* for this to be so.

Figure 7 is a histogram showing the distribution of probabilities of the numbers of heads obtained when a fair coin is tossed 30 times (using a binomial model with $n = 30$, $a = 0 \cdot 5$, $b = 0 \cdot 5$).

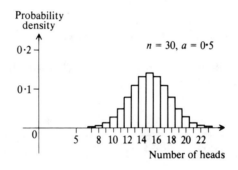

Fig. 7

What are the principal similarities and differences between the histograms of Figures 6 and 7?

**4.3 The inductive relationship generalized.** There is no difficulty in showing by the method of Section 4.1 that, with our usual notation,

$$\binom{n}{i+1} = \binom{n}{i} \times \frac{n-i}{i+1},$$

and

$$p_{i+1} = p_i \times \frac{n-i}{i+1} \times \frac{a}{b}.$$

### Exercise D

**1.** (*a*) For the sixth row of Pascal's triangle (1, 6, 15, 20, 15, 6, 1), the ratios of consecutive numbers can be written $\frac{6}{1}, \frac{5}{2}\left( = \frac{15}{6} \right), \frac{4}{3}\left( = \frac{20}{15} \right), \frac{3}{4}, \frac{2}{5}, \frac{1}{6}$. Check that the numbers in the tenth row are related in a similar way.

(*b*) Given that $\binom{22}{9} = 497\,420$, find $\binom{22}{10}$ and $\binom{22}{11}$.

**2.** Given that $\binom{100}{20} \approx 5\cdot36 \times 10^{20}$, find $\binom{100}{21}$ and $\binom{100}{19}$.

**3.** Devise a flow chart for the calculation of $\binom{30}{1}, \binom{30}{2}, \binom{30}{3}, \ldots$

**4.** (a) For a binomial model with $n = 20$, $a = 0\cdot3$, $b = 0\cdot7$, show that $p_1 = p_0 \times \dfrac{60}{7}$ and $p_2 = p_1 \times \dfrac{57}{14}$.

   (b) Find similar relations connecting (i) $p_3$ and $p_2$, (ii) $p_4$ and $p_3$, (iii) $p_5$ and $p_4$, (iv) $p_6$ and $p_5$, (v) $p_7$ and $p_6$.

   (c) Deduce from your work so far which of the $p_i$ (for $i = 0$ to 20) is the largest.

   (d) Show (by logarithms or a calculator) that $p_0 \approx 7\cdot98 \times 10^{-4}$.

   (e) Using this value for $p_0$, compute the values of $p_1, p_2, \ldots, p_{10}$ and draw a probability histogram.

**5.** A die is rolled 100 times. Write down a formula for $p_i$, the probability of getting $i$ sixes, and prove that the ratio of $p_{i+1}$ to $p_i$ is $\dfrac{100 - i}{5(i+1)}$.

   Given that $p_{10}$ is approximately $0\cdot0214$, calculate (with the help of a calculator or slide rule) the probabilities of various numbers of sixes from 11 to 25, and show your results graphically.

**6.** A pack of cards is shuffled and cut 50 times. About how many times would you expect to show a spade? Write down a formula for the probability of obtaining $i$ spades, and find the ratio of the probabilities of $i+1$ spades and $i$ spades. Use this to find the number with the highest probability.

**7.** Suppose that, in a factory making women's tights, 8% of the output are substandard. Calculate the probabilities that, of a random sample of 50, there will be 0, 1, 2, 3, ..., 10 substandard items.

**8.** With the usual notation, show that $p_{i+1} > p_i \iff i < na - b$. Explain what this implies about the most probable number of successes in Questions 4, 5, 6, and 7.

**9.** For binomial models with the following parameters, calculate $p_j$ where $j$ is equal to $na$ or the nearest integer to $na$, and then deduce $p_{j+1}$, $p_{j+2}, \ldots$ Calculate also $p_{j-1}, p_{j-2}, \ldots$ For both sequences, stop when values less than $0\cdot001$ are reached. Draw the probability histograms.

   (a) $n = 10$, $a = 0\cdot4$, $b = 0\cdot6$;      (b) $n = 20$, $a = 0\cdot4$, $b = 0\cdot6$;
   (c) $n = 10$, $a = 0\cdot8$, $b = 0\cdot2$;      (d) $n = 50$, $a = 0\cdot8$, $b = 0\cdot2$;
   (e) $n = 10$, $a = 0\cdot35$, $b = 0\cdot65$.

**10.** Write a computer program (or flow chart) to carry out the calculations of Question 4(d) and (e).

**11.** Select 60 blocks of ten digits from a table of random numbers, and record the number of multiples of 3 (i.e. 0, 3, 6, 9) that each contains. Calculate the relative frequencies of different scores in your population, and the mean value.

   Display your results in a histogram.

   Calculate the probabilities of the various scores and display these in a probability histogram.

**4.4   Binomial histograms for large *n*.** We have seen in Section 4.2 and Exercise D that a set of binomial probabilities give a humped histogram with mode at or near *na*. If $a \approx 0 \cdot 5$, the histogram is approximately symmetrical about the mode for quite small values of *n*, and becomes more symmetrical as *n* increases (see Exercise D, Question 9(*a*) and (*b*)). For larger or smaller values of *a*, the histogram is skew for relatively small *n*, but becomes symmetrical if *n* is large enough (see Exercise D, Question 9(*c*) and (*d*)).

# 5.  BINOMIAL THEOREM

**5.1   An algebraic expansion.** Copy and complete this pattern (where *b* and *a* are *any* real numbers) and extend it for three more lines.

$$(b+a)^2 = b^2 + 2ba + a^2,$$

$$(b+a)^3 = b^3 + 3b^2a + 3ba^2 + a^3,$$

$$(b+a)^4 = b^4 + \ldots.$$

Clearly the coefficients 1, 5, 10, 10, 5, 1 which appear in the expansion

$$(b+a)^5 = b^5 + 5b^4a + 10b^3a^2 + 10b^2a^3 + 5ba^4 + a^5$$

are the same *binomial coefficients* which we have used in our binomial probability model with five trials (probability of success *a*, probability of failure *b*). In terms of probability, since then $b + a = 1$, this equation states that the sum of the probabilities of 0, 1, 2, 3, 4 and 5 successes is 1.

But these expansions are valid whether or not *a* and *b* represent probabilities, and are useful algebraic results in their own right.

In general we have

$$(b+a)^n = \binom{n}{0}b^n + \binom{n}{1}b^{n-1}a + \binom{n}{2}b^{n-2}a^2 + \ldots + \binom{n}{n}a^n$$

$$= \sum_{i=0}^{n} \binom{n}{i} b^{n-i}a^i$$

for any $n \in \mathbb{N}$, a result known as the *binomial theorem*.

**5.2   Binomial expansions and Taylor approximations.** In Chapter 22 we saw that the Taylor approximation to $(1+h)^n$ near $h = 0$ was

$$(1+h)^n \approx 1 + nh + \frac{n(n-1)}{2!}h^2 + \frac{n(n-1)(n-2)}{3!}h^3 + \ldots$$

where *n* may be *any* rational number.

786

Comparing this with our binomial expansion, with $b = 1$ and $a = h$, which is (for $n \in \mathbb{N}$)

$$(1+h)^n = \binom{n}{0} + \binom{n}{1}h + \binom{n}{2}h^2 + \ldots + \binom{n}{n}h^n$$

$$= 1 + nh + \frac{n(n-1)}{2!}h^2 + \ldots + h^n,$$

we see that the two series are identical when $n$ is a natural number. For in that case the Taylor approximation stops at the power $h^n$, with coefficient $\dfrac{n!}{n!} = 1$, all further coefficients being zero.

When $n$ is *not* a natural number, the Taylor approximation shows us how we can generalize the binomial theorem for rational $n$. Polynomials of the form

$$1 + nh + \frac{n(n-1)}{2!}h^2 + \frac{n(n-1)(n-2)}{3!}h^3 + \ldots,$$

taken as far as some power $h^k$, give approximations to $(1+h)^n$ for small values of $h$ for $n \in \mathbb{Q}$.

Important special cases include:

$$\frac{1}{1+h} = (1+h)^{-1} \approx 1 - h + h^2 - h^3 + \ldots,$$

$$\frac{1}{(1+h)^2} = (1+h)^{-2} \approx 1 - 2h + 3h^2 - 4h^3 + \ldots,$$

$$\sqrt{(1+h)} = (1+h)^{\frac{1}{2}} \approx 1 + \tfrac{1}{2}h - \tfrac{1}{8}h^2 + \tfrac{1}{16}h^3 + \ldots.$$

The interval of values of $h$ over which these approximations are valid can be shown to be $-1 < h < 1$, and, provided enough terms of the series are taken, their sum can be made as near $(1+h)^n$ as we like. This result is known as the *general binomial theorem*.

### Exercise E

**1.** Find approximations in the form of cubic polynomials to the following functions for small values of $h$:

(a) $\dfrac{1}{(1+h)^3}$;     (b) $\dfrac{1}{\sqrt{(1+h)}}$;     (c) $\sqrt[3]{(1+h)}$;

(d) $\dfrac{1}{1+\frac{1}{2}h}$;     (e) $\sqrt{(1-h)}$;     (f) $\sqrt{(1-\frac{1}{3}h)}$.

**2.** (a) Writing $\sqrt{(4+h)}$ as $2\sqrt{(1+\frac{1}{4}h)}$, find a cubic polynomial which approximates to $\sqrt{(4+h)}$ for small $h$.

(b) Evaluate $\sqrt{4\cdot2}$ to three places of decimals.

**3.** Writing $\sqrt{15}$ as $\sqrt{(16-1)}=4\sqrt{(1-\frac{1}{16})}$, find $\sqrt{15}$ to three places of decimals.

**4.** Evaluate $1/\sqrt{50}$ and deduce the value of $\sqrt{2}$ to three places of decimals.

**5.** Five dice are rolled. Write down the probabilities of 0, 1, 2, 3, 4, 5 sixes. Compare your answers with the coefficients of $t^0$, $t^1$, $t^2$, $t^3$, $t^4$ and $t^5$ in the binomial expansion of $(\frac{5}{6}+\frac{1}{6}t)^5$.

**6.** A die is rolled repeatedly until a six appears. Write down the probability that: (a) a six appears on the first roll; (b) a non-six is rolled, followed by a six; (c) two non-sixes are followed by a six; (d) three non-sixes are followed by a six.

Compare your answers with the coefficients of $t$ in the binomial expansion of

$$\frac{1}{6-5t}.$$

### *Miscellaneous Exercise*

**1.** (a) Evaluate $1+4\times2+6\times2^2+4\times2^3+2^4$

and $\qquad 1+5\times2+10\times2^2+10\times2^3+5\times2^4+2^5$.

Comment on your answers.

(b) Write down expressions for $p_0, p_1, \ldots,$ where $p_i$ is the probability of $i$ dice showing three, four, five or six when four dice are thrown together. What light does this throw on the first part of (a)? Explain the second part of (a) in a similar way.

**2.** If 20 pennies are tossed together, find the probabilities of getting 0, 1, 2, ..., 20 heads. (Use a table of binomial coefficients, and note that $2^{20}\approx1\cdot05\times10^6$.)

(a) If you want to assert that there is about a 95% probability that the number of heads will be between $10\pm d$, what value would you give for $d$?

(b) If you want to assert that there is about one chance in a thousand that there will be fewer than $k$ heads, what value would you give for $k$?

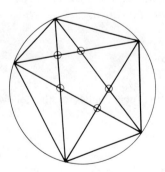 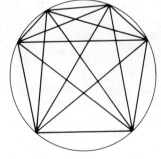

Fig. 8

**3.** Prove that, if $p$ is a prime number, then $\binom{p}{i}$ is a multiple of $p$ for $1 \le i \le p-1$. Is the converse true? Justify your answer.

**4.** When five points on a circle are joined by straight lines in all possible ways, the lines meet in five interior points (ringed in Figure 8). When six points in general position are taken on the circle, there are fifteen such interior points.

When $n$ points in general position on a circle are joined by straight lines in all possible ways, the lines meet in $s$ interior points. Complete the following table and describe your values of $s$ as binomial coefficients.

| $n$ | 4 | 5 | 6 | 7 | 8 |
|-----|---|---|----|---|---|
| $s$ |   | 5 | 15 |   |   |

Explain why these numbers are all binomial coefficients.

**5.** (a) Four dice are rolled and the number of sixes recorded. If the experiment is repeated 25 times, on how many occasions would you expect to get 0, 1, 2, 3, 4 sixes?

(b) If four dice are rolled 25 times, on how many occasions would you expect to get a triple or better (not necessarily of sixes)?

Carry out the experiments and compare the frequencies with the estimates you have made from the theory of probability.

**6.** An American city is designed on a square grid of streets, the intersections being labelled by integral Cartesian coordinates. The number of routes from $(0, 0)$ to $(r, s)$ with the shortest possible distance of $r+s$ 'blocks' is denoted by $f(r, s)$. Prove that

$$f(r, s) = f(r-1, s) + f(r, s-1), \quad r > 0, s > 0,$$

and give the values of $f(r, 0)$ and $f(0, s)$.

Draw a diagram of the lattice of street intersections, and mark against each the number of possible routes of this kind from $(0, 0)$. Guess a formula for $f(r, s)$, and then prove it either by induction or by some other argument.

**7.** The judges at a local baby show have to choose five babies out of a total entry of 80 to go on to the county finals. How many different selections can they make?

If 50 boys and 30 girls are entered for the contest, what are the probabilities that they will choose (a) five boys, (b) two boys and three girls, if the sex of the babies does not influence their choice?

**8.** A football pools coupon lists 48 matches, and contestants are expected to name four which they think will result in draws. How many different selections are possible?

If when the results are published it turns out that there are eleven draws altogether, what is the probability of winning if the selection was made at random?

**9.** A pack of cards is thoroughly shuffled. What is the probability that the top thirteen cards are all spades?

**10.** A bookshelf holds a family Bible and $k$ volumes of an encyclopaedia. A child takes down $i$ books at random. Use this illustration to justify in terms of combinations the relation $\binom{k+1}{i} = \binom{k}{i-1} + \binom{k}{i}$.

## SUMMARY

In a sequence of $n$ independent trials, each having probability $a$ of 'success' and $b$ of 'failure', the probability of $i$ successes is

$$p_i = \binom{n}{i} a^i b^{n-i},$$

where the *binomial coefficient*

$$\binom{n}{i} = \frac{n!}{i!(n-i)!}$$

$$= \frac{n(n-1)(n-2)\ldots(n-i+1)}{i(i-1)(i-2)\ldots 1}.$$

$\binom{n}{i}$ is also the number of subsets of size $i$ contained in a set of $n$ elements.

$$\binom{n}{i} = \binom{n}{n-i}.$$

The binomial coefficients form *Pascal's triangle*, in which each number in the middle of the table is the sum of the number immediately above it and the one to its left,

i.e.
$$\binom{n+1}{i} = \binom{n}{i} + \binom{n}{i-1}.$$

```
          1
          1   1
          1   2   1
          1   3   3   1
          1   4   6   4   1
          1   5  10  10   5   1
          1   6  15  20  15   6   1
          1   7  21  35  35  21   7   1
```

When calculating a sequence of binomial probabilities, it is helpful to use the ratio of consecutive terms:

$$p_{i+1} = p_i \times \frac{n-i}{i+1} \times \frac{a}{b}.$$

A set of binomial probabilities gives a humped histogram with mode at or close to $na$.

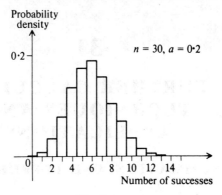

Fig. 9

*The binomial theorem*

$$(b+a)^n = \sum_{i=0}^{n} \binom{n}{i} b^{n-i} a^i$$

where $n \in \mathbb{N}$, and, for rational $n$, the series

$$1 + nh + \frac{n(n-1)}{2!} h^2 + \ldots + \binom{n}{k} h^k$$

converges to $(1+h)^n$ as $k \to \infty$, for $-1 < h < 1$.

# 31

# FURTHER CALCULUS TECHNIQUES AND APPLICATIONS

## 1. SUMMATION AND INTEGRATION

### *Exercise A*

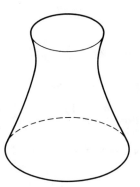

Fig. 1

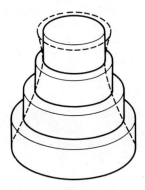

Fig. 2

**1.** The cooling tower in Figure 1 has a maximum radius of 18 m and a minimum radius of 9 m. It is 40 m high.

(*a*) Calculate an upper bound for the volume of the tower by finding the volume of the smallest cylinder that will just enclose it.

(b) Improve your estimate of the volume of the tower by calculating the volume of the four cylinders shown in Figure 2, using this data:

| Height above ground (m) | 0 | 10 | 20 | 30 | 40 |
|---|---|---|---|---|---|
| Radius (m) | | 18 | 13 | 10 | 9 | 10 |

**2.** (a) Obtain an upper bound for the volume of liquid that the glass in Figure 3 contains when full, if it is 4 cm deep and has maximum radius 2 cm.

Fig. 3

(b) Every vertical cross-section through the glass in Figure 3 fits the curve $y = x^2$. Calculate the radius of each of the four cylinders 1 cm high which envelop the glass in Figure 4. Calculate their volumes and hence estimate the volume of liquid.

(c) Improve your estimate in part (b) by taking cylinders $\frac{1}{2}$ cm high.

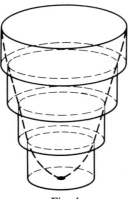

Fig. 4

(*d*) Write a flow diagram to calculate the value of the volume to any desired degree of accuracy. If you have computing facilities, run a program to calculate the volume to 4 significant figures.

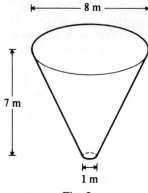

Fig. 5

**3.** A grain hopper is in the shape of an inverted right circular cone with the bottom removed (see Figure 5). Use the method of Question 2 with seven cylinders to obtain an estimate of the volume of the hopper. Compare your answer with the value obtained using the formula $v = \frac{1}{3}$(height)×(area of base) for any complete pyramid.

**4.** The cross-sectional area $C$ cm$^2$ of a rugby football which is 30 cm long is given by

$$C = x(30-x)$$

where $x$ cm is the distance from one end. Estimate the volume of air inside the ball by finding the total volume of the six cylinders shown in section in Figure 6. Improve your estimate by using twelve cylinders of half the thickness.

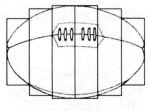

Fig. 6

**5.** The surface area of water in a bath (see Figure 7) at different heights above the plug-hole is as follows:

| Height (*y* cm) | 10 | 20 | 30 | 40 | 50 |
|---|---|---|---|---|---|
| Area ($C$ cm$^2$) | 7200 | 9800 | 11 600 | 13 000 | 14 200 |

Estimate the capacity of the bath when filled to a depth of 50 cm by calculating the total volume of the 'slices' shown in section in Figure 8.

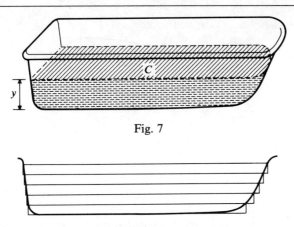

Fig. 7

Fig. 8

**6.** The vertical cross-sectional area of a car boot (see Figure 9) at various distances from the front is as follows:

| Distance ($x$ m) | 0 | 0·2 | 0·4 | 0·6 | 0·8 | 1·0 |
|---|---|---|---|---|---|---|
| Area ($C$ m$^2$) | 0·90 | 0·90 | 0·87 | 0·79 | 0·64 | 0·40 |

The overall distance from the front to the back of the boot is 1 m. Estimate the volume of the boot.

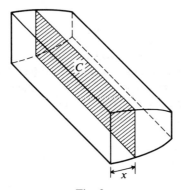

Fig. 9

**7.** The following table shows the cross-sectional area at distance $x$ m from the bows of a sailing boat 10 m long (see Figure 10, overleaf).

| Distance ($x$ m) | 0 | 2 | 4 | 6 | 8 | 10 |
|---|---|---|---|---|---|---|
| Area ($C$ m$^2$) | 0 | 1·1 | 1·8 | 2·0 | 1·7 | 1·2 |

Estimate the volume of the hull.

795

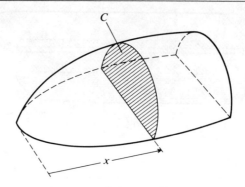

Fig. 10

**1.1**   In Exercise A, our method of estimating the volume of a solid was to add up the volumes of a series of slices which touched the outline of the solid, but each of which had *constant* cross-sectional area, so that the volume of an individual slice was simply area × thickness.

Figure 11 shows a typical slice for the rugby ball of Question 4.

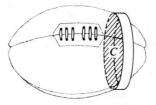

Fig. 11

This process should remind you of how we calculated approximate values for areas under graphs in Chapter 10 (see Figure 12). The *exact* area under the graph from $x = a$ to $x = b$ in Figure 12, is the limit of the sum as the rectangles are taken thinner and thinner. This limit is denoted by the definite integral

$$\int_a^b y\, dx.$$

Likewise the exact *volume* of the solid in Figure 13 (which is the limit of the sum as the slices get thinner and thinner), is denoted by the definite integral

$$\int_a^b C\, dx$$

where the cross-sectional area $C$ is a function of $x$.

796

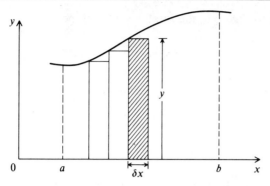

Fig. 12   The area of a typical thin
          rectangle is $y\,\delta x$. The
          approximate total area is
          the sum of the areas of thin
          rectangles, i.e. $\displaystyle\mathop{\mathbf{S}}_{x=a}^{x=b} y\,\delta x$.

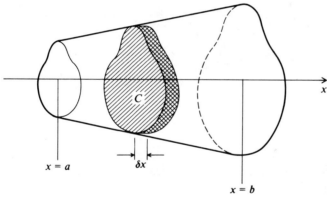

Fig. 13   The volume of a typical
          thin slice is $C\,\delta x$. The
          approximate total volume
          is the sum of the volumes of
          thin slices, i.e. $\displaystyle\mathop{\mathbf{S}}_{x=a}^{x=b} C\,\delta x$.

*Example* 1

If the cross-sectional area $C$ m$^2$ at distance $x$ m from the front of the car
boot in Exercise A, Question 6, is given by

$$C = \frac{9 - 5x^3}{10},$$

find by integration the total volume of the boot.

797

Referring to Figure 9, the total volume will be

$$\int_0^1 C\,dx = \int_0^1 \left(\frac{9-5x^3}{10}\right) dx$$

$$= \frac{1}{10}\left[9x - \frac{5x^4}{4}\right]_0^1$$

$$= 0\cdot775.$$

So the volume of the boot is about $0\cdot78\ \mathrm{m}^3$.

**\*1.2**    The justification for using integration in this way follows the same pattern as our proof in Chapter 10 (see p. 219).

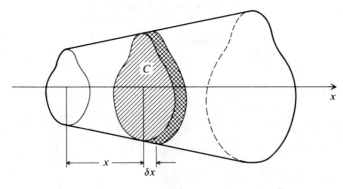

Fig. 14

If $V$ is the volume of the solid in Figure 14 up to distance $x$ from one end, and $C$ is the cross-section area at $x$, then both $V$ and $C$ are functions of $x$.

The shaded slice has volume $\delta V$ which will be greater than $C\,\delta x$ (the edges are not horizontal but in this example slope up from left to right).

So $$\delta V > C\,\delta x.$$

Similarly, if $C + \delta C$ is the area of the other face of the slice, we have

$$(C + \delta C)\,\delta x > \delta V.$$

Putting these two inequalities together,

$$(C + \delta C)\,\delta x > \delta V > C\,\delta x,$$

or $$C + \delta C > \frac{\delta V}{\delta x} > C.$$

798

Now, as $\delta x$ tends to zero, $C + \delta C$ tends to $C$ and $\dfrac{\delta V}{\delta x}$ tends to $\dfrac{dV}{dx}$. It follows that, in the limit,

$$\frac{dV}{dx} = C.$$

**1.3  Volumes of solids of revolution.** A solid the same shape as the wine glass in Figure 3 can be produced by spinning the area between the graph of $y = x^2$, the line $y = 4$ and the $y$-axis, about the $y$-axis (see Figure 15).

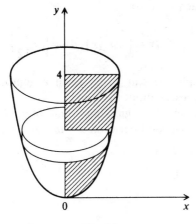

Fig. 15

The cross-sections of the slices we used to estimate the volume were particularly simple—they were all circles (whose radii, and therefore areas, are simple functions of $y$).

Such solids are called *solids of revolution.*

*Example* 2

Calculate the volume of the cone formed by rotating the area between $y = \frac{1}{2}x$, the line $x = 4$ and the $x$-axis, about the $x$-axis (see Figure 16, overleaf).

The slice shown—a disc—touches the cone at $(x, y)$. The radius of this disc is $y$, its cross-section area is $\pi y^2$ and its volume $\pi y^2 \, \delta x$.

So the total volume will be

$$V = \int_{x=0}^{x=4} \pi y^2 \, dx.$$

799

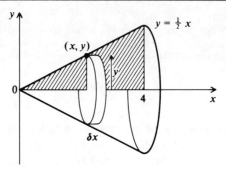

Fig. 16

But we are told that $y = \frac{1}{2}x$, so

$$V = \int_0^4 \pi y^2 \, dx = \int_0^4 \pi (\tfrac{1}{2}x)^2 \, dx = \left[ \pi \frac{x^3}{12} \right]_0^4 = \frac{16\pi}{3}.$$

From this example we can write down a general result for solids formed by rotating areas about the $x$-axis.

If the curve bounding the region has equation $y = f(x)$ (see Figure 17), then the volume of the solid between $x = a$ and $x = b$ will be

$$\int_{x=a}^{x=b} \pi y^2 \, dx = \int_a^b \pi \{f(x)\}^2 \, dx.$$

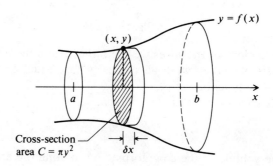

Fig. 17

Several of the solid shapes in Exercise A were solids of revolution with *vertical* axes. Sometimes we can turn such a solid through a right angle and use the method of Example 2 to find the volume, but sometimes it is more convenient to adapt the method and rotate about the $y$-axis instead of the $x$-axis, as the following example shows.

800

*Example* 3

The shape of the nose-cone of a rocket is obtained by rotating the area between the curve $y = 3(1 - x^2)$ and the axes about the *y*-axis (see Figure 18). Find the volume of the nose-cone.

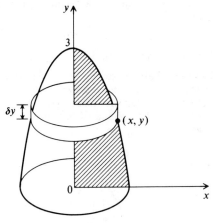

Fig. 18

The cross-section area of the disc shown touching the curve at the point $(x, y)$ in Figure 18 is $\pi x^2$. If its thickness is $\delta y$ then its volume will be

$$\pi x^2 \, \delta y.$$

The total volume of the cone will be the limit as $\delta y \to 0$ of the sum of the volumes of all such discs, or

$$V = \int_{y=0}^{y=3} \pi x^2 \, dy.$$

But, from $y = 3(1 - x^2)$, we obtain $x^2 = 1 - \tfrac{1}{3}y$.

So

$$V = \int_0^3 \pi(1 - \tfrac{1}{3}y) \, dy$$

$$= \pi \left[ y - \tfrac{1}{6}y^2 \right]_0^3$$

$$= \tfrac{3}{2}\pi.$$

### Exercise B

**1.** In Exercise A, Question 4, the cross-sectional area $C$ cm$^2$ at a distance $x$ cm from one end of the rugby football 30 cm long was given by

$$C = x(30 - x).$$

Find by integration an accurate value for the volume of the ball.

801

**2.** The cross-sectional area $C$ m$^2$ at a distance $x$ m from the bows of the hull of the sailing boat, total length 10 m, in Exercise A, Question 7, is given by

$$C = 2 - \tfrac{1}{18}(x - 6)^2.$$

Find by integration an accurate value for the volume of the hull.

**3.** The surface area $C$ cm$^2$ of the water at a height $y$ cm in the bath of Exercise A, Question 5, is given by

$$C = 2500\sqrt{y} - 70y.$$

Find the volume of the water in the bath to a height of 50 cm by integration.

**4.** Figure 19 shows a square-based pyramid, height 5 m and base edge 2 m. The shaded slice is $y$ m below the vertex. Write down in terms of $y$ an expression for the length of the edge of the shaded slice and hence the slice's area. If this slice has thickness $\delta y$, write down the volume of the slice. Find by integration the volume of the pyramid.

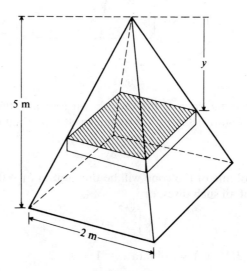

Fig. 19

**5.** A cone has base-area $A$ and height $h$ (see Figure 20). Show that the area of cross-section $C$ at depth $y$ below the vertex is given by

$$C = \frac{y^2}{h^2}A.$$

Show by integration that the volume of the cone is $\tfrac{1}{3}Ah$.

**6.** The radius of a tree-trunk decreases uniformly from 0·5 m at the base to 0·3 m at a height of 20 m above the ground. Give a formula for the radius at a height $y$ metres and find by integration the volume of wood in the trunk to a height of 20 m.

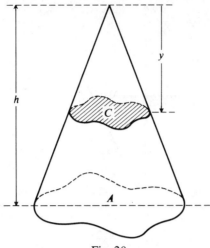

Fig. 20

**7.** If we turn the cooling tower of Exercise A, Question 1, on its side, the shape is generated by rotating the curve

$$y = \tfrac{1}{100}x^2 + 9$$

about the $x$-axis between $x = -10$ and $x = 30$. Find by integration the volume of the tower.

**8.** Find by integration the volume of water required to fill a hemispherical bowl, radius 10 cm, to a depth of 6 cm.

**9.** Show that the volume of a typical thin disc for the wine glass (see Figure 4) obtained by rotating $y = x^2$ about the $y$-axis between $y = 0$ and $y = 4$ is $\pi y\, \delta y$. Calculate by integration the total volume of liquid required to fill the glass.

**10.** The grain hopper of Exercise A, Question 3, is obtained by rotating the line $y = 2x$ about the $y$-axis between $y = 1$ and $y = 8$ (see Figure 21 for a vertical section). Show that the typical thin cylinder (shown shaded) has volume $\tfrac{1}{4}\pi y^2\, \delta y$. Show by integration that the volume of the hopper is $134\,\text{m}^3$ to 3 significant figures.

**11.** The region between the curve $y = 2 - x^2$ and the $x$ and $y$ axes is rotated (*a*) about the $y$-axis, and (*b*) about the $x$-axis. Sketch the solids formed and calculate their volumes.

**12.** (*a*) The region from $x = 1$ to $x = n$ between $y = \dfrac{1}{x}$ and the $x$-axis is rotated about the $x$-axis. Calculate the volume of the solid formed in terms of $n$. What happens to the volume as $n$ increases? Is there a limiting value?

(*b*) Repeat the question using $y = \dfrac{1}{x^2}$.

**13.** Sketch the parabolas $y^2 = 4x$ and $y^2 = 5x - 4$ and find their points of intersection. A bowl is made by rotating the area enclosed by the curves about the $x$-axis. Find the volume of the material used to make the bowl.

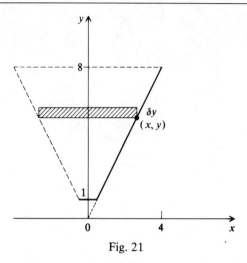

Fig. 21

**14.** A cylindrical hole, radius $b$ is bored symmetrically through a sphere of radius $a$ $(a > b)$. Find the volume remaining.

**15.** (a) Find the volumes of the solids formed when the following areas are rotated about the $x$-axis:

(i) $y = \sin x$   for $0 \le x \le \pi$;

(ii) $y = 2e^{-x}$   for $-1 \le x \le 1$;

(iii) $y = \dfrac{2}{\sqrt{x}}$   for $1 \le x \le 4$.

(b) Find the volumes of the solids formed when the following areas are rotated about the $y$-axis:

(i) $y = \ln(1+x)$   for $0 \le y \le 2$;

(ii) $y = \dfrac{2}{1+x^2}$   for $1 \le y \le 2$;

(iii) $y = \cos^{-1} x$   for $0 \le y \le \frac{1}{2}\pi$.

## 2. FIGURES WITH CIRCULAR SYMMETRY

**2.1   Area.** So far, all our summations have concerned rectangular strips or flat slices. Sometimes it is easier (or even essential) to use circular symmetry and add up thin annuli, or thin cylindrical or spherical shells.

For example, if we wish to derive the well-known formula $A = \pi a^2$ for the area of a circle, radius $a$, we can adopt the methods of previous sections and estimate the area using rectangular strips as in Figure 22.

Here it is convenient to calculate first the area of a quadrant and then multiply by four. The area of the quadrant is given by

$$\int_0^a y \, dx = \int_0^a \sqrt{(a^2 - x^2)} \, dx$$

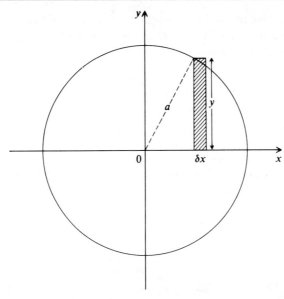

Fig. 22

and this integral is carried out using the substitution $x = a \sin \theta$ to give, eventually, $\frac{1}{4}\pi a^2$ as required.

An alternative method is to divide up the circle into circular slices as in Figure 23. We estimate the area $\delta A$ of each slice by imagining it to be

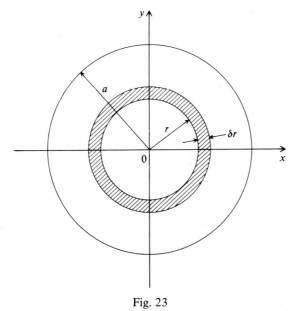

Fig. 23

straightened out to give a rectangle of area approximately $2\pi r\,\delta r$. The sum of the areas of all such rectangles for $0 \leqslant r \leqslant a$ will approach the total area of the circle as $\delta r \to 0$. In the limit

$$A = \int_0^a 2\pi r\,dr = \pi a^2.$$

**2.2   Volume.** Similarly, to calculate the volume of a sphere, radius $a$, we could choose flat, disc-shaped slices, but an alternative integral is obtained using thin concentric hollow cylinders (see Figure 24). If the radius of such a cylinder is $r$, and thickness $\delta r$, its height will be $2\sqrt{(a^2 - r^2)}$.

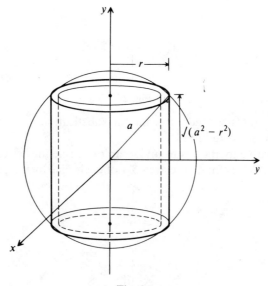

Fig. 24

Flattened out, its volume $\delta V$ will approximate to that of a rectangular slab of length $2\pi r$, width $2\sqrt{(a^2 - r^2)}$ and thickness $\delta r$, i.e.

$$\delta V \approx 4\pi r\sqrt{(a^2 - r^2)}\,\delta r.$$

Integrating,

$$V = \int_{r=0}^a 4\pi r\sqrt{(a^2 - r^2)}\,dr = -4\pi\left[\tfrac{1}{3}(a^2 - r^2)^{\frac{3}{2}}\right]_0^a = \tfrac{4}{3}\pi a^3.$$

**2.3**   In the next example we extend the scope of application of these ideas of summation using circular symmetry.

*Example* 4

A mathematical model of a city gives it a circular shape, radius 2 km, with a density of population which falls uniformly from 20 000 persons per square kilometre at the centre to 2000 per square kilometre at the outer edge. Estimate the population of the city.

Inhabitants of a city form a set of discrete units, but the number is large enough for it to be reasonable to represent this by a continuous distribution over the area of the city. With this model the population density, $\rho$ persons per square kilometre, at points distant $r$ km from the centre is given by the formula

$$\rho = 20\,000 - 9000r.$$

Let Figure 23 (see p. 805) be a diagram of the city. If $P$ is the population within a circle radius $r$ km, then the population $\delta P$ within the shaded annulus will be given by

$$\delta P \approx \rho \delta A$$
$$\approx \rho 2\pi r\, \delta r = (20\,000 - 9000r)\,.\, 2\pi r\, \delta r.$$

Integrating, the total population will be

$$P = \int_0^2 (20\,000 - 9000r)\,.\, 2\pi r\, dr$$
$$= \left[ \pi(20\,000r^2 - 6000r^3) \right]_0^2$$
$$= 32\,000\pi,$$

or about 100 000 inhabitants.

### Exercise C

**1.** The thickness $t$ cm of a discus (see Figure 25) at a distance $r$ cm from the centre is given by the formula

$$t = \frac{100 - r^2}{40}.$$

Figure 25 shows a hollow cylindrical slice whose inner radius is $r$ cm, and outer radius $(r + \delta r)$ cm. Write down an expression for the volume of this slice and integrate to find the total volume of the discus.

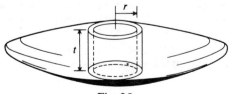

Fig. 25

**2.** The region between the $x$ and $y$ axes and the line $y = c + mx$ is rotated about the $y$-axis to form a right circular cone (see Figure 26). Find the constants $c$ and $m$ if the cone has height $h$ and base radius $a$.

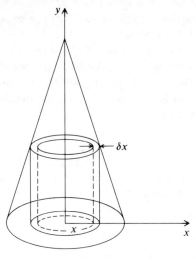

Fig. 26

The cone is divided into cylindrical slices as shown in Figure 26. By considering a typical slice, outer radius $x$, thickness $\delta x$, obtain the expression

$$V = \int_0^a 2\pi x h \left(1 - \frac{x}{a}\right) dx$$

for the volume $V$ of the cone. Evaluate this integral.

**3.** Find the volume of the solid formed by rotating about the $y$-axis the region bounded by the axes and the graph of $y = \cos x$ over the interval $0 \leq x \leq \frac{1}{2}\pi$. [Hint: you are advised to use the method of hollow cylinders.]

**4.** Find the volume of the wine glass in Exercise B, Question 9, using the method of hollow cylinders.

**5.** Find the volume of the solid generated by rotating the region bounded by the two axes, the graph $y = \exp(-x^2)$ and the line $x = b$ about the $y$-axis. Show that the volume approaches a finite limit as $b$ tends to infinity.

**6.** A further method of finding the volume of a sphere is to divide it into a series of thin concentric spherical shells. Write down an approximate expression for the volume $\delta V$ of such a shell, inner radius $r$, thickness $\delta r$. Integrate your expression to find the total volume of a sphere radius $a$. (You may use the formula for the surface area of a sphere, $A = 4\pi r^2$.)

**7.** Repeat the calculation of Example 4 for a city of radius 2 km whose population density $\rho$ falls from 20 000 per square kilometre at the centre according to the formula

$$\rho = 20\,000\, e^{-r}.$$

**8.** A competition was held at a darts club to find who could most consistently score a bull in the centre of the board. Measurements on the dartboard (outer radius 20 cm) afterwards showed that the density of holes per square centimetre in the board decreased according to the formula $\rho = \dfrac{k}{(r+1)^2}$ for $0 \leqslant r \leqslant 20$. If 500 darts were thrown, find the value of $k$. [Hint: you may find the substitution $u = r+1$ helpful.]

## 3. SUMMATION IN GENERAL

The replacement of the limit of a finite sum by a definite integral has many applications apart from the calculation of areas and volumes. Example 4 dealt with population density; the following examples show applications to mass and the flow of liquids. The technique will be used again in later chapters on mechanics and probability.

**3.1  Mass.** If the density of a solid is constant, its mass can be found by calculating the volume and then multiplying by the density. If, however, the density varies from point to point it may be very difficult to estimate the mass unless the variation is a known function of distance.

*Example 5*

The interior of a large jug has the shape formed by rotating about the $y$-axis the area between the graph of $y = 4x - 20$ and the $y$-axis for $0 \leqslant y \leqslant 20$. (See Figure 27.)

The jug is filled to the brim with orange juice which is allowed to settle. If, after some time, the variation of density $\rho$ g/cm$^3$ with height $y$ cm is given by

$$\rho = 1 \cdot 6 \, e^{-y/50},$$

find the total mass of orange juice in the jug.

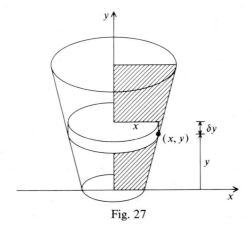

Fig. 27

809

Consider the typical cylindrical slice shown in Figure 27. Its volume $\delta V$ is $\pi x^2 \, \delta y$ cm$^3$. The density at height $y$ is $1 \cdot 6 \, e^{-y/50}$ g/cm$^3$. If the slice is very thin we can use this value throughout the slice, giving an approximate value for the mass $\delta m$ g of the slice:

$$\delta m \approx \rho \, \delta V = 1 \cdot 6 \, e^{-y/50} \times \pi x^2 \, \delta y.$$

But the geometry of the jug gives

$$y = 4x - 20 \;\Rightarrow\; x = \frac{y+20}{4} \;\Rightarrow\; x^2 = \left(\frac{y+20}{4}\right)^2.$$

So
$$\delta m \approx 1 \cdot 6 \pi \, e^{-y/50} \left(\frac{y+20}{4}\right)^2 \delta y.$$

The total mass will be the limiting value of the sum of all such slices from the bottom of the jug to the top, as their thickness tends to zero. That is,

$$m = \int_0^{20} 1 \cdot 6 \pi \, e^{-y/50} \left(\frac{y+20}{4}\right)^2 dy.$$

Integrating by parts twice, we finally obtain

$$m = 4630.$$

**3.2  Flow.** When liquid flows along a channel, whether it is a natural river or a domestic drainage pipe, the speed of flow is less near the walls and floor of the channel. The next example calculates the overall rate of flow using a very simple model for the variation of speed.

*Example 6*

Figure 28 shows the cross-section of an open water channel, overall height 1 m and width $2\sqrt{2}$ m. The outline of the cross-section fits the curve $y = \frac{1}{2}x^2$. The speed $v$ m/s of flow at height $y$ m above the bottom of the channel is given by

$$v = 1 + y.$$

Find the total volume of water per second flowing along the channel, when the water depth is $0 \cdot 8$ m.

Consider the volume of water per second crossing the thin rectangle at height $y$ m shown shaded in the cross-section of Figure 28. This volume will be found by multiplying the area by the speed of flow across it. If the rectangle is thin we can say that the speed is approximately $(1+y)$ m/s. The area is $2x \, \delta y = 2\sqrt{(2y)} \, \delta y$, so the volume which flows across the shaded rectangle per second is $(1+y)2\sqrt{(2y)} \, \delta y$ m$^3$.

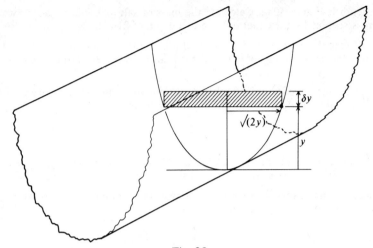

Fig. 28

The total volume of flow across the section per second will be the sum of the contributions from all such rectangles, or

$$\int_0^{0\cdot8} (1+y)2\sqrt{(2y)}\,dy = 2\sqrt{2}\int_0^{0\cdot8} (y^{\frac{1}{2}}+y^{\frac{3}{2}})\,dy$$

$$= 2\sqrt{2}\left[\tfrac{2}{3}y^{\frac{3}{2}}+\tfrac{2}{5}y^{\frac{5}{2}}\right]_0^{0\cdot8}$$

$$= 2\cdot0\ \text{m}^3\ \text{to 2 significant figures.}$$

### Exercise D

**1.** The density $\rho$ g/cm$^3$ of paint in a cylindrical tin (15 cm high and 8 cm in radius) at a depth $y$ cm from the top is given by

$$\rho = 1 + \tfrac{1}{150}y^2.$$

Find the total mass of paint in the tin.

**2.** Shortly after the beginning of a chemical test on the diffusion of bromine vapour, measurements of the density of a column of vapour in a cylindrical jar 20 cm high and 2 cm in radius show that the density at the bottom is $7 \times 10^{-3}$ kg/dm$^3$, and at the top it is $2 \times 10^{-3}$ kg/dm$^3$. Calculate the mass of bromine in the cylinder assuming either

(a) that the decrease in density is linear, or

(b) that the density $\rho$ kg/dm$^3$ fits the relation $\rho = 7 \times 10^{-3} e^{-ky}$ where $k$ is a constant to be determined, and $y$ cm is the height above the bottom of the jar.

**3.** The amount of salt in the sea at a particular place is $\left(12 + \dfrac{630}{x^2}\right)$ kg/m$^3$, where $x$ m is the depth from the surface and $x$ is greater than 30, and 12·7 kg/m$^3$ at

811

any depth less than 30 m. Calculate the mass of salt in a column of sea water of cross-section 1 square metre down to a depth of 210 m.

**4.** Calculate the total mass of a circular disc of constant thickness 0·02 m, radius 0·5 m, if the density $\rho$ kg/m$^3$ at radius $r$ m is given by $\rho = 3r^2$. [Hint: use annular slices.]

**5.** Calculate the mass of a ring of thickness 1 cm with inner radius 2 cm and outer radius 10 cm if the density $\rho$ g/cm$^3$ at radius $r$ cm is given by

$$\rho = \frac{12}{r}.$$

**6.** Calculate the mass of a sphere of radius 3 units when the density is given by: (i) $\rho = 2r$; (ii) $\rho = r^2$. (Use thin spherical shells; see Exercise C, Question 6.)

**7.** Suppose that a sphere of gas comprising a star of radius $a$ has a density at a distance $r$ from the centre given by

$$\frac{k(a-r)}{r},$$

where $k$ is a positive constant. Calculate the mass of the star. (Use thin spherical shells.)

**8.** The speed of flow $s$ cm/s of water along a drainage channel with a concrete floor and metal sides varies with height $x$ cm above the bottom of the channel according to the relation $s = 20 + 1·5x$. The channel is 50 cm wide and has total depth of water of 20 cm. Write down an expression in terms of $x$ for the volume of water that flows in one second through a rectangle in the section shown in Figure 29 which is $\delta x$ thick at a height $x$. Integrate to find the total volume per second of water flowing along the channel.

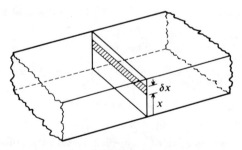

Fig. 29

**9.** Liquid flows in a circular pipe of radius $r$, the speed of flow at a distance $x$ from the axis being given by the formula

$$v = k(r^2 - x^2).$$

Give a formula for the total rate of flow of the liquid in the pipe. [Hint: consider the flow across a thin annulus of the cross-section as shown in Figure 30.]

**\*10.** A certain quantity of illumination is spread uniformly over a disc of radius $r$. Compare its effect at a point on the perpendicular axis, distance $s$ from the

812

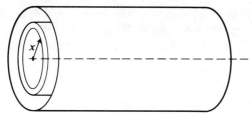

Fig. 30

centre of the disc, with the effect of a point source of light of the same intensity placed at the centre of the disc. (Note: the effect of a given source of illumination may be taken to vary inversely as the square of the distance from the source; use thin annuli.)

**11.** The rate $p$ people per hour at which customers enter a supermarket between 2 p.m. and 6 p.m. (the store opens after lunch at 2 p.m. and closes at 6 p.m.) is given by

$$p = 350t \sin\left(\frac{\pi t}{4}\right)$$

where $t$ is the time in hours after 2 p.m. Find the total number of people who enter the shop in this time.

**12.** Figure 31 shows the cross-section of a river, with the width of the river at intervals of 2 m in depth above the bed. Water flows through the river to a depth of 8 m, the average speed of flow at $x$ m above the bed being given by the formula

$$\frac{40x - x^2}{150}\ \text{m/s}.$$

Give an estimate of the quantity of water per second flowing down the river. [Hint: approximate to the cross-section by a series of rectangles, or use Simpson's rule.]

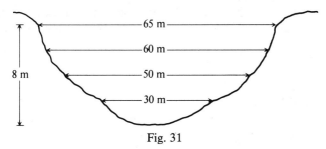

Fig. 31

## 4. AVERAGES

**4.1   Average speed.** The speed $v$ m/s of a car as it accelerates past a line of slow lorries is given by

$$v = 18 + 2t,$$

813

where $t$ is the time in seconds after the driver starts to accelerate. Figure 32 shows the speed/time graph. If the acceleration lasts 5 seconds, calculate the distance travelled in this time and the *average speed* $\bar{v}$ over these 5 seconds.

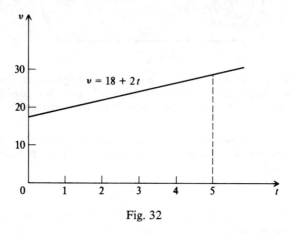

Fig. 32

Copy Figure 32 and mark on it a horizontal line showing the graph of motion with this constant average speed over the whole 5 seconds. Explain why the areas under the two graphs are identical.

Suppose that, instead of the simple linear formula $v = 18 + 2t$, the speed is given by the quadratic

$$v = 18 + 0{\cdot}4t^2.$$

What now will be the average speed over the interval $0 \leqslant t \leqslant 5$?

Figure 33 shows the graph of $v = 18 + 0{\cdot}4t^2$. The total distance travelled in the interval $0 \leqslant t \leqslant 5$ will be the area under the graph (shown shaded). Dividing this distance by the length of the time interval gives

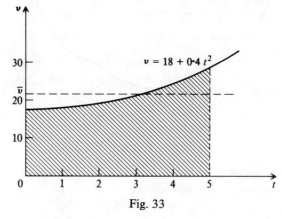

Fig. 33

814

the average speed.

$$\bar{v} = \frac{\displaystyle\int_0^5 (18 + 0 \cdot 4t^2)\, dt}{5}$$

$$= \frac{1}{5}\left[ 18t + \frac{0 \cdot 4t^3}{3} \right]_0^5$$

$$= 21\tfrac{1}{3}\ \text{m/s}.$$

The dotted horizontal line in Figure 33 shows this average speed, maintained over the 5 seconds. The area under the dotted line for $0 \leqslant t \leqslant 5$ is equal to the area under the original curve for the same interval.

**4.2**   The same method can be used to calculate average values in other contexts.

*Example* 7

An alternating current is given by the expression

$$I = 5 \sin 100\pi t.$$

Find the average current over the time interval $0 \leqslant t \leqslant 0 \cdot 01$.

We interpret 'average value' here, as we did in Section 4.1, to be the constant value $\bar{I}$ that would give the same area as that under the original graph (see Figure 34).

$$\bar{I} = \frac{\displaystyle\int_0^{0 \cdot 01} 5 \sin 100\pi t\, dt}{0 \cdot 01}$$

$$= 500 \left[ \frac{-1}{100\pi} \cos 100\pi t \right]_0^{0 \cdot 01}$$

$$= \frac{10}{\pi}$$

$$\approx 3 \cdot 18.$$

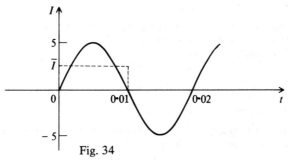

Fig. 34

**4.3   The average value of a function.** More generally, we define the average value $\bar{y}$ of a continuous function $y = f(x)$ over the interval $a \leqslant x \leqslant b$ to be

$$\bar{y} = \frac{\displaystyle\int_a^b f(x)\,dx}{b-a}$$

and, in terms of the graph, this average value is the height of a rectangle having the same area as the area under the graph over the interval $a \leqslant x \leqslant b$ (Figure 35).

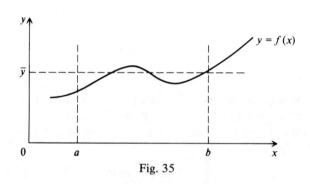

Fig. 35

### *Exercise E*

**1.** Find the average speed over the interval $0 \leqslant t \leqslant 5$ for the following speed functions. Sketch a graph for each and mark the average as a horizontal line.
(a) $v = 15t$;  (b) $v = 20 - 3t$;  (c) $v = 25 - t^2$;
(d) $v = 24 + 4 \sin\left(\frac{1}{5}\pi t\right)$;  (e) $v = 28(1 - e^{-t})$.

**2.** Find the average speed of a body falling under gravity from rest for 5 seconds. (Take $g$ as $10 \text{ m/s}^2$.)

**3.** Find the average values of the following functions over the given intervals. Illustrate each with a sketch graph.
(a) $x \to \sin x$    over $0 \leqslant x \leqslant \frac{1}{2}\pi$;
(b) $x \to \sqrt{(1-x^2)}$    over $-1 \leqslant x \leqslant 1$;
(c) $x \to \dfrac{1}{1+x^2}$    over $-1 \leqslant x \leqslant 1$;
(d) $x \to e^x + e^{-x}$    over $-2 \leqslant x \leqslant 2$.

**4.** Sketch the graph of $y = x \sin x$ over the interval $0 \leqslant x \leqslant \pi$. Find the average value of $x \to x \sin x$ over this interval.

816

**5.** Sketch the graph of $y = \dfrac{1}{x}\ln x$. Find $\displaystyle\int_a^b \dfrac{1}{x}\ln x \, dx$ using integration by parts and hence find the average value of $x \to \dfrac{1}{x}\ln x$ over $2 \leqslant x \leqslant 4$.

**6.** A body is cooling and its temperature is given by $T = 60e^{-t/2}$ where $T$ is in degrees Celsius and $t$ is in minutes. What is its average temperature over the first 10 minutes of cooling?

**7.** An oscillating current is given by the expression

$$i = 240 \sin 100\pi t.$$

What is its period? What is its mean value over that period?

This mean value is clearly not much use in practice; instead people use the *root mean square* (r.m.s.) value. Find the mean value of $i^2$ over $0 \leqslant t \leqslant 0{\cdot}02$ and then take its square root. Show that this value equals $240/\sqrt{2}$ and prove that the root mean square of any function of the form $y = A \sin kx$ must be $A/\sqrt{2}$ over $0 \leqslant x \leqslant 2\pi/k$.

**8.** A quantity of gas expands under pressure $p$ N/m$^2$ according to the law

$$pv^{0{\cdot}9} = 300.$$

What is the average pressure as the volume $v$ m$^3$ changes from $\frac{1}{4}$ to 1?

If the change in volume in terms of time is given by $v = 2t + 1$, what is the average pressure as the time changes from 0 to 1?

## 5. CENTRE OF MASS

**5.1**   An especially important kind of average is the centre of mass of a mechanical system. In Chapter 24 the centre of mass $\mathbf{r}_G$ of a system of $n$ discrete particles with masses $m_1, m_2, \ldots, m_n$ and position vectors $\mathbf{r}_1, \mathbf{r}_2, \ldots, \mathbf{r}_n$ was defined by

$$M\mathbf{r}_G = \sum m_i \mathbf{r}_i \tag{1}$$

where $M = \sum m_i$ is the total mass of the system. The centre of mass defines a mean position for the elements of the system, giving prominence to each according to its mass.

Particularly important properties of the centre of mass noted in Chapter 24 were:

(i) For the purposes of Newton's second law, a system of particles could be regarded as a *single* particle mass $M$ concentrated at the centre of mass. That is, in applying the formula

$$\mathbf{F} = M\mathbf{a}$$

to a system of total mass $M$, $\mathbf{F}$ is the vector sum of forces acting on the system and $\mathbf{a}$ is the acceleration of the centre of mass.

(ii) If the system is in a uniform gravitational field, the centre of mass is the *centre of gravity*, the point at which the weight of the system can be assumed to act.

The concept of summation developed in this chapter makes it possible to extend the idea of centre of mass to solid bodies (where the mass is continuously distributed) and to replace the summation by integration.

*Example* 8

Find the centre of mass of a semicircular piece of plastic of uniform thickness and radius 5 cm.

Clearly the centre of mass will lie along the line of symmetry of the semicircle (see the x-axis in Figure 36).

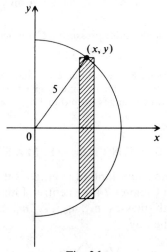

Fig. 36

To find the coordinate $x_G$ of the centre of mass we imagine the semicircle replaced by a set of rectangular strips. It is most convenient for the central vertical of each to end on the boundary, so that a typical strip has height $2y$ and width $\delta x$. If the surface density is $s$, the mass of this strip will be $2sy\, \delta x$ and its centre of mass will be at $(x, 0)$.

From equation (1), the x-coordinate of the centre of mass $x_G$ of the whole semicircle will be given by

$$Mx_G = \sum m_i x_i$$

where $m_i$ is the mass of a typical strip and $x_i$ is the position of its centre of mass. So

$$Mx_G = \mathop{\textbf{S}}_{x=0}^{x=5} 2sy\, \delta x \times x = \int_{x=0}^{x=5} 2sxy\, dx$$

818

in the limit as $\delta x \to 0$. But $x^2 + y^2 = 25$ for the semicircle, so $y = \sqrt{(25 - x^2)}$
and

$$Mx_G = \int_0^5 2sx\sqrt{(25 - x^2)}\,dx$$

$$\Rightarrow Mx_G = 2s\left[-\tfrac{1}{3}(25 - x^2)^{\frac{3}{2}}\right]_0^5$$

$$= \frac{250s}{3}.$$

But
$$M = \tfrac{1}{2}\pi 5^2 s = \tfrac{25}{2}\pi s$$

so
$$x_G = \frac{20}{3\pi} \approx 2\cdot 1.$$

Notice that, since the density is uniform, $s$ cancels out.

**5.2  Symmetry.** In practice it is often possible to use such arguments based on geometrical symmetry to help locate the centre of mass of a body whose density is uniform. But with more difficult shapes it is usually necessary to write equation (1) in component form

$$M\begin{pmatrix} x_G \\ y_G \\ z_G \end{pmatrix} = \Sigma\, m_i \begin{pmatrix} x_i \\ y_i \\ z_i \end{pmatrix}$$

and to deal with the three components separately. The following example is typical.

*Example 9*

The rudder shown in Figure 37, 4 metres high and 2 metres wide, is cut in the shape of the parabola

$$y = 4 - x^2$$

from a thin metal sheet. Find the position of its centre of mass.

Let the surface density of the metal sheet be $s$ kg per square metre. We replace the rudder by a set of rectangular strips (see Figure 38). The mass of a typical strip will be $sy\,\delta x$ and its centre of mass will be at $(x, \tfrac{1}{2}y)$. Applying our definition of centre of mass in two dimensions,

$$M\begin{pmatrix} x_G \\ y_G \end{pmatrix} = \begin{pmatrix} \Sigma\, m_i x_i \\ \Sigma\, m_i y_i \end{pmatrix}.$$

819

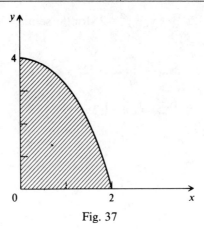

Fig. 37

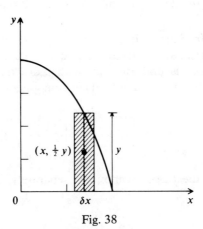

Fig. 38

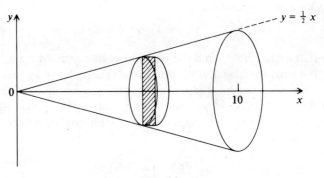

Fig. 39

820

We first calculate

$$M = \int_{x=0}^{x=2} sy\,dx$$

$$= \int_0^2 s(4-x^2)\,dx = \frac{16s}{3}.$$

Now, substituting $m_i = sy\,\delta x,\ x_i = x,\ y_i = \frac{1}{2}y$ for our typical strip,

$$\frac{16s}{3}\binom{x_G}{y_G} = \begin{pmatrix} \mathbf{S}\ sy\,\delta x\,.\,x \\[2mm] \mathbf{S}\ sy\,\delta x\,.\,\dfrac{y}{2} \end{pmatrix}$$

$$= \begin{pmatrix} s\displaystyle\int_{x=0}^2 xy\,dx \\[3mm] \dfrac{s}{2}\displaystyle\int_{x=0}^2 y^2\,dx \end{pmatrix} = \begin{pmatrix} s\displaystyle\int_0^2 (4x-x^3)\,dx \\[3mm] \dfrac{s}{2}\displaystyle\int_0^2 (4-x^2)^2\,dx \end{pmatrix}$$

$$\Rightarrow \frac{16s}{3}\binom{x_G}{y_G} = \binom{4s}{\frac{128}{15}s}$$

$$\Rightarrow \binom{x_G}{y_G} = \binom{0\cdot75}{1\cdot6}.$$

### Exercise F

**1.** Find the centre of mass of a piece of cardboard in the shape of an isosceles triangle of height 10 cm, base 6 cm.

**2.** Find the centre of mass of a piece of cardboard bounded by the $x$-axis and the graph of $y = \cos x$ for $-\frac{1}{2}\pi \leqslant x \leqslant \frac{1}{2}\pi$.

**3.** Find the centre of mass of a piece of cardboard in the shape of a quadrant of a circle.

**4.** Find the centre of mass of a piece of card cut to fit the area enclosed between the graphs of $y = x^2$ and $x = y^2$.

**5.** The centre of mass of any solid of revolution must lie along its axis. Find by integration based on cylindrical slices (see Figure 39) the position of the centre of mass of the cone 10 cm high generated by $y = \frac{1}{2}x$. (You may assume the cone is of uniform density.)

**6.** Find the centre of mass of a solid hemispherical bowl radius 10 cm.

### Miscellaneous Exercise

**1.** A water trough is 2 m long and the shape of its cross-section is given by $h = 0\cdot2 \sin x$ for $\frac{1}{2}\pi \leqslant x \leqslant \frac{3}{2}\pi$, where $h$ m is the height above a fixed level. Find the volume of water it holds when filled to the brim.

**2.** A plastic beaker is formed by rotating the curve $y^2 = \frac{1}{2}x + 3$ for $0 \leqslant x \leqslant 12$ about the $x$-axis, and removing the volume generated by rotating the curve $y^2 = \frac{1}{2}x + 2$ for $\frac{1}{2} \leqslant x \leqslant 12$ about the $x$-axis. (Units are centimetres.) Find the volume of plastic needed to make twenty such beakers. To what depth must a beaker be filled in order to half fill it (by volume) with tea?

**3.** A doughnut has a shape made by rotating a circle of radius $r$ about a line distance $d$ from its centre. Show that the area of cross-section at a height $x$ above its central horizontal section (supposing the doughnut to be on a horizontal plate) is $4\pi d\sqrt{(r^2 - x^2)}$. Hence show that the volume of the doughnut is $2\pi^2 r^2 d$.

**4.** Find the volume and centre of mass of the frustum of a solid cone formed by rotating the line segment $5x + y = 10$, $0 \leqslant y \leqslant 4$, about the $y$-axis.

**5.** As a result of an atomic explosion at a height $h$ above a flat desert, radioactive atoms are deposited on the ground. ($a$) If the number of atoms deposited per unit area at distance $r$ from the explosion is $a \exp(-kr^2)$, show that the total number deposited is $\pi a \exp(-kh^2)/k$. ($b$) Find the area of the circle which contains just half the number of atoms.

**6.** A town, total population $N$ people, is in the shape of a circle radius 4 km. The population density is uniform. Find the mean distance of a resident from the centre of the town.

**7.** A swarm of bees is clustered round the queen in a sphere of radius 10 cm. Find the average distance of a bee from the queen.

## SUMMARY

*Volume*

Volumes may be found approximately by summing slices whose volumes are cross-sectional area × thickness.

When the cross-sectional area $C$ is a known function of $x$, the volume of a solid between $x = a$ and $x = b$ is given by the definite integral

$$\int_a^b C\,dx.$$

Slices may also be taken which are thin annuli, cylinders or spherical shells.

*Solids of revolution*

The volume of the solid (see Figure 40) obtained by rotating the area between $y = f(x)$ and the $x$-axis for $a \leqslant x \leqslant b$ about the $x$-axis is

$$\int_a^b \pi y^2\,dx$$

where $y = f(x)$.

822

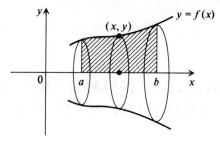

Fig. 40

If the area between $y = f(x)$ and the $y$-axis is rotated about the $y$-axis for $c \leq y \leq d$, the volume is $\displaystyle\int_c^d \pi x^2 \, dy$.

### Averages

The average value of the continuous function $x \to f(x)$ over $a \leq x \leq b$ is

$$\frac{\displaystyle\int_a^b f(x) \, dx}{b - a} \ .$$

### Centre of mass

For a solid body whose mass is continuously distributed, the centre of mass $\mathbf{r}_G$, defined by

$$M\mathbf{r}_G = \sum m_i \mathbf{r}_i \quad \text{or} \quad M \begin{pmatrix} x_G \\ y_G \\ z_G \end{pmatrix} = \sum m_i \begin{pmatrix} x_i \\ y_i \\ z_i \end{pmatrix},$$

is found by integration.

# 32

# COMPLEX NUMBERS AND POLYNOMIAL EQUATIONS

## 1. INTRODUCTION

We have already studied polynomial functions at some length because of their applicability to mathematical modelling, and their use in approximations.

We now take a closer look at the solution of polynomial *equations*. In Chapter 17 we evolved techniques for solving quadratic equations which we re-examine in Exercise A. We also saw that, although there was no simple general method for solving cubic equations, every cubic has at least one real root. If this root can be found, the solution of our cubic equation can be reduced to the solution of a quadratic. The main tool we developed for such reduction of cubic and higher degree polynomials was the factor theorem:

If $P(b/a) = 0$, then $(ax - b)$ is a factor of $P(x)$.

*Example* 1

Factorize $P(x) = x^3 - 3x^2 + 20$ over the real numbers, and find the real roots of $x^3 - 3x^2 + 20 = 0$.

Possible linear factors are $(x \pm 1)$, $(x \pm 2)$, $(x \pm 4)$, $(x \pm 5)$, $(x \pm 10)$ and $(x \pm 20)$. We calculate $P(\pm 1)$, $P(\pm 2)$, ... until we find a zero:

$$P(1) = 18, \ P(-1) = 16, \ P(2) = 16, \ P(-2) = 0.$$

We now know that $(x + 2)$ is a factor. Division gives

$$P(x) = (x + 2)(x^2 - 5x + 10)$$

and we can proceed no further since $x^2 - 5x + 10$ cannot be factorized over the real numbers.

Our calculations have given us the coordinates of four points on the graph of $P$. It is also clear that $P(0) = 20$. Check by differentiation that the maximum and minimum points of $P$ are at $(0, 20)$ and $(2, 16)$ as shown in Figure 1.

The only real root of $P(x) = 0$ is $x = -2$.

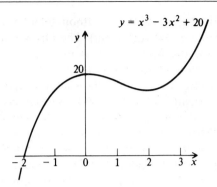

$$y = x^3 - 3x^2 + 20$$

Fig. 1

### Exercise A

**1.** Factorize the following polynomials over the real numbers where possible:
(a) $x^2 + 7x + 12$;  (b) $2x^2 - 7x + 5$;
(c) $x^2 - 2x + 1$;  (d) $x^2 + 3$;
(e) $x^3 - x$;  (f) $x^3 - x^2 + x - 1$;
(g) $x^4 - 2x^3 - 3x^2 + 8x - 4$.

**2.** For each part of Question 1, find all the zeros over the real numbers. Sketch the graph of each polynomial.

**3.** In Chapter 17 we derived the formula $x = \dfrac{-b \pm \sqrt{(b^2 - 4ac)}}{2a}$ for the solutions of the quadratic equation $ax^2 + bx + c = 0$. Use this formula to find the real roots of the following equations:
(a) $x^2 - 6x + 6 = 0$;  (b) $x^2 - 4x + 2 = 0$;
(c) $x^2 - 2x + 2 = 0$;  (d) $3x^2 + x + 1 = 0$;
(e) $x^2 + 6x + 9 = 0$.
State how many real roots you found for each equation.

**4.** Find the real roots of the following cubic equations:
(a) $x^3 - 6x^2 + 11x - 6 = 0$;  (b) $x^3 + 2x^2 - 4x - 8 = 0$;
(c) $x^3 + 1 = 0$.
Sketch a graph to illustrate each equation. What can you say in general about the number of real roots of a cubic equation?

**5.** Write down a quartic (fourth-degree) polynomial equation which has *no* real roots. [Hint: use two quadratics which have no real roots.] Illustrate with a graph.

## 2. COMPLEX NUMBERS

**2.1 Inventing new numbers.** Problems associated with the solution of polynomial equations have absorbed the attention of mathematicians since the earliest times. The simplest equations such as $x - 7 = 0$ or $12x - 5 = 0$ could be solved in the positive integers or rationals, both of which were in common use by 1000 B.C. (although modern notation for fractions dates only from about A.D. 1500). The Greeks in the 5th and 4th centuries B.C. made the first important extension to the number system by laying the foundations of irrational numbers, enabling equations like $x^2 - 5 = 0$ to be solved. Since their interest came principally from a geometric viewpoint, the Greeks did not appreciate that there might be *two* roots—indeed negative numbers in their present form were not fully established until the 16th century. At about that time also, the modern system of classification of polynomial equations according to their degree was introduced and it was realized (as we have seen in Exercise A) that there was no neat theory to account for the number of roots. A quadratic might have 0 or 2 roots (counting a repeated root as 2), a cubic might have 1 or 3 roots, a quartic might have 4, 2 or 0 and so on. Obviously it would be ideal if *every* quadratic had exactly 2 roots, every cubic 3 roots and every equation of degree $n$ had exactly $n$ roots.

Cardan in 1545 was the first to attempt to deal with the solution of an equation like $x^2 + 4 = 0$, but it was more than 250 years later that the invention of complex numbers was completed by Gauss (who went on to show that no further numbers need be invented to solve equations of any degree).

In fact, as we saw in Chapter 19, only one *new* number is needed, denoted by $j$, such that $j^2 = -1$. You will remember that we combined $j$ with the real numbers to obtain numbers of the form $a + bj$ called *complex numbers* ($a, b \in \mathbb{R}$). We made the assumption that the usual rules for addition and multiplication applied to complex numbers.

The square roots of all negative numbers are multiples of $j$. For example, since

$$(2j)^2 = 4j^2 = -4,$$

and

$$(-2j)^2 = 4j^2 = -4,$$

the square roots of $-4$ are $+2j$ and $-2j$. Similarly the square roots of $-7$ are $\pm\sqrt{7}j$.

**2.2  Equality of complex numbers.** The rational number $2/5$ is equivalent to the rational number $6/15$. In general the condition for $a/b$ to equal $c/d$ is that $ad = bc$. What is the condition for the complex number $a + bj$ to equal $c + dj$?

The usual rules of arithmetic give

$$a - c = (d - b)j.$$

Squaring,                           $$(a - c)^2 = -(d - b)^2.$$

826

Since the quantities in brackets are real numbers, the left side cannot be negative and the right side cannot be positive, hence they must both be zero. Hence the conditions are $a = c$ and $b = d$.

Can you think of any other structures in which equality requires two conditions like this?

**2.3 Roots of polynomials.** Since $-4$ has the two square roots $\pm 2j$, the quadratic $x^2 + 4 = 0$ has the two distinct roots $2j$ and $-2j$. Similarly, all other quadratic equations with real coefficients which have no real solutions have two distinct solutions in the complex numbers. For example,

$$x^2 - 2x + 5 = 0,$$

which can be written $\qquad (x - 1)^2 = -4,$

has the two roots $1 + 2j$ and $1 - 2j$. Substituting $1 + 2j$ into $x^2 - 2x + 5$ we have

$$(1 + 2j)^2 - 2(1 + 2j) + 5$$
$$= 1 + 4j + (2j)^2 - 2 - 4j + 5$$
$$= 1 + 4j - 4 - 2 - 4j + 5$$
$$= 0$$

which confirms that $1 + 2j$ is a root.

Note that this also means that $x - (1 + 2j)$ is a factor of $x^2 - 2x + 5$. Check that $1 - 2j$ also satisfies the quadratic equation and that

$$x^2 - 2x + 5 = [x - (1 + 2j)][x - (1 - 2j)].$$

Returning to Example 1, we can now find two more roots of the equation

$$x^3 - 3x^2 + 20 = 0.$$

Factorization over the real numbers gave

$$x^3 - 3x^2 + 20 = (x + 2)(x^2 - 5x + 10),$$

and $\quad (x + 2)(x^2 - 5x + 10) = 0 \quad \Rightarrow \quad x = -2 \quad$ or $\quad x^2 - 5x + 10 = 0,$
giving
$$x = -2 \text{ or } \frac{5 \pm \sqrt{15}j}{2}.$$

### Exercise B

**1.** What are the squares of $3j$, $\sqrt{7}j$, $-4j$, $-\sqrt{12}j$?

**2.** Write down the square roots of $-9$, $-16$, $-12$ and $-20$.

**3.** Solve the quadratic equations: $(a)$ $x^2+2x+10=0$; $(b)$ $x^2+4x+20=0$; $(c)$ $x^2-x-6=0$; $(d)$ $2x^2-2x+1=0$; $(e)$ $3x^2-7x+2=0$. Check one of the solutions in each case.

**4.** In Chapter 17, it was shown that for the equation $ax^2+bx+c=0$, the sum of the roots is $-b/a$, and the product of the roots is $c/a$. Verify these results for the equations in Question 3.

**5.** Using the results quoted in Question 4, write down quadratic equations with roots: $(a)$ $2+j$, $2-j$; $(b)$ $3+4j$, $3-4j$; $(c)$ $1+\sqrt{2}j$, $1-\sqrt{2}j$; $(d)$ $\frac{1}{2}\pm\frac{1}{2}\sqrt{3}j$.

**6.** Factorize: $(a)$ $x^2+9$; $(b)$ $x^2+2x+5$; $(c)$ $x^2+4x+20$; $(d)$ $x^2-6x+10$; $(e)$ $x^2-x-2$.

**7.** $(a)$ Evaluate $P(x)=x^2-jx+(1-3j)$ when (i) $x=1+2j$; (ii) $x=1+j$; (iii) $x=3-2j$. Solve $P(x)=0$ in the complex numbers.
   $(b)$ Evaluate $P(x)=x^3-5x^2+8x-6$ when (i) $x=2$; (ii) $x=3$; (iii) $x=1+j$; (iv) $x=2+j$; (v) $x=1-j$. Solve $P(x)=0$ in the complex numbers.

**8.** Show that $-1$ is a root of the cubic equation $x^3+4x+5=0$, and find the other two roots.

**9.** Show that $j$ is a root of the cubic equation $x^3+2x^2+x+2=0$, and find the other two roots.

**10.** Show that $x=j$ and $x=2$ are roots of $x^4-5x^3+7x^2-5x+6=0$. Find the other two roots and hence give the factors of $x^4-5x^3+7x^2-5x+6$.

**11.** Does the equation $x^4+5x^2+4=0$ have any real roots? Show that $j$ and $-j$ are roots and solve the equation completely. Hence factorize $x^4+5x^2+4$ over the complex numbers.

## 3. GEOMETRIC REPRESENTATION

**3.1 The Argand diagram.** Since any complex number $a+bj$ is uniquely associated with the ordered pair of real numbers $(a, b)$, we could use the abbreviated notation $(a, b)$ to stand for $a+bj$. This notation suggests that we can represent $a+bj$ by the point on the Cartesian plane whose coordinates are $(a, b)$. For example (see Figure 2),

$$2+3j \text{ will be represented by } (2, 3),$$

$$-1+4j \text{ will be represented by } (-1, 4),$$

$$7-j \text{ will be represented by } (7, -1).$$

This Cartesian representation of the complex numbers is called the *complex plane* or *Argand diagram* (after J. R. Argand, 1768–1822). Plot the numbers $3+2j$, $1+4j$ and their sum $4+6j$. Of what other process does this addition remind you?

**3.2 An isomorphism.** The rule for addition

$$(a+bj)+(c+dj)=(a+c)+(b+d)j$$

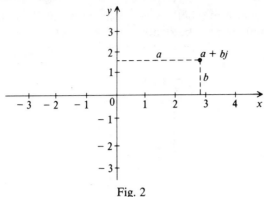

Fig. 2

may remind you of

$$\binom{a}{b} + \binom{c}{d} = \binom{a+c}{b+d}$$

and suggest a link with vector addition. Indeed, if we make the correspondence

$$\binom{a}{b} \leftrightarrow a + bj$$

then

$$\binom{c}{d} \leftrightarrow c + dj$$

and

$$\binom{a+c}{b+d} \leftrightarrow (a+c) + (b+d)j$$

leading to the correct addition.

Thus the correspondence defines an isomorphism between complex numbers under addition, and two-dimensional vectors under addition. So we can represent the complex number $a + bj$ by the vector $\binom{a}{b}$, and any result true for addition of vectors has a corresponding result for complex numbers.

Note that the isomorphism is with vectors, i.e. displacements or translations, though a complex number $a + bj$ is usually represented by the point $(a, b)$ whose position vector $\binom{a}{b}$ is the vector in question. Does the isomorphism also hold under subtraction?

**3.3   Notation.** Just as a vector is often expressed by a single symbol, in heavy type, in the same way a complex number, as we saw in Chapter 19, is frequently expressed by a single symbol and thought of as an entity. The general number $x + yj$ is usually denoted by the symbol $z$. Particular numbers may be denoted by using suffices. For example, in Section 3.1 we might have written: Plot $z_1 = 3 + 2j$, $z_2 = 1 + 4j$ and also $z_1 + z_2$ (see Figure 3).

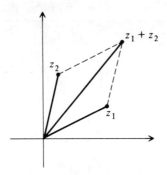

Fig. 3

**3.4  Subtraction.** Draw a copy of Figure 3 and mark on it the point representing $z_1 - z_2$. How is the position vector of this point related to the shift vector from $z_2$ to $z_1$?

## Exercise C

**1.** Plot the following pairs of complex numbers. Plot also their sum in each case.
    (a) $2 + j, 3 + 2j$;    (b) $-2 - 2j, 3 + 4j$;    (c) $4 - j, 1 + 3j$;
    (d) $1 + 2j, 1 - 2j$;    (e) $7 - 4j, 4 + 7j$.

**2.** If the first number in each pair in Question 1 is denoted by $z_1$ and the second by $z_2$, plot $z_1 - z_2$ and $z_2 - z_1$ for each pair. What geometrical relationship is there between the points representing the numbers $z_1 - z_2$ and $z_2 - z_1$?

**3.** Using the same scale for both axes, plot the points representing the pairs of complex numbers in Question 1 and their product $z_1 z_2$. Measure the lengths of each of the vectors representing $z_1$, $z_2$ and $z_1 z_2$. What do you find?
    Measure also the anticlockwise angle between the positive $x$-axis and each of the position vectors representing $z_1$, $z_2$ and $z_1 z_2$. What do you find?

**4.** Plot the following complex numbers as points on an Argand diagram: $2j$, $-5j$, $2 + 3j$, $1 + 4j$, $-2 + j$, $-1 + 5j$. Show the position vectors of these points on the diagram.
    Multiply each of the numbers by $j$, and plot the results on the same diagram. Draw in the position vectors of these points also. What is the geometric effect of multiplication by $j$?

**5.** Repeat Question 4, multiplying each number this time by $2j$. What is the geometric effect of multiplying by $2j$?

**6.** Plot on an Argand diagram the points representing the complex numbers $2 + j$ and $2 + 2j$. Denote these points by $A$ and $B$. Complete the triangle $OAB$ and draw in the vector $\mathbf{OP}$ where $P$ represents the complex number $1 + 2j$.

Calculate the products (i) $(1+2j)(2+j)$, (ii) $(1+2j)(2+2j)$. Plot the corresponding points on the Argand diagram, and denote them by $A'$ and $B'$ respectively. Complete the triangle $OA'B'$.

Making such measurements from your diagram as necessary, describe fully the transformation of the complex number plane effected by multiplication by $1+2j$. How is this transformation related to the position vector **OP** of the point representing $1+2j$ on the Argand diagram?

**7.** Repeat Question 6, plotting points $A$ and $B$ representing $3-j$ and $2-2j$ and drawing **OP** where $P$ represents $1+j$.

Calculate (i) $(1+j)(3-j)$ and (ii) $(1+j)(2-2j)$. Plot the corresponding points $A'$ and $B'$, draw the triangles $OAB$ and $OA'B'$ and describe the transformation effected by multiplication by $1+j$.

**8.** Check that your results in Questions 6 and 7 are valid for a triangle whose vertices are the points representing the numbers $2+0j$, $6-j$, $5+2j$.

**9.** Represent on an Argand diagram the complex numbers $z$, $z^2$, $z^3$ when
(a) $z = 2j$; (b) $z = 1+j$; (c) $z = 1+2j$. Comment.

# 4. MODULUS-ARGUMENT FORM FOR COMPLEX NUMBERS

The results of Exercise C suggest that there may be a simple rule for multiplying two complex numbers.

**4.1 Spiral similarities.** As seen in Question 6 of Exercise C, the geometric effect on the Argand diagram of multiplication by $1+2j$ appears to be equivalent to a rotation, centre $O$, of about $63°$, combined with an enlargement, centre $O$, of scale factor approximately $2 \cdot 2$. This transformation is known as a *spiral similarity* about the origin. Figure 4 shows the effect of such a transformation. The two shaded shapes are similar.

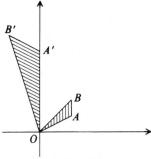

Fig. 4

**4.2 Modulus and argument.** Measurements of the vector $\begin{pmatrix} 1 \\ 2 \end{pmatrix}$ in Figure 4, Question 6 of Exercise C, give its length as approximately $2 \cdot 2$

units, and the angle which it makes with the positive $x$-axis as about 63°. Compare these measurements with the specification of the spiral similarity (Section 4.1). It would seem that for the purpose of multiplying complex numbers it would be useful to find the *polar coordinates r* and $\theta$ of the point on the Argand diagram representing a complex number $z$. In Figure 5, $z = a + bj$ is represented by the point $(a, b)$, whose polar coordinates are $(r, \theta)$. So

$$z = a + bj \text{ is equivalent to}$$

$$z = r\,(\cos \theta + j \sin \theta)$$

where $\qquad r = \sqrt{(a^2 + b^2)}$

is known as the *modulus* of the complex number $z$ and written $|z|$. ($r$ is non-negative.) The angle $\theta$ (in radian measure) which $OP$ makes with the positive $x$-axis is called the *argument* of $z$, written $\arg(z)$.

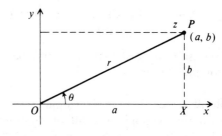

Fig. 5

Thus $r = |z|$, and $\theta = \arg(z)$.

As the circular measure of angle $X\hat{O}z$ can be equal to $\theta + 2k\pi$ for any integer $k$, we clarify matters by defining a *principal value* of the argument, and usually require that $0 \le \arg(z) < 2\pi$. Sometimes a more useful interval is $-\pi < \arg(z) \le \pi$.

We write $z = [r, \theta]$ as shorthand for $z = r(\cos \theta + j \sin \theta)$. This is known as the *modulus-argument* form for $z$.

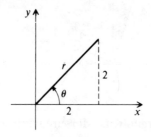

Fig. 6

*Example* 2

Express the complex number $z = 2 + 2j$ in modulus-argument form.
Figure 6 shows that $r = \sqrt{8}$, and that $\theta = \frac{1}{4}\pi$. Thus $z = [\sqrt{8}, \frac{1}{4}\pi]$.

*Example* 3

Express the complex number $z = -1 - \sqrt{3}j$ in modulus-argument form.
Figure 7 shows that $r = 2$, and that $\theta = \frac{4}{3}\pi$. Thus $z = [2, \frac{4}{3}\pi]$.

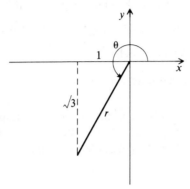

Fig. 7

*Example* 4

Express the complex number $z = [5, \frac{1}{3}\pi]$ in the form $a + bj$.
Figure 8 shows that $a = 5\cos\frac{1}{3}\pi = \frac{5}{2}$, and $b = 5\sin\frac{1}{3}\pi = \frac{5}{2}\sqrt{3}$. Thus $z = \frac{5}{2} + \frac{5}{2}\sqrt{3}j$.

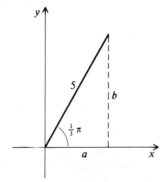

Fig. 8

**4.3 Multiplication in modulus-argument form.** Section 4.1 suggests the following rule for multiplying complex numbers:

If $z_1 = [r_1, \theta_1]$ and $z_2 = [r_2, \theta_2]$, then $z_1 z_2 = [r_1 r_2, \theta_1 + \theta_2]$.

833

It is quite easy to establish this result formally. For

$$z_1 = r_1 \cos \theta_1 + jr_1 \sin \theta_1$$

and
$$z_2 = r_2 \cos \theta_2 + jr_2 \sin \theta_2$$

and hence
$$
\begin{aligned}
z_1 z_2 &= (r_1 \cos \theta_1 + jr_1 \sin \theta_1)(r_2 \cos \theta_2 + jr_2 \sin \theta_2) \\
&= r_1 r_2 (\cos \theta_1 \cos \theta_2 - \sin \theta_1 \sin \theta_2) \\
&\quad + jr_1 r_2 (\cos \theta_1 \sin \theta_2 + \sin \theta_1 \cos \theta_2) \\
&= r_1 r_2 \cos(\theta_1 + \theta_2) + jr_1 r_2 \sin(\theta_1 + \theta_2) \\
&= [r_1 r_2, \theta_1 + \theta_2]
\end{aligned}
$$

(where $\theta_1 + \theta_2$ is reduced mod $2\pi$ if necessary).

**4.4  Division.** Since division is the inverse of multiplication, it is not difficult to deduce (see Exercise D, Question 8) that the rule for division is to *divide* the moduli and *subtract* the arguments.

### Exercise D

**1.** Represent the following complex numbers as points on a single Argand diagram, and find their moduli and arguments. Rewrite the numbers in the form $[r, \theta]$.

(a) $3+4j$;   (b) $-1+j$;   (c) $2-j$;   (d) $-\sqrt{3}-j$;
(e) $2+j$;   (f) $1-2j$;   (g) $-4-3j$;   (h) $-5+12j$;
(i) $-2-3j$.

**2.** The following numbers are given in modulus-argument form. Rewrite them in the form $a+bj$.

(a) $[3, 0]$;   (b) $[4, \frac{1}{3}\pi]$;   (c) $[2, \frac{1}{8}\pi]$;   (d) $[2, \frac{2}{3}\pi]$;
(e) $[1, \pi]$;   (f) $[\sqrt{2}, \frac{5}{4}\pi]$;   (g) $[2, \frac{2}{3}\pi]$;   (h) $[5, \frac{13}{10}\pi]$;
(i) $[4, \frac{1}{2}\pi]$.

**3.** Rewrite the following complex numbers in modulus-argument form.

(a) $\frac{1}{2}\sqrt{3} + \frac{1}{2}j$;   (b) $\frac{1}{\sqrt{2}} - \frac{1}{\sqrt{2}}j$;   (c) $-j$.

Plot the corresponding points on an Argand diagram. What do they have in common? Construct some more complex numbers with this property, and represent them on the Argand diagram.

**4.** What is the modulus of the complex number $\cos \theta + j \sin \theta$? What is the geometrical effect of multiplying by this complex number?

**5.** Find the products (a) $(4+5j)(1-2j)$, (b) $(2+j)(3-4j)$. Check your answers in each case by finding the modulus and argument of each complex number, and using the rule of Section 4.3.

**6.** Calculate the products:

(a) $[3, \frac{1}{6}\pi] \times [2, \frac{1}{3}\pi]$;  (b) $[2, \frac{2}{9}\pi] \times [1, \frac{1}{2}\pi]$;

(c) $[4, \frac{2}{3}\pi] \times [2, \frac{5}{9}\pi]$;  (d) $[3, \frac{19}{12}\pi] \times [1, \frac{5}{12}\pi]$;

(e) $[2, \frac{7}{6}\pi] \times [2, \frac{1}{6}\pi]$.

Give your answers both in modulus-argument form, and in the form $a + bj$.

**7.** Find $[r, \theta]$ in the following:

(a) $[3, \frac{1}{3}\pi] \times [r, \theta] = [6, \frac{1}{2}\pi]$;

(b) $[2, \frac{1}{4}\pi] \times [r, \theta] = [10, \frac{5}{4}\pi]$;

(c) $[4, \frac{11}{6}\pi] \times [r, \theta] = [2, \frac{1}{2}\pi]$;

(d) $[\sqrt{2}, \frac{2}{5}\pi] \times [r, \theta] = [4, \frac{9}{5}\pi]$;

(e) $[r_1, \theta_1] \times [r, \theta] = [r_2, \theta_2]$.

**8.** (a) Use the ideas of Question 7 to show that if $z_2 = [r_2, \theta_2]$ and $z_1 = [r_1, \theta_1]$ then

$$z_2 \div z_1 = \left[\frac{r_2}{r_1}, \theta_2 - \theta_1\right].$$

(b) Show also that $\dfrac{1}{z_1} = \left[\dfrac{1}{r_1}, -\theta_1\right]$.

**9.** Write down the second, third, fourth, and $n$th powers of:

(a) $[1, \frac{1}{3}\pi]$;  (b) $[1, \frac{2}{3}\pi]$;  (c) $[2, \frac{1}{4}\pi]$;  (d) $[\sqrt{2}, \frac{1}{6}\pi]$.

**10.** For each of the following pairs of complex numbers $z$, $w$, plot the points on the Argand diagram representing $z$, $w$, $zw$, $z/w$ and $1/w$.

(a) $z = [3, \frac{1}{6}\pi]$, $w = [2, \frac{1}{3}\pi]$;  (b) $z = [2, \frac{2}{9}\pi]$, $w = [1, \frac{1}{2}\pi]$;

(c) $z = [4, \frac{2}{3}\pi]$, $w = [2, \frac{5}{9}\pi]$;  (d) $z = [3, \frac{19}{12}\pi]$, $w = [1, \frac{5}{12}\pi]$;

(e) $z = [2, \frac{7}{6}\pi]$, $w = [2, \frac{1}{6}\pi]$.

**\*11.** (a) Calculate the products

(i) $(a + bj)(c + dj)$,

and

(ii) $\begin{pmatrix} a & -b \\ b & a \end{pmatrix}\begin{pmatrix} c & -d \\ d & c \end{pmatrix}$.

Hence show that the correspondence

$$a + bj \leftrightarrow \begin{pmatrix} a & -b \\ b & a \end{pmatrix}$$

between the set of complex numbers under multiplication and the set of matrices of the form $\begin{pmatrix} a & -b \\ b & a \end{pmatrix}$ under matrix multiplication is an isomorphism.

(b) Write down the matrices of (i) a rotation of $\theta$ about the origin; (ii) an enlargement, scale factor $r$, centre the origin; (iii) the spiral similarity which is the combination of (i) and (ii).

(c) Explain the connection between (a) and (b).

## 5. DE MOIVRE'S THEOREM

In this section we link some of the geometrical ideas we have been developing with our earlier theme of solving polynomial equations.

**5.1  Complex numbers of unit modulus.** Using the rule for multiplying complex numbers derived in Section 4, we obtain the following:

$$[1, \theta]^2 = [1, \theta] \times [1, \theta]$$
$$= [1, 2\theta],$$
$$[1, \theta]^3 = [1, \theta] \times [1, \theta]^2$$
$$= [1, \theta] \times [1, 2\theta]$$
$$= [1, 3\theta],$$

and it is not hard to see that, in general,

$$[1, \theta]^n = [1, n\theta]$$

(where the arguments are reduced mod $2\pi$ as necessary) which can be proved formally by induction.

Expressing this in the standard form for complex numbers gives

$$(\cos \theta + j \sin \theta)^n = \cos n\theta + j \sin n\theta,$$

for $n \in \mathbb{N}$; this is known as de Moivre's theorem.

*Example 5*

De Moivre's theorem with $n = 2$ gives

$$\cos 2\theta + j \sin 2\theta = [\cos \theta + j \sin \theta]^2$$
$$= \cos^2 \theta + 2j \sin \theta \cos \theta - \sin^2 \theta.$$

Hence
$$\cos 2\theta = \cos^2 \theta - \sin^2 \theta,$$

and
$$\sin 2\theta = 2 \sin \theta \cos \theta.$$

Similarly other values of $n$ lead to other real trigonometrical results. Calculating powers of complex numbers is, like multiplication, best done in modulus-argument form.

*Example 6*

For $z = -1 + \sqrt{3}j$, find $z^2$ and $z^3$ and plot the points representing $z$, $z^2$ and $z^3$ on an Argand diagram.

Now $z = -1 + \sqrt{3}j = [2, \frac{2}{3}\pi]$, so $z^2 = [4, \frac{4}{3}\pi]$ and $z^3 = [8, 2\pi] = [8, 0]$ (see Figure 9).

**5.2  Finding $n$th roots.** By reversing the process shown in the last example, we can find a cube root of 8.

Clearly there is one *real* cube root: $\sqrt[3]{8} = 2$.

836

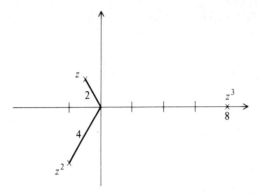

Fig. 9

But we have seen that $8 = [8, 2\pi] = [2, \frac{2}{3}\pi]^3$, giving a second root $[2, \frac{2}{3}\pi]$ or $-1 + \sqrt{3}j$.

We can find a third root by writing 8 as $[8, 4\pi]$, taking another whole turn, and then $[8, 4\pi] = [2, \frac{4}{3}\pi]^3$, indicating that $[2, \frac{4}{3}\pi]$ or $-1 - \sqrt{3}j$ is also a cube root of 8.

The process cannot be repeated indefinitely. If we take $8 = [8, 6\pi] = [2, 2\pi]^3$ we are back to our first root, 2, and any other representation only gives further duplication. Why?

Thus 8 is found to have exactly three distinct cube roots

$$2, \ -1 + \sqrt{3}j, \ -1 - \sqrt{3}j$$

which are symmetrically placed as we can see from Figure 10.

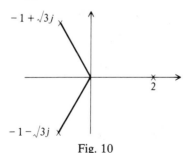

Fig. 10

Notice that we have found the solutions to the equation $z^3 = 8$. That is to say $z^3 - 8 = 0$ has the roots $2, -1 + \sqrt{3}j, -1 - \sqrt{3}j$. Hence $z^3 - 8$ has the factors $(z - 2), (z + 1 - \sqrt{3}j), (z + 1 + \sqrt{3}j)$.

The next example shows how the working can be condensed.

*Example 7*

Find the roots of $z^5 = 4 + 4j$.

837

Write $z = [r, \theta]$. Then, since $4 + 4j = [\sqrt{32}, \frac{1}{4}\pi + 2k\pi]$, $k \in \mathbb{Z}$, the equation becomes

$$[r, \theta]^5 = [\sqrt{32}, \tfrac{1}{4}\pi + 2k\pi]$$

or  $\qquad\qquad [r^5, 5\theta] = [\sqrt{32}, \tfrac{1}{4}\pi + 2k\pi].$

So $r^5 = \sqrt{32}$, giving $r = \sqrt{2}$ (as $r$ is real and non-negative), and $5\theta = \frac{1}{4}\pi + 2k\pi$. Taking $k = 0, 1, 2, 3$, and $4$ we obtain the five distinct values $\theta = \frac{1}{20}\pi, \frac{9}{20}\pi, \frac{17}{20}\pi, \frac{25}{20}\pi$ and $\frac{33}{20}\pi$. Check that further values of $k$ give repeats.

The five distinct roots of $z^5 = 4 + 4j$, which are $[\sqrt{2}, \frac{1}{20}\pi]$, $[\sqrt{2}, \frac{9}{20}\pi]$, $[\sqrt{2}, \frac{17}{20}\pi]$, $[\sqrt{2}, \frac{25}{20}\pi]$, and $[\sqrt{2}, \frac{33}{20}\pi]$, are shown in Figure 11. Describe the symmetry of the figure.

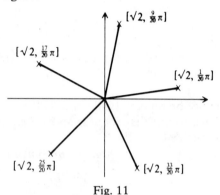

Fig. 11

### Exercise E

**1.** Check by direct multiplication that the three complex numbers $[1, 0]$, $[1, \frac{2}{3}\pi]$ and $[1, \frac{4}{3}\pi]$ are roots of the equation $z^3 = 1$. Plot the three roots on an Argand diagram. Describe the symmetry of your diagram. State the factors of $z^3 - 1$.

**2.** Check that $[2, \frac{1}{6}\pi]$, $[2, \frac{5}{6}\pi]$ and $[2, \frac{9}{6}\pi]$ are all roots of the equation $z^3 = 8j$. Plot the roots and describe the symmetry of the diagram.

**3.** Check that $[3, \pi]$ is one root of $z^3 = -27$. Use the symmetry you have found in Questions 1 and 2 to plot all three roots on an Argand diagram *without* calculation. Write down the other two roots and check them. Factorize $z^3 + 27$.

**4.** Use the ideas of Question 3 to find the other two roots to a cubic equation, of the form $z^3 = a$, one of whose roots is $z = -5$. Write down the original cubic equation.

**5.** Find all the complex roots of $z^4 + 1 = 0$. Plot the roots on an Argand diagram.

**6.** Find all the roots of the following equations. In each case plot the roots on an Argand diagram and describe the symmetry:
  (a) $z^4 = j$;  (b) $z^4 = 1 + j$;  (c) $z^5 = -1$;
  (d) $z^5 = 32$;  (e) $z^5 = 4 + 4j$.

Did the diagrams for (i) all the fourth-degree equations, (ii) all the fifth-degree equations, have the same symmetry?

**7.** Given $z^5 = 1 + j$, find the possible values of $z$ and factorize $z^5 - 1 - j$ into its five factors.

**8.** Show that $1 + 2j$ is a root of $z^4 = -7 - 24j$. Write down the other three roots.

**5.3  Summary.** The results of Section 5.2 and Exercise E suggest that any polynomial equation of form $z^n = a + bj$ will have exactly $n$ complex roots. This is indeed true, and part of a more powerful result which we will meet in Section 7.

# 6. CONJUGATE COMPLEX NUMBERS

**6.1  Roots of quadratic equations.** Look back at the complex solutions to the equations

$$x^2 - 2x + 5 = 0 \quad \text{and} \quad x^2 - 5x + 10 = 0$$

in Section 2.3. Find also the solutions to (a) $x^2 - 2x + 2 = 0$ and (b) $x^2 - 4x + 5 = 0$. What have all the pairs of solutions in common?

The non-real solutions of quadratic equations with real coefficients occur in pairs $a + bj$, $a - bj$. A pair of complex numbers related in this way are called *conjugates*: $a - bj$ is the conjugate of $a + bj$ and vice versa.

If $z = a + bj$, its conjugate is written $z^* = a - bj$. Note that $z$ and $z^*$ have the $x$-axis as an axis of symmetry, and

$$z = [r, \theta] \Leftrightarrow z^* = [r, -\theta] = [r, 2\pi - \theta].$$

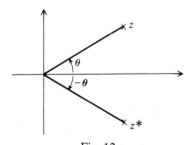

Fig. 12

## *Exercise F*

**1.** Write down the conjugates of: (a) $5 + 2j$; (b) $2 + j$; (c) $3 - 4j$; (d) $-7j$; (e) $-3$; (f) $-3 - 2j$.

**2.** When $z = 3 + 4j$, represent the following complex numbers on the same Argand diagram: $z$, $z^*$, $z + z^*$, $z - z^*$, $zz^*$.

**3.** When $z = a + bj$, find (i) $z + z^*$, (ii) $z - z^*$, (iii) $zz^*$.

**4.** $z = a + bj$, where $b \neq 0$. Find all the complex numbers $w$ which satisfy the two conditions: (i) $z + w$ is real; (ii) $zw$ is real.

**5.** Using the method of completing the square, find the complex numbers $z$ satisfying (a) $z^2 - 2jz - 5 = 0$; (b) $z^2 + jz - 1 = 0$. Comment on your answers, with reference to Section 6.1. Factorize the polynomials $z^2 - 2jz - 5$ and $z^2 + jz - 1$.

**6.** Show, taking $z = a + bj$, that
(a) $(z^3)^* = (z^*)^3$,
(b) $(z^3 + 5z^2 - 7z + 8)^* = (z^*)^3 + 5(z^*)^2 - 7z^* + 8$.

**7.** Given $z = a + bj$ and $w = c + dj$, show that
(a) $z^* + w^* = (z + w)^*$;
(b) $(z^*)^n = (z^n)^*$ (use de Moivre's theorem);
(c) $(zw)^* = z^* w^*$;
(d) $zz^* = |z|^2$.

**8.** Show by direct substitution that the conjugate pair $(1 + 2j)$, $(1 - 2j)$ are roots of $x^3 - 3x^2 + 7x - 5 = 0$. What is the third root?

## 6.2 Polynomials over the real numbers.

It is not hard to see why the non-real roots of quadratic equations with real coefficients always occur in conjugate pairs. For in the method of completing the square to solve the equations, we eventually arrive at $(x - p)^2 = d$ for some real numbers $p$ and $d$, and the equation will have real solutions unless $d < 0$. In this case, we have

$$(x - p)^2 = -q^2 \quad \text{for real numbers } p \text{ and } q$$
$$\Rightarrow x - p = \pm qj$$
$$\Rightarrow x = p \pm qj.$$

However, this is only an example of a more powerful result:

Roots of a real polynomial equation (of any degree) which are not themselves real numbers, occur in conjugate pairs.

Consider a general polynomial of degree $n$ with real coefficients:

$$P(z) \equiv a_n z^n + a_{n-1} z^{n-1} + a_{n-2} z^{n-2} + \cdots + a_1 z + a_0.$$

If $z_1$ is a root, $P(z_1) = 0$. We have to prove that $P(z_1^*) = 0$. Now,

$$P(z_1^*) = a_n (z_1^*)^n + a_{n-1}(z_1^*)^{n-1} + a_{n-2}(z_1^*)^{n-2} + \cdots + a_1 z_1^* + a_0$$

$$= a_n (z_1^n)^* + a_{n-1}(z_1^{n-1})^* + a_{n-2}(z_1^{n-2})^* + \cdots + a_1 z_1^* + a_0$$

(using Exercise F, Question 7(b))

$$= (a_n z_1^n)^* + (a_{n-1} z_1^{n-1})^* + (a_{n-2} z_1^{n-2})^* + \cdots + (a_1 z_1)^* + (a_0)^*$$

(since the $a_i$ are real)

$$= (a_n z_1^n + a_{n-1} z_1^{n-1} + a_{n-2} z_1^{n-2} + \cdots + a_1 z_1 + a_0)^*$$

(using Exercise F, Question 7(a) repeatedly)

$$= (P(z_1))^*$$

$$= 0^* = 0.$$

*Example* 8

Given that $2+3j$ is a root of $z^4 - 4z^3 + 12z^2 + 4z - 13 = 0$, find the other roots.

If $2+3j$ is a root, $2-3j$ will be a root as well. This enables us to write down a quadratic factor of $P(z) = z^4 - 4z^3 + 12z^2 + 4z - 13$ using the result (quoted in Exercise B, Question 4) about the sum and product of roots.

Since $$(2+3j) + (2-3j) = 4$$

and $$(2+3j)(2-3j) = 13,$$

$(z^2 - 4z + 13)$ is a factor of $P(z)$.

We can find another quadratic factor by inspection:

$$(z^2 - 4z + 13)(z^2 - 1) = z^4 - 4z^3 + 12z^2 + 4z - 13.$$

Hence two more linear factors of $P(z)$ are $(z-1)$ and $(z+1)$, giving a total of four roots for $P(z) = 0$:

$$1, -1, 2+3j, 2-3j.$$

### 6.3 Use of conjugates in division of complex numbers.

If $z = [r, \theta] = a + bj$, then $z^* = [r, -\theta] = a - bj$.

Hence, $zz^* = [r^2, 0] = a^2 + b^2$. So $zz^*$ is always a *real* number. This fact enables us to find the multiplicative inverse of a complex number, and to divide complex numbers. For

$$(a + bj)(a - bj) = a^2 + b^2$$

$$\Rightarrow (a + bj) \cdot \left( \frac{a}{a^2 + b^2} - \frac{b}{a^2 + b^2} j \right) = 1$$

$$\Rightarrow \frac{a}{a^2 + b^2} - \frac{b}{a^2 + b^2} j \text{ is the inverse of } a + bj \text{ under multiplication.}$$

$\Bigg($Another way of putting this is to say: if $z = a + bj$, then

$$\frac{1}{z} = \frac{a}{a^2+b^2} - \frac{b}{a^2+b^2}j.$$

Check that this is consistent with our earlier result $\frac{1}{z} = \left[\frac{1}{r}, -\theta\right].$$\Bigg)$

*Example 9*

Write the complex number $\dfrac{3+4j}{1+2j}$ in the form $a + bj$.

We can make the denominator real by multiplying top and bottom by the conjugate of the denominator. Hence

$$\frac{3+4j}{1+2j} = \frac{3+4j}{1+2j} \times \frac{1-2j}{1-2j}$$

$$= \frac{3-6j+4j-8j^2}{5}$$

$$= \frac{11}{5} - \frac{2}{5}j.$$

### Exercise G

**1.** Show that $\frac{1}{2} + \frac{1}{2}\sqrt{3}j$ is a root of the quartic equation $z^4 + 3z^3 - 2z^2 + 3z + 1 = 0$. Write down another root of this equation. Factorize the quartic into two quadratics with real coefficients. Hence find the other two roots.

**2.** Use the factor theorem to find a real factor of the cubic $z^3 - 4z^2 + 6z - 4$. Hence find the two non-real zeros of the polynomial. What are its factors over $\mathbb{C}$?

**3.** Find a real root of the equation $z^5 + 2z^3 + 10z^2 + z + 10 = 0$. Verify that $j$ is another root of this equation. Find the three other complex roots, and hence factorize the equation into five factors over $\mathbb{C}$. What are the factors over $\mathbb{R}$?

**4.** Write in the form $a + bj$:

(i) $\dfrac{1}{1+j}$;  (ii) $\dfrac{2+3j}{1+j}$;  (iii) $\dfrac{j}{2+3j}$;

(iv) $\dfrac{1-3j}{2-j}$;  (v) $\dfrac{3+4j}{j}$;  (vi) $\dfrac{4+6j}{1-5j}$.

**5.** Show that $2 - j$ is a root of the equation $z^3 - 2z^2 - 3z + 10 = 0$. Use the result of Section 6.2 to write down another root. Find the third root.

**6.** Repeat Question 5 for the root $-\frac{1}{2} + \frac{1}{2}\sqrt{3}j$ of the cubic $z^3 - z^2 - z - 2 = 0$.

**7.** Show that $\{a + bj : a, b \in \mathbb{R}\}$ is closed under division if $0 + 0j$ is excluded.

## 7. THE FUNDAMENTAL THEOREM OF ALGEBRA

**7.1   Factors and roots.** Here, we collect together some of our previous examples of factorization:

$$x^3 - 3x^2 + 20 = (x+2)(x + \tfrac{5}{2} - \tfrac{1}{2}\sqrt{15}j)(x + \tfrac{5}{2} + \tfrac{1}{2}\sqrt{15}j),$$

$$x^2 - 2x + 5 = (x - 1 + 2j)(x - 1 - 2j),$$

$$z^4 - 4z^3 + 12z^2 + 4z - 13 = (z-1)(z+1)(z-2-3j)(z-2+3j),$$

$$z^2 - 2jz - 5 = (z - j + 2)(z - j - 2).$$

What do these results suggest about the number of linear factors of a polynomial of degree $n$? And if we count repeated roots separately, what does our experience so far suggest about the number of roots of a polynomial equation of degree $n$?

**7.2   The fundamental theorem.** In Chapter 19 we stated that the complex number system is algebraically complete, in the sense that it is sufficient to solve all polynomial equations (with real or complex coefficients). This means that, for every polynomial $P(z)$, there exists at least one value of $z$ in the complex numbers for which $P(z) = 0$, i.e.

Every polynomial equation over $\mathbb{C}$ has a root in $\mathbb{C}$.

This is known as the *fundamental theorem of algebra*. The proof of this theorem is beyond the scope of this course, but it is a simple matter to deduce an important consequence of the theorem:

A polynomial equation of degree $n$ has exactly $n$ roots in $\mathbb{C}$ (allowing for repeated roots).

We show this by the following argument.

If $P(z)$ is a polynomial of degree $n$, by the fundamental theorem it has a zero, say $\alpha$, and hence a factor $(z - \alpha)$.

So $P(z) = (z - \alpha)Q(z)$, where $Q(z)$ is a polynomial of degree $n - 1$.

But $Q(z)$ must *itself* have a zero, and so the process can be repeated until $P(z)$ is expressed as a product of $n$ linear factors. Each factor gives rise to a root of $P(z) = 0$.

Notice that the fundamental theorem tells us nothing about *how* to find the roots of a polynomial equation.

## 8. LOCI

Our main purpose in this chapter has been to investigate polynomial equations and their roots, although we have also looked at geometrical representations of complex numbers wherever it was relevant.

In this section we follow up some of the geometrical ideas for their own sakes. Other applications of complex numbers are introduced in Chapter 37.

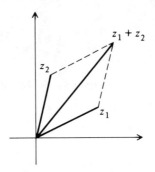

Fig. 13

**8.1 The triangle inequality.** Figure 13 shows any two complex numbers $z_1 = a + bj$, $z_2 = c + dj$ and their sum $z_1 + z_2 = (a+c) + (b+d)j$. These three points will form a parallelogram with the origin. Hence, considering either of the two triangles, we have

$$|z_1| + |z_2| \geqslant |z_1 + z_2|$$

since the sum of the lengths of two sides will always be greater than the length of the third side. This is known as the *triangle inequality*. Algebraically it is

$$\sqrt{(a^2 + b^2)} + \sqrt{(c^2 + d^2)} \geqslant \sqrt{[(a+c)^2 + (b+d)^2]},$$

which is not easy to establish by algebra.

Make a similar statement about $|z_1 - z_2|$.

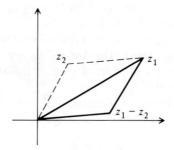

Fig. 14

**8.2. Loci.** If $z_1 = 7 + 5j$ and $z_2 = 2 + 4j$, then $z_1 - z_2 = 5 + j$. Figure 14 shows that $z_1 - z_2$ has the position vector of the displacement from

$z_2$ to $z_1$. $|z_1 - z_2|$ is the length of this displacement, which is $\sqrt{26}$. Similarly, for any complex number $z = x + yj$, $|z - z_2|$ is the distance from $z_2$ to $z$.

*Example* 10

Find the locus of $z$ if $|z - (2 + 4j)| = 5$.

This is merely another way of saying that the position of $z$ is restricted so that the distance from $z$ to $2 + 4j$ is 5. Thus the locus of $z$ would be a circle of radius 5 with centre at the point $(2, 4)$, as shown in Figure 15.

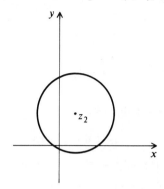

Fig. 15

Algebraically,
$$|z - z_2| = 5$$
$$\Rightarrow |(x + yj) - (2 + 4j)| = 5$$
$$\Rightarrow |(x - 2) + (y - 4)j| = 5$$
$$\Rightarrow \sqrt{[(x - 2)^2 + (y - 4)^2]} = 5$$
$$\Rightarrow (x - 2)^2 + (y - 4)^2 = 25$$

and you should recognize this as the circle $x^2 + y^2 = 5^2$, translated by $\binom{2}{4}$.

*Example* 11

Illustrate in the complex plane the set $P$ where

$$P = \{x : |z - 3| = |z + 2j|\}.$$

This means that the distance from $z$ to $(3, 0)$ is the same as its distance from $(0, -2)$. Thus $P$ is the mediator of these two points, as shown in Figure 16.

845

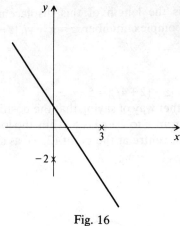

Fig. 16

This too may be confirmed algebraically:

$$|z-3| = |z+2j|$$
$$\Rightarrow \sqrt{[(x-3)^2 + y^2]} = \sqrt{[x^2 + (y+2)^2]}$$
$$\Rightarrow x^2 - 6x + 9 + y^2 = x^2 + y^2 + 4y + 4$$
$$\Rightarrow 6x + 4y - 5 = 0$$

which passes through the midpoint $(1\cdot5, -1)$ with gradient $-\frac{3}{2}$.

*Example* 12

Find the locus in the complex plane of $z$, where

$$\arg(z-2) = \tfrac{3}{4}\pi.$$

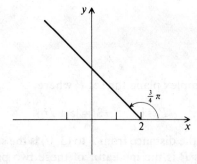

Fig. 17

Here the displacement from $(2, 0)$ to $z$ makes an angle $\frac{3}{4}\pi$ with the $x$-axis. The locus is thus the half-line shown in Figure 17. Check that the other half of this line would be given by

$$\arg(z-2) = -\tfrac{1}{4}\pi = \tfrac{7}{4}\pi$$

or
$$\arg(2-z) = \tfrac{3}{4}\pi.$$

### Exercise H

**1.** Illustrate the following loci in the complex plane:
(a) $\{z: |z-2| = 3\}$;      (b) $\{z: |z| \geqslant 4\}$;
(c) $\{z: |z-j| = 2\}$;      (d) $\{z: |z+4| \leqslant 1\}$;
(e) $\{z: |z+3j| > 3\}$;     (f) $\{z: |z+1+j| = \sqrt{2}\}$;
(g) $\{z: |z-3-4j| = 4\}$;   (h) $\{z: |z-2+j| > 1\}$.

**2.** Illustrate the following loci in the complex plane:
(a) $\{z: |z-1| = |z+2|\}$;    (b) $\{z: |z+j| = |z+1|\}$;
(c) $\{z: |z-2j| \geqslant |z-3|\}$;   (d) $\{z: |z-2| < |z-j|\}$.

**3.** Illustrate the following loci in the complex plane:
(a) $\{z: \arg(z-3) = \tfrac{1}{2}\pi\}$;   (b) $\{z: \arg(z-j) = \tfrac{1}{4}\pi\}$;
(c) $\{z: \arg(z+4) = \tfrac{5}{4}\pi\}$;   (d) $\{z: \tfrac{1}{2}\pi \leqslant \arg(z-2) \leqslant \tfrac{2}{3}\pi\}$;
(e) $\{z: \arg(z+1+j) = \tfrac{2}{3}\pi\}$;  (f) $\{z: 0 \leqslant \arg(z-1-j) \leqslant \tfrac{1}{2}\pi\}$.

**4.** Find the Cartesian equations of the following loci:
(a) $|z-2| = 3$;         (b) $|z-3-4j| = 4$;
(c) $|z-4| = |z-6j|$;    (d) $|z+j| = |z+1|$;
(e) $|z| = 2|z-6|$.

**5.** (a) Illustrate the locus $|z-8| = 4$.
(b) Explain the connection between part (a) and Question 4(e).

**\*6.** Using the result $|z|^2 = zz^*$ (see Exercise F, Question 7(d)), show that $2|z-1| = |z-4|$ may be reduced to $zz^* = 4$. Describe the locus $\{z: 2|z-1| = |z-4|\}$.

**\*7.** Sketch the following loci, giving as many details as you can:
(a) $\{z: |z+1| + |z-1| = 3\}$;
(b) $\{z: |z+1| - |z-1| = 1\} \cup \{z: |z+1| - |z-1| = -1\}$;
(c) $\{z: \arg(z-1) - \arg(z+1) = \tfrac{1}{2}\pi\} \cup \{z: \arg(z-1) - \arg(z+1) = -\tfrac{1}{2}\pi\}$.
How would you alter the definition of the loci of parts (a) and (c) so that the regions enclosed by the loci become the solution sets?

**\*8.** We know that $|z| + |w| \geqslant |z+w|$ where $z$ and $w$ are complex numbers. Can this inequality be generalized? If so, give the generalization. Use a representation in the complex plane to substantiate your arguments and state the geometrical fact that you use.

### Miscellaneous Exercise

**1.** Find the quotient and remainder when $z^3 - 2jz^2 + (3+j)z - 5$ is divided by $z-1-j$.

**2.** How many roots of $z^n + 1 = 0$ are real if $(a)$ $n$ is even, $(b)$ $n$ is odd? Repeat for $z^n - 1 = 0$.

**3.** Which complex number represents a rotation of a third of a turn about $O$? An equilateral triangle has its vertices on the circle $|z| = 2$. One vertex is the point representing $z = [2, \frac{1}{6}\pi]$. Find the other two vertices.

**4.** Show that $\{a + bj, +, \times\}$ is isomorphic to $\{aI + bJ, +, \times\}$ where $I = \begin{pmatrix} 1 & 0 \\ 0 & 1 \end{pmatrix}$ and $J = \begin{pmatrix} 0 & -1 \\ 1 & 0 \end{pmatrix}$.

**5.** Investigate de Moivre's theorem for $(a)$ $n = -2$, $(b)$ $n = \frac{1}{3}$.

**6.** $(a)$ Given $z = 1 + j$, find $z^2$, $z^3$ and $z^4$ in modulus-argument form, and plot on an Argand diagram the points representing $1$, $1 + z$, $1 + z + z^2$, $1 + z + z^2 + z^3$ and $1 + z + z^2 + z^3 + z^4$.

$(b)$ Repeat part $(a)$ for $z = \frac{1}{2}(1 + j)$. Explain the difference between the two spirals you obtain.

$(c)$ For $z = \frac{1}{2}(1 + j)$, plot $\dfrac{1}{1 - z}$. How does this point appear to be connected with the spiral of part $(b)$? Can you explain the connection?

**7.** Given $w = \frac{1}{2}(-1 + \sqrt{3}j)$, find $w^2$. Show that $w^4 = w$. Write $w$ and $w^2$ in modulus-argument form and explain, with a vector diagram, why $1 + w + w^2 = 0$.

**8.** Show that the equation of the circle $(x - a)^2 + (y - b)^2 = r^2$ can be written in the form $zz^* - c^*z - cz^* + cc^* = r^2$ where $c = a + bj$.

## SUMMARY

The set of complex numbers $\mathbb{C} = \{a + bj: a, b \in \mathbb{R}; j^2 = -1\}$ contains the solutions of all polynomial equations.

Two complex numbers $a + bj$ and $c + dj$ are equal if and only if $a = c$ and $b = d$.

The complex number $a + bj$ can be represented by the point $(a, b)$ in the Argand diagram, and by the vector $\begin{pmatrix} a \\ b \end{pmatrix}$.

The modulus-argument form of $z = a + bj$ is $z = r(\cos \theta + j \sin \theta)$ or $z = [r, \theta]$ where $0 \leqslant \theta < 2\pi$ or $-\pi < \theta \leqslant \pi$, and $r = |z|$, the modulus of $z$, and $\theta = \arg z$.

*Multiplication*       $[r_1, \theta_1] \times [r_2, \theta_2] = [r_1 r_2, \theta_1 + \theta_2]$.

*Division*            $[r_1, \theta_1] \div [r_2, \theta_2] = [r_1/r_2, \theta_1 - \theta_2]$.

*Reciprocal*          $1/[r_1, \theta_1] = [1/r_1, -\theta_1]$.

*Isomorphisms*

The complex numbers under addition are isomorphic to two-dimensional vectors under vector addition.

The complex numbers under multiplication are isomorphic to the spiral similarities (enlargements combined with rotations) with a fixed centre.

*De Moivre's theorem*  $[\cos \theta + j \sin \theta]^n = \cos n\theta + j \sin n\theta$ for $n \in \mathbb{N}$.

The *conjugate* of $z = a + bj$ is $z^* = a - bj$.

Roots of a polynomial equation with real coefficients occur in conjugate pairs.

Every polynomial over $\mathbb{C}$ has a root in $\mathbb{C}$.

# REVISION EXERCISES

## 29. LOGARITHMIC AND EXPONENTIAL FUNCTIONS

**1.** Find the values of:

(a) $\int_{2}^{5} \frac{1}{x} dx$;

(b) $\int_{0}^{3} \frac{1}{x+2} dx$;

(c) $\int_{2}^{5} \frac{x+1}{x} dx$;

(d) $\int_{3}^{4} \frac{1}{2x-5} dx$;

(e) $\int_{-2}^{-1} \frac{1}{2x} dx$.

**2.** Differentiate: (a) $\ln 2x$; (b) $\ln(x+6)$; (c) $\ln(3x-2)$; (d) $\ln(2/x)$; (e) $\ln \sin^2 x$; (f) $\ln 7x^2$; (g) $\ln(5-x^2)$; (h) $x^2 \ln x^2$.

**3.** Find:

(a) $\int \frac{x}{4+x^2} dx$;

(b) $\int \frac{2}{1-x^2} dx$;

(c) $\int \frac{dx}{x(x^2-1)}$;

(d) $\int_{0}^{\pi/2} \frac{\cos x}{2+\sin x} dx$;

(e) $\int_{6}^{10} \frac{x-1}{x^2-7x+12} dx$.

**4.** Given that $y = e^x + e^{-x}$, show that $\frac{d^2y}{dx^2} = y$.

**5.** Find the maximum value of the function $f: x \to x^2 e^{-x}$ and sketch the graph of $y = f(x)$ for $x \geq 0$. Find the total area between the curve and the positive $x$-axis.

**6.** Evaluate:

(a) $\int_{0}^{2} 10 e^{-2x} dx$;

(b) $\int_{-1}^{1} x \exp\left(-\tfrac{1}{5}x^2\right) dx$;

(c) $\int_{0}^{1} x e^{2x} dx$.

**7.** Find the solution sets of:
(a) $100 \exp(-x^2) < 0 \cdot 1$;  (b) $e^{2x-5} = 100$;  (c) $e^{t/10} > 10^3$.

**8.** A mathematical model is constructed to describe the situation in a factory. The number of workers $w$ which an employer requires is a function of the wage rate £$r$ per week for each worker, where $w = 100 e^{-0 \cdot 04r}$. If the union wishes to maximize the total pay of its members, what rate will it ask for? (Assume all workers belong to the union.)   (OC)

## 30. BINOMIAL MODELS

**1.** Assuming that boys and girls are born with equal probability, what is the probability that a family of six children has more boys than girls?

**2.** Three married couples went to a dance together. They decided that before each dance they would draw lots to determine partners. Mr A would draw first, followed by Mr B, leaving Mr C his partner. There were 24 dances.

(a) What is the probability that Mr A danced with his wife exactly three times?

(b) What is the probability that no husband danced with his wife all evening?

(c) What is the probability that each husband had the last dance with his own wife?

**3.** If the probability of rain on any given day is $\frac{1}{3}$, what are the probabilities that in a given week:

(a) there is no rain;

(b) there are exactly three consecutive dry days;

(c) there are at least two dry days?

**4.** If on average one person in fifty is colour-blind, how many people would you need to have together in order to be 95% certain of having at least one colour-blind person in the group? With this group, what is the chance that there will in fact be just two colour-blind people?

**5.** Use the binomial theorem to calculate $(1 \cdot 024)^{-0 \cdot 1}$ to three places of decimals.

Show that $(1 \cdot 024)^{-0 \cdot 1} = \dfrac{10^{0 \cdot 3}}{2}$ and hence find $10^{0 \cdot 3}$ to three places of decimals.

Check your answer using tables of logarithms.

**6.** A mechanic has a box containing a large number of bolts in three sizes, $A$, $B$, and $C$, in the ratio 2 to 3 to 5. He has another box containing nuts to fit these three sizes of bolt. The numbers of nuts are in the ratio 4 to 5 to 1.

(a) If he picks out one bolt and one nut at random, what is the probability that they will fit?

(b) If he picks out two bolts and two nuts, what is the probability that he has at least one bolt and nut which fit?

# 31. FURTHER CALCULUS
# TECHNIQUES AND APPLICATIONS

**1.** Figure 1 shows a view of a dome of square cross-section and height 20 m. If at height $h$ above ground level the square section has side $x$, which of the following expressions gives the volume contained within the dome?

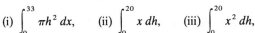

$$\text{(i) } \int_0^{33} \pi h^2 \, dx, \qquad \text{(ii) } \int_0^{20} x \, dh, \qquad \text{(iii) } \int_0^{20} x^2 \, dh,$$

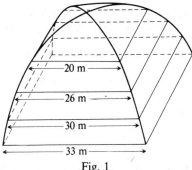

Fig. 1

(iv) $\int_0^{33} h^2 \, dx,$   (v) $\int_0^{20} \pi x^2 \, dh.$

The dimensions given in the figure show the values of $x$ at ground level and at heights $h = 5$, 10 and 15 m. Use Simpson's rule to show that the volume contained is about 12 700 m$^3$. (OC)

**2.** The internal cross-section area $C$ m$^2$ of a concrete-mixer is given approximately as a function of the distance $x$ m from one end by $C = \frac{1}{2}x(7 - 2x)$. Given that the total length of the mixer is 3·5 m, find the volume of concrete it holds when completely full.

**3.** (a) Find the volumes of the solids formed when the following areas are rotated about the $x$-axis: (i) $y = x^2$ for $0 \leqslant x \leqslant 2$; (ii) $y = \dfrac{x^2 + 1}{x}$ for $\frac{1}{2} \leqslant x \leqslant 1\frac{1}{2}$.

(b) Find the volumes of the solids formed when the following areas are rotated about the $y$-axis: (i) $x^2 + 4y^2 = 4$ for $0 \leqslant y \leqslant 1$; (ii) $y = \ln(1 - x)$ for $0 \leqslant y \leqslant 2$.

**4.** (a) Find the coordinates of the points of intersection of the graphs $y^2 = 8x$ and $y = 2x$.

(b) Find the volume of the solid formed when the area enclosed by the graphs in part (a) is rotated 360° about the $x$-axis.

**5.** Sketch the graph of $y^2 = 4x^2(1 - x)$. Find the area enclosed by the loop. If a piece of uniform card is cut to the shape of this loop, where would its centre of mass be?

**6.** A city of 600 000 inhabitants has for its boundary a circle of radius 4 miles centred on the City Hall. A model of the population distribution assigns to the population density $p$ people per square mile at a distance $x$ miles from the City Hall, the formula

$$p = k(4 - x)\sqrt{x},$$

where $k$ is a numerical constant. Explain briefly why this model gives the total population as

$$\int_0^4 2\pi k x(4 - x)\sqrt{x} \, dx,$$

and hence find the approximate value of $k$ to 2 significant figures. (OC)

## 32. COMPLEX NUMBERS AND POLYNOMIAL EQUATIONS

**1.** (a) Show that $3 - 2j$ is a root of $x^3 - 5x^2 + 7x + 13 = 0$. Find the other two roots.

(b) Factorize $x^3 - 5x^2 + 7x + 13$ (i) over the reals, (ii) over the complex numbers.

**2.** Solve the equations

$$z + (1 - j)w = j,$$
$$(1 + j)z + jw = -1,$$

for the complex numbers $z$ and $w$, giving each answer in the form $a + bj$. (OC)

**3.** What is the connection between arg $(z_1 z_2)$, arg $z_1$ and arg $z_2$?

Figure 2 shows points $P_1$, $P_2$ representing complex numbers $z_1$, $z_2$ in the complex plane. The points $A$, $B$, $C$, $D$, $E$ represent $z_1 + z_2$, $z_1 - z_2$, $z_1 z_2$, $z_1/z_2$, $1/z_1 + 1/z_2$ in some order.

Identify which point represents each expression. (OC)

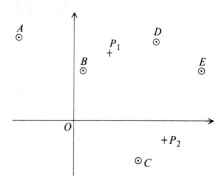

Fig. 2

**4.** Let $z$ be a (non-real) complex number with modulus $r$ and argument $\theta$. Write down its complex conjugate $z^*$ in modulus-argument form.

Find arg $(z^*/z)$ (i) when $z = 1 + \sqrt{3}j$, (ii) when $z = -1 + \sqrt{3}j$. (OC)

**5.** Find in modulus-argument form the value of

$$\frac{E}{R + (pL - 1/pC)j}$$

when $E = 390$, $R = 12$, $L = 0 \cdot 06$, $C = 0 \cdot 0004$, $p = 250$. (OC)

**6.** Solve the following equations in the complex numbers:
(a) $z^4 + 64 = 0$; (b) $2z^3 + (\sqrt{3} - j) = 0$; (c) $z^3 - (1 + j) = 0$.
Show the roots on an Argand diagram in each case.

**7.** Illustrate the following loci in the complex plane:
(a) $|z + 2j| = 2$; (b) $|z + 1| = |z - 1|$; (c) arg $(z - 2j) = 0$;
(d) $\frac{1}{2}\pi \le \arg(z - 1 - j) \le \frac{3}{4}\pi$; (e) $|z - 2| = 2|z - 5|$.

# 33

# INTRODUCTION TO
# DIFFERENTIAL EQUATIONS

## 1. WHAT IS A DIFFERENTIAL EQUATION?

Suppose we start with 20 milligrams of a radioactive substance, and its mass $m$ milligrams after $t$ days is given by

$$m = 20 \exp(-0 \cdot 3t). \tag{1}$$

Then the decay rate is given by the derivative

$$\frac{dm}{dt} = -6 \exp(-0 \cdot 3t). \tag{2}$$

Now $\exp(-0 \cdot 3t) = m/20$, so equation (2) can be written

$$\frac{dm}{dt} = -0 \cdot 3m. \tag{3}$$

Equations like (2) and (3) which tell us something about a derivative are called *differential equations*.

Equation (3) tells us that the rate of decay (i.e. the gradient of the $t \to m$ graph in Figure 1) is proportional to the mass. This is what we would expect—the fewer atoms there are, the fewer will decay in the next day.

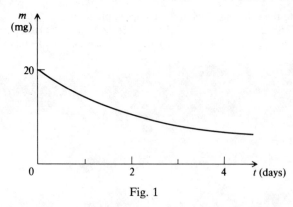

Fig. 1

Very often our knowledge of a situation or of scientific laws is in terms of a rate, and this will enable us to set up a model as a differential

854

equation. We shall then wish to obtain an explicit relation between the variables; this is called *solving* the differential equation. In terms of our radioactivity example, it means starting with equation (3) and deducing equation (1).

Whenever we attempt to reverse results involving differentiation, our basic method is to use our experience of differentiation and see if we can find an answer by trial and error.

Study of the example above would help us solve the differential equation

$$\frac{dx}{dt} = 4x.$$

It seems that $x$ is some number times $e^{4t}$. By differentiation we can check that

$$x = Ae^{4t}$$

satisfies the equation for all values of $A$. As with simple integration, we have a constant which can be determined if we know the initial conditions. In this case, $A$ is itself the initial value of $x$, i.e. the value of $x$ when $t = 0$.

## Example 1

The rate at which a rumour spreads through a school depends upon the number of people who have already heard it. Devise a mathematical model to describe what happens, assuming that there are 1000 pupils in the school and that each person who knows the rumour passes it on to five others every hour.

At a time when $z$ people have already heard the rumour, only a fraction $(1000-z)/1000$ of those who are told the rumour will be hearing it for the first time; therefore each carrier will add

$$5 \times \frac{1000-z}{1000} = \frac{1000-z}{200}$$

pupils per hour to the number in the know. Since there are at that time $z$ carriers, the rate at which the rumour is spreading is $z$ times this number; that is,

$$\frac{dz}{dt} = \frac{z(1000-z)}{200}.$$

Can we solve this differential equation by inspection, i.e. find a suitable relation between $z$ and $t$? Unfortunately not.

855

Other exact methods do exist, some of which we shall develop in Chapter 38, but we shall often find differential equations which cannot be solved by *any* exact means. We shall then fall back on a numerical method, and it is this that we explain next. If we cannot obtain an explicit relation, we shall aim instead for a table of values and a graph—a *solution curve*.

## Exercise A

**1.** A parachutist falls freely from rest at $t = 0$. Find his velocity when he pulls his rip-cord 8 seconds later, and sketch the velocity-time graph for this interval. (Take the acceleration due to gravity as $10 \text{ m/s}^2$ and neglect air resistance.)

**2.** The air resistance to a parachutist is not a constant force but increases directly with velocity. Show that if air resistance is taken into account, a possible expression for the acceleration during free fall might be

$$\frac{dv}{dt} = 10 - 0.2v,$$

where the parachutist's velocity is $v$ m/s vertically downwards after $t$ seconds. Superimpose a rough sketch of the velocity-time graph for this differential equation on your graph for Question 1 by comparing the gradients at various values of $v$.

**3.** The motion of the parachutist after his parachute has opened is described by

$$\frac{dv}{dt} = 10 - 0.1v^2,$$

and $v = 15$ vertically downwards initially. What is his initial acceleration? If at a later stage his velocity is almost constant (the *terminal velocity*), what is his acceleration then, and what is his velocity? Sketch the solution curve.

**4.** Show that $y = \dfrac{1}{\sqrt{(k - 2x)}}$ is a solution of $\dfrac{dy}{dx} = y^3$ for all values of $k$.

Can you find a solution of $\dfrac{dy}{dx} = y^2$?

**5.** Use the quotient rule to differentiate

$$v = 10\left(\frac{5 + e^{-2t}}{5 - e^{-2t}}\right)$$

and show that this is a solution of

$$\frac{dv}{dt} = 10 - 0.1v^2.$$

Sketch the $t \rightarrow v$ graph.

856

## 2. THE STEP-BY-STEP METHOD

### 2.1  A pursuit curve problem

*Example* 2

A dog capable of running at 10 m/s sees a hare running in a straight line some distance away at 8 m/s. He sets off in pursuit, heading always directly towards the hare. Trace his path.

To fulfil the conditions of the problem, the dog must change course continually, and his path will be a curve. To find the exact form of this curve is a difficult problem; but we can easily find an approximation in the form of a path made up of line segments.

Suppose that the dog is rather slow-witted, and that he sights on the hare only once a second; then during the intervals between re-sighting he will run 10 m in a straight line towards the point where he last saw the hare. The paths of the hare and the dog are illustrated in Figure 2.

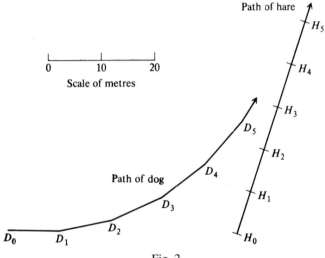

Fig. 2

During the first second the hare runs from $H_0$ to $H_1$, and the dog from $D_0$ to $D_1$ in the direction of $H_0$. He then adjusts his course, and while the hare runs from $H_1$ to $H_2$ the dog runs from $D_1$ to $D_2$ in the direction of $H_1$; and so on.

The polygon $D_0 D_1 D_2 \ldots$ is an approximation to the solution of the original problem. Clearly a better approximation could be made by correcting course more frequently; thus by re-sighting ten times a second the dog would steer a better path.

857

**2.2 Step-by-step solutions of differential equations.** A similar method will now be applied to find (in the form of a table of values) a solution to the parachutist's differential equation of Exercise A, Question 2,

$$\frac{dv}{dt} = 10 - 0 \cdot 2v,$$

in which $t$ is measured from the instant he leaves the aircraft (when $v = 0$).

We can see from the differential equation that initially the air resistance is negligible and the acceleration (entirely due to gravity) is $10 \text{ m/s}^2$. The velocity then builds up and as it does so the acceleration $dv/dt$ decreases. As $v$ approaches 50, the acceleration tends to 0. It seems that the velocity-time graph should look like Figure 3, though the man would be well advised to open his parachute when his velocity is well short of his terminal velocity!

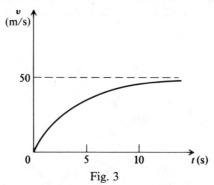

Fig. 3

We should like to obtain the coordinates of a set of points $A, B, C, D, E, F$ which when joined up will give a graph close to that of Figure 3. To start with, we shall take time intervals of 2 seconds. At $A$, the acceleration is 10 so we set off (rather like the dog) along a line with gradient 10.

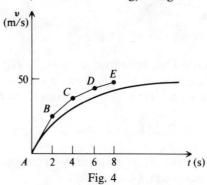

Fig. 4

858

At this rate $v$ increases by 20 in the interval $0 \leqslant t \leqslant 2$. So $B$ is the point $(2, 20)$.

When $v = 20$, $dv/dt = 6$, so we set off from $B$ towards $C$ along a line with gradient 6, leading to an increase of 12 in $v$. So the value of $v$ at $C$ is $20 + 12 = 32$.

All this is best set out in a table.

| Interval | Gradient, $dv/dt$ | Increase in $v$ | $t$ | $v$ | Point |
|---|---|---|---|---|---|
| | | | 0 | 0 | A |
| $0 \leqslant t \leqslant 2$ | 10 | 20 | | | |
| | | | 2 | 20 | B |
| $2 \leqslant t \leqslant 4$ | 6 | 12 | | | |
| | | | 4 | 32 | C |
| $4 \leqslant t \leqslant 6$ | 3·6 | 7·2 | | | |
| | | | 6 | 39·2 | D |
| $6 \leqslant t \leqslant 8$ | 2·16 | 4·32 | | | |
| | | | 8 | 43·52 | E |

Our estimate of the speed after 8 seconds is about 43·5 m/s.

It is clear that a better estimate would be obtained if we took shorter time intervals. Compile a table similar to the one above using intervals of 1 second. You should find that your new estimate for the speed at $t = 8$ is approximately 41·6 m/s. Intervals of 0·5 second give 40·7 m/s. Successively smaller intervals give values which approach the value of 39·9 m/s which can be obtained by integration.

Obviously it is undesirable to make the time intervals so small that a very large number of steps have to be calculated; in every solution, we shall have to compromise between accuracy and tedium. On the other hand, it is an easy matter to write a computer program to calculate successive entries in the table. If we compare the results this gives with two different step lengths, we can get a good assessment of the accuracy.

### Exercise B

Use the method of Section 2.2 to answer the following questions. Set out your answers in a similar tabular form, writing the gradients and 'increases in $v$' on the line between calculated values of the variables. At each stage round your answers to 3 significant figures. Use the tables to draw approximate graphs of the solution curves.

1. $\dfrac{dv}{dt} = 10 - 0 \cdot 3v$, with $v = 0$ when $t = 0$. Obtain values of $v$ for $0 \leqslant t \leqslant 10$, taking intervals of 2 seconds.

**2.** (*a*) Repeat Question 1 taking intervals of 1 second.

(*b*) Repeat Question 1 taking intervals of 2 seconds but starting with $v = 5$ when $t = 0$.

**3.** $\dfrac{dv}{dt} = 10 - 0 \cdot 1v^2$, with $v = 15$ when $t = 0$. Obtain values of $v$ for $0 \leqslant t \leqslant 1$ taking intervals of 0·2 second.

**4.** (*a*) Repeat Question 3 taking intervals of 0·1 second.

(*b*) Repeat Question 3 taking intervals of 0·2 second but starting with $v = 0$ when $t = 0$.

(*c*) Repeat Question 3 taking intervals of 0·1 second and starting with $v = 0$ when $t = 0$.

**5.** A country has a constant birth rate of 19 per thousand, and a constant death rate of 15 per thousand. If $P$ is the population at time $t$ years, obtain the differential equation

$$\frac{dP}{dt} = 0 \cdot 004P.$$

If the total population at the 1976 census was 10 million, estimate the population at 20 year intervals to the year 2076.

**6.** A cyclist is proceeding along a level road at 4 m/s. Seeing green traffic lights ahead the cyclist first of all puts on a spurt, then brakes as the lights change. The net accelerating force at the wheels is as follows:

| Time (s) | 0 | 10 | 20 | 30 | 40 | 50 |
|----------|----|----|----|----|----|----|
| Force (N) | 22 | 28 | 45 | 20 | −3 | −67 |

Deduce a table of accelerations, given that the mass of the man and his cycle is 100 kg, and estimate how the speed varies during the first 60 seconds.

**7.** Write a flow chart to carry out the calculations of Question 1. Modify it for other interval lengths. If you have computing facilities, write and run a program, finally obtaining an answer correct to 1 decimal place.

**2.3 The general method.** Let us consider the technique we have been using in more detail, arguing in terms of the graph of Figure 5.

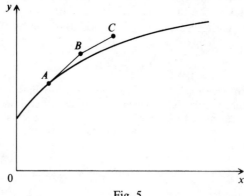

Fig. 5

We wish to obtain the solution curve which passes through our starting point $A$. We set off along the tangent at $A$ until our displacement in the $x$-direction is our chosen step length, which we shall call $\delta x$. The consequent increase in $y$, written $\delta y$, is estimated to be

$$\frac{dy}{dx} \times \delta x.$$

As long as the tangent remains close to the curve, the approximation will be reasonably accurate.

From $B$ we proceed to $C$ along a second straight step in the direction found by substituting the coordinates of $B$ into the differential equation. In general this will *not* be a tangent to the solution curve, as we can see in Figure 5, but hopefully it will stay near to it. We calculate the increase in $y$ as before.

*Example* 3

Apply a step-by-step method of solution to $\dfrac{dy}{dx} = \dfrac{1}{x}$ starting with $y = 0$ when $x = 1$ and taking intervals of $0 \cdot 2$ up to $x = 2$.

| Interval | $\delta x$ | $\dfrac{dy}{dx}$ | $\delta y$ | $x$ | $y$ | $\ln x$ |
|---|---|---|---|---|---|---|
| | | | | 1 | 0 | 0 |
| $1 \leqslant x \leqslant 1\cdot2$ | $0\cdot2$ | 1 | $0\cdot2$ | | | |
| | | | | $1\cdot2$ | $0\cdot2$ | $0\cdot182$ |
| $1\cdot2 \leqslant x \leqslant 1\cdot4$ | $0\cdot2$ | $0\cdot833$ | $0\cdot166$ | | | |
| | | | | $1\cdot4$ | $0\cdot366$ | $0\cdot336$ |
| $1\cdot4 \leqslant x \leqslant 1\cdot6$ | $0\cdot2$ | $0\cdot714$ | $0\cdot143$ | | | |
| | | | | $1\cdot6$ | $0\cdot509$ | $0\cdot470$ |
| $1\cdot6 \leqslant x \leqslant 1\cdot8$ | $0\cdot2$ | $0\cdot625$ | $0\cdot125$ | | | |
| | | | | $1\cdot8$ | $0\cdot634$ | $0\cdot588$ |
| $1\cdot8 \leqslant x \leqslant 2\cdot0$ | $0\cdot2$ | $0\cdot556$ | $0\cdot111$ | | | |
| | | | | $2\cdot0$ | $0\cdot745$ | $0\cdot693$ |

You will have realized that this differential equation can be integrated directly to give

$$y = \ln |x| + k$$

and the requirement that $y = 0$ when $x = 1$ gives $k = 0$. Comparing the exact values with our estimates enables us to see what errors are introduced by the approximate method. The relevant values of $\ln x$ are given in the last column of the table and Figure 6 shows the correct solution curve and the one given by the step-by-step method.

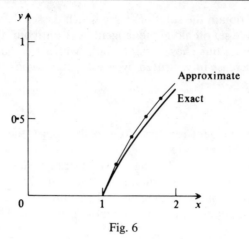

Fig. 6

The errors arise, of course, from using the gradient at the left-hand end of an interval instead of some sort of average gradient for the interval. We can tell in retrospect the scale of the errors by looking at the $dy/dx$ column in the table. If the values do not change too rapidly, the technique is reasonably accurate.

## 3. FAMILIES OF CURVES

With each differential equation we need to specify the starting values. If the starting values are changed we should expect to get a different solution and a different solution curve. For the differential equation of Section 2.2,

$$\frac{dv}{dt} = 10 - 0\cdot 2v,$$

the pattern of solution curves corresponding to different initial conditions is shown in Figure 7. We call this a *family* of curves.

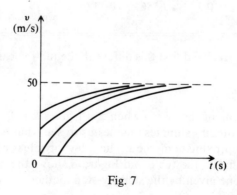

Fig. 7

862

### Exercise C

**1.** The water in a kettle is brought to the boil and then allowed to cool. Its temperature $\theta$ °C at a time $t$ minutes after the heat is turned off is governed by the differential equation

$$\frac{d\theta}{dt} = -0{\cdot}02(\theta - 15).$$

Explain the significance of this equation in physical terms. Estimate the temperature 30 minutes later. Is your estimate too high or too low?

**2.** A ball is thrown vertically upwards with velocity 8 m/s. For how long will it rise if air resistance is negligible?

If in fact air resistance is such that the velocity satisfies the equation

$$\frac{dv}{dt} = -(10 + 0{\cdot}2v),$$

calculate the approximate time taken for the ball to reach its highest point.

**3.** Given that $\dfrac{dy}{dx} = \dfrac{1}{\sqrt{x}}$ and that $y = 0$ when $x = 1$, estimate the value of $y$ when $x = 2$, taking steps $\delta x = 0{\cdot}2$ and working throughout to 2 decimal places. Integrate to find $y$ as a function of $x$ to check the accuracy of your estimate. Illustrate with a graph.

**4.** Given that $\dfrac{dy}{dx} = \dfrac{10}{x^2}$ and $y = 7{\cdot}5$ when $x = 4$, estimate the value of $y$ when $x = 10$ using steps of (a) $\delta x = 2$, (b) $\delta x = 1$. Check your accuracy by integration. Suggest a suitable step length to give accuracy to 2 significant figures.

**5.** Given that $\dfrac{dy}{dx} = \dfrac{x}{x^2 - 3}$ and that $y = 0$ when $x = 2$, estimate the value of $y$ when $x = 3$ using two intervals. Show by integration that in fact $y = 0{\cdot}90$ to 2 significant figures when $x = 3$ and explain why your estimate was so poor.

**6.** If $\dfrac{dy}{dx} = \dfrac{x}{5 - y}$ and $y = 1$ when $x = 0$, take steps $\delta x = 0{\cdot}5$ to estimate the value of $y$ when $x = 3$. Show that $x^2 + (y - 5)^2 = 16$ satisfies the differential equation and the initial conditions. Draw the graph of this relation and on the same diagram show your successive estimates.

**7.** Market research shows that the demand for a certain article varies with price according to the equation

$$\frac{dn}{dP} = -\frac{10^6}{P^3}$$

where $n$ is the number of articles sold per week at a price of £$P$. If a price of £10 gives weekly sales of 5000 articles, estimate to 2 significant figures the number of articles sold if the price is increased to £12.

**8.** Take five steps with $\delta x = 0 \cdot 4$ for $\dfrac{dy}{dx} = \sqrt{(1 + y^2)}$ with each of the following

starting points. Draw the graphs with the same axes.
   (*a*) $(3, 0)$;   (*b*) $(2, 0)$;   (*c*) $(1, 0)$;   (*d*) $(0, 0)$;   (*e*) $(-1, 0)$.

**9.** Take five steps with $\delta x = 0 \cdot 4$ for $\dfrac{dy}{dx} = \sqrt{(1 + x^2)}$ with the following different

starting points. Draw the graphs with the same axes.
   (*a*) $(0, 3)$;   (*b*) $(0, 2)$;   (*c*) $(0, 1)$;   (*d*) $(0, 0)$;   (*e*) $(0, -1)$.

**10.** Repeat Question 9 for the differential equations:

   (i) $\dfrac{dy}{dx} = y - 2x$;      (ii) $\dfrac{dy}{dx} = x - y + 1$;

  (iii) $\dfrac{dy}{dx} = 2\,e^{-x} - 2y$;    (iv) $\dfrac{dy}{dx} = y^2$.

The full benefit of this question can be obtained painlessly if the twenty calculations are divided among the class. The sets of curves of each family should be displayed together.

## 4. FAMILY PORTRAITS

If you assembled some of the solution curves of Exercise C, Question 10(i), you will not be surprised by Figure 8 which shows more completely the *family portrait* of $\dfrac{dy}{dx} = y - 2x$. There are two important features of such a diagram. First, no two solution curves intersect since at each point there is a unique value of the gradient (given, of course, by the differential equation). Secondly, the solution curves completely cover the plane; in other words there exists a curve through any point you care to name.

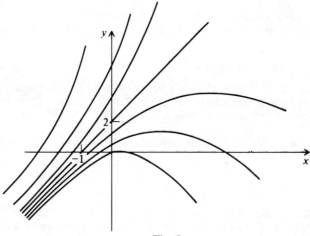

Fig. 8

Furthermore, we see that a small difference in the starting value could make a crucial difference to the solution. From $(0, 1\cdot9)$ the solution curve is concave downwards and after reaching a maximum the value of $y$ decreases more and more rapidly. But from $(0, 2\cdot1)$, the solution curve gets steeper and steeper.

**4.1  Sketching family portraits.** It is sometimes useful to be able to sketch a family portrait without any laborious calculations.

*Example* 4

Sketch the solution curve for the rumour-spreading model of Example 1 for which

$$\frac{dz}{dt} = \frac{z(1000 - z)}{200}.$$

This involves a school of 1000 pupils so we are only concerned with positive $t$ and positive values of $z$ up to 1000. The rumour is started by one or more pupils; while $z$ is small, so is $dz/dt$ and the rumour spreads slowly. When about half the school have heard it, there are many carriers and many receptive hearers so the number grows rapidly. As $z$ nears 1000, the rate of change of $z$ becomes small again. So we have a solution curve like Figure 9.

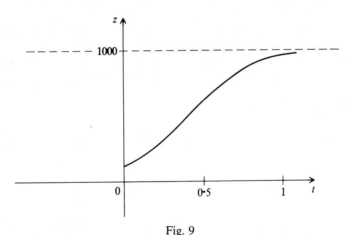

Fig. 9

Similar arguments apply for different starting values and the relevant curves are parts of the fuller picture of Figure 10. Can you explain why the graphs here are images of each other under translations parallel to the $t$-axis (cf. Exercise C, Question 8)?

865

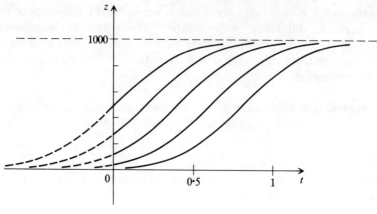

Fig. 10

*Example 5*

Investigate the family of curves defined by $\dfrac{dy}{dx} = x + y$.

Substitution of the coordinates of a point into this equation gives a value for $dy/dx$. For example, $(1, 2)$ gives $dy/dx = 3$. This means that the member of the family which passes through $(1, 2)$ has gradient 3 at that point.

If we carry out a similar calculation for a selection of points with integer coordinates, we can sketch in the skeleton of the family of curves by marking small 'compass needles' at the lattice points showing these gradient directions (Figure 11). See if you can sketch in some of the members of the family in this region. If in doubt, draw in the lattice lines at half intervals and put on intermediate compass needles.

**4.2 Use of the second derivative.** The main features of the family portrait can often be established fairly simply even without the compass-needle diagram. We can start by noting where the gradient is zero. This occurs for

$$\frac{dy}{dx} = x + y$$

at all points on the line $x + y = 0$. But, more important, it forms a boundary between the upper region where the gradient is positive everywhere and the lower region where it is negative (see Figure 12).

Now by differentiating

$$\frac{dy}{dx} = x + y,$$

866

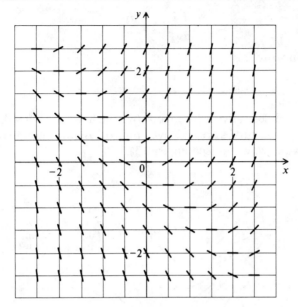

Fig. 11

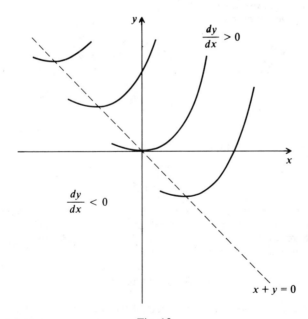

Fig. 12

we obtain

$$\frac{d^2y}{dx^2} = 1 + \frac{dy}{dx}$$

and we can write this

$$\frac{d^2y}{dx^2} = 1 + x + y.$$

So the second derivative is positive above the line $1 + x + y = 0$, meaning that the solution curves are concave upwards. Below this line the curves are concave downwards (see Figure 13).

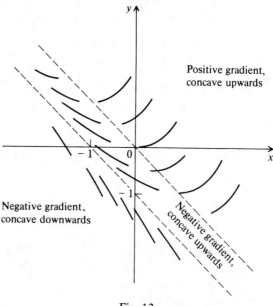

Fig. 13

The line $1 + x + y = 0$ is itself one of the solution curves and is an asymptote for each of the others. The full diagram is given in Figure 14.

### Exercise D

**1.** In a chemical reaction, substances $A$ and $B$ combine to give a substance $C$. Initially 50 grams of $A$ are present, 60 grams of $B$ and none of $C$. After $t$ minutes, there are $50 - x$ grams of $A$, $60 - 2x$ grams of $B$ and $3x$ grams of $C$.
  The rate of reaction is given by

$$\frac{dx}{dt} = 0 \cdot 001(50 - x)(60 - 2x),$$

i.e. the rate is proportional to the product of the concentrations of the reacting molecules.

868

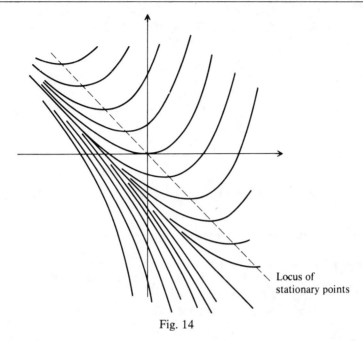

Fig. 14

Explain why $x$ never exceeds 30. Without detailed calculations, sketch the solution curve.

**2.** Give a rough sketch of the solution curve (for positive $t$) for each of the following, avoiding detailed calculation.

(a) $\dfrac{dv}{dt} = 3 - 0 \cdot 2v$, given $v = 0$ when $t = 0$;

(b) $\dfrac{dv}{dt} = 3 - 0 \cdot 2v$, given $v = 50$ when $t = 0$;

(c) $\dfrac{dy}{dt} - \dfrac{2-y}{1+y}$, given $y = 0$ when $t = 0$;

(d) $\dfrac{dy}{dt} = \dfrac{2-t}{1+t}$, given $y = 0$ when $t = 0$.

**3.** Use the compass-needle method to sketch the family portrait of $\dfrac{dy}{dx} = x^2$. Check your result by integration.

**4.** Use the compass-needle method to sketch the family of solutions of:

(a) $\dfrac{dy}{dx} = -\dfrac{1}{x}$;     (b) $\dfrac{dy}{dx} = y$;     (c) $\dfrac{dy}{dx} = -xy$;

(d) $\dfrac{dy}{dx} = xy$;     (e) $\dfrac{dy}{dx} = y - 5$;     (f) $\dfrac{dy}{dx} = xy - 1$.

**5.** Given $\dfrac{dz}{dt} = 2t - z$, show that $\dfrac{d^2z}{dt^2} = 2 - 2t + z$. Explain why $2 - 2t + z = 0$ is a solution of the original differential equation. Indicate on a diagram the signs of

869

$\dfrac{dz}{dt}, \dfrac{d^2z}{dt^2}$ in the regions $2t - z < 0$, $0 < 2t - z < 2$, $2 < 2t - z$. Sketch the family portrait.

**6.** For the differential equation $\dfrac{dy}{dx} = y - x^2$, show clearly the boundaries where $\dfrac{dy}{dx} = 0$ and where $\dfrac{d^2y}{dx^2} = 0$ and the sign of the first and second derivatives in the four regions formed by these boundaries. Hence sketch the family of solution curves.

**7.** For the differential equation $\dfrac{dy}{dx} = -\dfrac{y}{x}$, show the sign of the first derivative in each of the four quadrants, noting that both axes form boundaries. Hence sketch the family portrait.

**8.** Sketch the family portrait for the equation $\dfrac{dy}{dx} = \dfrac{x}{y}$.

**9.** Explain why at any point where a member of the family of Question 7 meets a member of the family of Question 8, the curves cross at right-angles. The families are said to be *orthogonal*.

**10.** Sketch, with the same axes, the orthogonal families given by

$$\frac{dy}{dx} = \frac{1}{x} \quad \text{and} \quad \frac{dy}{dx} = -x.$$

**11.** Sketch, with the same axes, the orthogonal families given by

$$\frac{dy}{dx} = \frac{y}{x} \quad \text{and} \quad \frac{dy}{dx} = -\frac{x}{y}.$$

## 5. AN IMPROVED METHOD

We have already remarked that the accuracy of the simple step-by-step method depends on how quickly the gradient is changing. That is, the divergence between tangent and curve is not too great provided $d^2y/dx^2$ is small.

We can improve the accuracy by using ideas from Chapter 22 where we met almost exactly the same problem. Then we were using polynomials to calculate approximate values near known points of other more complicated functions. We first used linear approximation (taking the tangent at the known point) and then improved our estimates using quadratic and higher degree polynomials.

The step-by-step method of Section 2 can be regarded as the replacement of the solution curve by its local linear approximation at the left-hand end of the interval. If the equation of the solution curve is

$$y = f(x)$$

then the increment $\delta y$ has been calculated from

$$\delta y \approx f'(x)\,\delta x.$$

If we fit a *quadratic* function to the curve instead, i.e. use the second Taylor approximation, then

$$\delta y \approx f'(x)\,\delta x + \tfrac{1}{2}f''(x)(\delta x)^2,$$

and we might expect to get a more accurate approximation for a given step length. We show the method for the differential equation of Section 2.2.

If

$$f'(x)=\frac{dy}{dx}=10-0\cdot2y$$

then

$$f''(x)=\frac{d^2y}{dx^2}=-0\cdot2\frac{dy}{dx}.$$

Starting at $(0, 0)$ and taking $\delta x = 2$, we get the following table:

| $f'(x)$ | $f''(x)$ | $\delta x$ | $f'(x)\,\delta x$ | $\tfrac{1}{2}f''(x)(\delta x)^2$ | $\delta y$ | $x$ | $y$ |
|---------|----------|------------|-------------------|----------------------------------|------------|-----|-----|
|         |          |            |                   |                                  |            | 0   | 0   |
| 10      | $-2$     | 2          | 20                | $-4$                             | 16         |     |     |
|         |          |            |                   |                                  |            | 2   | 16  |
| 6·8     | $-1·36$  | 2          | 13·6              | $-2·72$                          | 10·88      |     |     |
|         |          |            |                   |                                  |            | 4   | 26·9 |
| 4·62    | $-0·92$  | 2          | 9·24              | $-1·84$                          | 7·40       |     |     |
|         |          |            |                   |                                  |            | 6   | 34·3 |
| 3·14    | $-0·62$  | 2          | 6·29              | $-1·26$                          | 5·03       |     |     |
|         |          |            |                   |                                  |            | 8   | 39·3 |

This estimate is considerably better than the *linear* approximation with the same step length, 2, and in fact it is better than the linear approximation with step length 0·5 (see p. 859). In this example, the use of the quadratic term produces a consistent underestimate. Can you see what would happen if we took a further, cubic, term?

Apart from providing improved answers, this method throws light on the simple linear method. The latter works well with longish step lengths if the second and higher derivatives are small enough. Otherwise, as with all Taylor approximations, the increment (step length) must be sufficiently small for the terms of the polynomial approximations to get smaller rapidly.

## Exercise E

**1.** Given that $\dfrac{dy}{dx} = \dfrac{1}{x}$ and that $y = 0$ when $x = 1$, use the method of Section 5 to estimate the value of $y$ when $x = 3$ (use step length $\delta x = 0 \cdot 5$). Compare this with the answer given by the linear method and with the answer given by integration.

**2.** Use the method of Section 5 to obtain solutions of the following differential equations in the given intervals taking the suggested step lengths.

(a) $\dfrac{dy}{dx} = 2y - 1$ for $0 \leqslant x \leqslant 1$ with $\delta x = 0 \cdot 2$; start from $(0, 1)$.

(b) $\dfrac{dy}{dx} = x + y$ for $0 \leqslant x \leqslant 2$ with $\delta x = 0 \cdot 4$; start from $(0, 1)$.

(c) $\dfrac{dy}{dx} = y - x^2$ for $0 \leqslant x \leqslant 1$ with $\delta x = 0 \cdot 2$; start from $(0, 2 \cdot 5)$.

(d) $\dfrac{dy}{dx} = xy - 1$ for $0 \leqslant x \leqslant 1$ with $\delta x = 0 \cdot 2$; start from $(0, 1)$.

In each part, comment on the choice of step length and assess the accuracy of your final $y$-value.

**3.** Write a flow chart or computer program for one of the parts of Question 2, making provision for the use of various step lengths, starting points and final values of $x$.

## Miscellaneous Exercise

**1.** Show that $x + y = \frac{1}{2}$ is one solution of

$$\frac{dy}{dx} = 1 - \frac{1}{x+y}.$$

Find an expression for the second derivative and its sign in the regions for which $x + y < 0$, $\;0 < x + y < \frac{1}{2}$, $\;\frac{1}{2} < x + y$.

Sketch the family portrait, noting the locus of turning points and where the gradient is discontinuous.

**2.** Apply the methods of Sections 2 and 5 to the solution of $\dfrac{dy}{dx} = y$ with $y = 1$ when $x = 0$. Show that with intervals of $0 \cdot 1$ the solutions are equivalent to multiplying by $1 \cdot 1$ and $1 \cdot 105$ respectively at each stage. Deduce equations satisfied by corresponding values of $x$ and $y$. Write them in the form $y = c^x$ and compare with the correct solution $y = e^x$.

**3.** Discuss suitable step lengths for numerical solution of the following differential equations using (i) the linear method, (ii) the method of Section 5.

(a) $\dfrac{dy}{dx} = -xy$; \qquad (b) $\dfrac{dx}{dt} = 0 \cdot 01(20 - x)^2$.

**4.** The methods of this chapter can be extended for use with simultaneous differential equations. Use a step length $\delta x = 0 \cdot 2$ with

$$\frac{dy}{dx} = -z, \qquad \frac{dz}{dx} = y$$

given $y = 1$, $z = 0$ when $x = 0$. Show that $y = \cos x$, $z = \sin x$ satisfy the equations and the initial values, and compare your values for $y$ and $z$ with those given in the circular function tables.

**5.** The *second-order* differential equation

$$\frac{d^2y}{dt^2} + 2\frac{dy}{dt} + 17y = 0,$$

which describes the damped oscillations of a certain physical system, can be written as a pair of simultaneous first-order differential equations by introducing a variable $z$ such that

$$\frac{dy}{dt} = 4z - y.$$

Show that then

$$\frac{dz}{dt} = -z - 4y.$$

Obtain a numerical solution over the interval $0 \leqslant t \leqslant 2$ if initially $y = 4$ and $dy/dt = 0$ (use $\delta t = 0 \cdot 1$).

## SUMMARY

The solution set of the differential equation

$$\frac{dy}{dx} = f(x, y)$$

is a family of non-intersecting curves.

The family portrait can be sketched by determining the boundaries where $\frac{dy}{dx} = 0$ and where the second derivative $\frac{d^2y}{dx^2} = 0$. The sign of the derivatives in the regions formed by these boundaries gives the shape of the curves in each region, as shown in Figure 15. Compass-needle calculation of the direction $\frac{dy}{dx}$ at specific points will give finer detail.

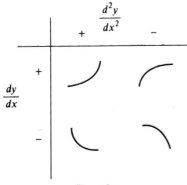

Fig. 15

Points on a particular member of the family can be estimated numerically by the step-by-step method; stepping in the direction of the tangent, with a suitable interval $\delta x$, using the linear approximation

$$\delta y \approx \frac{dy}{dx}\delta x.$$

A computer program can be written for this step-by-step method and, by taking sufficiently small step intervals, can give any required degree of accuracy. Higher order derivatives can be used to refine the process, using for example

$$\delta y \approx \frac{dy}{dx}\delta x + \tfrac{1}{2}\frac{d^2 y}{dx^2}(\delta x)^2.$$

# 34

## MOMENTUM AND IMPULSE

Why does it take the QE 2 such a long time to slow down as she approaches port? Why do car passengers sustain such serious injuries in crashes, even at quite low speeds? In this chapter we look at simple models for situations of this sort. So far we have looked at the motion of particles from two separate points of view: we have described motion with no reference to its causes (Chapter 7) and we have looked at those causes when we studied Newton's laws (Chapters 12 and 24). We now consider motion as the effect of specific forces acting for finite intervals of time.

## 1. INTERACTION AND CONSTANT FORCES

The forces we consider in this chapter will sometimes be external to the body or system of bodies we are considering, but often they will arise from an *interaction* between two or more bodies (for instance, the collision between a car and a rigid barrier, or the gravitational inter-action between the earth and the moon, or the forces between gun and bullet when the gun is fired). In Chapter 24 the *interaction principle* was stated for such forces: if a body $A$ exerts a force on body $B$, body $B$ in turn exerts an equal and opposite force on body $A$. We shall apply this principle frequently in the present chapter.

**1.1 Straight-line motion with constant acceleration.** The following exercise explores a variety of situations where the forces acting are all assumed to be constant. In cases where the force would in reality change during the time considered, we use an average force. Variable forces are discussed in Section 4.

### Exercise A

**1.** (*a*) Research into car crashes shows that when a car travelling at 20 m/s (about 40 m.p.h.) hits a solid concrete barrier, it is reduced to rest in a very short time. Find this time, assuming that a constant force of $5 \times 10^5$ N is exerted on the car (mass 1000 kg).

(*b*) Fitting impact-absorbing bodywork reduces the force to $3 \times 10^5$ N. How long does the car take to come to rest now?

**2.** A car, total mass 1200 kg, has an engine which will produce a constant tractive force of 6000 N. How long does it take to accelerate from 20 m/s to 30 m/s?

**3.** To answer Questions 1 and 2, why is it unnecessary to find the acceleration explicitly? Eliminate $a$ between $v = u + ta$ and $F = ma$ and make $t$ the subject of your new equation. Use it to answer Question 4.

**4.** (*a*) An empty barge, mass 200 tonnes, is approaching a lock at 3 m/s and must come to a complete stop before entering. A constant retarding force of 2400 N is produced by reversing the thrust of the engines. How long will it take to bring the barge to rest?

   (*b*) How long would it take the barge, if loaded to total mass 600 tonnes, to come to rest from the same speed using the same retarding force?

   (*c*) How long would it take the empty barge to come to rest from 6 m/s under the same retarding force?

**5.** A ship, mass 4000 tonnes is moving sideways towards a pier at 0·03 m/s. Find the force (assumed constant) that must be exerted by the pier if the ship is brought to rest in 2 seconds. What force (again assumed constant) would be required if, as a result of hanging rubber tyres on the pier, the time is increased to 5 seconds?

**6.** A railway truck, mass 5 tonnes, runs into fixed buffers at 2 m/s and rebounds at 0·5 m/s. If the contact time is 4 seconds, find the force (assumed constant) exerted by the buffers on the truck. (Take care to choose a positive direction of motion, and remember the direction of the velocity reverses after collision.)

## 2. THE IMPULSE-MOMENTUM EQUATION

**2.1**  We have seen in Exercise A that it is not necessary to calculate the acceleration in circumstances where a constant force acting for a finite time brings about a change of velocity; elimination of **a** between

$$\mathbf{v} = \mathbf{u} + t\mathbf{a} \quad \text{and} \quad \mathbf{F} = m\mathbf{a}$$

gives
$$\mathbf{v} = \mathbf{u} + t\frac{\mathbf{F}}{m}$$

or
$$m\mathbf{v} = m\mathbf{u} + t\mathbf{F}. \tag{1}$$

All our forces and velocities so far have been deliberately one-dimensional, so we have only been concerned with the components of these vector quantities in one direction. We consider motion in two dimensions in Section 2.4.

The product $t\mathbf{F}$ is called the *impulse* of the force **F**, and $m\mathbf{v}$ is the *momentum* of the particle, mass $m$, when its velocity is **v**. Note that both momentum and impulse are vector quantities.

By writing equation (1) as

$$m\mathbf{v} - m\mathbf{u} = t\mathbf{F},$$

we can equate the change in momentum ($m\mathbf{v} - m\mathbf{u}$) with the impulse $t\mathbf{F}$ that caused it. This equation is called the *impulse-momentum equation* and this chapter will be devoted to applying it to a variety of situations.

**2.2   Units.** The SI unit of impulse is the newton-second (written Ns). Since each term of the impulse-momentum equation must have the same dimensions, it follows that the SI unit for momentum is also the Ns. Check for yourself that the expressions in terms of the basic dimensions $\mathbf{M}$, $\mathbf{L}$ and $\mathbf{T}$ for $[mv]$ and $[tF]$ are identical. (See Chapter 12, p. 281.)

*Example 1*

The driver of a car entering a speed-limit applies his brakes and reduces his speed from 25 m/s to 14 m/s. in 6 seconds. What is the average retarding force of the brakes if the mass of the car is 1 tonne?

If $\mathbf{i}$ is a unit vector in the direction of motion, the impulse-momentum equation gives

$$1000 \times 14\mathbf{i} - 1000 \times 25\mathbf{i} = 6\mathbf{F}$$

$$\Rightarrow \mathbf{F} = -1833\mathbf{i},$$

i.e. a force of magnitude 1833 N opposing the motion.

**2.3   Impulse.** In many situations we can observe a change in momentum but are unable to measure either $t$ or $\mathbf{F}$ separately (for instance when the momentum of a tennis ball is changed by impact with the racquet). Under these conditions we can only calculate the total impulse, denoted by the letter $\mathbf{I}$, and we write the impulse-momentum equation as

$$\mathbf{I} = m\mathbf{v} - m\mathbf{u}.$$

*Example 2*

A cricket ball, mass 0·16 kg, reaches the batsman travelling horizontally at 25 m/s. Find the impulse that is needed to: (*a*) bring the ball to rest; (*b*) return it toward the bowler at 20 m/s.

Let $\mathbf{i}$ be a unit vector in the initial direction of motion of the ball (see Figure 1).

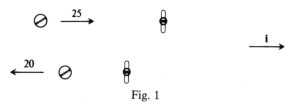

Fig. 1

877

(a) $\mathbf{I} = 0.16 \times 0\mathbf{i} - 0.16 \times 25\mathbf{i} = -4\mathbf{i}$,

that is, an impulse of 4 Ns towards the bowler.

(b) Assuming that the ball leaves the bat at 20 m/s in the $-\mathbf{i}$ direction,

$$\mathbf{I} = 0.16 \times (-20)\mathbf{i} - 0.16 \times 25\mathbf{i} = -7.2\mathbf{i}.$$

As we would expect, a much larger impulse is needed to *reverse* the direction of motion rather than just bring the ball to rest.

**2.4  Extensions to two dimensions.** The next example investigates how we apply the impulse-momentum equation to a situation where the particle is deflected by the impulse.

*Example* 3

A billiard ball moving at 2 m/s hits a cushion at 60°. The ball maintains contact for 0·2 seconds, during which time the cushion exerts a constant force perpendicular to the side of the table of magnitude 1·5 N. If the mass of the ball is 0·1 kg, find its velocity just after impact.

Two methods are given for the solution. The first extends the drawing methods we have encouraged in previous chapters; the second provides an equivalent calculation using the impulse-momentum equation in column vectors.

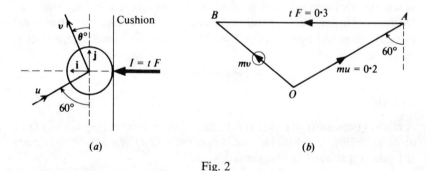

(a)                                              (b)

Fig. 2

*Method* (i). Figure 2(a) gives a diagrammatic representation of the cushion and ball; Figure 2(b) is an impulse-momentum vector diagram in which the initial momentum is represented in magnitude and direction by **OA**, the impulse by **AB**, and

$$\mathbf{OA} + \mathbf{AB} = \mathbf{OB} \quad \text{represents} \quad m\mathbf{u} + t\mathbf{F} = m\mathbf{v}.$$

We use the impulse-momentum equation in this form—where we *add* the initial momentum to the impulse to give the resultant momentum—because addition of vectors is easier on the vector diagram: arrow **AB** follows on after **OA** to meet the resultant **OB**.

By measurement from the diagram, $mv = 0 \cdot 16$ and angle $OBA = 38°$, giving a final velocity of $1 \cdot 6$ m/s at $52°$ to the cushion.

*Method* (ii). Take unit vectors **i** and **j** as shown in Figure $2(a)$ and let $\mathbf{v} = \begin{pmatrix} v_1 \\ v_2 \end{pmatrix}$. The impulse-momentum equation $m\mathbf{v} = m\mathbf{u} + t\mathbf{F}$ gives

$$0 \cdot 1 \begin{pmatrix} v_1 \\ v_2 \end{pmatrix} = 0 \cdot 1 \begin{pmatrix} -2 \sin 60° \\ 2 \cos 60° \end{pmatrix} + 0 \cdot 2 \begin{pmatrix} 1 \cdot 5 \\ 0 \end{pmatrix}$$

$$\Rightarrow \begin{pmatrix} v_1 \\ v_2 \end{pmatrix} = \begin{pmatrix} -1 \cdot 732 \\ 1 \end{pmatrix} + \begin{pmatrix} 3 \\ 0 \end{pmatrix} = \begin{pmatrix} 1 \cdot 268 \\ 1 \end{pmatrix}.$$

From this, $v = \sqrt{(1 \cdot 268^2 + 1^2)} \approx 1 \cdot 61$ and $\tan \theta° = \dfrac{1 \cdot 268}{1} \Rightarrow \theta \approx 51 \cdot 7$.

**2.5  Continuous change of momentum: jets.** Have you ever wondered why the water sprinklers used to spray tennis courts and cricket pitches keep on rotating (see Figure 3)?

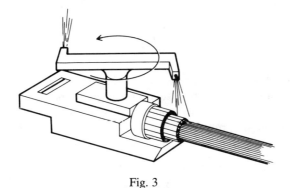

Fig. 3

The following example shows how we use the impulse-momentum equation when a continuous flow of matter changes its velocity.

*Example* 4

Water in a domestic supply flows at 8 m/s round a bend between two straight sections of pipe which change the direction of flow by $70°$. If the cross-section of the pipe is $2 \times 10^{-4}$ m$^2$, find the force of the water on the pipe at the bend. (1 m$^3$ of water has mass 1000 kg.)

The mass of water flowing round the bend is $8 \times 2 \times 10^{-4} \times 1000 =$ 1·6 kg in each second. The momentum of this mass of water has magnitude $8 \times 1·6 = 12·8$ Ns, and it is changed in direction at the bend by 70°.

Figure 4(b) shows the momentum-impulse diagram for one second. Measurement from the diagram gives an impulse of magnitude 14·7 Ns per second along the bisector of the angle between the sections of pipe.

This impulse on the water is provided by a steady force of 14·7 N exerted by the wall of the pipe on the water, and the pipe 'feels' an equal and opposite force. If the pipe is not securely fixed, the force will cause it to move.

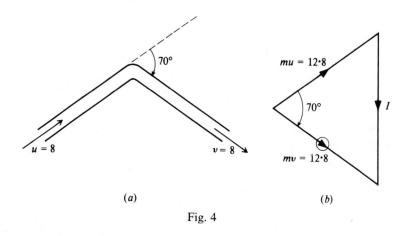

(a)                                                        (b)

Fig. 4

**2.6 Other forces.** In almost all examples where we apply the momentum-impulse equation several forces will be acting on the body concerned, but we are only concerned with the force which actually changes the momentum (for instance we have made no mention of gravity in Examples 1, 2, 3, or 4).

### Exercise B

**1.** Calculate, in Ns, the magnitude of the momentum of each of the following:
 (a) a railway train, total mass 400 tonnes, travelling at 45 m/s;
 (b) a bullet, mass 40 g, travelling at 500 m/s;
 (c) a sprinter, mass 70 kg, running at 10 m/s;
 (d) a barge, mass 200 tonnes, moving at 3 m/s;
 (e) an electron, mass $9 \times 10^{-31}$ kg, travelling at $3 \times 10^7$ m/s.

**2.** Four boys push a car, mass 0·9 tonne, each with a constant force of magnitude 250 N parallel to the direction of motion. How long will it be before the car reaches a speed of 2 m/s, if the total resistance to motion is a constant 400 N in the opposite direction to the push?

**3.** An engine exerts a constant force of $8 \times 10^4$ N on a train of total mass 300 tonnes, moving against a resistance of $3 \times 10^4$ N on a straight level track. Find the increase in speed in the first 25 seconds.

**4.** A squash ball, mass 25 g, hits the front wall of the court perpendicularly at 45 m/s. It rebounds along the same line at 30 m/s. Find the impulse of the wall on the ball.

**5.** A stone of mass 0·05 kg, falling vertically, hits the surface of a pond at 6 m/s. If the impact reduces its speed to 2·5 m/s, find the impulse at the water surface.

**6.** Use the impulse-momentum equation $m\mathbf{u} + \mathbf{I} = m\mathbf{v}$ to answer the following questions. You are recommended to work each question in component form *and* by drawing a vector diagram on graph paper.

(a) $m = 4, \mathbf{u} = \begin{pmatrix} 1 \\ 2 \end{pmatrix}, \mathbf{I} = \begin{pmatrix} 8 \\ -12 \end{pmatrix}$, find $\mathbf{v}$;

(b) $m = 2, \mathbf{u} = \begin{pmatrix} 0 \\ -3 \end{pmatrix}, \mathbf{I} = \begin{pmatrix} -4 \\ 9 \end{pmatrix}$, find $\mathbf{v}$;

(c) $m = 0\cdot5, \mathbf{u} = \begin{pmatrix} 12 \\ 0 \end{pmatrix}, \mathbf{v} = \begin{pmatrix} 0 \\ 12 \end{pmatrix}$, find $\mathbf{I}$;

(d) $m = 30, \mathbf{v} = \begin{pmatrix} 1 \\ -2 \end{pmatrix}, \mathbf{I} = \begin{pmatrix} -30 \\ -20 \end{pmatrix}$, find $\mathbf{u}$;

(e) $\mathbf{u} = \begin{pmatrix} -4 \\ 5 \end{pmatrix}, \mathbf{I} = \begin{pmatrix} 9 \\ -3 \end{pmatrix}, \mathbf{v} = \begin{pmatrix} -1 \\ 4 \end{pmatrix}$, find $m$.

**7.** A squash ball, mass 25 g, hits a side wall of the court at 20 m/s at an angle of 30° to the wall. If the impulse of the wall on the ball is 0·4 Ns in a direction perpendicular to the wall, estimate the direction and speed at which the ball leaves the wall by drawing a momentum-impulse diagram to scale.

**8.** Check the accuracy of your answer to Question 7 by reworking using the column-vector method of Example 3.

**9.** A bullet, mass 30 g, is travelling at 500 m/s when it ricochets from a steel plate at 375 m/s and is deflected through 90°. Find the impulse on the bullet (*a*) from a momentum-impulse diagram, (*b*) using column vectors.

**10.** A ball of mass 0·8 kg strikes a wall. Unit vectors **i** and **j** are chosen as shown in Figure 5. If

$$\mathbf{u} = \begin{pmatrix} -12 \\ 5 \end{pmatrix} \text{ m/s} \quad \text{and} \quad \mathbf{v} = \begin{pmatrix} 4 \\ 3 \end{pmatrix} \text{ m/s},$$

calculate the impulse on the ball due to the impact.

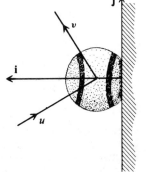

Fig. 5

**11.** An electron, mass $9 \times 10^{-31}$ kg, is moving at a steady speed of $10^8$ m/s along the axis of an oscilloscope tube (see Figure 6). It is deflected by a constant force perpendicular to the axis while it passes between a set of plates of width 0·01 m and emerges at 30° to the axis.

Explain why the component of the velocity parallel to the axis is unaltered and find the time taken to pass between the plates. Find also, by drawing or by calculation, ($a$) the speed of the electron when it emerges from the plates, and ($b$) the magnitude of the force.

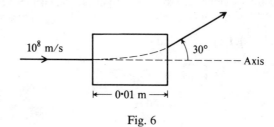

Fig. 6

**12.** Explain in terms of momentum and impulse:
   ($a$) why railway buffers are sprung and not solid;
   ($b$) why parachutists bend their knees as they land;
   ($c$) how to catch a fast, heavy ball.

**13.** ($a$) A ball, mass 0·2 kg, with velocity $\begin{pmatrix} 5 \\ 0 \\ -1 \end{pmatrix}$ m/s is in contact with a bat for 0·01 s, as a result of which its new velocity is $\begin{pmatrix} 3·5 \\ 2 \\ 0 \end{pmatrix}$ m/s. Calculate the average force exerted by the bat on the ball.

   ($b$) An impulse of $\begin{pmatrix} 3 \\ -9 \\ 6 \end{pmatrix}$ Ns causes the final momentum of a 3 kg body to be $\begin{pmatrix} 6 \\ 3 \\ 9 \end{pmatrix}$ Ns. Calculate the initial velocity of the body.

**14.** A comet of mass $6 \times 10^{22}$ kg approaches the sun at 40 km/s. It passes by at a great distance and is deflected through an angle of 120°. If its speed is unaltered, find the impulse of the gravitational force of the sun on the comet. If the effective 'contact time' is 14 days, calculate the mean force exerted by the sun on the comet.

**15.** A jet of water issues horizontally from a fire hose at 15 m/s. The nozzle is 1·5 cm in diameter; find the force the fireman must exert to keep the hose still.

**16.** The water from the hose in Question 15 strikes a wall perpendicularly and rebounds along the same line at 3 m/s; find the force on the wall.

**17.** Bullets of mass 45 g are fired from a machine gun at a stationary tank. The velocity of each bullet is 600 m/s and the gun fires them at a constant rate of 300 per minute. Find the force on the tank, assuming they hit it at the same speed, at right-angles to its side and do not rebound.

**18.** A model boat has a fountain pump in it which draws water from outside the boat and squirts it horizontally over the stern at a speed of 10 m/s from a nozzle 0·3 cm in diameter. Find the propulsive force on the boat (*a*) when the boat is stationary, and (*b*) when the boat is moving forwards at 2 m/s.

**19.** A horizontal conveyor belt at a power station delivers coal at a rate of 100 tonnes per hour. Find the force required to keep the belt moving at a steady 2 m/s.

# 3. CONSERVATION OF MOMENTUM

## 3.1   Two-body collisions in a straight line

*Example* 5

A miniature railway wagon, mass 5 kg, moving at 4 m/s, collides with a smaller truck, mass 2 kg, moving in the same direction at 2 m/s. After the collision the truck moves on at a speed of 4·5 m/s. Assuming that they are in contact for $\frac{1}{2}$ s, find the average force on the truck.

Use the principle of interaction to find the final velocity of the wagon.

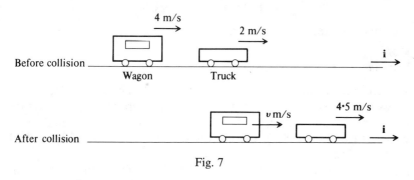

Fig. 7

With **i** in the direction shown in Figure 7, the impulse-momentum equation for the *truck* is

$$2\times4\cdot5\mathbf{i}-2\times2\mathbf{i}=0\cdot5\mathbf{F}\Rightarrow\mathbf{F}=10\mathbf{i}.$$

That is, there is a force of 10 N on the truck in the **i**-direction. Now the interaction principle tells us that the force on the *wagon* is equal and opposite to that on the truck, so for the wagon we have

$$5 \times \mathbf{v} - 5 \times 4\mathbf{i} = 0.5 \times (-10)\mathbf{i}$$

where $\mathbf{v}$ is the velocity of the wagon after the collision. Solving for $\mathbf{v}$ we obtain

$$\mathbf{v} = 3\mathbf{i}$$

indicating a final speed of 3 m/s in the $\mathbf{i}$-direction.

Now calculate the *total* momentum of the truck and wagon before the collision. Calculate the total momentum after the collision. Explain why it was unnecessary in this example to calculate the force.

**3.2** In fact we need not have calculated the impulse in the above example, because the interaction principle for forces extends to ensure that the impulses of the forces, acting for the same time, are themselves equal and opposite. Since there is no other impulse acting on the two bodies, one gains momentum and the other loses an equal amount so that their total momentum before collision is the same as afterwards.

This special case of a more general *principle of conservation of momentum* is very useful in solving problems about collisions: if the only impulses are 'internal', interaction ones, the method of solution is to equate total momentum before with total momentum after.

In the example above,

$$\text{total momentum before} = 2 \times 2\mathbf{i} + 5 \times 4\mathbf{i}$$

$$\text{total momentum after} \quad = 2 \times 4.5\mathbf{i} + 5 \times \mathbf{v}$$

and equating these gives $\mathbf{v} = 3\mathbf{i}$ as before.

*Example 6*

A space module moving at 3 m/s collides with another moving in the opposite direction at 1 m/s. The two spacecraft couple together automatically and move on in the direction of the first module at 1.25 m/s (see Figure 8). If the mass of the first module is 1200 kg, find the mass of the second.

Equating total momentum before collision with total momentum after, we have

$$1200 \times 3\mathbf{i} + m \times (-1)\mathbf{i} = (1200 + m) \times 1.25\mathbf{i}$$

where $m$ kg is the mass of the second module. This reduces to

$$2.25m = 2100 \quad \text{or} \quad m = 933.$$

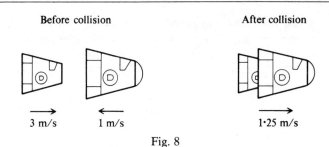

Fig. 8

**3.3 Collisions in two dimensions.** The principle of conservation of momentum can be extended to more general collisions at oblique angles.

*Example* 7

As two stock-cars come out of a bend on a slippery, watered track, side by side, one driver loses control of his car, which slides into the other. Car *A* (mass 750 kg) hits car *B* (mass 1000 kg) at an angle of 30° to the direction of *B*'s motion. Before the collision they are both travelling at 20 m/s.

Assuming that the efforts of both drivers have no effects on their motion, and that the cars may be treated as particles *with no horizontal external forces* on them, find the direction and speed of car *A* immediately after the impact if *B* is deflected through 25° and has its speed increased to 22 m/s.

Figure 9 shows the situation before and after collision. We can draw a momentum-impulse diagram for car *B* using the data given (see Figure 10).

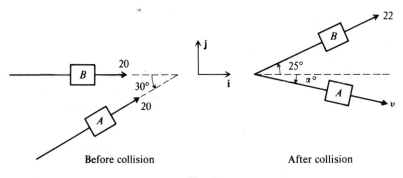

Fig. 9

885

Now, by the interaction principle, the impulse **I** on $B$ is equal and opposite to the impulse **J** on $A$, so copying the impulse vector from Figure 10, but reversing the direction of the arrow we can draw the momentum-impulse diagram for $A$ (see Figure 11($a$)).

Figure 10 shows

$$m_B\mathbf{u}_B + \mathbf{I} = m_B\mathbf{v}_B. \tag{2}$$

Figure 11($a$) shows

$$m_A\mathbf{u}_A + \mathbf{J} = m_A\mathbf{v}_A. \tag{3}$$

If we reverse the order of the terms in the left-hand side of equation (3), our vector triangle is redrawn as in Figure 11($b$). We can now fit Figure 10 and Figure 11($b$) together to form a momentum quadrilateral (Figure 12). The diagonals **PQ** and **QP** give the impulses on $A$ and $B$ respectively. The diagonal **RS** represents the total momentum of the

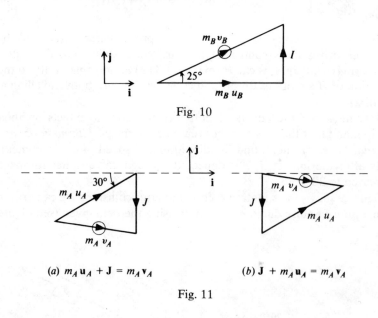

Fig. 10

(a) $m_A\mathbf{u}_A + \mathbf{J} = m_A\mathbf{v}_A$  (b) $\mathbf{J} + m_A\mathbf{u}_A = m_A\mathbf{v}_A$

Fig. 11

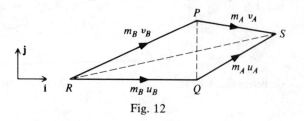

Fig. 12

886

two-body system which has remained constant; from triangle $RQS$ we see that **RS** represents the total momentum *before* impact, from triangle *RPS* we see it is also the total momentum *afterwards*.

Adding equations (2) and (3), remembering that $\mathbf{J} = -\mathbf{I}$, we obtain

$$m_B\mathbf{u}_B + m_A\mathbf{u}_A = m_B\mathbf{v}_B + m_A\mathbf{v}_A \tag{4}$$

showing again that the total momentum before collision equals the total momentum afterwards.

To complete the solution of Example 7, we either measure the length *PS* and the angle *PS* makes with **i** from an accurate drawing, or we substitute the appropriate column vectors into equation (4). Using unit vectors **i** and **j** as shown in Figure 9,

$$1000\begin{pmatrix}20\\0\end{pmatrix} + 750\begin{pmatrix}20\cos 30°\\20\sin 30°\end{pmatrix} = 1000\begin{pmatrix}22\cos 25°\\22\sin 25°\end{pmatrix} + 750\begin{pmatrix}v\cos\alpha\\-v\sin\alpha\end{pmatrix} \tag{5}$$

giving
$$\begin{pmatrix}v\cos\alpha\\-v\sin\alpha\end{pmatrix} = \begin{pmatrix}17{\cdot}4\\-2{\cdot}4\end{pmatrix}$$

from which $v \approx 17{\cdot}6$ and $\alpha \approx 7{\cdot}8$.

In this two-dimensional example we have seen that, in a situation where there is no external impulse, the total momentum of the system is conserved in both directions we have chosen to consider: the **i**-components of equation (5) show that the momentum in the **i**-direction is the same before as afterwards; likewise the **j**-components. We shall see in Section 6.2 that, in an example of this sort, momentum is in fact conserved in *any* direction.

### 3.4 Explosions and relative velocity.

In Example 6, two space modules collided and coupled together. If we had made a ciné film of the event and ran it backwards, we should see what we might call an *explosion*— two bodies flying apart after an *internal* impulse. Since the interaction principle ensures that the explosive forces (just like collision forces) are equal and opposite for the two bodies, explosions where there are no external impulses are governed by the same law of conservation of momentum as collisions.

*Example 8*

A rifle, mass 3·6 kg, fires a bullet of mass 10 g at 900 m/s (see Figure 13). Find the velocity at which the rifle recoils (assuming it is not held in any way).

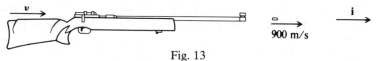

Fig. 13

The total momentum before firing is zero. The conservation of momentum equation gives

$$0 = 0.01 \times 900\mathbf{i} + 3.6\mathbf{v}$$

$$\Rightarrow \mathbf{v} = -2.5\mathbf{i}$$

i.e. the gun recoils at 2·5 m/s in the opposite direction to the bullet.

In this example the velocity of the bullet was given relative to the earth. All velocities up to this point in the chapter have also been understood in that way. Sometimes the velocity of a projectile is given *relative to the gun* which fired it (the velocity is then called the *muzzle velocity*). If the velocities relative to the earth of the bullet and the gun are $\mathbf{v_b}$ and $\mathbf{v_g}$ respectively, then the velocity of the bullet relative to the gun will be $\mathbf{v_b} - \mathbf{v_g}$. In Example 8 the velocity of the bullet relative to the gun is $900\mathbf{i} - (-2.5)\mathbf{i} = 902.5\mathbf{i}$.

A further complication is that the gun is often constrained to move in only one direction, and momentum is only conserved in that direction. The following example illustrates both these difficulties.

*Example 9*

A gun, mass 1000 kg, mounted on a horizontal railway track so that it can recoil freely, has its barrel inclined at an angle of 40° to the horizontal. It fires a shell, mass 50 kg, which leaves the barrel at a speed of 250 m/s relative to the gun (see Figure 14). Calculate the speed at which the gun recoils.

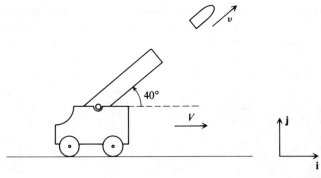

Fig. 14

If the gun were free to recoil in any direction, it would move in the opposite direction to the shell. The rails prevent it from doing this by providing an external impulse vertically. Momentum is only conserved horizontally (i.e. in the direction where there is no external impulse).

888

The velocity of the shell relative to the earth will be the vector sum of the velocity of the gun relative to the ground and the velocity of the shell relative to the gun: i.e.

$$\mathbf{v} = \mathbf{V} + \begin{pmatrix} 250\cos 40° \\ 250\sin 40° \end{pmatrix}$$

where $\mathbf{V}$ is the velocity of the gun. Putting $\mathbf{V} = V\mathbf{i}$, this becomes

$$\mathbf{v} = \begin{pmatrix} 250\cos 40° \\ 250\sin 40° \end{pmatrix} + \begin{pmatrix} V \\ 0 \end{pmatrix} = \begin{pmatrix} 250\cos 40° + V \\ 250\sin 40° \end{pmatrix}.$$

The equation for conservation of momentum in the $\mathbf{i}$-direction gives

$$0 = 1000\,V\mathbf{i} + 50(250\cos 40° + V)\mathbf{i}$$

from which          $V = -9{\cdot}12.$

So the gun recoils at about $9{\cdot}1$ m/s.

### Exercise C

**1.** A Dodgems car of mass 120 kg, moving at 3 m/s with its power switched off, hits another car of mass 140 kg directly from behind. The second car was originally at rest, and moves forward after the collision at 2 m/s. Find the subsequent velocity of the first car.

**2.** A descent module, mass 400 kg, is docking with its command module, mass 1200 kg. Before they come together they are both moving at constant speed in the same direction, the command module at 4 m/s and the descent module at 5 m/s. Find the speed of the recombined spaceship after docking.

**3.** In a game of bowls, one wood of mass 0·9 kg hits a stationary jack. Its speed is reduced from 2 m/s to 1·5 m/s. The whole motion takes place in the same line and the jack moves off at 3·2 m/s; what is its mass?

**4.** Two punts collide head-on. The total mass of punt $A$, including passengers, is 500 kg, and that of $B$ is 300 kg. Before the collision $A$ was moving at 0·75 m/s and $B$ at 0·5 m/s in the opposite direction. After the collision $B$ rebounds at 0·5 m/s. How fast and in which direction does $A$ travel afterwards?

**5.** Use the conservation of momentum equation $m_1\mathbf{u}_1 + m_2\mathbf{u}_2 = m_1\mathbf{v}_1 + m_2\mathbf{v}_2$ to answer the following questions. You are recommended to draw a vector quadrilateral like Figure 12 for each on graph paper, *and* to work each question in component form. Draw also a rough sketch like Figure 9 showing the colliding bodies before and after impact.

(a) $m_1 = 3,\ m_2 = 3,\ \mathbf{u}_1 = \begin{pmatrix} 3 \\ -1 \end{pmatrix},\ \mathbf{u}_2 = \begin{pmatrix} 1 \\ 2 \end{pmatrix},\ \mathbf{v}_1 = \begin{pmatrix} 3 \\ 1 \end{pmatrix}$, find $\mathbf{v}_2$;

(b) $m_1 = 2,\ m_2 = 3,\ \mathbf{u}_1 = \begin{pmatrix} 6 \\ -3 \end{pmatrix},\ \mathbf{u}_2 = \begin{pmatrix} 0 \\ 0 \end{pmatrix},\ \mathbf{v}_1 = \begin{pmatrix} 1\frac{1}{2} \\ -3 \end{pmatrix}$, find $\mathbf{v}_2$;

(c) $m_1 = 2,\ \mathbf{u}_1 = \begin{pmatrix} 1 \\ 2 \end{pmatrix},\ \mathbf{u}_2 = \begin{pmatrix} 3 \\ 0 \end{pmatrix},\ \mathbf{v}_1 = \begin{pmatrix} 3 \\ 0 \end{pmatrix},\ \mathbf{v}_2 = \begin{pmatrix} 2 \\ 1 \end{pmatrix}$, find $m_2$.

**6.** A shell, mass 6 kg, is travelling horizontally at 400 m/s when it breaks into two fragments, masses 4 kg and 2 kg, which continue to travel in the same horizontal plane. The 4 kg mass moves off at 500 m/s at 30° to the original direction. Find from a momentum vector diagram the speed and direction of the other fragment.

**7.** An $\alpha$-particle enters a bubble-chamber filled with liquid helium. A photograph of its track shows that, after collision with a stationary helium atom, it is deflected through 20° and measurements show that its speed is reduced from $2.5 \times 10^7$ m/s to $2.35 \times 10^7$ m/s. The helium atom moves off at right-angles to the final direction of the $\alpha$-particle, at $8.55 \times 10^6$ m/s. Show that the two particles appear to be equal in mass.

**8.** A satellite of mass 200 kg is attached to a nose-cone of mass 12·5 kg. When travelling at 9600 m/s the two are separated by an internal impulse of $1.6 \times 10^5$ Ns in a direction at right-angles to the line of flight. Find the subsequent speeds of the satellite and nose-cone and the deflection of each from the original line of flight.

**9.** Two billiard balls, A and B, both of mass 0·1 kg, collide. A is moving at 2·5 m/s and B at 2 m/s at 120° to the direction of A's velocity. A is deflected through 80° by the collision and B is then moving perpendicular to it. Draw a momentum vector diagram and measure the momenta of A and B after the collision. Deduce the final velocities.

**10.** Check the accuracy of your answer to Question 9 by calculation using column vectors.

**11.** The Scottish game of curling is played by sliding stones on ice. Stone A, mass 3 kg, travelling at 2 m/s, hits a stationary stone B, mass 2·5 kg. The angle between the original direction of A's motion and the line of centres at impact is 30° (see Figure 15(a)). Since the impulse acts along the line of centres, stone B must move off along that direction. A moves off at 75° to B (Figure 15(b)). Draw the momentum vector diagram and find by measurement the final velocities of the two stones. Find also the impulse on A.

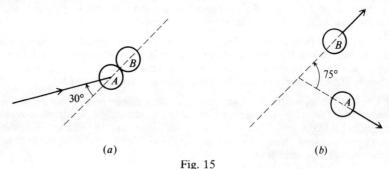

(a)                                                                    (b)

Fig. 15

**12.** A smooth sphere A of mass 0·8 kg, moving at 4 m/s, collides with another smooth sphere B of mass 0·4 kg, moving at 2 m/s. Their velocities before impact are inclined at 30° and 60° to the line PQ (see Figure 16) joining their centres at the moment of impact. A moves off after the impact at 3 m/s at an angle of 42° to PQ; find the subsequent velocity of B. Find also the impulse of A on B.

890

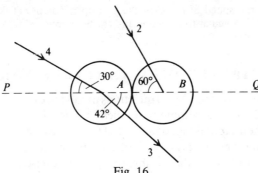

Fig. 16

**13.** The two curling stones of Question 11 hit each other at the angle shown in Figure 17. $A$ is moving at 2 m/s at 60° to the line of centres and $B$ is moving at $V$ m/s at $\alpha°$. $A$ moves off at 2·1 m/s at 56° to the line of centres at impact and $B$ moves off at 1 m/s at 43°. Find the initial velocity $V$ m/s for $B$.

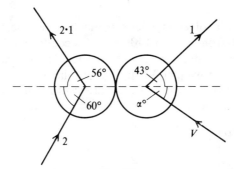

Fig. 17

**\*14.** A cannon of mass 10 tonnes is free to recoil in the direction of the barrel. It fires a shot, mass 80 kg, with a speed of 200 m/s relative to the gun. Find the velocity of recoil of the gun.

The recoil is resisted by a constant force so that the gun moves back only 20 cm. Find the magnitude of this force.

**\*15.** A gun of mass 20 tonnes rests on a slope inclined at 30° to the horizontal. It is prevented from moving down the slope, but can recoil freely up it (see Figure 18). It fires a shot of mass 100 kg horizontally at a muzzle speed of

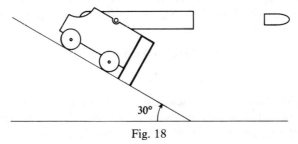

Fig. 18

400 m/s. Find the speed of recoil of the gun up the slope. (Take unit vectors parallel and perpendicular to the slope and consider conservation of momentum parallel to the slope.)

## 4. IMPULSE OF A VARIABLE FORCE

**4.1** So far we have considered questions involving only a constant force. Clearly this is a considerable simplification: for instance, experiment shows that when a tennis ball bounces the force between it and the ground increases as the ball distorts. Similarly, research into car crashes shows great variation of force during impact. (See Exercise D, Question 1.) Even billiard balls distort each other slightly when they collide!

We investigate a simple case of variable force in one dimension in the next example.

*Example* 10

A space capsule involved in a docking manoeuvre is acted on by a thrust which builds up from zero to 1400 N in 4 seconds and then decreases to zero at the same rate. Find the final speed if the capsule has mass 2000 kg and was moving at 3·5 m/s before the 'burn'.

Figure 19 shows how the thrust $F$ varies with time. Clearly a constant force of 700 N is the mean value which will produce the same effect as

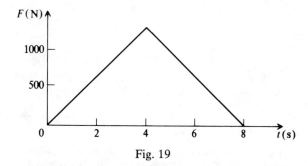

Fig. 19

the variable force we are given. Such a mean force would have an impulse of $700 \times 8 \, \text{Ns} = 5600 \, \text{Ns}$, giving from the impulse-momentum equation a final speed $v$ m/s:

$$2000v = 2000 \times 3 \cdot 5 + 5600$$

$$\Rightarrow v = 6 \cdot 3.$$

How does this example help us to approach situations where the variation of force with time is more complicated? Superimposing a graph of the mean force 700 N on the original force graph of Figure 19

892

(see Figure 20) gives us the clue we need, for the impulse we have calculated is represented by the area under $F = 700$ over the 8 second interval involved, which is the same as the area under the original force-time graph.

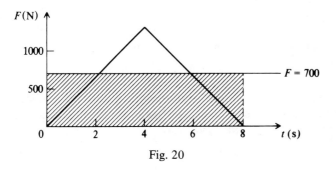

Fig. 20

For a more general variation of force with time we make use of the discussion in Chapters 10 and 31, where we replaced the limit of a sum of small elements of area under a graph by an integral. In Figure 21 the total impulse between $t_1$ and $t_2$ will be the limiting value of the sum of successive small impulses $F\,\delta t$:

$$\overset{t_2}{\underset{t_1}{\mathbf{S}}}\ F\,\delta t.$$

This limit as $\delta t \to 0$ is the definite integral

$$\int_{t_1}^{t_2} F\,dt.$$

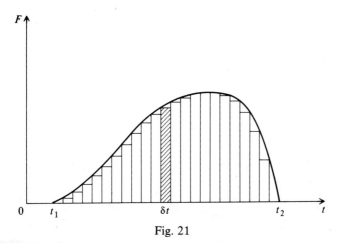

Fig. 21

Further, at any instant, $F = ma = m \dfrac{dv}{dt}$.

So
$$\int_{t_1}^{t_2} F\, dt = \int_{t_1}^{t_2} m \frac{dv}{dt}\, dt = \left[ mv \right]_{t_1}^{t_2} = mv_2 - mv_1,$$

where $v_2$ and $v_1$ are the speeds at $t_2$ and $t_1$ respectively.

So, as before, the change in momentum is equal to the impulse that caused it.

**4.2** Since this one-dimensional reasoning can be applied to each component in two or three dimensions, we can extend the result immediately to the vector form

$$\int_{t_1}^{t_2} \mathbf{F}\, dt = m\mathbf{v}_2 - m\mathbf{v}_1.$$

Note that we are still restricted to situations in which the mass is constant. Variable-mass situations are the subject of a project exercise on p. 1116.

*Example* 11

The force $F$ N on a golf ball of mass 45 g when it is struck is given approximately by $F = kt\,e^{-1000t}$ for $0 \leqslant t \leqslant 0.004$. If $k = 2.4 \times 10^6$, find the impulse on the ball, and the speed at which it leaves the club.

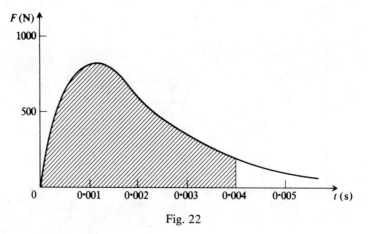

Fig. 22

The impulse is represented by the area shaded in Figure 22, which is

$$k \int_0^{0 \cdot 004} t\,e^{-1000t}\,dt = k\left\{\left[\frac{-t}{1000}e^{-1000t}\right]_0^{0 \cdot 004} + \frac{1}{1000}\int_0^{0 \cdot 004} e^{-1000t}\,dt\right\}$$

$$\approx k\left\{-7 \cdot 33 \times 10^{-8} - \left[10^{-6} \times e^{-1000t}\right]_0^{0 \cdot 004}\right\}$$

$$\approx k \times 9 \cdot 08 \times 10^{-7}$$

$$\approx 2 \cdot 18 \text{ Ns.}$$

Using the impulse-momentum equation,

$$0 \cdot 045v - 0 = 2 \cdot 18$$

$$\Rightarrow v \approx 48,$$

giving a speed of 48 m/s.

### Exercise D

**1.** Measurements taken during a simulation of a car crash produce a force-time graph as shown in Figure 23. Estimate the area under the graph by counting squares or using the trapezium rule. If the mass of the car is 1200 kg, find the original speed if it came to rest after $0 \cdot 1$ seconds.

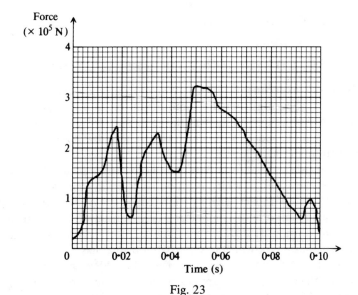

Fig. 23

**2.** A ball of mass 90 g strikes a wall at right-angles when moving at 8 m/s and rebounds with a speed of 6 m/s. Assuming that the thrust between the wall and

895

the ball increases uniformly with time up to a maximum and then decreases at the same rate, find the maximum thrust in newtons, if the total time of contact is 0·002 s.

**3.** A car, mass 1 tonne, started from rest and accelerated for 60 s. During this time the propulsive force was measured at 10 s intervals and found to be:

| Force (N) | 1050 | 650 | 480 | 260 | 170 | 130 | 80 |
|-----------|------|-----|-----|-----|-----|-----|-----|
| Time (s)  | 0    | 10  | 20  | 30  | 40  | 50  | 60 |

Use Simpson's rule or the trapezium rule to estimate the total impulse on the car during the 60 s and estimate its final speed.

**4.** A horse-drawn tram has a mass of 4000 kg. When starting from rest, the pull of the horse is initially 1050 N. This pull decreases uniformly with time until after 10 s the pull is 350 N. Sketch the force-time graph and calculate the impulse on the tram during the first 10 s. What speed will the tram acquire if it started from rest?

**5.** When a car runs off the road into a certain type of wire crash-barrier, the force exerted by the barrier on the car is approximately given by the function $F = 42\,000 \sin 2\pi t$ (where $F$ is measured in newtons and $t$ in seconds). This force acts perpendicular to the barrier. A car, mass 1200 kg, hits such a barrier at an angle of 30° while travelling at 20 m/s. Find the impulse of the barrier on the car if the impact lasts 0·5 s and find the subsequent velocity of the car.

**6.** A particle is acted on by a variable force

$$\mathbf{F} = \begin{pmatrix} 2t \\ \sin 2t \end{pmatrix}.$$

Find by integration the change in momentum from $t = 0$ to $t = 1$.

## *5. COEFFICIENT OF RESTITUTION

**5.1 Newton's experimental law.** If you drop a tennis ball, a lump of putty or a ball-bearing from the same height on to a horizontal stone floor, they will all reach the floor at the same speed. But we know from experience that the speeds with which they rebound will be different for the different materials.

Experiment shows that for a particular body striking a fixed surface at right-angles, the speed at which it rebounds is always the same fraction of the speed before impact. This fraction (called the *coefficient of restitution* and usually denoted by the letter $e$) is a constant for the particular materials in collision. It is clear that $0 \leqslant e \leqslant 1$; for example, putty dropped on stone has $e = 0$, while a 'Superball' on steel has $e \approx 0·95$.

What happens when two moving bodies collide? We can approach the answer by considering what happens when we drop a tennis ball on to the floor of a lift moving at constant speed. Common sense suggests and experiment confirms that it is the speed of the ball *relative* to the lift which is reduced by the same fraction as when the ball was dropped on to a stationary floor. By taking speeds relative to the lift we do in effect imagine that it is at rest.

In a similar way, when *any* two bodies collide *in a straight line*, their relative velocity after impact is *e* times their relative velocity before, and in the opposite direction, i.e.

$$(\mathbf{v}_2 - \mathbf{v}_1) = -e(\mathbf{u}_2 - \mathbf{u}_1).$$

*Example* 12

A miniature railway truck, mass 2 kg, moving at 5 m/s, collides with an engine, mass 8 kg, moving in the same direction at 0·5 m/s. After the collision the truck rebounds at 1 m/s (see Figure 24). Find the subsequent velocity of the engine and the value of *e* for these two bodies.

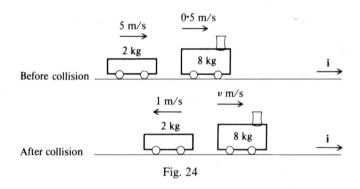

Fig. 24

The conservation of momentum equation gives

$$2 \times 5\mathbf{i} + 8 \times 0\cdot5\mathbf{i} = 2 \times (-1)\mathbf{i} + 8 \times v\mathbf{i}$$

$$\Rightarrow \mathbf{v} = 2\mathbf{i}.$$

The velocity of the truck relative to the engine before collision is

$$5\mathbf{i} - 0\cdot5\mathbf{i} = 4\cdot5\mathbf{i}$$

and the velocity of the truck relative to the engine after the collision is

$$(-1)\mathbf{i} - 2\mathbf{i} = (-3)\mathbf{i}.$$

So                           $$(-3)\mathbf{i} = -e \times 4\cdot5\mathbf{i}$$

$$\Rightarrow e = \frac{-3}{-4\cdot5} = \tfrac{2}{3}.$$

897

**5.2  Oblique collisions.** For a more general collision in two or three dimensions, the same experimental law holds if we take the *component* of the relative velocity *along the line of impact*; i.e.

$$(\mathbf{v}_2 - \mathbf{v}_1) \cdot \mathbf{n} = -e(\mathbf{u}_2 - \mathbf{u}_1) \cdot \mathbf{n}$$

where **n** is a unit vector along the line of impact.

*Example* 13

Two small smooth spheres $A$ and $B$ of mass 3 kg and 2 kg collide when their velocities are $\begin{pmatrix} 4 \\ 3 \end{pmatrix}$ m/s and $\begin{pmatrix} -5 \\ 12 \end{pmatrix}$ m/s and their line of centres is parallel to **i** (see Figure 25). If $e = \frac{2}{3}$ for these spheres, calculate their subsequent velocities.

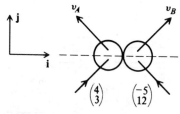

Fig. 25

Let
$$\mathbf{v}_A = \begin{pmatrix} a_1 \\ a_2 \end{pmatrix} \quad \text{and} \quad \mathbf{v}_B = \begin{pmatrix} b_1 \\ b_2 \end{pmatrix}.$$

The velocity of $A$ relative to $B$ before collision is

$$\begin{pmatrix} 4 \\ 3 \end{pmatrix} - \begin{pmatrix} -5 \\ 12 \end{pmatrix} = \begin{pmatrix} 9 \\ -9 \end{pmatrix}$$

and the velocity of $A$ relative to $B$ after collision is

$$\begin{pmatrix} a_1 \\ a_2 \end{pmatrix} - \begin{pmatrix} b_1 \\ b_2 \end{pmatrix} = \begin{pmatrix} a_1 - b_1 \\ a_2 - b_2 \end{pmatrix}.$$

Newton's experimental law tells us that the component of relative velocity along **i** will be reduced by a factor of $-\frac{2}{3}$, so

$$9 \times (-\tfrac{2}{3}) = a_1 - b_1$$

$$a_1 - b_1 = -6. \tag{1}$$

898

There are no external impulses so the conservation of momentum equation gives

$$3\binom{4}{3} + 2\binom{-5}{12} = 3\binom{a_1}{a_2} + 2\binom{b_1}{b_2}$$

$$\Rightarrow 2 = 3a_1 + 2b_1 \tag{2}$$

and $$33 = 3a_2 + 2b_2. \tag{3}$$

From equations (1) and (2) we obtain $a_1 = -2$ and $b_1 = 4$. Since the impulse is perpendicular to $\mathbf{j}$, the components of the velocity of each ball in the $\mathbf{j}$-direction will be unaltered by the collision, so $a_2 = 3$ and $b_2 = 12$.

Hence the final velocities of $A$ and $B$ are $\binom{-2}{3}$ and $\binom{4}{12}$.

## *6. PARTICLE SYSTEMS

**6.1 Systems of particles and bodies.** We have so far discussed the momentum of a single particle and that of pairs of particles. We now investigate how the impulse-momentum equation can be applied to systems of particles and solid bodies and in particular look to see whether momentum is conserved in situations where there *is* an external impulse.

First, consider a mass $m_1$ which, as a result of an impulse $\mathbf{I}_1$, changes its velocity from $\mathbf{u}_1$ to $\mathbf{v}_1$. It follows that

$$\mathbf{I}_1 = m_1\mathbf{v}_1 - m_1\mathbf{u}_1.$$

Similar equations may be written for the action of other impulses $\mathbf{I}_2, \mathbf{I}_3, \mathbf{I}_4, \ldots$ on the other particles of masses $m_2, m_3, m_4, \ldots$ . If we have $n$ particles we may summarize the effects of these impulses by the equations

$$\mathbf{I}_i = m_i\mathbf{v}_i - m_i\mathbf{u}_i \quad (i = 1, 2, \ldots, n)$$

and summing these equations we obtain

$$\sum \mathbf{I}_i = \sum m_i\mathbf{v}_i - \sum m_i\mathbf{u}_i. \tag{1}$$

If the particles are independent of each other there is little more we can say, but if they interact we can appeal to the interaction principle. Forces between pairs of particles will be equal and opposite, so that the net contributions of the impulses of such internal forces to the sum on the left-hand side of equation (1) will be zero.

In particular, if the system of particles is a solid body, the left-hand side of equation (1) consists of the sum of the external impulses only.

899

In order to simplify the right-hand side of the equation we consider a general system of particles. Let the position vector of the point where the $i$th particle is situated be $\mathbf{r}_i$. Then at time $t$

$$\mathbf{v}_i = \frac{d}{dt}(\mathbf{r}_i).$$

As the mass of this particle, $m_i$, is assumed to be constant, we have

$$m_i\mathbf{v}_i = m_i\frac{d}{dt}(\mathbf{r}_i) = \frac{d}{dt}(m_i\mathbf{r}_i)$$

and

$$\sum m_i\mathbf{v}_i = \sum \frac{d}{dt}(m_i\mathbf{r}_i) = \frac{d}{dt}(\sum m_i\mathbf{r}_i).$$

In our earlier work on centres of mass (Chapter 24, p. 593) we defined the position vector $\mathbf{r}_G$ of the centre of mass of a system of particles by

$$M\mathbf{r}_G = \sum m_i\mathbf{r}_i$$

where $M = \sum m_i$ is the total mass. Consequently,

$$\sum m_i\mathbf{v}_i = \frac{d}{dt}(\sum m_i\mathbf{r}_i) = \frac{d}{dt}(M\mathbf{r}_G) = M\mathbf{v}_G$$

where $\mathbf{v}_G$ is the velocity of the centre of mass of the system. Similarly,

$$\sum m_i\mathbf{u}_i = M\mathbf{u}_G.$$

Hence for a system of particles of total mass $M$, equation (1) simplifies to

$$\mathbf{I} = M\mathbf{v}_G - M\mathbf{u}_G, \tag{2}$$

where $\mathbf{I}$ is the total external impulse and $\mathbf{u}_G$ and $\mathbf{v}_G$ are the initial and final velocities of the centre of mass of the system.

Now we can see why it was reasonable to treat bodies as particles earlier in the chapter: we have in effect been regarding the bodies as particles of mass $M$ located at the centre of mass and moving with it. (Note: we are specifically ignoring rotation.)

Finally we can sum all the equations we get from applying equation (2) to several bodies to give

$$\sum \mathbf{I}_i = \sum M_i\mathbf{v}_i - \sum M_i\mathbf{u}_i. \tag{3}$$

And in solving problems we can consider the total momentum of the system of bodies before and after the total impulse acts.

900

**6.2  Conservation of linear momentum.** If we form the scalar product of both sides of equation (3) with a unit vector **n** we obtain

$$\mathbf{n} \cdot (\textstyle\sum \mathbf{I}_i) = \mathbf{n} \cdot (\textstyle\sum M_i \mathbf{v}_i) - \mathbf{n} \cdot (\textstyle\sum M_i \mathbf{u}_i) \qquad (4)$$

which gives us the components of total impulse and change in momentum in the direction of **n**. This equation is particularly useful in the two cases when $\mathbf{n} \cdot \sum \mathbf{I}_i = 0$. This happens either when $\sum \mathbf{I}_i = \mathbf{0}$ (the net impulse is zero) or when **n** is perpendicular to the resultant impulse. In both cases we can rewrite equation (4) as

$$\mathbf{n} \cdot (\textstyle\sum m_i \mathbf{v}_i) = \mathbf{n} \cdot (\textstyle\sum M_i \mathbf{u}_i)$$

which shows that the component of the total momentum of the system in the direction of **n** is constant.

So we can now generalize the principle of conservation of linear momentum:

The total momentum of a system is constant if no external forces act on it. When there is an external force, the component of the total momentum perpendicular to the resultant impulse is constant.

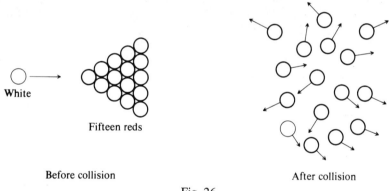

Before collision                                            After collision

Fig. 26

A striking example of conservation of momentum for a system of bodies is provided at the first shot of a game of snooker (see Figure 26). If we ignore outside impulses, then the total momentum of all sixteen balls after the white hits the fifteen reds must equal the original momentum of the white ball.

### Exercise E

**1.** A golf ball strikes a concrete floor at 5 m/s and rebounds at 3·5 m/s. Find $e$ for the ball and the floor.

**2.** Find $e$ for the wagon and truck of Example 5.

3. A miniature railway truck, mass $m$ kg and velocity $\mathbf{i}$ m/s, collides with another truck, mass 2 kg and velocity $-3\mathbf{i}$ m/s. If $e = \frac{1}{4}$ and the second truck is brought to rest by the collision, find the subsequent velocity of the first truck. Find also its mass.

4. A wooden ball, mass 2 kg, moving with velocity $3\mathbf{i}$, strikes a similar ball, mass 1 kg, which is at rest. If $e = \frac{1}{2}$ and they both move off in the $\mathbf{i}$-direction, find the speed of each ball after the collision.

5. Find $e$ for Exercise C, Question 3.

6. Find $e$ for Exercise C, Question 10.

7. Two wooden balls, each of mass $0\cdot 1$ kg, collide. The line of centres at impact is along $\begin{pmatrix} 1 \\ 0 \end{pmatrix}$. If their velocities before the collision are $\mathbf{u}_1 = \begin{pmatrix} 1 \\ 3 \end{pmatrix}$ m/s and $\mathbf{u}_2 = \begin{pmatrix} -2 \\ 1 \end{pmatrix}$ m/s, and $e = \frac{1}{3}$, find their velocities after collision.

8. A billiard ball strikes another identical ball initially at rest. If the velocity of the moving ball before collision is 2 m/s at 45° to the line of centres at impact, and $e = 0\cdot 6$, find the velocities of the two balls after the collision.

9. Two billiard balls of equal mass are lying in contact on a smooth table and a third ball of the same mass, moving with velocity $v$ m/s along their common tangent, strikes them simultaneously (see Figure 27). Prove that the speed of the third ball is reduced to $\frac{1}{5}(2 - 3e)v$, where $e$ is the coefficient of restitution for each pair of balls, and find the velocities of the other two balls.

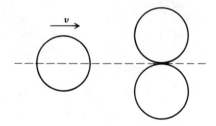

Fig. 27

## Miscellaneous Exercise

1. Two balls of the same mass, one hard and the other soft, strike you at the same speed. Explain why the hard ball is more painful.

2. A ball is thrown vertically downwards so as to strike a horizontal floor with speed 12 m/s. It rebounds and strikes a horizontal ceiling 4 m above the floor. Find the speed at which it again hits the floor, given that the coefficient of restitution at each impact is $0\cdot 8$. Will it hit the ceiling again?

3. A smooth sphere collides obliquely with another sphere at rest. The two spheres are of equal mass and perfectly elastic ($e = 1$). Show that after the collision their velocities are mutually perpendicular.

**4.** A particle of mass $m$ is enclosed in a straight tube of length $a$ and mass $2m$. The tube has enclosed ends and lies on a smooth table. The coefficient of restitution between the particle and the ends of the tube is $\frac{2}{3}$. The particle is projected along the tube with speed $v$. Find the distance moved by the tube between the first and second impacts and the time interval between the second and third.

**5.** A bullet of mass $m$ is fired horizontally into a block of wood of mass $M$, resting on a smooth horizontal table, with a velocity $v$. If the resistance to the motion of the bullet through the block is constant and equal to $P$, find the velocity of the block and the bullet when the latter has come to rest relative to the block. Find the time taken to do so.

**6.** A line of pennies rests on a smooth table, each penny touching its neighbours. A single penny, moving along the direction of the line at 10 cm/s, strikes an end penny. Explain what is observed to happen.

If the experiment is conducted with two striking pennies, two pennies usually are seen to detach themselves from the line. Can you explain this?

If there are ten pennies originally in the line, and the last penny moves off at 5 cm/s, ($a$) explain what has happened to the conservation of momentum, and ($b$) give an estimate of the coefficient of restitution.

**7.** A billiard ball hits two adjacent edges of a billiard table in succession. Show that if the coefficient of restitution in each case is $e$, then the final direction of travel of the billiard ball is parallel to its initial direction.

**8.** A raindrop is falling vertically through a cloud of very fine drops which are themselves falling vertically with constant velocity $u$. At time $t$ the drop, of mass $m$, is falling with velocity $v$ and is about to coalesce with a small element of the cloud of mass $\delta m$. After coalescing at time $t + \delta t$, the drop so formed moves down with velocity $v + \delta v$. By considering the change in momentum and following a limiting argument, obtain the equation

$$m\frac{dv}{dt} + (v - u)\frac{dm}{dt} = mg.$$

If the accumulation of mass is such that $\dfrac{dm}{dt} = k$, show that

$$mv - mu - (g/2k)m^2 = \text{constant}.$$

# SUMMARY

*The impulse-momentum equation*

For a constant force

$$t\mathbf{F} = m\mathbf{v} - m\mathbf{u}$$

where $t\mathbf{F}$ is the *impulse* of the force $\mathbf{F}$ acting for time $t$, which produces the change in *momentum* $(m\mathbf{v} - m\mathbf{u})$ in a body, mass $m$, whose velocity changes from $\mathbf{u}$ to $\mathbf{v}$.

## Units

The units of both impulse and momentum are newton-seconds (written Ns).

## Impulse of a variable force

When the force is fixed in direction, the impulse is represented by the area under the force-time graph. In general,

$$\int_{t_1}^{t_2} \mathbf{F} \, dt = m\mathbf{v}_2 - m\mathbf{v}_1.$$

## Coefficient of restitution, e

For the collision of two bodies moving along the same straight line,

(relative velocity after) $= -e \times$ (relative velocity before).

For oblique impacts, take the component of the relative velocities along the line of impact:

$$e = \frac{-(\mathbf{v}_2 - \mathbf{v}_1) \cdot \mathbf{n}}{(\mathbf{u}_2 - \mathbf{u}_1) \cdot \mathbf{n}}.$$

## Conservation of momentum

The linear momentum of a system of bodies is conserved in a direction perpendicular to the net external impulse, or in any direction if the net external impulse is zero.

# 35

# PROBABILITY DISTRIBUTIONS

## 1. INTRODUCTION

**1.1 Win or lose?** Take out four coins. Shake them in your hands, and put all four down on your desk. How many heads have you got? I'll give you 1p for one head, 2p for two heads, 4p for three heads and 8p for four. The only snag is that you must pay me 3p for playing this game! Who do you think is going to win in the long run, you or me? Without trying to work it out, write down who you guess will win. Also guess how much you might expect to win (or lose) over, say, 100 games.

Now try the game sixteen times to see what happens. Are your guesses being confirmed?

**1.2 Using a probability model.** You might have guessed that you would win in the long run since you can win 1p, 2p, 4p or 8p depending on getting 1, 2, 3 or 4 heads, whereas you only pay 3p a game. But is this an accurate way of looking at the game? It is quite unlikely you'd get four heads and win 8p. The best way to find out is to use a *probability model* for the game and see if your guesses match its predictions.

We saw in Chapter 30 that getting heads or tails on tossing coins was a *binomial* probability situation which we could model using Pascal's triangle. In this case we have four coins so the probabilites of getting 0, 1, 2, 3, 4 heads are given by

| Number of heads | 0 | 1 | 2 | 3 | 4 |
|---|---|---|---|---|---|
| Probability | $\frac{1}{16}$ | $\frac{4}{16}$ | $\frac{6}{16}$ | $\frac{4}{16}$ | $\frac{1}{16}$ |

Suppose we play the game sixteen times. The model predicts that we will win nothing on one game, 1p on four games, 2p on six games, 4p on four games and 8p on just one game i.e. a *total* of 40p from 16 games. So we *expect* to win $2\frac{1}{2}$p per game and since the stake is 3p per game we *lose* in the long run.

Compare the predictions of the model with what actually happened when you played the game sixteen times. What was your *mean* win (or loss) per game?

## Exercise A

**1.** Write down the probabilities of getting 0, 1, 2, 3 heads when you toss three coins. Suppose you win 1p for every head; work out your predicted winnings for eight games. What fee to play the game will make it fair?

**2.** (*a*) On a fruit machine, the mechanism is arranged so that you win £1 one time out of 100, 20p six times out of 100, and 5p thirty times out of 100. Work out how much you would expect to win out of 100 tries. How much do you expect to win *on average* each try?

(*b*) You have to pay 5p for each try of the fruit machine. Do you or the machine win in the long run? How much do you expect to win (or lose) in 100 tries? How much do you expect to win (or lose) *on average* each try?

**3.** In Question 2 write down the *probabilities* of winning £1, 20p and 5p. Multiply each winning by its probability. Add up the three quantities. Explain why this gives you the same result as the final answer to part (*a*) of Question 2.

**4.** Write a table listing the sums of the scores on two dice. Underneath each sum put the probability (as a fraction in 36ths). If you receive £2 for a sum of 2, £3 for a sum of 3 and so on, calculate how much you expect to receive in 36 throws of two dice. What do you receive on average for a single throw of two dice? Use the method of Question 3 to check your answer.

## 2. EXPECTED VALUE

**2.1 A theoretical mean.** If we were to play the game in Section 1 $n$ times, we should expect to win 0p in $\frac{1}{16}n$ games, 1p in $\frac{4}{16}n$ games, 2p in $\frac{6}{16}n$ games, 4p in $\frac{4}{16}n$ games and 8p in $\frac{1}{16}n$ games, and our total winnings would be

$$0 \times \tfrac{1}{16}n + 1 \times \tfrac{4}{16}n + 2 \times \tfrac{6}{16}n + 4 \times \tfrac{4}{16}n + 8 \times \tfrac{1}{16}n \text{ pence.}$$

So our average winnings *per game* we would expect to be

$$\frac{1}{n}[0 \times \tfrac{1}{16}n + \cdots + 8 \times \tfrac{1}{16}n] = 0 \times \tfrac{1}{16} + 1 \times \tfrac{4}{16} + 2 \times \tfrac{6}{16} + 4 \times \tfrac{4}{16} + 8 \times \tfrac{1}{16}$$

$$= 2\tfrac{1}{2}\text{p.}$$

(Notice that we get the same value whatever $n$ is.)

This 'theoretical mean' we call the *expected value* of the winnings (and in a gambling game this would be the value of the stake to make the game *fair*). Notice that the expected value is calculated by multiplying each outcome (win or loss) by its probability, and adding up the products.

The expected value is denoted by the Greek letter $\mu$, and in general $\mu = \sum x_i p(x_i)$ where $p(x_i)$ is the probability of outcome $x_i$.

906

*Example* 1

An experiment consists of taking samples of five from a box containing a large number of beads, 30% of which are yellow. The following table gives the results for 100 samples.

| Number of yellow beads in a sample | Frequency |
|:---:|:---:|
| 0 | 14 |
| 1 | 38 |
| 2 | 40 |
| 3 | 7 |
| 4 | 1 |
| 5 | 0 |
|   | 100 |

(*a*) Calculate the mean from the table of experimental results.

(*b*) Calculate the probability of each number of yellow beads (hereafter called the *score*). Calculate the expected value of the score.

(*c*) Illustrate the experimental data and the probability model.

(*a*) Mean $m = \frac{1}{100}(0 \times 14 + 1 \times 38 + 2 \times 40 + 3 \times 7 + 4 \times 1)$
$= 1 \cdot 43.$

(*b*) Using a binomial model,

$$p_0 = (0 \cdot 7)^5 = 0 \cdot 168,$$

$$p_1 = 5 \times 0 \cdot 3 \times 0 \cdot 7^4 = 0 \cdot 360,$$

$$p_2 = 10 \times 0 \cdot 3^2 \times 0 \cdot 7^3 = 0 \cdot 309,$$

$$p_3 = 10 \times 0 \cdot 3^3 \times 0 \cdot 7^2 = 0 \cdot 132,$$

$$p_4 = 5 \times 0 \cdot 3^4 \times 0 \cdot 7 = 0 \cdot 028,$$

$$p_5 = 0 \cdot 3^5 = 0 \cdot 002.$$

Expected value

$$\mu = \sum x_i p(x_i)$$

$$= 0 \times 0 \cdot 168 + 1 \times 0 \cdot 360 + 2 \times 0 \cdot 309 + 3 \times 0 \cdot 132 + 4 \times 0 \cdot 028$$

$$+ 5 \times 0 \cdot 002$$

$$= 1 \cdot 496.$$

(We get exactly $1 \cdot 5$ if rounding errors in the probabilities are eliminated.)

(*c*) To make the two histograms of Figure 1 directly comparable, we scale the frequency diagram down so that the total area is 1. The area of each rectangle then represents a *relative frequency*; that is, a proportion of the total sample. In the second diagram, the vertical axis represents the *probability density* so that the areas of the rectangles represent probabilities.

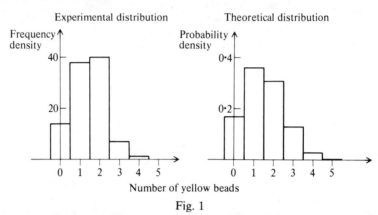

Number of yellow beads

Fig. 1

**2.2  Probability models.** The models of the game in Section 1 and the sampling experiment in Example 1 were both binomial. Although it often happens that a standard model fits the situation in this way, in general the construction of a probability model is much more of a practical process. The statistics of an experiment are used to assign probabilities, which then form the basis of a probability model. This model is tested by comparing predicted frequencies with those actually obtained when the experiment is repeated.

*Example* 2

Observations of the flow of traffic along a road suggest that about 30% of the vehicles travel at speeds around 100 km/h, 58% at around 80 km/h, 10% at 55 km/h and 2% at 15 km/h. Set up a probability model and calculate the expected frequencies for a sample of 2000 vehicles. What is the expected value of the speed of the vehicles?

| Speed | Probability | Expected frequency |
|-------|-------------|--------------------|
| 15    | 0·02        | 40                 |
| 55    | 0·10        | 200                |
| 80    | 0·58        | 1160               |
| 100   | 0·30        | 600                |

908

The expected value

$$\mu = \sum x_i p(x_i)$$

$$= 15 \times 0 \cdot 02 + 55 \times 0 \cdot 10 + 80 \times 0 \cdot 58 + 100 \times 0 \cdot 30$$

$$= 82 \cdot 2 \text{ km/h.}$$

Clearly there are many factors which need to be considered to refine this model, though we shall not pursue them here. Suggest some of them.

The important thing is to be clear about the distinction between statistical observations on the one hand and predictions from a probability model on the other hand. We adopt notation which helps keep this distinction constantly in mind, using Roman letters for *statistics* and the corresponding Greek letters for the associated *probability parameters*.

Thus $m = \dfrac{1}{N} \sum x_i f_i$ gives the *mean* of observed data where $\sum f_i = N$, while $\mu = \sum x_i p(x_i)$ gives the *expected value* from a probability model in which, of course, $\sum p(x_i) = 1$.

**2.3   Interpretation of expected value.** In probability theory we use the word 'expected' in a technical sense which does not carry all its everyday associations. First, it is important to notice that $\mu$ corresponds to the mean and not to the mode. For example, if before making a trial in the experiment of Example 1 you were asked how many successes you expect to get, you might well answer 1, this being the 'most probable' value in the possibility space. The expected value $\mu = 1 \cdot 5$ as we have defined it is not even a value that can be obtained in a single trial. The meaning of the statement 'the expected value is $1 \cdot 5$' is that over a large number of trials, we expect to get about $1 \cdot 5$ successes per trial *on average*.

### Exercise B

**1.** The probabilities of winning money on a fruit machine are given by this table:

| Winnings | 50p | 20p | 10p | 5p | 2p |
|---|---|---|---|---|---|
| Probability | $\frac{1}{200}$ | $\frac{2}{100}$ | $\frac{5}{100}$ | $\frac{10}{100}$ | $\frac{15}{100}$ |

Calculate the expected value of the winnings. If the machine is designed to make a small profit, suggest the likely charge for each play.

**2.** Random checks were carried out at a factory making an electronic component. A large number of samples were taken, with ten components in each sample. From the results a probability model was constructed for the various numbers of defective components in a sample of ten:

| Number of defective components | 0 | 1 | 2 | 3 | 4 | 5 | 6 | 7 or more |
|---|---|---|---|---|---|---|---|---|
| Probability | | 0·41 | 0·26 | 0·12 | 0·11 | 0·07 | 0·02 | 0·01 | 0 |

Find the expected number of defective components in a sample of ten.

**3.** A manufacturer makes shoes in sizes 7 to 11, and markets them at a standard price of £8·00. The costs to him of making the five sizes are £5·30, £5·40, £5·60, £5·80 and £5·90, and he estimates the demand at 12%, 35%, 28%, 14%, and 11% respectively of his total order. Calculate the expected value of his profit per pair.

**4.** A player rolls two dice and receives from the bank a prize of as many pennies as the difference between his score and 7. Make a table of the probabilities of each size of prize and find his expected winning. Would 2p be a fair entry fee, and if not whom would it favour (the player or the bank), and at what rate in the long run?

Carry out three runs, each of twenty plays of the game, and find the mean profit per game for each of your runs, assuming an entry fee of 2p per game.

**5.** A game consists of three successive tosses of a coin. A player receives 1p for the first head, 2p for the second and finally 3p for the third (so that if he tosses *HTH* he gets $(1+2)$p). What would be a fair forfeit for 'no heads' if the game is to be fair without an entrance fee?

Carry out three runs, each of ten plays of the game, and find the mean receipts per game in each of your runs. (If you prefer it, simulate the game with a table of random numbers.)

**6.** The time taken for a building job depends on the weather and many other factors. The following probabilities are assigned:

| Duration in weeks | 20 | 23 | 24 | 25 | 26 | 28 | 30 |
|---|---|---|---|---|---|---|---|
| Probability | 0·10 | 0·20 | 0·24 | 0·18 | 0·13 | 0·10 | 0·05 |

(*a*) Find the expected value of the duration.
(*b*) Would it be sensible to base the estimated labour costs on this?

**7.** Compare these two games:
(*a*) Pay a stake of 2p to roll two dice. If you roll a double six you get 50p; otherwise you lose your stake.
(*b*) Pay a stake of 1p to roll two dice. If you roll a total of 10 or more your stake is returned, plus another 2p; otherwise you lose your stake.

Which game is more attractive? Calculate the expected value of the amount you receive for each.

910

**8.** For each of these games using two dice, find the expected value of the *winnings* (note: the stake is only returned where specifically stated).

(*a*) Stake 3p; £1 given for a double six.

(*b*) Stake 3p; 15p prize for total score of 2 or 12; 10p for 3 or 11; stake returned for 6 or 8.

(*c*) Stake 3p; 25p prize for 3 or 11.

Which game is most attractive?

**9.** Place a set of ten marbles, two of which are blue, in a bag. Draw one at a time at random without replacement until the first blue marble is picked. If this happens on the fourth draw, record a score of 4, etc. Repeat the experiment 90 times, calculate the mean score, and show this on a relative frequency histogram of your results.

Calculate the probabilities of all the possible scores and the predicted frequencies in a set of 90 trials. Compare with your observed frequencies.

Find the expected value and show this on a probability histogram.

**10.** Repeat Question 9, starting with three blue marbles and seven others.

***11.** In a game of bridge, I know that my opponents hold five trumps between them. What is the probability that four rounds will be needed to clear trumps (in which case one opponent holds one trump and the other four trumps)? What is the expected value of the number of rounds of trumps I shall have to lead in order to clear both their hands of this suit?

## 3. STANDARD DEVIATION

The analogy we have developed between the mean of a statistical population and the theoretical mean for a corresponding probability model can be extended to other statistics such as measures of spread.

It will be recalled that the standard deviation is the root mean square deviation from the mean, given by the formula

$$s^2 = \frac{1}{N} \sum (x_i - m)^2 f_i.$$

This expression can be written as

$$\sum (x_i - m)^2 \frac{f_i}{N},$$

$\frac{f_i}{N}$ being the relative frequency of the score $x_i$.

In defining a corresponding parameter for a probability model we replace the mean of the sample by the theoretical mean for the model, and relative frequencies by probabilities. Thus the spread in the probability model can be described by the parameter $\sigma$ such that

$$\sigma^2 = \sum (x_i - \mu)^2 p(x_i).$$

As in statistics, we use the words *standard deviation* and *variance* to describe $\sigma$ and $\sigma^2$ respectively. Again the parameter for the probability model is denoted by the Greek letter corresponding to the Roman letter used for the analogous statistic.

**3.1 The alternative formula.** Just as in the statistical calculations we found that

$$s^2 = \frac{1}{N} \sum (x_i - m)^2 f_i$$

simplified to

$$s^2 = \left[ \frac{\sum x_i^2 f_i}{N} \right] - m^2,$$

it is easy to show that

$$\sigma^2 = \sum (x_i - \mu)^2 p(x_i) \text{ can be rewritten as}$$
$$\sigma^2 = \left[ \sum x_i^2 p(x_i) \right] - \mu^2.$$

This alternative form is usually easier to use.

*Example* 3

Calculate the standard deviation of the winnings in the game in Section 1 (ignore the stake).

It is convenient to tabulate the calculation:

| $x_i$ | $p(x_i)$ | $x_i^2 p(x_i)$ |
|-------|----------|----------------|
| 0 | $\frac{1}{16}$ | 0 |
| 1 | $\frac{4}{16}$ | $\frac{4}{16}$ |
| 2 | $\frac{6}{16}$ | $\frac{24}{16}$ |
| 4 | $\frac{4}{16}$ | $\frac{64}{16}$ |
| 8 | $\frac{1}{16}$ | $\frac{64}{16}$ |
| | | $\frac{156}{16}$ |

$$\sigma^2 = \left[ \sum x_i^2 p(x_i) \right] - \mu^2$$
$$= \frac{156}{16} - \frac{25}{4}$$
$$= \frac{56}{16},$$

$$\sigma \approx 1 \cdot 87.$$

**3.2 'Two-standard-deviation' check.** In Chapter 11 (p. 260), we saw that if a statistical population has a humped histogram which is reasonably symmetrical, then *about* two-thirds of the population would have values within 1 standard deviation either side of the mean, and *about* 95% would be within 2 standard deviations from the mean. We used these approximate figures as a rough check on our answers for standard deviations.

Likewise we can apply this check to a probability model as a quick way of ensuring that our answers for expected value and standard deviation for the model are reasonable.

### *Exercise C*

**1.** Calculate the standard deviation of the winnings on the fruit machine of Exercise B, Question 1.

**2.** A probability model of a queue gives the probabilities of finding 0, 1, 2, ... , 6 people in the queue on arrival as $0·14$, $0·27$, $0·27$, $0·18$, $0·09$, $0·04$, $0·01$. Find the expected value of the length of the queue on arrival, and the standard deviation.

**3.** Calculate the standard deviation for the profits per pair of shoes in Exercise B, Question 3.

**4.** Calculate the standard deviation for the vehicle speeds in the probability model described in Example 2.

**5.** With the data of Question 4 of Exercise B:
   (*a*) find the variance of the player's winnings ignoring the entrance fee;
   (*b*) if the entrance fee is 2p, find the variance of his profits;
   (*c*) draw probability histograms of (i) the winnings ignoring the entrance fee and (ii) the profits when the entrance fee is 2p. Explain why the answers to (*a*) and (*b*) are the same.

**6.** Calculate the standard deviation for the duration of the building job in Exercise B, Question 6. Draw a probability histogram and mark in lines at $\mu$, $\mu \pm \sigma$ and $\mu \pm 2\sigma$.

**7.** Calculate the standard deviation of the receipts in each of the games in Exercise B, Question 7. Do your answers help you to decide which game is more attractive? If so, how?

**8.** Repeat Question 7 for the three games in Exercise B, Question 8.

**9.** Use the two-standard-deviation check idea to estimate the standard deviation for the model of Exercise B, Question 9, and then calculate $\sigma$ in the usual way.

**10.** A casino offers its patrons a choice between three games, for each of which there is an entry fee of 1 franc. The possible winnings are:

*Game 1.* A 2% probability of winning 20 francs.
*Game 2.* An 8% probability of winning 5 francs.
*Game 3.* A 1% probability of winning 20 francs and a 4% probability of winning 5 francs (but you cannot win both).

In each game a winner also has his entry fee returned. For each game calculate the mean gain to the casino and the variance. How should a casino proprietor adjust the mean and variance if ($a$) he wishes to ensure a steady income for himself, ($b$) he is interested in making a long-term profit while making the game superficially attractive to the player?

**11.** Blocks of five digits are selected from a table of random numbers, and the number of even digits in each block recorded. Calculate the probabilities of obtaining the various possible scores, and hence find the expected value and variance.

Repeat this calculation if the digits counted are ($a$) fives, ($b$) multiples of three (including zero), ($c$) those greater than two. Can you recognize any general pattern in your answers? If so, express it algebraically.

**12.** Calculate $\mu$ and $\sigma^2$ for binomial models with the following parameters:
($a$) $n = 3$,       $a = 0.7$,       $b = 0.3$;
($b$) $n = 4$,       $a = \frac{1}{4}$,       $b = \frac{3}{4}$;
($c$) $n = 5$,       $a = \frac{3}{5}$,       $b = \frac{2}{5}$;
($d$) $n = 10$,     $a = \frac{1}{2}$,       $b = \frac{1}{2}$.
Can you find simple formulae for $\mu$ and $\sigma^2$ in terms of $n$, $a$ and $b$?

## 4. PARAMETERS OF A BINOMIAL MODEL

The following table shows $\mu$ and $\sigma^2$ for five different binomial models.

| $n$ | $a$ | $b$ | $\mu$ | $\sigma^2$ |
|---|---|---|---|---|
| 5 | 0.4 | 0.6 | 2 | 1.2 |
| 10 | 0.9 | 0.1 | 9 | 0.9 |
| 20 | $\frac{1}{4}$ | $\frac{3}{4}$ | 5 | $\frac{15}{4}$ |
| 100 | 0.85 | 0.15 | 85 | 12.75 |
| 400 | $\frac{1}{2}$ | $\frac{1}{2}$ | 200 | 100 |

You may have already found in Exercise C, Questions 11 and 12, that for the binomial probability model there are simple formulae which enable us to calculate expected value and standard deviation. Check that

$$\mu = na, \qquad \sigma^2 = nab$$

are satisfied by each of the models in the table.

A general proof of these formulae will be found in Section 8.2. Here we limit ourselves to a small value of $n$.

914

Take $n = 4$, with $a$ the probability of success and $b$ the probability of failure (so that $a + b = 1$). Calculating $\mu$ and $\sigma^2$ using a table (see Example 3), we have:

| $x_i$ | $p(x_i)$ | $x_i p(x_i)$ | $x_i^2 p(x_i)$ |
|---|---|---|---|
| 0 | $b^4$ | 0 | 0 |
| 1 | $4b^3 a$ | $4b^3 a$ | $4b^3 a$ |
| 2 | $6b^2 a^2$ | $12b^2 a^2$ | $24b^2 a^2$ |
| 3 | $4ba^3$ | $12ba^3$ | $36ba^3$ |
| 4 | $a^4$ | $4a^4$ | $16a^4$ |

Notice that the sum of the probabilities is

$$b^4 + 4b^3 a + 6b^2 a^2 + 4ba^3 + a^4.$$

But we saw in Chapter 30, Section 5.1, that

$$(b + a)^4 = b^4 + 4b^3 a + 6b^2 a^2 + 4ba^3 + a^4.$$

Since $b + a = 1$, the probabilities sum to 1 as we should expect.
The expected value $\mu$ is the total of the third column.

$$\mu = 4b^3 a + 12b^2 a^2 + 12ba^3 + 4a^4$$
$$= 4a(b^3 + 3b^2 a + 3ba^2 + a^3)$$
$$= 4a(b + a)^3$$
$$= 4a,$$

since $b + a = 1$. This is what we hoped for; the formula $\mu = na$ with $n = 4$.

Similarly, adding the last column of the table, we can show that $\sum x_i^2 p(x_i) = 4a(b + a)^3 + 12a^2(b + a)^2$, and, using $\sigma^2 = \sum x_i^2 p(x_i) - \mu^2$, that $\sigma^2 = 4ab$.

## Example 4

A die is rolled ($a$) 12 times, ($b$) 120 times. Calculate in each case the expected number of sixes, and the standard deviation.

Write down how many standard deviations from the mean the following results are: 3 sixes out of 12 rolls; 30 sixes out of 120.

Comment on your answers.

For $n = 12$, $\mu = \frac{12}{6} = 2$ and $\sigma = \surd(12 \times \frac{1}{6} \times \frac{5}{6}) \approx 1 \cdot 29$.
For $n = 120$, $\mu = \frac{120}{6} = 20$ and $\sigma = \surd(120 \times \frac{1}{6} \times \frac{5}{6}) \approx 4 \cdot 08$.

So we quickly can see that the second result, 30 out of 120, is more surprising since 30 is well over two standard deviations from the expected value, 20. In contrast, for 3 out of 12, 3 is within one standard deviation from the expected value 2.

## Example 5

It is thought that in the country as a whole, 40% of the voters support Labour. If a random sample of 2000 voters is taken, find the expected value and standard deviation of the number of Labour supporters in the sample. Discuss the likely spread of results.

Taking a binomial model with $n = 2000$, $a = 0\cdot4$, $b = 0\cdot6$, we get

$$\mu = na = 800$$

and
$$\sigma = \sqrt{(nab)} = \sqrt{480} \approx 22.$$

Using a two-standard-deviation criterion, we can say that we are unlikely to obtain a sample containing more than 844 or less than 756 Labour supporters.

### Exercise D

**1.** A coin is tossed (*a*) 10 times, (*b*) 100 times, (*c*) 1000 times. Calculate in each case the expected number of heads, and the standard deviation.

Which would surprise you more—3 heads and 7 tails in 10 tosses, or 300 heads and 700 tails in 1000 tosses?

**2.** A die is rolled 100 times. It is estimated that there is about 95% probability that the number of sixes lies between $\mu - 2\sigma$ and $\mu + 2\sigma$. What numbers of sixes lie within this interval?

**3.** A fully trained card-punch operator makes on average ten mistakes a day. If she punches $N$ symbols per day in all, what is the probability that she makes a mistake in punching any single symbol? Prove that the standard deviation of the number of mistakes per day is very nearly $\sqrt{10}$.

**4.** Thirty sets of four random digits were examined, and a success was recorded if a digit $i$ satisfied $0 \le i \le k$, where $k$ is some integer. The results were:

| Number of successes in a set of 4 digits | 0 | 1 | 2 | 3 | 4 |
|---|---|---|---|---|---|
| Frequency | 5 | 14 | 10 | 0 | 1 |

Calculate the mean number of successes in a set of four digits.

What do you think was the value of $k$? With this value of $k$ calculate the probabilities of each score and compare them with the observed relative frequencies.

Calculate also the variance of the observed population and the corresponding parameter for your probability model.

**5.** It is thought that 60% of the people in a town are protected from smallpox through sufficiently recent vaccination. Tests on a random sample of 300 show that 140 are *not* protected. Does this throw serious doubt on the original belief?

916

**6**. In the experiment of Example 1, calculate what numbers of 0s would be surprisingly low or high, using a two-standard-deviation criterion.

**7**. Our company makes meat pies. We have a new recipe and will switch to this if a market research survey shows that 60% of customers prefer the new meat pies.

290 out of a sample of 500 say they prefer the new pies. Is this good enough?

**8**. Samples of 200 from the output of a factory making ladies' tights are tested at regular intervals to check the quality. It is usual for 5% to be substandard for one reason or another.

If the number of substandard tights in a sample exceeds $x$, the quality-control supervisor must be called immediately. Suggest, with reasons, a sensible value for $x$.

## 5. PROBABILITY DENSITY FUNCTIONS

So far in this chapter the *variables* we have used have almost all been *discrete*, e.g. number of heads, number of pence, number of people in a sample. Figure 2 is a relative frequency histogram of the results from measurements of the lifetimes of 1000 calculator batteries. The horizontal axis now represents a *continuous* variable, time, and we have had to group our measurements. In Figure 2 we have chosen groupings of width 50 hours and, to take an example, the largest rectangle has area 0·39, indicating that 390 batteries had a life of between 150 and 200 hours. We could have taken intervals of smaller width; Figure 3 shows the same set of observations grouped in intervals of 10 hours.

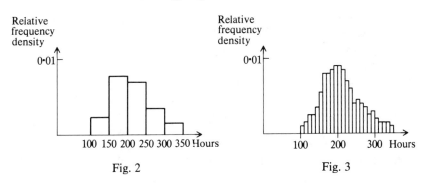

Fig. 2                                    Fig. 3

These two histograms convey much the same message. Can we use them to set up a probability model to answer questions like 'Find the probability of two batteries in a calculator both lasting more than 240 hours'?

We shall use a *continuous probability model* (see Figure 4), a curve giving the same general impression as Figures 2 and 3. Since the number of batteries in our sample with a life of less than 240 hours is given approximately by the total area of each histogram to the left of $x = 240$, it is reasonable to *define* the corresponding probability as the area under the curve of our probability model to the left of $x = 240$.

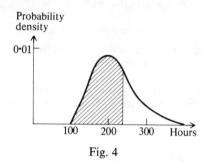

Fig. 4

The equation of the curve, $y = \phi(x)$, is called a *probability density function*, and if this approach is to be useful it will be a function we can easily integrate to find the areas we need.

How we select an equation $y = \phi(x)$ as the 'best' probability density function for a particular situation is a question we shall defer for the moment, but we need to note two important constraints:

(i) $\phi(x) \geq 0$ throughout the domain;

(ii) $\displaystyle\int_{-\infty}^{\infty} \phi(x)\, dx = 1$, representing the fact that the total probability is 1.

**5.1** It is also important to note that because the probability that a battery will last between 240 and 250 hours is represented by the area under $y = \phi(x)$ *between* these times, a question like 'What is the probability that a battery will last exactly 240 hours?' must have the answer zero since there is zero area under the graph at a point. Such questions are meaningless anyway because we cannot measure time *exactly*. Probability density functions enable us to find the probability that a variable takes a value within a given interval, and in fact questions about measurements are always in that form. If we are measuring to the nearest hour, a life of 240 hours will include all results in the interval

$$239 \cdot 5 \leq x < 240 \cdot 5.$$

*Example 6*

Gamma ray sources are screened by surrounding them with lead. A probability model for the depth to which a gamma ray of fixed energy from a given source penetrates the lead assigns the probability density function

$$\phi(x) = A\, e^{-0 \cdot 05x} \quad (x \geq 0)$$

918

to the distance $x$ mm the gamma ray will penetrate. Find $(a)$ the value of the constant $A$, and $(b)$ the probability that a gamma ray will penetrate more than 30 mm. Hence find the proportion of gamma rays from this source that will go straight through a shield 30 mm thick.

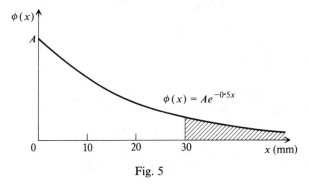

Fig. 5

$(a)$ Figure 5 shows the graph of the density function. The total area under the graph must be 1, so

$$\int_0^\infty A e^{-0\cdot05x}\,dx = 1$$

$$\Rightarrow \left[-\frac{A}{0\cdot05}e^{-0\cdot05x}\right]_0^\infty = 1$$

$$\Rightarrow 0 - \frac{-A}{0\cdot05} = 1$$

$$\Rightarrow A = 0\cdot05.$$

$(b)$ The probability is represented by the area shaded in Figure 5 and is given by

$$\int_{30}^\infty 0\cdot05\, e^{-0\cdot05x}\,dx = \left[-e^{-0\cdot05x}\right]_{30}^\infty$$

$$\approx 0\cdot22.$$

This indicates that 22% of the rays will penetrate a 30 mm shield.

### Exercise E

**1.** The function $\phi$ is given by

$$\begin{aligned}
\phi(x) &= 0 && \text{for } x < 0,\\
\phi(x) &= kx && \text{for } 0 \leqslant x < 5,\\
\phi(x) &= k(10-x) && \text{for } 5 \leqslant x < 10,\\
\phi(x) &= 0 && \text{for } x \geqslant 10.
\end{aligned}$$

919

Sketch $\phi(x)$ and find the value of $k$ if $\phi(x)$ is to be a probability density function. Find $(a)\, p(x<2)$, $(b)\, p(5<x<6)$.

**2.** Find the values of the constant $k$ if the following are to be probability density functions with the given domains.

$(a)\ \phi(x)=kx^2(3-x)$,       $0\leqslant x\leqslant 3$;
$(b)\ \phi(x)=kx(3-x)^2$,       $0\leqslant x\leqslant 3$;
$(c)\ \phi(x)=kx^3(3-x)$,       $0\leqslant x\leqslant 3$;
$(d)\ \phi(x)=kx^2(3-x)^2$,      $0\leqslant x\leqslant 3$.

In each case, sketch the graph (giving the coordinates of the maximum point) and find the probability of getting a number less than 1.

**3.** The quarantine period for a certain disease is between 5 and 11 days after contact. The probability of showing the first symptoms at various times during the quarantine period is described by the probability density function

$$\phi(t)=\tfrac{1}{36}(t-5)(11-t)$$

Sketch the graph of this function.

$(a)$ Find the probability that the symptoms will appear within 7 days of contact.

$(b)$ Five people catch the disease at a party. Find the probability that all of them first show symptoms between $t=7$ and $t=9$.

**4.** A probability model for the mass $x$ kg of two-year-old children is given by

$$\phi(x)=A\sin\left[\tfrac{1}{10}\pi(x-7)\right]\quad\text{for}\quad 7\leqslant x\leqslant 17.$$

Show that $A=\tfrac{1}{20}\pi$.

Find the percentage of two-year-olds whose mass is $(a)$ greater than 16 kg, $(b)$ between 12 and 13 kg.

**5.** A mathematical model for the age $x$ years to which a new-born infant will live assigns to this a probability density function

$$\phi(x)=kx^3(90-x)\quad\text{for}\quad x>0.$$

On this basis, calculate:

$(a)$ the proportion of the population who would live to be over 80;
$(b)$ the commonest age at which people would die.

**6.** A probability density function for the life $t$ hours of Luxa light bulbs is

$$\phi(t)=k\exp(-t/1200)\qquad(t>0).$$

$(a)$ Find the value of the constant $k$.
$(b)$ Find the probability that a bulb will last more than 2000 hours.
$(c)$ Find the age beyond which only 10% of Luxa bulbs survive.

**7.** Sketch the graph of $y=x\sin x$ for $0\leqslant x\leqslant \pi$ and find $k$ if

$$\phi(x)=kx\sin x$$

is a probability density function with the same domain. Find the probability that $x<2$.

**8.** A possible equation for the probability density function to model the data in Section 5 is

$$\phi(x)=k(x-100)(x-400)^2\quad\text{for}\ 100\leqslant x\leqslant 400.$$

920

Find the value of $k$ and calculate:

(a) the probability that a battery will last less than 240 hours;

(b) the probability that the next three batteries I use will all last longer than 300 hours.

**9.** Show that

$$\phi(x)=\frac{2}{(1+4|x|)^2}$$

satisfies the two criteria in Section 5 for a probability density function for $x$. Sketch the graph and answer the following questions, marking the relevant areas on your graph.

(a) Find $a>0$ such that $p(x\geqslant a)=0\cdot05$.

(b) Find $b>0$ such that $p(|x|\geqslant b)=0\cdot05$.

# 6. PARAMETERS OF CONTINUOUS MODELS

When we try to fit a continuous probability model to statistical data it is important that the model and the data have approximately the same mean and spread.

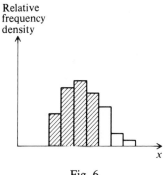

Fig. 6

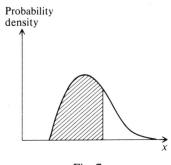

Fig. 7

We have seen how probabilities associated with an interval of the domain are found in the discrete case by *summation* (simple adding up of areas of rectangles) and in the continuous case by *integration*.

This suggests immediately how the definitions of $\mu$ and $\sigma$ might be extended.

$$\mu=\sum x_i p(x_i) \qquad (\text{with } \sum p(x_i)=1)$$

in the discrete case, so we define

$$\mu=\int x\phi(x)\,dx \quad \left(\text{with } \int \phi(x)\,dx=1\right)$$

in the continuous case. In the discrete case, the summations are over the whole *possibility space*—the set of possible values—and similarly the integrals are over the whole domain of the probability density function.

Again, by analogy with the formula

$$\sigma^2 = \sum (x_i - \mu)^2 p(x_i)$$

in the discrete case, we define

$$\sigma^2 = \int (x - \mu)^2 \phi(x)\, dx,$$

and find that there is an alternative form which is usually more convenient:

$$\sigma^2 = \int x^2 \phi(x)\, dx - \mu^2.$$

*Example 7*

Find the expected value for the probability model of Example 6 where $\phi(x) = 0.05\, e^{-0.05x}$ for $x \geq 0$.

$$\mu = \int x\phi(x)\, dx = \int_0^\infty 0.05x\, e^{-0.05x}\, dx.$$

Integration by parts gives

$$\mu = \left[ -x\, e^{-0.05x} \right]_0^\infty + \int_0^\infty e^{-0.05x}\, dx$$

$$= \left[ \frac{-1}{0.05}\, e^{-0.05x} \right]_0^\infty$$

$$= \frac{1}{0.05} = 20,$$

representing an expected depth of 20 mm.

*Example 8*

Sketch the graph of the density function $\phi(x) = \dfrac{1}{2\pi}(1 + \cos x)$ with domain $-\pi \leq x \leq \pi$. Find the expected value and the standard deviation. Show that 65% of the area lies within $\mu \pm \sigma$ and 97% within $\mu \pm 2\sigma$.

Figure 8 shows the graph; by symmetry, the mean is zero.

$$\sigma^2 = \int_{-\pi}^{\pi} \frac{x^2}{2\pi}(1 + \cos x)\, dx = \frac{1}{2\pi}\left[ \frac{x^3}{3} + x^2 \sin x \right]_{-\pi}^{\pi} - \frac{1}{2\pi}\int_{-\pi}^{\pi} 2x \sin x\, dx$$

$$= \frac{1}{2\pi}\left( \frac{2\pi^3}{3} - 4\pi \right) \approx 1.29,$$

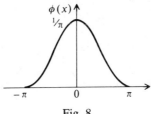

Fig. 8

which gives $\sigma \approx 1 \cdot 14$.

Now $\qquad \int_{-1\cdot14}^{1\cdot14} \frac{1}{2\pi}(1+\cos x)\,dx = \frac{1}{2\pi}\Big[x+\sin x\Big]_{-1\cdot14}^{1\cdot14} \approx 0\cdot65,$

and $\qquad \int_{-2\cdot28}^{2\cdot28} \frac{1}{2\pi}(1+\cos x)\,dx = \frac{1}{2\pi}\Big[x+\sin x\Big]_{-2\cdot28}^{2\cdot28} \approx 0\cdot97.$

### Exercise F

**1.** Find the expected value and standard deviation of the life of Luxa light bulbs, using the probability model of Exercise E, Question 6.

**2.** Find $\mu$ and $\sigma$ for the model of Exercise E, Question 7.

**3.** Find $\mu$ and $\sigma$ for each of the models in Exercise E, Question 2.

**4.** Find the expected age of death using the model of Exercise E, Question 5.

**5.** Find the expected value of the masses of the children in Exercise E, Question 4. Could you have predicted the answer without doing any calculations? If so, how?

**6.** A positive variable has probability density

$$\phi(x)=x\,e^{-x}.$$

Verify that this satisfies the conditions for a density function, and find the expected value of $x$ and the standard deviation. What is the probability that (a) $x > \mu$, (b) $x > \mu + 2\sigma$? Draw a sketch graph and comment on your answers.

**7.** The following three equations define probability density functions over the interval $-a \leqslant x \leqslant a$:
  (a) $\phi(x)=k(a^2-x^2)$;      (b) $\phi(x)=k(a^2-x^2)^2$;      (c) $\phi(x)=k(a-|x|)$.
For each equation draw the graph and find $k$ in terms of $a$. Calculate the standard deviation, and find the probability that $x$ lies within two standard deviations of the mean.

## 7. CONSTRUCTING PROBABILITY DENSITY FUNCTIONS

If the histogram from observed data suggests a probability density function with a graph like Figure 9, we could adapt Example 8 by applying a stretch followed by a translation.

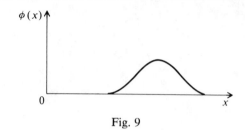

Fig. 9

But the graphs of several other functions have the same general shape, for example $y = \dfrac{1}{1+x^2}$ and $y = \exp(-x^2)$. How do we choose a probability density function in practice?

Statisticians have an extensive range of suitable functions, the properties of which are well known. In the vast majority of cases they judge that one of these 'ready-to-wear' models is adequate for their purposes and only rarely do they choose to construct a 'tailor-made' model.

We can take the analogy with tailoring a stage further. To take a simple example,

$$\phi(x) = k(x-a)^c(b-x), \quad a \leq x \leq b,$$

gives a family of probability density curves of similar type, differences resulting from one's choice of values for $a, b, c$. A shop may stock many jackets made from the same material and of the same style. To find one that fits well enough, one might start by insisting upon the right chest size and arm length. These are the *parameters* of the range of jackets.

A common way to select a particular model from a family of probability density functions is to make the parameters $\mu$ and $\sigma$ equal to the statistics $m$ and $s$ calculated from some observed data. Of course other parameters can be used, just as there are other measurements of the human body a tailor would like to be able to match. Can you say why the mode and extreme values will generally be less satisfactory than $\mu$ and $\sigma$?

### Example 9

Experimental data from observations of the gestation period of 1000 rabbits bred in captivity are set out in the table below. Find the mean and standard deviation of these results and construct a probability density function of the form $\phi(x) = px^2 + qx + r$ with the same parameters. Compare the frequencies predicted by your model with those obtained experimentally.

924

| Gestation period (x days) | Frequency |
|---|---|
| $25 \cdot 5 \leqslant x < 26 \cdot 5$ | 4 |
| $26 \cdot 5 \leqslant x < 27 \cdot 5$ | 55 |
| $27 \cdot 5 \leqslant x < 28 \cdot 5$ | 99 |
| $28 \cdot 5 \leqslant x < 29 \cdot 5$ | 127 |
| $29 \cdot 5 \leqslant x < 30 \cdot 5$ | 140 |
| $30 \cdot 5 \leqslant x < 31 \cdot 5$ | 158 |
| $31 \cdot 5 \leqslant x < 32 \cdot 5$ | 142 |
| $32 \cdot 5 \leqslant x < 33 \cdot 5$ | 125 |
| $33 \cdot 5 \leqslant x < 34 \cdot 5$ | 90 |
| $34 \cdot 5 \leqslant x < 35 \cdot 5$ | 52 |
| $35 \cdot 5 \leqslant x < 36 \cdot 5$ | 8 |

Check that the mean and variance for the data are
$$m = 30 \cdot 98 \quad \text{and} \quad s^2 = 4 \cdot 94.$$
The histogram of the results is shown in Figure 10.

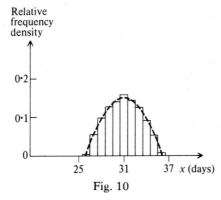

Fig. 10

We wish to fit a parabolic density function (shown dotted) with $\mu = 31$ and $\sigma^2 = 5$. It is convenient to shift our origin to the mean ($\mu = 31$) and work with the density function
$$\phi(x) = b^2 - a^2 x^2$$
(see Figure 11) whose mean is zero.

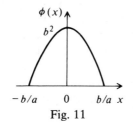

Fig. 11

925

If $\phi(x)$ is to be a density function, the area under the graph must be unity. Thus

$$\int_{-b/a}^{b/a} (b^2 - a^2 x^2)\, dx = \left[ b^2 x - a^2 \frac{x^3}{3} \right]_{-b/a}^{b/a} = \frac{4b^3}{3a} = 1.$$

Also we require $\sigma^2$ to be 5, so

$$\sigma^2 = \int_{-b/a}^{b/a} x^2 \phi(x)\, dx - \mu^2 = \int_{-b/a}^{b/a} x^2 (b^2 - a^2 x^2)\, dx - 0$$

$$= \frac{4b^5}{15a^3} = 5.$$

Combining these results, $b^2 = \frac{3}{20} = 0\cdot 15$ and $a^2 = 0\cdot 006$, giving

$$\phi(x) = 0\cdot 15 - 0\cdot 006 x^2.$$

The following table shows the comparison between frequencies given by the model and those obtained experimentally.

| $x$ | Experimental frequency | Theoretical frequency |
|---|---|---|
| $25\cdot 5 \leqslant x < 26\cdot 5$ | 4 | 0 |
| $26\cdot 5 \leqslant x < 27\cdot 5$ | 55 | 54 |
| $27\cdot 5 \leqslant x < 28\cdot 5$ | 99 | 96 |
| $28\cdot 5 \leqslant x < 29\cdot 5$ | 127 | 126 |
| $29\cdot 5 \leqslant x < 30\cdot 5$ | 140 | 144 |
| $30\cdot 5 \leqslant x < 31\cdot 5$ | 158 | 150 |
| $31\cdot 5 \leqslant x < 32\cdot 5$ | 142 | 144 |
| $32\cdot 5 \leqslant x < 33\cdot 5$ | 125 | 126 |
| $33\cdot 5 \leqslant x < 34\cdot 5$ | 90 | 96 |
| $34\cdot 5 \leqslant x < 35\cdot 5$ | 52 | 54 |
| $35\cdot 5 \leqslant x < 36\cdot 5$ | 8 | 0 |

Here, as in Section 5, our situation involved a continuous variable. We shall see in Chapter 39 that continuous probability models are often useful for *discrete* variables too (see also Exercise H, Question 6).

**\*7.1   Continuous models based on symmetry.** We have often remarked on the two main ways in which probabilities are assigned: (i) based on past experience, using relative frequencies calculated from observed statistical data; (ii) using arguments involving symmetry, as with dice and other gaming equipment.

The last section in effect discussed the setting up of continuous models of type (i). There are also some important special models of type (ii) which we now investigate.

926

*Example* 10

An airline map gives distances between cities to the nearest 10 km. Set up a probability model for the rounding errors introduced, and find the probability of the errors in the distances given for the four stages of a particular long journey all being greater than 3 km.

Since individual errors lie between −5 and 5 km and, for example, an error between 3 and 4 is neither more nor less likely than an error between −1 and 0, we choose a rectangular model as in Figure 12, the probability density of $\frac{1}{10}$ being required to give a total area of 1. Compare with the probability histogram for single throws of a fair die.

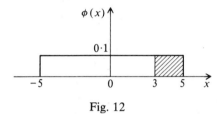

Fig. 12

The probability of a single error being greater than 3 km is 0·2, so the required probability for a four-stage journey is $0·2^4$.

*Example* 11

Find the probability of the total error for the sum of two distances as in Example 10 being between 2 and 3 km. Set up a probability model for this total error.

The journey might be London–Rome–Cairo. There is an error in the distance recorded for London to Rome, and a further error in the distance recorded for Rome to Cairo. All combinations of two such errors can be represented by points of the square in Figure 13, where $p$ stands for the first error and $q$ for the second. In the first instance

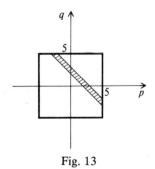

Fig. 13

927

we are interested in points between the lines $p+q=2$ and $p+q=3$. These form an area of $\frac{1}{2}\times 8^2 - \frac{1}{2}\times 7^2 = 7 \cdot 5$ and the required probability is $\dfrac{7 \cdot 5}{100} = 0 \cdot 075$.

This argument is reminiscent of the way we find the probability $\frac{7}{36}$ of a total of 9 or 10 when two dice are thrown, using the ringed set of discrete points in Figure 14.

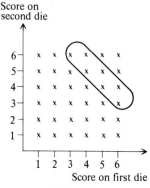

Fig. 14

It is clear from Figure 13 (and no surprise at all) that total errors close to 0 are more likely than extreme values near $-10$ or 10. To obtain the complete model we first consider the *cumulative probability function*, the probability that $p+q < x$. This is written $\Phi(x)$. From Figure 16 we see that, for values of $x$ greater than 0,

$$\Phi(x) = 1 - \tfrac{1}{2}(10-x)^2 \div 100.$$

Show that, for values of $x$ less than 0,

$$\Phi(x) = \tfrac{1}{2}(10+x)^2 \div 100.$$

Figure 15 shows the relationship in general between the functions $\phi$ and $\Phi$.

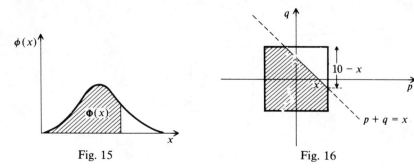

Fig. 15                                   Fig. 16

Since $\Phi$ is found from $\phi$ by integration, it follows that we can find $\phi$ from $\Phi$ by the reverse process, differentiation.

In our example,

$$\phi(x) = \tfrac{1}{100}(10+x), \qquad -10 < x < 0,$$

$$\phi(x) = \tfrac{1}{100}(10-x), \qquad 0 \leqslant x < 10.$$

We have a triangular distribution (see Figure 17), as you would doubtless have predicted, bearing in mind the familiar discrete model for the total score from two dice (see Figure 18).

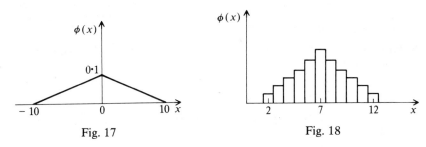

Fig. 17                                      Fig. 18

Finding the cumulative function first and then differentiating to get the probability density function is a common technique. It is necessary because in a continuous model, as we saw in Section 5.1, the probability of obtaining any one value is always zero. We have to consider instead the probability of a value in a *specified interval*.

## Exercise G

**1.** (a) Show that the probability density function $\phi(x) = k\,e^{-k(x+0\cdot5)}$ $(x > -0\cdot5)$ has expected value $\dfrac{1}{k} - 0\cdot5$.

(b) Typewriters leaving the final assembly line at a factory are all tested for faults. The results of tests on a batch of 1000 typewriters were as follows:

| Number of faults | 0 | 1 | 2 | 3 | 4 | 5 | 6 |
|---|---|---|---|---|---|---|---|
| Frequency | 618 | 265 | 87 | 18 | 7 | 3 | 2 |

Calculate the mean number of faults. Construct a probability density function of the form $\phi(x) = k\,e^{-k(x+0\cdot5)}$ with the same mean. Compare the frequencies predicted by your model with those in the table. Compare also the two standard deviations.

**2.** The records of a driving school over a year gave the following data:

| Number of tests before passing | 1 | 2 | 3 | 4 | 5 | 6 | 7 | 8 |
|---|---|---|---|---|---|---|---|---|
| Frequency | 84 | 50 | 31 | 12 | 12 | 5 | 4 | 2 |

Calculate the mean number of tests taken before a person passed.

929

Fit a probability density function of the form $\phi(x) = k\,e^{-k(x-0\cdot5)}$ $(x > 0\cdot5)$ to this data, having the same mean. Calculate the predicted frequencies and compare with the results in the table.

**3.** A probability density function is given by

$$\phi(x) = k(a^2 - x^2) \quad \text{for } |x| < a,$$
$$\phi(x) = 0 \qquad\qquad \text{for } |x| > a.$$

Find $k$ in terms of $a$. Find the values of $k$ and $a$ which give a standard deviation of 2.

**4.** (*a*) For the triangular model of Example 11, find $p(-1 < x < 1)$.

(*b*) The distances from $A$ to $B$, from $B$ to $C$ and from $A$ to $C$ via $B$ are each written to the nearest 10 km. Find the probability that the sum of the first two numbers is different from the third.

**5.** Find the variance for the rectangular model of Example 10, and also for the triangular model of Example 11. Comment on your answers.

**6.** It can be shown that, for the sum of three independent errors as in Example 10, the probability density function is

$$\phi(x) = \tfrac{1}{2000}(15 + x)^2 \quad \text{for } -15 < x < -5,$$
$$\phi(x) = \tfrac{1}{1000}(75 - x^2) \quad \text{for } -5 < x < 5,$$
$$\phi(x) = \tfrac{1}{2000}(15 - x)^2 \quad \text{for } 5 < x < 15.$$

Draw the graph of $\phi(x)$ carefully, and calculate the variance by integration.

**7.** A stick of length 100 cm is broken into three pieces at points $P$ and $Q$ chosen at random on the stick. If these are $p$ cm and $q$ cm from the left-hand end, the various combinations can be represented by the points of the square in Figure 20.

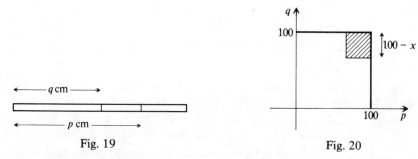

Fig. 19                                                   Fig. 20

(*a*) Explain why the set of points for which the left-hand section of the stick is longer than $x$ cm is given by the shaded square in the diagram.

On copies of the square show:

(*b*) the set of points for which the middle section is longer than $x$ cm;

(*c*) the set of points for which none of the sections is longer than $x$ cm, assuming $50 < x < 100$.

If $\Phi(x)$ is the probability that the longest section is less than $x$ cm, show that

$$\Phi(x) = 1 - \tfrac{3}{10000}(100 - x)^2 \quad \text{for } 50 < x < 100,$$

and $\Phi(x)=\frac{1}{10000}(3x-100)^2$     for $33\frac{1}{3}<x<50$.

Deduce the probability density function and draw its graph.

## *8. PROBABILITY GENERATORS

In this section we describe briefly a technique helpful in setting up some discrete models and finding their parameters.

If the probabilities of obtaining $0, 1, 2, \ldots, n$ successes as the result of some experiment are $p_0, p_1, p_2, \ldots, p_n$, then we form the expression

$$G(t)=p_0+p_1t+p_2t^2+\ldots$$

and call this the *probability generator* for that experiment. The 'dummy variable' $t$ has no special significance, but the power of $t$ acts as a label for the probability. For example, the probability generator for the total scores when two dice are rolled $(2, 3, 4, \ldots, 12)$ is

$$G(t)=\frac{1}{36}t^2+\frac{2}{36}t^3+\frac{3}{36}t^4+\ldots+\frac{2}{36}t^{11}+\frac{1}{36}t^{12}.$$

Note that when $t=1$, for all probability generators,

$$G(1)=p_0+p_1+p_2+\ldots+p_n=1.$$

**8.1 Calculation of expected value and standard deviation.** If we differentiate $G(t)$ we obtain

$$G'(t)=0+p_1+2p_2t+3p_3t^2+\ldots+np_nt^{n-1}.$$

The coefficients of $t$ in this derived function are precisely the terms we add to find the expected value of the number of successes:

$$\mu=\sum ip_i=p_1+2p_2+3p_3+\ldots+np_n.$$

So, putting $t=1$,

$$\mu=G'(1).$$

Further differentiation leads to a formula on similar lines for the variance. We have

$$G(t)=\sum p_it^i$$
$$\Rightarrow G'(t)=\sum ip_it^{i-1}$$
$$\Rightarrow G''(t)=\sum i(i-1)p_it^{i-2}$$

giving
$$G''(1)=\sum i(i-1)p_i$$
$$=\sum i^2p_i-\sum ip_i$$
$$=\sum i^2p_i-\mu.$$

931

We recall that $\sigma^2 = \sum i^2 p_i - \mu^2$, and we can now write this as

$$\sigma^2 = G''(1) + \mu - \mu^2.$$

*Example* 12

A pair of dice is thrown and the number of sixes recorded. The probability of no sixes is $(\frac{5}{6})^2 = \frac{25}{36}$, of one six is $2 \times \frac{5}{6} \times \frac{1}{6} = \frac{10}{36}$, of two sixes is $(\frac{1}{6})^2 = \frac{1}{36}$. Hence

$$G(t) = \tfrac{25}{36} + \tfrac{10}{36}t + \tfrac{1}{36}t^2.$$

It follows that

$$G'(t) = \tfrac{10}{36} + \tfrac{2}{36}t,$$

$$G''(t) = \tfrac{2}{36}.$$

Hence $\qquad \mu = G'(1) = \tfrac{12}{36} = \tfrac{1}{3},$

and $\qquad \sigma^2 = G''(1) + \mu - \mu^2 = \tfrac{1}{18} + \tfrac{1}{3} - \tfrac{1}{9}$

$$= \tfrac{5}{18}.$$

**8.2 Parameters for the binomial probability model.** An important application of generators is to the general binomial model for which the proofs suggested in Section 4 were cumbersome. For samples of size 3,

$$G(t) = b^3 + 3b^2 at + 3ba^2 t^2 + a^3 t^3,$$

and this can be written $G(t) = (b + at)^3$. Similarly, for samples of size $n$,

$$G(t) = (b + at)^n \quad \text{(see Chapter 30).}$$

For this function,

$$G'(t) = na(b + at)^{n-1},$$

$$G''(t) = n(n - 1)a^2(b + at)^{n-2}.$$

Since $b + a = 1$, it follows that

$$G'(1) = na,$$

$$G''(1) = n(n - 1)a^2 = n^2 a^2 - na^2,$$

so that $\qquad \mu = na,$

and $\qquad \sigma^2 = G''(1) + \mu - \mu^2$

$$= n^2 a^2 - na^2 + na - n^2 a^2$$

$$= na - na^2$$

$$= na(1 - a),$$

whence $\qquad \sigma^2 = nab.$

932

These are the formulae we used earlier, of course. The success of this method of proof was assured once the generator was expressed in a simple, concise form.

### Exercise H

**1.** Write down the probability generator for the game of Exercise B, Question 4, with no entry fee, and deduce the mean and standard deviation of the player's winnings. Repeat with an entry fee of 2p.

**2.** For the game described in Exercise B, Question 5, assume that there is a forfeit of 18p if no heads show up. Write down a probability generator for the player's receipts and losses, and deduce the variance.

**3.** For a certain game the probabilities of winning various sums are specified by the generator $G(t)$, the expected value of the winnings is $\mu$ and the variance $\sigma^2$. Explain why the imposition of an entry fee of $r$ units changes the generator for the player's profits to $t^{-r}G(t)$; and deduce values for the expected profits and the variance in terms of $\mu$ and $\sigma$.

**4.** (a) Show that if $|u| < 1$, the sum of the geometric progression

$$1 + u + u^2 + \ldots + u^{n-1}$$

tends to $(1-u)^{-1}$ as $n$ tends to infinity.

(b) A die is rolled repeatedly until a six appears. Write down the probability that $r$ non-sixes are thrown before the first six, and show that the generator for this is $(6-5t)^{-1}$. Deduce the expected number of non-sixes and the standard deviation.

**5.** A gambler goes on playing until he loses a game, and then stops. If his probability of winning a game is $0 \cdot 4$, find a probability generator for the number of games he will play in all. Deduce the mean and standard deviation.

**6.** A continuous model is required to approximate to the situation of Question 4. We take

$$\phi(x) = k\,e^{-ax} \quad \text{with domain } -\tfrac{1}{2} < x.$$

Explain why $e^{-a}$ should be chosen as $\tfrac{5}{6}$, and find the value of $k$. Draw the histogram for Question 4(b) and superimpose the graph of the probability density function. Calculate $\mu$ and $\sigma$ for the continuous model and compare with the values from the discrete model.

**7.** A die is rolled repeatedly until two sixes have appeared. Find the probability that there will be $r$ non-sixes before the second six shows up, and find a generator for the probability function. How could your answer have been forecast from the generator of Question 4?

**8.** The probability generators for the numbers of successes in two independent experiments are

$$G = p_0 + p_1 t + p_2 t^2 + \ldots$$

and

$$H = q_0 + q_1 t + q_2 t^2 + \ldots .$$

Interpret the expression

$$p_0 q_3 + p_1 q_2 + p_2 q_1 + p_3 q_0$$

(i) as a probability, (ii) as a coefficient in the expression $GH$. Hence interpret $K = GH$ as a probability generator.

Using the probability generator for the totals on two dice, deduce the probability generator for the totals on four dice.

**9.** Prove the following results directly from the relation $K = GH$ from Question 8, and interpret them.

(a) $K(1) = 1$.

(b) $K'(1) = G'(1) + H'(1)$.

(c) $K''(1) + K'(1) - [K'(1)]^2 =$
$$G''(1) + G'(1) - [G'(1)]^2 + H''(1) + H'(1) - [H'(1)]^2.$$

**10.** Sets of $n$ digits are taken from a table of random numbers. Show that the generator for their totals is

$$G(t) = [F(t)]^n$$

where $F(t)$ is the generator for single digits.

Deduce that the variance of the totals is $n$ times the variance for single digits.

**11.** The rules of a gambling game once played at St Petersburg were as follows. A player tosses a coin repeatedly until a head appears; if the head first appears on the $n$th toss, he receives $2^{n-1}$ units of prize money from the bank.

(a) In one version of the game there is a limit of ten tosses. If the player never throws a head then he wins no prize. What would be a suitable entry fee?

(b) What would be a suitable entry fee if the coin may be tossed an unlimited number of times?

(c) Find the probability generator for the total number of tosses in the unlimited game, and deduce the mean and variance of the length of run.

(d) If the bank will only pay 10 000 units to any one player because of a shortage of funds, what is the probability that a player will 'break the bank'?

(e) If the game is played 256 times a night, what is the probability that the bank will not be broken during the course of the night? (Use the binomial theorem to get an approximate answer.)

(f) What is the probability that the bank will be broken in a season of 64 nights?

# SUMMARY

| Statistical population | Discrete probability model | Continuous probability model |
|---|---|---|
| Relative frequency $f_i/N$ | Probability $p(x_i)$ | Probability density $\phi(x)$ |
| $\sum f_i/N = 1$ | $\sum p(x_i) = 1$ | $\int \phi(x)\,dx = 1$ |
| Mean $m = \sum x_i(f_i/N)$ | Mean (expected value) $\mu = \sum x_i p(x_i)$ | Mean (expected value) $\mu = \int x\phi(x)\,dx$ |
| Variance $s^2 = \sum (x_i - m)^2(f_i/N)$ | Variance $\sigma^2 = \sum (x_i - \mu)^2 p(x_i)$ | Variance $\sigma^2 = \int (x - \mu)^2 \phi(x)\,dx$ |
| $= \sum x_i^2(f_i/N) - m^2$ | $= \sum x_i^2 p(x_i) - \mu^2$ | $= \int x^2 \phi(x)\,dx - \mu^2$ |

## Binomial model

$$\mu = na, \qquad \sigma^2 = nab.$$

## Cumulative probability

This is the total probability of a value less than or equal to $x$. For a continuous model this is denoted by $\Phi(x)$, and $\Phi'(x) = \phi(x)$.

## Probability generators

The definition is $G(t) = p_0 + p_1 t + p_2 t^2 + \ldots = \sum p_i t^i$. Then $G(1) = 1$, and

$$\mu = G'(1), \qquad \sigma^2 = G''(1) + \mu - \mu^2.$$

# 36

# WORK AND ENERGY

In Books 1 and 2 we described the motion of bodies when accelerated and the relationship between acceleration and force embodied in Newton's second law. Chapter 34 investigated the effects on bodies of forces acting for known periods of *time* and the principle of conservation of momentum was introduced. In this final mechanics chapter we look at the effects on bodies of forces acting through known *distances*.

### *Exercise A*

(It is important to attempt *all* of Questions 1–7.)

**1.** A stone falls vertically with a constant acceleration of $10 \text{ m/s}^2$ in a straight line, and when $t = 0$ it has a speed of 5 m/s.
(*a*) How far has it travelled when $t = 3$?
(*b*) How fast is it moving when it has travelled 100 m?

**2.** A body moving in a straight line has a constant acceleration of $a \text{ m/s}^2$, and when $t = 0$ it has a speed of $u$ m/s.
(*a*) Show that at time $t$ the speed $v$ m/s is given by $v = u + at$ and that the body has travelled a distance $s$ m where $s = ut + \frac{1}{2}at^2$.
(*b*) Eliminate $t$ from the two equations in (*a*) to derive the equation $v^2 = u^2 + 2as$.

**3.** (*a*) A diver steps off a springboard which is 5 m above the surface of a swimming pool. Assuming a constant downward acceleration of $10 \text{ m/s}^2$, find how fast he is moving when he hits the water.
(*b*) The diver in (*a*) springs upwards with an initial speed of $7\frac{1}{2}$ m/s. How high above the board will he be when he comes to instantaneous rest? What will be his final speed when he hits the water?
(*c*) What would be his final speed if he is thrown off the springboard with an initial speed vertically downwards of $7\frac{1}{2}$ m/s?

**4.** The diver of Question 3 has an initial upward speed of $u$ m/s off a springboard height $h$ m above the water. If his final speed on hitting the water is $v$ m/s, find an expression for $v^2$ in terms of $u$, $g$ and $h$. Would your answer have been different if the initial speed $u$ m/s had been downwards?

**5.** A swimmer of mass 70 kg slides into a swimming pool down a straight chute inclined at an angle $\theta$ to the horizontal. Copy Figure 1 and show the forces acting on the swimmer.
(*a*) If air resistance and friction are ignored, what is the resultant force on the swimmer down the chute? What is his acceleration?
(*b*) If the top of the chute is a distance $h$ m above the water surface, find the length of the chute. If the initial speed of the swimmer is $u$ m/s and his speed on entering the water is $v$ m/s, find an expression for $v^2$ in terms of $u$, $g$ and $h$.

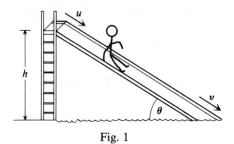

Fig. 1

(c) Did the value of $\theta$ affect $v^2$ in (b)? Would your answer have been the same if frictional forces had been taken into account?

(d) If the chute had been curved and did not reach right down to the water would the value of $v^2$ in (b) have been the same?

**6.** (a) A ski-jump consists of three parts as shown in Figure 2. The slopes $AB$, $BC$ and $CD$ are at angles 70°, 60° and 80° respectively to the vertical. $B$ is 5 m lower than $A$, $C$ is 10 m lower than $B$, and $D$ is 2 m lower than $C$. If the speed of a skier at $A$ is zero, use your answer to Question 5(b) to find the speed of the skier at $D$. (You may neglect friction, air resistance and 'bump' effects at $B$ and $C$.)

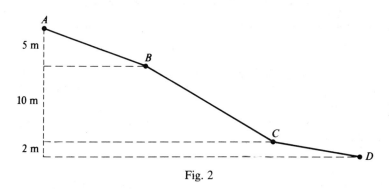

Fig. 2

(b) What would be the final speed of a skier at the foot of the ski-jump shown in Figure 3?

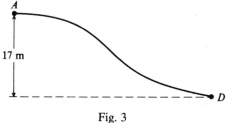

Fig. 3

937

**7.** Newton's second law for straight-line motion is $F = ma$. Use this together with $v^2 = u^2 + 2as$ to show that, for straight-line motion under a constant force in which a particle moves a distance $x$ from $A$ to $B$,

$$Fx = \tfrac{1}{2}mv_B^2 - \tfrac{1}{2}mv_A^2.$$

**8.** A body at point $A$ is moving initially ($t = 0$) with velocity $\mathbf{u}$ and is subject to a constant acceleration $\mathbf{a}$.

(a) If the body is at $B$, position vector $\mathbf{r}$ relative to $A$, at time $t$, integrate the relationships $\dfrac{d\mathbf{v}}{dt} = \mathbf{a}$ and $\dfrac{d\mathbf{r}}{dt} = \mathbf{v}$ to obtain the equations:

$$\text{(i) } \mathbf{v} = \mathbf{u} + t\mathbf{a}; \qquad \text{(ii) } \mathbf{r} = t\mathbf{u} + \tfrac{1}{2}t^2\mathbf{a}.$$

(b) Show that $\mathbf{a} \cdot \mathbf{r} = (t\mathbf{a}) \cdot \mathbf{u} + \tfrac{1}{2}(t\mathbf{a}) \cdot (t\mathbf{a})$ by taking the scalar product of (a) (ii) with $\mathbf{a}$. Eliminate $t$ by using (a) (i) to obtain an expression for $\mathbf{a} \cdot \mathbf{r}$ in terms of $v^2$ and $u^2$.

(c) Use this derived expression together with Newton's second law to show that $\mathbf{F} \cdot \mathbf{r} = \tfrac{1}{2}mv^2 - \tfrac{1}{2}mu^2$ for motion under a constant force $\mathbf{F}$ moving through displacement $\mathbf{r}$.

# 1. THE PRINCIPLE OF ENERGY

In Questions 4 and 5 of Exercise A you derived the result

$$v^2 = u^2 + 2gh \tag{1}$$

for the swimmers on the springboard and chute. In both cases we saw that the change in the square of the speed, $v^2 - u^2$, depended only on the vertical height $h$ through which the swimmers moved. The force of gravity was acting in both cases and, for a body of mass $m$, it is useful to recast equation (1) in the form

$$mgh = \tfrac{1}{2}mv^2 - \tfrac{1}{2}mu^2.$$

More generally (as you may have found in Question 8 of Exercise A), if a constant force $\mathbf{F}$ acts on a body of mass $m$ which accelerates from velocity $\mathbf{u}$ to velocity $\mathbf{v}$, changing its displacement by $\mathbf{r}$, we have

$$v^2 - u^2 = 2\mathbf{a} \cdot \mathbf{r}.$$

Also, by Newton's second law,

$$\mathbf{F} = m\mathbf{a}.$$

Elimination of $\mathbf{a}$ from these two equations gives us

$$\mathbf{F} \cdot \mathbf{r} = \tfrac{1}{2}mv^2 - \tfrac{1}{2}mu^2.$$

This is called the *equation of energy* and we will return to it after we have examined the terms involved more closely.

938

**1.1 Work.** When you push a heavy box along the floor it is hard 'work' and the further you push it the more 'work' you do. What is meant by 'work' here? Does it matter at what angle to the horizontal you push the box?

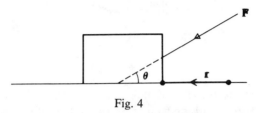

Fig. 4

If you pushed the box vertically downwards you might get tired but you would not have done any *useful* work. Obviously you try to push the box as nearly as possible in the direction in which you wish it to move because only the component of the force in that direction makes a useful contribution. This suggests that the relevant component of the applied force **F** should be multiplied by the distance moved to give a measure of 'useful' work, i.e. $F \cos \theta \times r$, or, as shown in Chapter 18, **F.r**. We therefore define mechanical work as follows:

The work done by a constant force **F** newtons when it moves its point of application through a displacement **r** metres is given by the scalar product **F.r**.

If **F** is measured in newtons and **r** in metres then the scalar product will be in newton-metres, and it is usual to define this unit as a joule (J).† That is, one joule is the work done when a force of one newton moves its point of application through one metre.

*Example* 1
Find the work done by a man who cycles for 50 m at a steady speed up a slope inclined at 10° to the horizontal, if the man and bicycle together have a mass of 80 kg and the total frictional forces are 30 N.

Figure 5 shows the forces acting on the bicycle and man. Since the bicycle is moving at a steady speed (i.e. acceleration is zero), Newton's second law gives

$$\mathbf{P} + \mathbf{F} + \mathbf{R} + m\mathbf{g} = \mathbf{0}.$$

Resolving parallel to the slope gives

$$P - 30 + 0 - 80g \sin 10° = 0$$

i.e.                       $P = 30 + 0 \cdot 174 \times 80g \approx 166.$

† This unit of work is named after Thomas Joule (1818–89) who contributed greatly to modern ideas of energy conversion and conservation.

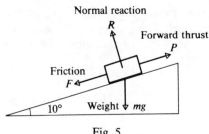

Fig. 5

The work done by the man is therefore $166 \times 50 = 8300$ J. (Note that the frictional forces and the weight between them do 8300 J of work in opposing the motion. The normal reaction does no work since it is perpendicular to the motion and $\mathbf{R} \cdot \mathbf{r}$ is zero.)

**1.2 Kinetic energy.** We now turn to the right-hand side of the equation of energy $\mathbf{F} \cdot \mathbf{r} = \frac{1}{2}mv^2 - \frac{1}{2}mu^2$ and note that it expresses a change in the scalar quantity $\frac{1}{2}mv^2$. This quantity is defined to be the *energy* of the body due to its motion. The word *kinetic* means due to motion' and the quantity $\frac{1}{2}mv^2$ is thus called the *kinetic energy* (KE) of the body. The body does work as it slows down and the kinetic energy is a measure of the amount of work the body would do in coming to rest. Note that kinetic energy is a *scalar* quantity depending on the magnitude, $v$, of the velocity $\mathbf{v}$ and not on the direction.

This equivalence of change of kinetic energy and work done (embodied in the equation of energy) is called the *principle of energy*:

The work done by a force acting on a body equals the change in kinetic energy of the body.

*Example 2*

A space capsule of mass 10 tonnes is moving towards the earth's surface at 50 m/s. It is required to reduce its speed to 5 m/s before splashdown by applying a constant retarding force $\mathbf{P}$ newtons provided by a series of parachutes. If the force is to act for a total distance of 1 km find (i) the kinetic energy of the capsule just before splashdown, and (ii) the magnitude of $\mathbf{P}$.

(i) Kinetic energy before splashdown $= \frac{1}{2}mv^2 = \frac{1}{2} \times 10\,000 \times 5^2$
$$= 125\,000 \text{ J}.$$

(ii) The resultant downward force on the capsule has magnitude $mg - P$. This must do work to reduce the kinetic energy, and the energy equation gives

work done = final KE − initial KE

Fig. 6

so    $(10\,000 \times 9 \cdot 8 - P) \times 1000 = \frac{1}{2} \times 10\,000 \times 5^2 - \frac{1}{2} \times 10\,000 \times 50^2$

$$\Rightarrow 98\,000 - P = 125 - 12\,500$$

$$\Rightarrow P = 110\,375.$$

In other words, the parachutes provide a retarding force of about 110 000 newtons.

*Example* 3

An electron of mass $10^{-30}$ kg is moving at a speed of $4 \times 10^5$ m/s when it enters an electrical field. $4 \times 10^{-9}$ s later it is moving in a direction perpendicular to its initial direction with a speed of $6 \times 10^5$ m/s. Find (*a*) the impulse, and (*b*) the work done on the electron during the interval.

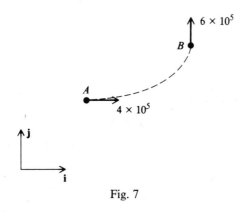

Fig. 7

941

Figure 7 illustrates the situation with the electron moving from $A$ to $B$ during the interval. Choosing **i** and **j** as shown we have

$$\mathbf{u} = \begin{pmatrix} 4 \times 10^5 \\ 0 \end{pmatrix} \text{ m/s} \quad \text{and} \quad \mathbf{v} = \begin{pmatrix} 0 \\ 6 \times 10^5 \end{pmatrix} \text{ m/s}.$$

($a$) Impulse $= m\mathbf{v} - m\mathbf{u} = m(\mathbf{v} - \mathbf{u})$

$$= 10^{-30} \begin{pmatrix} -4 \times 10^5 \\ 6 \times 10^5 \end{pmatrix} = 10^{-25} \begin{pmatrix} -4 \\ 6 \end{pmatrix} \text{ Ns}.$$

($b$) Work done $= \frac{1}{2}mv^2 - \frac{1}{2}mu^2 = \frac{1}{2}m(v^2 - u^2)$

$$= \frac{1}{2} \times 10^{-30} \left[ \begin{pmatrix} 0 \\ 6 \times 10^5 \end{pmatrix} \cdot \begin{pmatrix} 0 \\ 6 \times 10^5 \end{pmatrix} - \begin{pmatrix} 4 \times 10^5 \\ 0 \end{pmatrix} \cdot \begin{pmatrix} 4 \times 10^5 \\ 0 \end{pmatrix} \right]$$

$$= (18 - 8) \times 10^{-20}$$

$$= 10^{-19} \text{ J}.$$

Note that the path travelled by the electron was irrelevant in determining the work done.

*Example 4*

A particle of mass 5 kg is acted on by a force of $\begin{pmatrix} 12 \\ -5 \\ 5 \end{pmatrix}$ N whilst it is displaced through $\begin{pmatrix} 5 \\ 4 \\ 2 \end{pmatrix}$ m. If its final speed is 6 m/s, calculate its initial speed.

The equation of energy gives

$$\begin{pmatrix} 12 \\ -5 \\ 5 \end{pmatrix} \cdot \begin{pmatrix} 5 \\ 4 \\ 2 \end{pmatrix} = \frac{1}{2} \times 5 \times 6^2 - \frac{1}{2} \times 5 \times u^2$$

$$\Rightarrow 50 = 90 - \frac{5}{2}u^2 \quad \text{and} \quad u^2 = 16.$$

So the initial speed is 4 m/s.

### Exercise B

**1.** In ($a$), ($b$) and ($c$), find the work done by the force **F** N in displacement **r** m.

($a$) $\mathbf{F} = \begin{pmatrix} 1 \\ 2 \\ 3 \end{pmatrix}, \mathbf{r} = \begin{pmatrix} 3 \\ -4 \\ 1 \end{pmatrix};$ ($b$) $\mathbf{F} = \begin{pmatrix} -3 \\ 2 \\ 5 \end{pmatrix}, \mathbf{r} = \begin{pmatrix} 1 \\ -2 \\ 4 \end{pmatrix};$

(c) $\mathbf{F} = \begin{pmatrix} 3 \\ 5 \\ 2 \end{pmatrix}$, $\mathbf{r} = \begin{pmatrix} 5 \\ -4 \\ 1 \end{pmatrix}$;

(d) A particle of mass 5 kg is moved 12 m down a slope making an angle $\tan^{-1} \frac{3}{4}$ with the horizontal (see Figure 8). Find the work done by each of the forces shown.

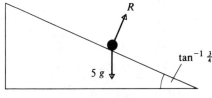

Fig. 8

**2.** In each case find the kinetic energy of the body with the given velocity or speed.

(a) A satellite of mass 2 tonnes with velocity $\begin{pmatrix} 7500 \\ 10\,000 \\ 5000 \end{pmatrix}$ km/h.

(b) A bullet of mass 30 g travelling at 500 m/s.

(c) A train of mass 400 tonnes travelling at 80 km/h.

(d) An electron of mass $10^{-27}$ g moving with velocity $\begin{pmatrix} 2 \times 10^7 \\ 3 \times 10^7 \\ 4 \times 10^7 \end{pmatrix}$ cm/s.

**3.** A particle of mass 200 g moves through a displacement $\mathbf{r}$ m under the action of a force $\mathbf{F}$ N. If its initial speed is $u$ and final speed $v$ m/s, find:

(a) the value of $v$ if $\mathbf{F} = \begin{pmatrix} -5 \\ 10 \\ 4 \end{pmatrix}$, $\mathbf{r} = \begin{pmatrix} 16 \\ -4 \\ -4 \end{pmatrix}$, $\mathbf{u} = \begin{pmatrix} 10 \\ 20 \\ 30 \end{pmatrix}$;

(b) the value of $u$ if $\mathbf{F} = \begin{pmatrix} 4 \\ -8 \\ 10 \end{pmatrix}$, $\mathbf{r} = \begin{pmatrix} -50 \\ 20 \\ -8 \end{pmatrix}$, $\mathbf{v} = \begin{pmatrix} -3 \\ 2 \\ 5 \end{pmatrix}$.

**4.** A ball of mass 25 g is moving north with a velocity of 60 cm/s. Some time later it is moving south-east at 80 cm/s.

(a) Find (i) the impulse and (ii) the work done during the interval.

(b) If the time interval is 2 s, find the force (assumed constant) acting on the ball. Hence find the ball's acceleration and displacement during the interval.

**5.** A bullet of mass 15 g passes horizontally through a piece of wood 2 cm thick. If its speed is reduced from 500 m/s to 300 m/s, find the average resisting force exerted by the wood.

**6.** A sledge of mass 240 kg is pulled on level ground from rest by dogs with a total forward force of 150 N against a resistance of 45 N. How fast will the sledge be moving after it has gone 56 m?

**7.** A destroyer slows down from 60 km/h to 40 km/h. Calculate (*a*) the loss in kinetic energy and (*b*) the retarding force if the mass of the destroyer is 5000 tonnes and it travels 200 m whilst slowing down.

**8.** The braking efficiency of a car is defined to be the percentage of the car's weight that the brakes can supply as a resistance to motion. Find how far a car travels whilst being slowed:
    (*a*) from 100 km/h to 50 km/h by brakes that are 75% efficient;
    (*b*) from 80 km/h to a standstill by brakes that are only 40% efficient.

**9.** A rocket of mass 1000 tonnes is standing ready for take off. Calculate its kinetic energy due to the rotation of the earth about its axis if the rocket is at latitude 50°N (take the radius of the earth to be 6400 km).

**10.** Find the kinetic energy of the earth due to its motion round the sun. (You may assume the mass of the earth to be $6 \cdot 04 \times 10^{24}$ kg, the mean radius of its orbit to be $1 \cdot 5 \times 10^{8}$ km and the length of the year to be 365 days.)

**11.** A toboggan of mass 5 kg slides from rest down an incline of 1 in 6. After travelling 80 m it has acquired a speed of 10 m/s. Find the resistance, assumed constant.

**12.** A cricket ball of mass 150 g is travelling horizontally at 20 m/s when it is struck by a batsman. Find the impulse and the work done when:
    (*a*) it is struck back to the bowler at 20 m/s;
    (*b*) it is deflected 20° to go through the slips at 20 m/s.
    Comment on your answers.

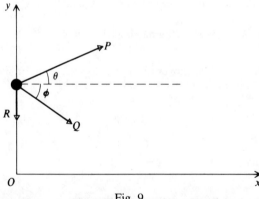

Fig. 9

**13.** (*a*) See Figure 9. A particle of mass *m* kg is at the origin *O* and is controlled by smooth guides so that it moves either along the *x*-axis or along the *y*-axis. Forces *P*, *Q* newtons act on the particle making angles $\theta$, $\phi$ with the direction of *Ox*. A force *R* newtons acts on the particle towards the origin. The diagram shows the forces when the particle is at an arbitrary position on the *y*-axis. In the following cases find the total work done by the forces and the final velocity of the particle:
    (i) $m = 2$, particle moves 3 m along the *x*-axis. Initial velocity $= 4$ m/s in the direction *Ox*.

$$P = 4, \qquad \theta = 10°, \qquad Q = 10, \qquad \phi = 30°, \qquad R = 3.$$

944

(ii) As for (i) but the particle moves 3 m along the $y$-axis with the initial velocity 4 m/s in the direction $Oy$.

(iii) As for (i) but the initial motion reversed.

(iv) As for (ii) but the initial motion reversed.

($b$) In which of the above motions would the particle eventually come to rest for an instant and how far would it have travelled before coming to rest?

**14.** A man pulls a 20 kg block along a rough road by a chain. He exerts a tension of 200 N in the chain. The resistance due to the ground is half the normal reaction between the road and the block. Find the final speed of the block after it has moved 4 m along the road in each of the cases where the chain makes an angle of (i) 0°, (ii) 30°, (iii) 60° with the ground.

**15.** A car of mass 1 tonne accelerates with a constant acceleration from 0 to 108 km/h in 15 s. If the net resistance to motion is a constant 500 N, find the forward thrust of the engine. If the engine is then switched off and the car is allowed to come to rest under the action of the 500 N resistance, find the total distance travelled by the car.

**16.** A car of mass 800 kg is capable of producing a tractive force of 3100 N in first gear, 2000 N in second gear, 1500 N in third gear, and 1100 N in top gear. Find the speed attained if the car is driven from rest for 10 m in first, 20 m in second, 30 m in third and 40 m in top gear, assuming the resistances to motion are a constant 400 N throughout.

**17.** A ball of mass 100 g is dropped from a height of 3 m. Find the speed on hitting the ground. The ball rebounds to a height of 2 m. Find the impulse of the ground on the ball. What force is exerted if the ball is made of:

(i) steel, with contact lasting for $\frac{1}{5000}$ s;

(ii) rubber, with contact lasting for $\frac{1}{100}$ s?

What would be the values of the forces if the heights were multiplied by 4?

**\*18.** A golf ball is dropped from a height $h$ onto a horizontal marble surface. If the coefficient of restitution between the ball and surface is $e$, write down the velocity of the ball immediately after impact and hence find the height to which it will rebound in terms of $e$ and $h$.

If the ball continues to bounce, write down the sum of a series representing the total distance travelled after $n$ bounces. Hence find the total distance travelled by the ball before it comes to rest. How long does it take for the ball to come to rest after it was initially released?

## 2. FORCES WHICH DO NO WORK

In Questions 5 and 6 of Exercise A you discovered that the final speeds of the swimmer and skier depended only on the *vertical* heights through which they moved. The gain in kinetic energy in each case was due to the work done by the weight moving downwards through a distance $h$. However, in each case, another force was acting—the normal reaction **R**. Why did it do no work?

Figure 10($a$) shows a particle of mass $m$ sliding down an inclined plane from $A$ to $B$. What is the component of **R** down the slope? What

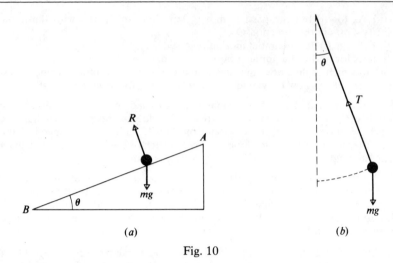

Fig. 10

is the value of **R** . **AB**? Forces which are always perpendicular to the direction of motion of a body do no work. Another common force which does no work is the tension in the string of a pendulum; it acts along the radius and is thus always perpendicular to the tangential motion of the bob (see Figure 10($b$)).

**2.1 Conservative forces.** The reader will be well aware that in practice the length of a slide or ski-slope *does* affect the final speed at the bottom of a vertical drop $h$—imagine a helter-skelter and compare jumping from the top with the more conventional method of arriving at the base. The effects of friction and air resistance vary greatly depending on the path taken.

When a particle moves from point $A$ to point $B$ under the action of a number of forces, the forces can be classified into two sets:

(i) those, such as the force of gravity, for which the work done in moving from $A$ to $B$ is *independent* of the path taken. They are called *conservative forces*;

(ii) those, such as friction, for which the work done depends on the path. These are *non-conservative forces*.

*Example 5*

A ball-bearing of mass $m$ is travelling in a horizontal tube at $A$ with speed $u$ when the tube gently alters direction so that at $B$, with coordinates $(b, h)$ referred to $A$, the tube is vertical. Calculate the speed of the ball-bearing at $B$ assuming that friction is negligible.

Figure 11 illustrates the situation where **R** is always perpendicular to the line of motion. In this case, **R** does no work, and the work done by

946

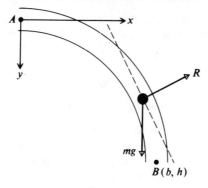

Fig. 11

$\mathbf{R} + m\mathbf{g}$, the total force acting on the ball-bearing, between $A$ and $B$ reduces to that done by the constant force $m\mathbf{g}$. Hence the equation of energy gives

$$m\mathbf{g} \cdot \binom{b}{h} = m\binom{0}{g} \cdot \binom{b}{h} = \tfrac{1}{2}mv^2 - \tfrac{1}{2}mu^2$$

from which                          $v^2 = u^2 + 2gh.$

*Example 6*

A boy whirls a conker of mass $m$ in a vertical circle by means of a string of length $l$. The speed of the conker is $u$ at the lowest point $A$ of the circle. (See Figure 12.)
   (i) Find the speed of the conker when its height above $A$ is $h$.
   (ii) Find the tension in the string at the top of the vertical circle.

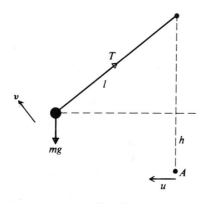

Fig. 12

947

(i) When the conker has risen a height $h$, the work done against gravity is $mgh$. The tension does no work. The equation of energy gives

$$\text{work done} = \text{change in KE}$$

$$-mgh = \tfrac{1}{2}mv^2 - \tfrac{1}{2}mu^2.$$

Hence $\qquad v^2 = u^2 - 2gh \Rightarrow v = \sqrt{(u^2 - 2gh)}.$

(ii) When the conker reaches the top, $h = 2l$ and the speed $v$ is given by $v^2 = u^2 - 4gl$. The total downward force on the conker is $T + mg$ and this must equal the mass-acceleration $mv^2/l$ for circular motion to be maintained. (See Chapter 24.) Hence

$$T + mg = \frac{mv^2}{l} = \frac{mu^2}{l} - 4mg$$

or $\qquad T = \frac{m}{l}(u^2 - 5gl).$

(Note that circular motion can only take place if $u^2 \geqslant 5\,gl$.)

*Example 7*

A man of mass 70 kg swings on a rope of length 8 m. He starts with the rope taut from a platform $A$ which is 1 m below the point of suspension of the rope.

(i) What must be the minimum breaking strain of the rope if he is to reach the lowest point $B$ without the rope snapping?

(ii) If the rope has a breaking strain of 1500 N, at what depth below $A$ will the man be when the rope snaps?

Figure 13 shows the forces on the man, when he has fallen a height $h$ below $A$.

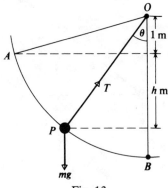

Fig. 13

948

(i) At $B$ the speed $v$ is given by

$$mg \times 7 = \tfrac{1}{2}mv^2$$

i.e.                    $$v^2 = 14g.$$

The net force towards the centre, $T - mg$, must equal the mass-acceleration $mv^2/r$:

$$T - 70g = \tfrac{1}{8} \times 70v^2 = \tfrac{1}{8} \times 70 \times 14g.$$

This gives

$$T \approx 70 \times 9 \cdot 8 + \tfrac{1}{8} \times 70 \times 14 \times 9 \cdot 8 \approx 1900,$$

i.e. a tension at the lowest point $B$ of about 1900 N.

(ii) Newton's second law for the man along $PO$ gives

$$T - mg \cos \theta = \frac{mv^2}{r} \Rightarrow T = 70g \cos \theta + \tfrac{70}{8}v^2.$$

Now                    $$\tfrac{1}{2}mv^2 = mgh$$

from the equation of energy. Hence

$$T = 70g \cos \theta + \tfrac{140}{8}gh.$$

Also                    $$\cos \theta = \frac{h+1}{8}$$

and when the rope snaps we have

$$1500 \approx 70 \times 9 \cdot 8 \times \frac{(h+1)}{8} + \frac{140 \times 9 \cdot 8}{8} \times h,$$

leading to                    $$h \approx 5 \cdot 5.$$

So the man is approximately 5·5 m below $A$ when the rope snaps.

### Exercise C

1. A child sitting on a mat slides down a helter-skelter. If the friction is negligible and the helter-skelter is 10 m high, what will be the child's speed at the bottom?

2. A boy swings on the end of a 5 m rope in a gymnasium. If he initially jumped off a 'horse' 2 m high at 3 m/s on a level 3·5 m below the point of suspension of the rope, which was taut, find:
   (a) his maximum speed;
   (b) his maximum height above ground;
   (c) the tension in the rope in the vertical position if his mass is 60 kg.

**3.** A Scout travels along an aerial runway starting from 10 m up a tree (see Figure 14). If the lowest point he reaches is 2 m off the ground and the friction of the system can be neglected, at what speed will he pass that point?

If you take into account the sag in the rope, what effect will this have on your answer?

If the end of the aerial runway is 4 m off the ground, with what speed will he reach it and what effect will the sag in the rope have on this answer?

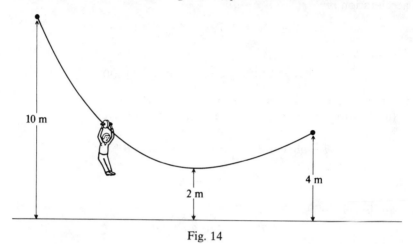

Fig. 14

**4.** A bridge over a river is in the form of a circular arc of radius 20 m. What is the greatest speed in km/h at which a motor cycle can cross the bridge without leaving the road at the highest point?

**5.** A demolition gang operates a crane with a 1 tonne bob on the end of a cable. The centre of mass of the bob is 10 m from the end of the jib and the mass of the cable can be neglected. Assuming that the bob travels along the arc of a vertical circle, centre the stationary extremity of the jib, starting 3 m above the lowest point, find an expression for $v^2$, the square of the speed of the bob, after it has descended 1 m, 2 m, and 3 m. At each of these points find the tension in the cable. If $\theta$ is the acute angle the cable makes with the vertical, find an expression for $v^2$ and hence for the tension in the cable for this general position.

Will the cable snap if it has a breaking strain of 20 000 N and the bob is released to swing from a height of 5 m above the lowest point of the arc?

Do you think the cable would snap if the bob was rested on a platform 5 m vertically below the jib and then released?

**6.** A rope of length 6 m is suspended from a high branch of a tree and a boy swings on the rope along the arc of a vertical circle starting from a branch 2 m above the lowest point of swing. When the rope is vertical it strikes against a branch situated 2 m below the point of suspension. If the boy releases his grip when the lower part of the rope makes an angle of 45° with the vertical, find the boy's speed at this instant.

**7.** A marble is placed on the top of a smooth up-turned hemispherical bowl and gently pushed off. If the radius of the outside of the bowl is 20 cm and the marble is of mass 2 g, find the speed after descending through a vertical distance

950

of 4 cm, 8 cm, 12 cm, 16 cm and 20 cm. If $\mathbf{R}$ is the normal reaction between the bowl and the marble, find $\mathbf{R}$ for each of the speeds found above. Comment on your results.

If the question was about a bead threaded on a smooth semicircular wire standing in a vertical plane, what modifications would you make to your answers?

**8.** An eskimo sits on the highest point of a smooth hemispherical igloo of radius 3 m. He eases himself gently from the top and slides down the outside of the igloo. Obtain an expression for the speed of the eskimo whilst he remains in contact with the igloo. Give your answer in terms of $\theta$, the angle made with the vertical by the position vector of the eskimo relative to the centre of the igloo.

Write down the acceleration of the eskimo in the direction of this position vector and hence obtain an expression giving the reaction between the eskimo and the igloo in terms of $\theta$. At what value of $\theta$ will the eskimo leave the surface of the igloo?

**9.** Repeat Question 8 for an eskimo who starts with an initial speed of 1 m/s at the top of the igloo.

**10.** A conker of mass 25 g is held on the end of a piece of string 22·5 cm long. Find, where possible, its speed and the tension in the string after rising 10 cm, 20 cm, 22·5 cm, 25 cm, 45 cm for the following initial speeds from the lowest point: (*a*) 1·4 m/s; (*b*) 2·1 m/s; (*c*) 2·5 m/s; (*d*) 4 m/s. Take $g = 9·8$ m/s². Comment on your results.

If the question was about a bead threaded onto a smooth circular wire standing in a vertical plane, what modifications would you make to your answers?

**11.** An olympic athlete of mass 70 kg is swinging in vertical circles on the high horizontal bar. Assuming that his motion can be described as the same as a mass of 70 kg concentrated at a distance of 120 cm from the bar, find the tension or thrust in his arms at the top and bottom of the circle given that the angular velocity of the athlete at the top is (*a*) 0·5 radians/second, (*b*) 1 radian/second.

What must be the angular velocity at the top if the athlete's arms are to remain in tension throughout the motion? What would be the tension in his arms at the lowest point of swing in this case? Comment on your answer.

**12.** A bob of mass $m$ is attached to one end $A$ of an inextensible string of length $l$, the other end of which is attached to a fixed point $O$. The particle is projected horizontally with a velocity $u$ when $OA$ is vertical with $A$ below $O$. Show that the velocity $v$ of the particle when $AO$ makes an angle of $\theta$ with the downward vertical through $O$ is given by the expression

$$v^2 = u^2 - 2gl\,(1 - \cos\theta)$$

provided that the string is still taut. Apply Newton's second law radially at this point to show that the tension $T$ in the string in terms of $m$, $g$, $\theta$, $u$ and $l$ is given by

$$T = mg(3\cos\theta - 2) + \frac{mu^2}{l}.$$

Now investigate the following situations:
(*a*) $u^2 < 2gl$;    (*b*) $u^2 = 2gl$;    (*c*) $2gl < u^2 < 5gl$;
(*d*) $u^2 = 5gl$;    (*e*) $u^2 > 5gl$.

951

**13.** A bead of mass $m$ is threaded on a smooth circular wire of radius $l$ situated in a vertical plane. By applying the methods suggested by Question 12 to the situation when the bead is projected from the lowest point with a horizontal velocity of $u$, establish corresponding equations for the velocity and reaction between the bead and the wire when the radius to the bead makes an angle $\theta$ with the downward vertical through the centre of the circle. Find:

(a) when the reaction becomes zero;

(b) the value of $u$ necessary for the bead to make a complete revolution. (N.B. it is not $u \geqslant \sqrt{(5gl)}$.)

Explain what happens in physical terms.

**14.** Using the relations for $v^2$ and $T$ obtained in Question 12, show that when $\pi \geqslant \theta > \frac{1}{2}\pi$, $T$ will always become zero before $v$.

## 3. VARIABLE FORCES WHICH DO WORK

You will have noticed that in the preceding sections we have only considered work done by forces that remained constant during the displacement. The only variable forces that we encountered were normal reactions or tensions and they did no work. We now investigate the principle of energy for variable forces.

**3.1 Straight-line motion.** One common example of a variable force is the tension in an elastic string as it is stretched. In Chapter 24 we saw that the tension $T$ in a spring or elastic string which had been extended a distance $x$ was given by the formula

$$T = kx$$

where $k$ is a constant depending on the material.

Suppose we take a piece of elastic, unstretched length 0·5 m, which stretches 0·02 m under a force of 10 N. If one end is attached to a fixed point, how much work is done in stretching the string to a total length of 0·7 m?

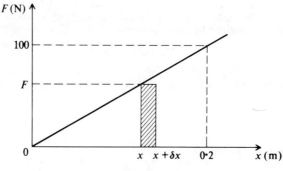

Fig. 15

The graph in Figure 15 shows how the pulling force $F$ N increases linearly with the extension $x$ m, from zero to 100 N at extension 0·2 m (total length 0·7 m).

The work done, $\delta W$, in stretching the string from an extension $x$, when the force is $F$, to $x + \delta x$ will be approximately $F\delta x$, which is the area of the shaded rectangle in Figure 15. It is easy to show, by the methods of Chapters 10 and 31, that the work done is given exactly by the area under the graph. Thus the total work done in stretching the string 0·2 m will be $\frac{1}{2} \times 100 \times 0\cdot2 = 10$ J.

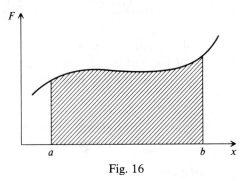

Fig. 16

For a general force (see Figure 16), we integrate to find the area under the force-displacement curve:

$$\text{work done by force } F \text{ moving from } a \text{ to } b = \int_a^b F\,dx.$$

Also, from Newton's second law,

$$F = ma = m\frac{dv}{dt} = m\frac{dv}{dx} \times \frac{dx}{dt} = mv\frac{dv}{dx},$$

we obtain $\displaystyle\int_a^b F\,dx = \int_{v_a}^{v_b} mv\,dv.$

The principle of energy for a variable force in straight-line motion becomes

$$\int_a^b F\,dx = \int_{v_a}^{v_b} mv\,dv = \tfrac{1}{2}mv_b^2 - \tfrac{1}{2}mv_a^2.$$

*Example 8*

Find the work done on a satellite of mass 1000 kg when it is lifted up to 200 km above the earth's surface. Take the radius of the earth to be $6\cdot4 \times 10^6$ m and the value of $g$ at the earth's surface to be 9·8 m/s$^2$.

953

The satellite is raised from $P_1$ to $P_2$ (see Figure 17) where

$$OP_1 = r_1 = 6 \cdot 4 \times 10^6 \, \text{m}$$

and
$$OP_2 = r_2 = 6 \cdot 4 \times 10^6 + 2 \times 10^5$$

$$= 6 \cdot 6 \times 10^6 \, \text{m}.$$

The magnitude $F$ of the force on the satellite is given by Newton's law of gravitation (see Chapter 12, p. 279) as

$$F = \frac{GmM}{r^2}$$

where $G$ is the universal constant of gravitation, $m$ is the mass of the satellite, $M$ is the mass of the earth, and $r$ the distance between their centres. The work done by the gravitational force as the satellite is raised is

$$W = \int_{P_1}^{P_2} F \, dx = \int_{P_1}^{P_2} -\frac{GmM}{r^2} \, dr \quad \text{(since } F \text{ acts in the opposite direction to the displacement)}$$

$$= \left[ GmM\left(\frac{1}{r}\right) \right]_{r_1}^{r_2}$$

$$= GmM\left(\frac{1}{r_2} - \frac{1}{r_1}\right)$$

$$= GmM \times \left(\frac{1}{6 \cdot 6 \times 10^6} - \frac{1}{6 \cdot 4 \times 10^6}\right)$$

$$= -\frac{GmM \times 0 \cdot 2}{6 \cdot 6 \times 6 \cdot 4 \times 10^6}. \tag{1}$$

Now at the earth's surface we know that

$$\frac{GmM}{r_1^2} = mg \approx 9 \cdot 8m = 9 \cdot 8 \times 1000.$$

Thus in (1) we have work done by gravity

$$= -\frac{9 \cdot 8 \times 1000 \times (6 \cdot 4 \times 10^6)^2 \times 0 \cdot 2}{6 \cdot 6 \times 6 \cdot 4 \times 10^6}$$

$$\approx -1 \cdot 9 \times 10^9 \, \text{J}.$$

The negative sign means that the force of gravity does negative work and an equal amount of positive work must be supplied by a rocket to raise the satellite to $P_2$.

954

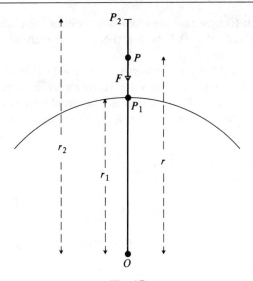

Fig. 17

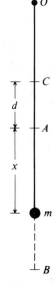

Fig. 18

## Example 9

A mass of 200 g is attached to a spring which is stretched 5 cm by a force of 1 N. The spring is attached to a fixed point $O$ and pulled down to a point $B$ so that the spring is extended by 30 cm. The mass is then released. Find: (i) how fast the mass is travelling at $A$ when the spring becomes unstretched; (ii) how far the mass travels above $A$ before coming to instantaneous rest.

We measure extension downwards from $A$ with $B$ being $0.3$ m below $A$ (see Figure 18). The value of $k$ for Hooke's law is clearly $20$ N/m.

(i) The net force in the direction of the acceleration is $F = mg - kx$ vertically downwards. The work done by the weight and the tension is given by

$$\int_B^A F\,dx = \int_{0.3}^0 (mg - kx)\,dx$$

$$= \left[ mgx - \tfrac{1}{2}kx^2 \right]_{0.3}^0$$

$$= \tfrac{1}{2} \times 20 \times 0.3^2 - 0.2 \times 9.8 \times 0.3$$

$$= 0.312$$

$$= \text{change in KE}$$

$$= \tfrac{1}{2}mv^2.$$

Hence the speed at $A$ is given by

$$\sqrt{\left( \frac{0.312}{\tfrac{1}{2} \times 0.2} \right)} \approx 1.8 \text{ m/s}.$$

(ii) Work done by weight and tension from $A$ to $C$ (where $C$ is $d$ metres above $A$, i.e. $x = -d$) is

$$\int_A^C F\,dx = \int_0^{-d} (-kx + mg)\,dx$$

$$= \left[ -\tfrac{1}{2}kx^2 + mgx \right]_0^{-d}$$

$$= -\tfrac{1}{2}kd^2 - mgd$$

$$= -10d^2 - 1.96d \text{ J}.$$

This equals the change in kinetic energy which is $-0.312$ J since the mass is now at rest. Thus

$$10d^2 + 1.96d = 0.312$$

which readily factorizes to

$$(d + 0.3)(10d - 1.04) = 0$$

since $d = -0.3$ represents the position $B$. Hence

$$d = \frac{1.04}{10} \approx 0.1.$$

That is, the mass travels about 10 cm before coming to instantaneous rest.

**\*3.2 Component form.** In two dimensions a variable force $\mathbf{F}$ can be separated into two perpendicular components $\mathbf{F} = \begin{pmatrix} X \\ Y \end{pmatrix}$ (see Figure 19).

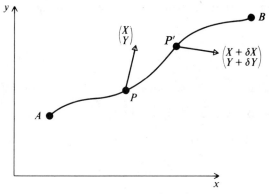

Fig. 19

As a particle moves under the action of $\mathbf{F}$, work will be done by $X$ when the $x$-coordinate of the particle changes but, since $Y$ is perpendicular to the $x$-axis, it will do no work for a change in $x$ alone; similarly $Y$ but not $X$ will do work when $y$ changes. If the particle moves from $P(x, y)$ to $P'(x + \delta x, y + \delta y)$ it is clear that the work done by $\mathbf{F}$ is given by

$$\delta W \approx X \, \delta x + Y \, \delta y = \begin{pmatrix} X \\ Y \end{pmatrix} \cdot \begin{pmatrix} \delta x \\ \delta y \end{pmatrix}.$$

The total work done by $\mathbf{F}$ on the particle when it moves from $A$ to $B$ is thus given by

$$W = \lim_{\substack{\delta x \to 0 \\ \delta y \to 0}} \sum_{A}^{B} (X \, \delta x + Y \, \delta y) = \int_{A}^{B} X \, dx + \int_{A}^{B} Y \, dy.$$

By expressing the acceleration of the particle in component form, Newton's second law gives

$$\mathbf{F} = \begin{pmatrix} X \\ Y \end{pmatrix} = m \begin{pmatrix} \ddot{x} \\ \ddot{y} \end{pmatrix}$$

and it is easy to show that

$$\int_A^B X\,dx = \tfrac{1}{2}m\dot{x}_B^2 - \tfrac{1}{2}m\dot{x}_A^2$$

and

$$\int_A^B Y\,dy = \tfrac{1}{2}m\dot{y}_B^2 - \tfrac{1}{2}m\dot{y}_A^2.$$

Thus, adding,

$$W = \int_A^B \binom{X}{Y}\cdot\binom{dx}{dy} = \tfrac{1}{2}m(\dot{x}_B^2 + \dot{y}_B^2) - \tfrac{1}{2}m(\dot{x}_A^2 + \dot{y}_A^2) = \tfrac{1}{2}mv_B^2 - \tfrac{1}{2}mv_A^2$$

and we again see that the work done by **F** equals the change in kinetic energy of the particle.

*Example* 10

A body of mass $m$ moves under the action of a force $\mathbf{F} = \begin{pmatrix} -mn^2x \\ -mn^2y \end{pmatrix}$ where $n$ is a constant. Initially the body is at $A(a, 0)$ and its velocity is $\begin{pmatrix} 0 \\ nb \end{pmatrix}$. Find its speed when it reaches the point $B(0, b)$.

$$\text{Work done} = \int_A^B \begin{pmatrix} -mn^2x \\ -mn^2y \end{pmatrix}\cdot\binom{dx}{dy}$$

$$= \int_a^0 -mn^2x\,dx + \int_0^b -mn^2y\,dy$$

$$= \left[-\tfrac{1}{2}mn^2x^2\right]_a^0 + \left[-\tfrac{1}{2}mn^2y^2\right]_0^b$$

$$= \tfrac{1}{2}mn^2(a^2 - b^2).$$

$$\text{Change in KE} = \tfrac{1}{2}mv_B^2 - \tfrac{1}{2}m(nb)^2$$

The equation of energy thus gives

$$\tfrac{1}{2}mv_B^2 - \tfrac{1}{2}mn^2b^2 = \tfrac{1}{2}mn^2a^2 - \tfrac{1}{2}mn^2b^2$$

$$\Rightarrow v_B^2 = n^2a^2.$$

The speed at $B$ is thus $na$.

This is an example of elliptic harmonic motion, being the combination of two perpendicular simple harmonic motions:

$$\ddot{x} = -n^2x;$$

$$\ddot{y} = -n^2y.$$

958

You may like to check back to Chapter 25, p. 626 and write down the full solution.

**\*3.3   Alternative forms for variable forces.** In Section 3.2, Figure 19, when the particle moved from $P$ to $P'$ its displacement changed by $\begin{pmatrix} \delta x \\ \delta y \end{pmatrix}$. Writing this as $\delta \mathbf{r}$ we have

$$\delta W \approx \begin{pmatrix} X \\ Y \end{pmatrix} . \begin{pmatrix} \delta x \\ \delta y \end{pmatrix} = \mathbf{F} . \, \delta \mathbf{r}. \tag{1}$$

The total work done from $A$ to $B$ could thus be written in the form

$$W = \underset{\delta r \to 0}{\text{limit}} \sum_A^B \mathbf{F} . \, \delta \mathbf{r} = \int_A^B \mathbf{F} . \, d\mathbf{r}. \tag{2}$$

In practice this can be awkward to use and an alternative form can be derived from (1):

$$\delta W \approx \mathbf{F} . \, \delta \mathbf{r} \Rightarrow \delta W \approx \left( \mathbf{F} . \frac{\delta \mathbf{r}}{\delta t} \right) \delta t,$$

giving
$$W = \underset{\delta t \to 0}{\text{limit}} \sum_A^B \left( \mathbf{F} . \frac{\delta \mathbf{r}}{\delta t} \right) \delta t$$

$$= \int_A^B (\mathbf{F} . \mathbf{v}) \, dt \quad \text{since} \quad \underset{\delta t \to 0}{\text{limit}} \frac{\delta \mathbf{r}}{\delta t} = \mathbf{v}.$$

This expression and equation (2) above are also valid in three dimensions—what would be the corresponding expressions for $W$ in component form?

## Exercise D

**1.** A particle of mass $m$ kg moves along the $x$-axis and when it is $x$ m from 0 it is acted on by a variable force $P$ N in the direction of $x$-increasing and by a force $Q$ N in the direction opposite to that of the velocity. The particle starts at $x = a$ with a velocity of $u$ m/s in the direction of $x$-increasing and travels to the point $x = b$ where it has a velocity of $v$ m/s in the same direction. If:

(a) $m = 90$, $P = 5x$, $Q = \frac{5}{3}$, $a = 0$, $u = 1$, $b = 6$, find $v$;
(b) $m = 90$, $P = -5x$, $Q = \frac{5}{3}$, $a = 0$, $u = \frac{5}{2}$, $b = 6$, find $v$;
(c) $m = 32$, $P = -5x$, $Q = \frac{2}{3}$, $a = 0$, $b = 6$, $v = 6$, find $u$;
(d) $m = 12$, $P = 3(10 - x)$, $Q = 0$, $a = 0$, $b = 2$, $v = 3$, find $u$ and the velocity when the particle is at $x = 4$;

(e) $m = 8$, $P = \dfrac{-120}{x^2}$, $Q = 3$, $a = 2$, $u = 4$, $b = 8$, find $v$ and (harder) the point where the particle comes instantaneously to rest.

**2.** A body of mass 10 kg is projected by a machine with the following force-distance relationship:

| Distance (m) | 0 | 1 | 2 | 3 | 4 | 5 | 6 | 7 | 8 |
|---|---|---|---|---|---|---|---|---|---|
| Force (N) | 400 | 300 | 240 | 210 | 190 | 160 | 130 | 80 | 0 |

Find the velocity of the body at intervals of one metre during the thrust.

**3.** A light spring of natural length 20 cm which requires a force of 1·5 N to stretch it 1 cm, is attached to a fixed point at one end and hangs freely. A 1 kg mass is hung from the lower end and it is released from rest with the spring unstretched. How long is the spring when the mass comes instantaneously to rest?

**4.** A spring of natural length 1·5 m will stretch 1 cm under a tension of 4 N. Find the work done in stretching the spring from:
(a) 1·5 m to 2·5 m;    (b) 1·5 m to 2·0 m;    (c) 2·0 m to 2·5 m;
(d) 2·5 m to 3·5 m;    (e) 3 m to 4 m.

**5.** A car which has a mass of 1 tonne experiences a constant resistance to motion of 150 N. When it has travelled a distance $x$ m, the force exerted by the engine is given by the following table:

| Distance (m) | 0 | 10 | 20 | 30 | 40 | 50 |
|---|---|---|---|---|---|---|
| Force (N) | 4000 | 3900 | 3750 | 3550 | 3300 | 3000 |

Draw a graph showing the acceleration of the car plotted against $x$ and find the speed of the car when it has travelled 50 m, assuming that it starts from rest.

**6.** It is often convenient to define the *elastic constant* $\lambda$ of an elastic string (or spring) as the tension in the string when it has been stretched to twice its natural length $l$. ($\lambda$ is sometimes wrongly called the modulus of elasticity.) Show that the work done in stretching a string from an unstretched position to twice its natural length is $\frac{1}{2}\lambda l$ and write down in terms of $\lambda$, $l$ and $x$ an expression for the work done in stretching a string an amount $x$.

**7.** (a) Two springs of natural lengths $a_1$, $a_2$ and each of elastic constant $\lambda$ (see Question 6) are attached end to end. Show that the combined spring has elastic constant $\lambda$.

(b) Two springs of elastic constants $\lambda_1$, $\lambda_2$ and each of natural length $a$ are attached side by side. Show that the combined spring has elastic constant $\lambda_1 + \lambda_2$.

**8.** A 7 kg mass lies on a rough table, the coefficient of friction being $\frac{1}{2}$. It is attached to a point $A$, 3 m away, by a string of natural length 1·5 m (N.B. It is *not* a spring; it becomes slack at less than 1·5 m.) The mass is projected towards $A$ with velocity 4 m/s and reaches $A$ with velocity 2 m/s. Find the elastic constant of the string (see Question 6).

**9.** Two masses are connected by a spring that has natural length $l$ and elastic constant $\lambda$ (see Question 6). Find the sum of their kinetic energies when the spring is unstretched if they are released from rest when they are $2l$ apart.

**10.** Two climbers each of mass 70 kg have 50 m of rope between them when the higher one falls. If he is 48 m vertically above the second who is firmly belayed to the rock face, find where the falling climber first comes to rest if the rope stretches 1 m under a tension of 300 N.

**11.** A spring whose natural length is 0·5 m and whose elastic constant is 200 N (see Question 6) has one end attached to a fixed support and the other end attached to a mass of 10 kg. The mass is released when it is 0·5 m below the support. Calculate the speed of the mass when it has fallen 0·2 m and find where it comes instantaneously to rest (two places).

**12.** A car of mass 1 tonne starts from rest on a level road. The propulsive force is initially 4000 N but this falls in proportion to the distance travelled so that after 200 m its value is 700 N. There is a constant frictional force of 700 N. Find the speed of the car every 25 m and sketch a graph to show the relation between the speed and the distance travelled.

**\*13.** Calculate the work done by a force $\mathbf{F} = \begin{pmatrix} -y \\ x \end{pmatrix}$ on a particle which moves from $(4, 0)$ to $(0, 4)$ along the line $x + y = 4$.

**\*14.** (*a*) Calculate the work done by a force $\mathbf{F}$ given by

$$\mathbf{F} = \begin{pmatrix} x^2 \\ y^2 \end{pmatrix}$$

in moving from $A(1, 0)$ to $B(0, 1)$ along:
   (i) the $x$-axis towards 0 and up the $y$-axis to $B$;
   (ii) the line $AB$;
   (iii) the quadrant of the circle $x^2 + y^2 = 1$.

   (*b*) Repeat (*a*) for the force $\mathbf{F} = \begin{pmatrix} y^2 \\ x^2 \end{pmatrix}$.

   Is either of these forces conservative?

**\*15.** An aeroplane of mass 10 tonnes lands on an aircraft carrier with a relative velocity of 45 m/s along the flight deck. It catches the mid-point of a cable 70 m long which is at right-angles to the line of flight. The cable is unstretched, but not slack, and the force in it is given by $F = kx$ where $x$ is the extension of the cable. If, on catching the cable, the aeroplane's engines have their thrust reversed, thus producing a constant retarding force of $10^4$ N, find the value of $k$ so that the aircraft is brought to rest in 40 m.

**\*16.** The force towards the earth on a rocket of mass $m$ is $\dfrac{mgd^2}{r^2}$ where $d$ is the radius of the earth, $r$ the distance of the rocket from the centre of the earth and $g$ the acceleration due to gravity at the earth's surface. Calculate the initial velocity required to lift the rocket to a height $x$ above the earth's surface. Hence find the initial velocity necessary if the rocket is to escape from the earth's gravitational field.

**\*17.** $Ox$ and $Oy$ are horizontal and vertical axes respectively. An aircraft is initially at $A$, position vector $\begin{pmatrix} 0 \\ h \end{pmatrix}$, flying horizontally with velocity $\begin{pmatrix} u \\ 0 \end{pmatrix}$, when the pilot alters the controls to produce a constant force $\mathbf{F} = \lambda mg \begin{pmatrix} \sqrt{3} \\ 1 \end{pmatrix}$ (the only other force acting on the aircraft being its weight $m\mathbf{g}$).

   Find the velocity $\mathbf{v}$ and the position vector $\mathbf{r}$ of the aircraft $t$ seconds later, and show that if $\lambda < 1$ the aircraft loses height.

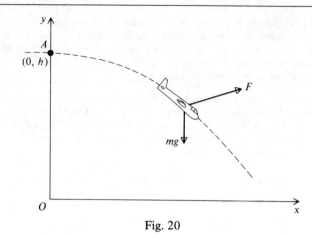

Fig. 20

Write down an expression for the work done by the force **F** between times $t = 0$ and $t = T$, and using this expression with $\lambda = \frac{1}{2}$ show that, as the plane descends to half its original height, **F** does work $W$, where

$$W = \tfrac{1}{2}mg\left[ h + u\sqrt{\left(\frac{6h}{g}\right)} \right].$$

(OC)

## 4. POWER

When we say that a sports car is more powerful than a Mini what do we mean? Which could travel up a hill quicker?

If two water-pumps pump water from a 10 m deep well and the supply pipes have equal diameters, what can you say about the relative amounts of water you would expect to be delivered every second if one pump is twice as powerful as the other?

Suppose a horse is pulling a barge along a canal as hard as it can and it is able to achieve a speed of 1 m/s, whereas a small tractor is able to achieve a speed of 2 m/s. How much more powerful would you say that the tractor is than the horse?

Your answers to these questions should have suggested that the power of an engine depends on the force it is capable of producing and the speed at which the force can be *usefully* applied, and that these questions are in some way linked to the *rate* at which the engine can do work.

In Section 3.1 we suggested that, for small $\delta x$, the work done $\delta W$ by a force $F$ was given by $\delta W \approx F \delta x$. Dividing by $\delta t$ we have

$$\frac{\delta W}{\delta t} \approx F\frac{\delta x}{\delta t}$$

962

which, in the limit, gives us

$$\frac{dW}{dt} = F\frac{dx}{dt} = Fv.$$

More generally $\delta W \approx \mathbf{F} \cdot \delta \mathbf{r}$ leads to $\dfrac{dW}{dt} = \mathbf{F} \cdot \dfrac{d\mathbf{r}}{dt} = \mathbf{F} \cdot \mathbf{v}$. We define *power* as the rate of doing work per unit time and it follows from the above that

$$P = \frac{dW}{dt} = \mathbf{F} \cdot \mathbf{v}$$

and we see the connection between the scalar quantity power and the vector quantities $\mathbf{F}$ and $\mathbf{v}$. What units shall we use for power?

We define 1 watt (W) as 1 joule per second and, since this is a fairly low rate of working, the kilowatt (kW) is often used. (Until recently the *horsepower* (hp) was widely used as a unit of power. It was approximately equal to $\frac{3}{4}$ kW. A typical car engine develops about 60 kW or 80 hp.)

*Example* 11

At what steady speed will an engine whose tractive force $\mathbf{P}$ can work at a rate of 480 kW pull a train of 200 tonnes $(a)$ along the level and $(b)$ up a slope of 1 in 125 if the resistance to motion $F$ is 80 N per tonne of train in each case? If the slope levels off when the train is travelling at its steady uphill speed what will be its initial acceleration?

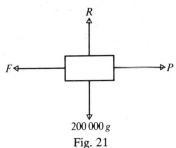

Fig. 21

$(a)$ See Figure 21. On the level the resultant force in the direction of motion is zero since there is no acceleration, i.e. $\mathbf{P} - \mathbf{F} = \mathbf{0}$. But $F = 80 \times 200$ so the tractive force also has magnitude $80 \times 200 = 16\,000$ N. The power of the engine is $\mathbf{P} \cdot \mathbf{v}$ kW $= 480$ kW. Hence, if the speed is $v$ m/s, we have $16\,000\,v = 480\,000$, giving $v = 30$.

$(b)$ See Figure 22. Newton's second law gives, at steady speed $v$ m/s (i.e. zero acceleration),

$$\mathbf{P} + \mathbf{F} + \mathbf{R} + 200\,000\,\mathbf{g} = \mathbf{0}.$$

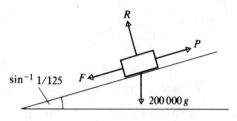

Fig. 22

Resolving up the incline this gives

$$P - 80 \times 200 - 200\,000 \times 9\cdot8 \times \tfrac{1}{125} = 0 \Rightarrow P \approx 32\,000.$$

The power $\mathbf{P} \cdot \mathbf{v}\,\text{kW} = 480\,\text{kW}$ gives $32\,000v = 480\,000$, from which $v = 15$.

When the train levels out we have from Figure 21 the resultant accelerating force is $P - F$. Now $P$ takes the value $32\,000$ and thus Newton's second law gives

$$32\,000 - 80 \times 200 = 200\,000a$$

$$\Rightarrow a = 0\cdot08,$$

where $a$ is the magnitude of the acceleration in $\text{m/s}^2$.

*Example* 12

A pump takes water at a certain speed and delivers it at the same speed 15 m higher at a flow rate of 100 kg/s. Find the power of the pump.

Since the water is not accelerated, the force of the pump on each particle of water must equal the weight of the particle. In $t$ seconds a mass of $100t$ kg is raised 15 m; the work done is thus $100t \times 9\cdot8 \times 15\,\text{J}$ giving the power of the pump as $100 \times 9\cdot8 \times 15\,\text{W}$, or about 15 kW.

*Example* 13

A parcel of mass $m$ is placed on a conveyor belt moving at a constant speed of $u$ such that on contact the parcel has negligible velocity. The parcel initially slips on the belt, the coefficient of friction being $\mu$. Investigate the situation and find the power required to maintain a belt speed of $u$ whilst the parcel is coming to rest relative to the belt.

Figure 23 shows the forces on the parcel and on the belt, where $T$ is the force transmitted to the belt to maintain speed $u$. Since the belt is moving with speed $u$ the power transmitted is $Tu$. The belt is not accelerating so that $T - \mu R = 0$ and the parcel is not accelerating vertically so that $R - mg = 0$. Consequently $T = \mu R = \mu mg$ and the required power is $\mu mgu$.

964

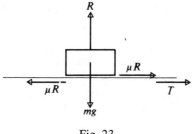

Fig. 23

Before we leave this example it is worth looking at the kinetic energy gained by the parcel and the work done by the conveyor. Applying the impulse-momentum equation to the parcel we can find the time taken for it to come to rest relative to the belt. This gives $\mu mgt = mu$ and hence $t = u/\mu g$. Now the parcel has acquired a kinetic energy of $\frac{1}{2}mu^2$ but the work done by $T$ whilst the parcel is coming to rest is given by

$$Tut = \mu mgu \times u/\mu g = mu^2.$$

Thus the mechanical energy supplied to the system is twice that gained by the system. What has happened to this 'missing' energy? Why wasn't mechanical energy conserved? We take this up in Section 5.

### Exercise E

**1.** A man steadily winds up the 2 kg 'weight' of a grandfather clock through 1·5 m in $\frac{1}{4}$ min. Find the power of the tension in this chain over the 'weight'. Is the power of the force between the man's finger and the key likely to be larger than this? At what minimum power must the man be working?

**2.** (a) A crane steadily raises a $7\frac{1}{2}$ tonne ingot at a rate of 2 m/s. What is the power of the force at the attachment? Is the power of the force on the chain at the drum likely to be larger than this?

(b) If the power of the force at the axle of the chain drum is increased to 220 kW and the power of the force at the point of attachment is 70% of this, what will be the acceleration of the ingot when the speed is 2 m/s?

(c) If the crane continues to produce this power what will be the final steady speed achieved by the ingot?

**3.** Find the power of the projector machine of Exercise D, Question 2, at intervals of 1 m during the thrust.

**4.** Find the power of the car of Exercise D, Question 5, at intervals of 10 m for the first 50 m of travel.

**5.** A pump takes water from rest in a hole in the road and delivers it 2 m higher on the road surface at 3 m/s at a flow rate of 25 kg/s. If the pump is 80% efficient, find the power of the pump in kW.

**6.** The following specification of British Rail passenger-haulage equipment is for a train of mass 475 tonnes: a steady speed of 150 km/h on the level and a steady speed of 100 km/h up a gradient of 1 in 70. Find the resistances to motion, assumed constant, in newtons per tonne of the train's mass, and the power rating of the locomotive in kilowatts required to deliver these performances.

**7.** Repeat Question 6 for British Rail freight-haulage equipment: the mass of the train is 950 tonnes, 110 km/h is required on the level and 70 km/h up a gradient of 1 in 70.

**8.** An engine is to be designed to pump water from a reservoir to fill a swimming bath 1 km away. The reservoir is 20 m below the level of the pump outlet and the filling process is to last no longer than 8 hours. The swimming bath measures 30 m by 10 m and slopes uniformly from a depth of 1 m to a depth of 2 m. Find the power of the pumping engine assuming that it is 70% efficient.

**9.** On a level road a car can develop 60 kW when travelling at a maximum speed of 120 km/h. Find the resistance to motion.

Assuming the resistance to be constant, at what maximum speed in the same gear can the car climb a gradient of 1 in 20? Assume the mass of the car to be 1 tonne.

**10.** The highest speed attained by any four-wheeled vehicle is 988·5 km/h. This was achieved in 1965 by an American jet-propelled car developing a thrust of 66 750 N. Find the power of the engine.

**11.** The speed of a train of mass 100 tonnes varies in accordance with the following table:

| Speed (km/h) | 0 | 29 | 46 | 58 | 66 | 70 | 72 |
|---|---|---|---|---|---|---|---|
| Time (s) | 0 | 10 | 20 | 30 | 40 | 50 | 60 |

The train is running down an incline of 1 in 490. Find the power exerted at the end of the first 20 s, and the first 40 s, if the total frictional and air resistances amount to 150 N per tonne throughout the motion.

**12.** A frigate is driven at a speed of 50 km/h by means of engines delivering an effective 25 000 kW. Calculate the resistance to the motion of the ship and, assuming that the resistance varies as the square of the speed, the effective power output required for a speed of 60 km/h.

**\*13.** The power of the wind resistance on a car at 55 km/h is −4 kW. The force of the resistance varies as the square of the speed; find the power of the resistance at 110 km/h. The power of the forces flexing the tyres rises approximately linearly with speed, being zero at rest and −5 kW at 55 km/h. Find the total power of these two forces at 110 km/h.

The total power of the driving force at 55 km/h is 30 kW and at 110 km/h is 50 kW. Find the acceleration of the car at each speed if its mass is 750 kg.

**\*14.** 50 kg of anthracite grains are deposited on a conveyor belt moving with a constant speed of 5 m/s horizontally. If the centre of mass of the load moves 2 m relative to the belt before coming to rest on the belt, calculate the power required to maintain the conveyor speed at 5 m/s whilst the load is being deposited. (Assume that the load will move bodily along the belt, although in practice this will not be the case.)

966

## 5. COLLISIONS AND EXPLOSIONS

We conclude the chapter with some examples that combine the concepts of work and kinetic energy with those of momentum and impulse from Chapter 34.

### Example 14

A satellite of mass 200 kg is attached to a nose-cone of mass 12·5 kg. When travelling at a speed of 9600 m/s the two are separated by an internal explosive impulse of $1·6 \times 10^5$ N s at right-angles to the line of flight. Assuming the masses of the satellite and nose-cone remain the same, calculate the total gain in kinetic energy due to the explosion.

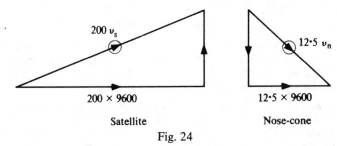

Fig. 24

Let $\mathbf{v}_s$ and $\mathbf{v}_n$ be the velocities after separation of the satellite and nose-cone respectively. Figure 24 shows the impulse-momentum triangles for the satellite and nose-cone. We have by Pythagoras's theorem

$$(200v_s)^2 = (200 \times 9600)^2 + (1·6 \times 10^5)^2 \text{ giving } v_s^2 = 9·28 \times 10^7,$$

$$(12·5v_n)^2 = (12·5 \times 9600)^2 + (1·6 \times 10^5)^2 \text{ giving } v_n^2 = 2·56 \times 10^8.$$

Now the total kinetic energy before separation is

$$\tfrac{1}{2} \times (200 + 12·5) \times 9600^2 = 9·792 \times 10^9,$$

and the total kinetic energy after separation is

$$\tfrac{1}{2} \times 200 \times v_s^2 + \tfrac{1}{2} \times 12·5 \times v_n^2 = 9·28 \times 10^9 + 1·60 \times 10^9$$

$$\approx 10·9 \times 10^9.$$

The gain in kinetic energy due to the explosion is thus about $1·1 \times 10^9$ J.

### Example 15

A railway truck of mass $M$ moving with speed $U$ strikes against buffers and rebounds with speed $V$. If the coefficient of restitution between the truck and buffers is $e$, find the loss of kinetic energy due to the impact. Comment on the cases $e = 1$, $e = 0$.

967

Newton's experimental law of impact tells us that $V = eU$. Hence the loss in kinetic energy of the truck is

$$\tfrac{1}{2}MU^2 - \tfrac{1}{2}MV^2 = \tfrac{1}{2}MU^2(1 - e^2).$$

If $e = 1$ there is no KE loss and we say that the impact is perfectly elastic. If $e = 0$ the KE loss is a maximum. The truck is stopped dead by the buffers and all the kinetic energy is destroyed.

These last two examples show that in explosions and collisions kinetic energy can be created or destroyed. It is only *conserved* in the very special case of perfectly elastic collisions.

### *Miscellaneous Exercise*

**1.** A truck of mass 3 tonnes moving at 3 m/s catches up and collides with one of mass 2 tonnes moving at 2 m/s. The trucks remain coupled together after the collision. With what speed will they be moving immediately after collision and how much kinetic energy is lost?

**2.** The speed of a bullet is measured by means of a 'ballistic pendulum'. This consists of a block of wood of mass $M$ suspended from a fixed point by an inelastic string of length $l$. The bullet of mass $m$ is fired with unknown speed $u$ into the middle of the block and the angle of deflection $\theta$ of the string with the downward vertical is measured at the top of the swing.

(*a*) Write down the momentum equation at impact and obtain an expression for the combined speed $V$ of block and bullet. What is the loss of kinetic energy on impact?

(*b*) Equate the kinetic energy after impact of block and bullet to the work done against gravity during the swing to obtain an expression for $u$ in terms of $m, M, \theta$.

(*c*) Evaluate your expression if $m = 30$ g, $M = 7$ kg, $l = 2$ m and $\theta = 30°$.

**3.** (*a*) A rugby player of mass 70 kg moving at 6 m/s tackles another player of mass 80 kg moving at 4 m/s in the same direction. Calculate their combined speed after collision and the loss of kinetic energy due to the impact. If they slither to a halt after travelling 2 m, calculate the frictional resistance of the ground, assumed constant throughout.

(*b*) If the players were moving in opposite directions at impact, calculate the loss in kinetic energy and, assuming the same frictional resistance as in (*a*), calculate how far they will slide before stopping.

**4.** A frog of mass 120 g is standing on a brick of mass 500 g which is free to move on the smooth ice of a frozen pond. The frog leaps with a horizontal velocity of 20 cm/s onto a second brick of mass 250 g, also free to move on the smooth ice of the pond. Discuss the subsequent motion of the two bricks giving their separate kinetic energies. If the total energy supplied by the frog for the leap is $\tfrac{1}{50}$ J, explain possible causes of the loss of energy.

**5.** A satellite of mass 1000 kg moving at 1200 m/s breaks up into two equal parts so that one part moves at 1202 m/s in a direction making an angle of $0.03°$

with the original direction. Give, correct to 4 significant figures, the new speed of the other part.

**6.** An airborne firework of mass $2\,m$ kg explodes into two equal parts. The firework's velocity before the explosion is $\mathbf{u}$ and the velocity of one part after the explosion is $\mathbf{v}$, where

$$\mathbf{u} = \begin{pmatrix} 5u \\ 0 \end{pmatrix} \quad \text{and} \quad \mathbf{v} = \begin{pmatrix} u \\ 3u \end{pmatrix}.$$

Find the velocity of the other part:
  (a) if $\mathbf{v}$ is relative to same frame of reference as $\mathbf{u}$;
  (b) if $\mathbf{v}$ is relative to the new velocity of the other part.
In each case calculate the increase in kinetic energy of the system.

**7.** A body of mass 6 kg moving with velocity $\begin{pmatrix} 3 \\ 6 \\ 11 \end{pmatrix}$ m/s collides with and sticks to a body of mass 10 kg moving with velocity $\begin{pmatrix} 3 \\ -2 \\ 3 \end{pmatrix}$ m/s. Find the change in kinetic energy due to the impact.

**8.** A plank $AB$ of length $l$ and mass $M$ is at rest on a smooth horizontal floor. A man of mass $m$ is originally at rest on the plank at the end $A$. He walks along the plank from $A$ to $B$ without slipping, at constant speed $V$ relative to the plank, stopping as he reaches $B$. Find:
  (a) the time of motion;
  (b) the distance moved by the plank;
  (c) the total kinetic energy of the system at any instant during the motion.

**9.** (a) A pile-driver of mass 100 kg is dropped through 2 m onto a pile of mass 1 tonne. The driver does not bounce. If the pile is driven 10 cm into the earth, what resistance does the earth offer if it is assumed constant?
  (b) Find the height from which a pile-driver of mass 200 kg must be dropped onto a pile of mass 1 tonne if the combined pile and driver drive the pile 15 cm into the earth. Assume the same resistance as in (a).

**10.** Find the velocity at height $h$ m above the nozzle of a water jet issuing $m$ kg of water per second vertically upwards at $v$ m/s. If this water impinges upon a surface at this height and is instantaneously brought to rest by the surface, find the force exerted by the water and hence find the height at which the jet will support a ball of mass $M$ kg.

**11.** A boat has to steam a given distance upstream. If it does so at constant speed, and if the power varies as the cube of the velocity relative to the water, write down the total time taken for the journey and the total work done during the journey. Hence show that the most economical speed is half that of the stream relative to the bank.

**12.** If a particle of mass $m$ is a distance $r$ from a particle of mass $M$ then there is a force of $GMm/r^2$ between them. Calculate the work done by a force $P$ which moves the particle of mass $m$ radially at constant speed from $r = a$ to $r = x$ whilst the mass $M$ remains fixed. (N.B. $m$ does *not* accelerate.) Put $x = a(1 + k)$ in the result and show that for $k$ small, so that $\dfrac{1}{x} \approx \dfrac{1}{a}(1-k)$, the work done by moving a mass $m$ a small distance $h$ radially near the earth's surface is given by $mgh$.

**\*13.** A man of mass 70 kg walking at 5 km/h walks onto a moving pavement travelling at 7 km/h. If the man eventually stands still on the pavement, find the power required to maintain the speed of the pavement. If you need to know the time taken for the man to come to rest on the pavement, assume it to be 5 s. Discuss the situation that arises if the man now starts to walk at 5 km/h relative to the moving pavement in the same direction.

**\*14.** The man of Question 13 steps instead onto an escalator and comes to rest before the escalator begins to ascend a 45° slope. Find the power required to maintain the speed of the escalator while the man is being carried up the incline. Discuss the situation that arises if the man starts to walk up the escalator at 5 km/h relative to it during the ascent.

# SUMMARY

*Work*

For a constant force, $W = \mathbf{F} . \mathbf{r}$.

*Principle of energy*

The work done on a body equals the change in kinetic energy.

*Equation of energy*

$$\tfrac{1}{2}mv^2 - \tfrac{1}{2}mu^2 = \mathbf{F} . \mathbf{r}.$$

For a non-constant force in straight-line motion

$$\tfrac{1}{2}mv^2 - \tfrac{1}{2}mu^2 = \int_A^B F\,dx,$$

and for a non-constant force $\begin{pmatrix} X \\ Y \end{pmatrix}$ in two dimensions

$$\tfrac{1}{2}mv^2 - \tfrac{1}{2}mu^2 = \int_A^B \begin{pmatrix} X \\ Y \end{pmatrix} . \begin{pmatrix} dx \\ dy \end{pmatrix}.$$

*Power*

Power is the rate of doing work:

$$P = \frac{dW}{dt} = \mathbf{F} . \mathbf{v}.$$

*Units*

Units of work and kinetic energy are *joules* (J):

$$1 \text{ joule} = 1 \text{ newton-metre.}$$

Units of power are *watts* (W) or *kilowatts* (kW):

$$1 \text{ watt} = 1 \text{ joule/second.}$$

# REVISION EXERCISES

## 33. INTRODUCTION TO DIFFERENTIAL EQUATIONS

When working out step-by-step solutions, all figures should be rounded to 2 decimal places.

**1.** A ball is thrown vertically upwards with velocity $8\,\mathrm{m/s}$, and its motion is given by the differential equation

$$\frac{dv}{dt} = -(10 + 0{\cdot}1v^2).$$

The solution curve is drawn in Figure 1.

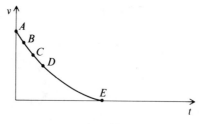

Fig. 1

(a) What are the coordinates of $A$?

(b) What is the gradient of the solution curve at $A$?

(c) What is the gradient of the solution curve at $E$?

(d) $B$, $C$, $D$ are the points on the solution curve for which $t = 0{\cdot}1$, $0{\cdot}2$, $0{\cdot}3$. Find approximately the velocities at these instants, using a simple step-by-step method.

(e) Continue the working of (d) to find approximately the time when the ball comes to rest (i.e. the $t$-value at the point $E$).

**2.** Obtain a more accurate answer to Question 1(e) by using a step length of $0{\cdot}05$.

**3.** Due to a chemical reaction, the amount $x$ grams of a substance after $t$ minutes is growing in a way described by the differential equation

$$\frac{dx}{dt} = \frac{1}{100}(30 - x)(20 - x).$$

(a) After 1 minute, $x = 5$; at what rate is $x$ then increasing?

(b) What will the value of $x$ be approximately when $t = 1{\cdot}5$?

(c) What will the value of $x$ be approximately when $t = 2$?

(d) Explain why $x$ cannot exceed 20.

(e) Sketch the solution curve.

**4.** Sketch the solution curves of:

(a) $\dfrac{dx}{dt} = \dfrac{1}{100}(30-x)(40-x)$, given that $x = 1$ when $t = 0$;

(b) $\dfrac{dy}{dt} = \dfrac{1}{60}(30-y)^2$, given that $y = 5$ when $t = 0$;

(c) $\dfrac{dv}{dt} = 10 - 0 \cdot 8v$, given that $v = 30$ when $t = 0$.

**5.** Obtain step-by-step solutions to the differential equations of Question 4, taking step lengths of $0 \cdot 5$ and continuing until $t = 3$.

**6.** (a) Obtain a step-by-step solution to

$$\frac{dx}{dt} + 2x = 10\,e^{-t}, \text{ given } x = 3 \text{ when } t = 0,$$

taking steps of length $0 \cdot 1$ and continuing until $t = 1$.

(b) Show that $x = 10\,e^{-t} - 7\,e^{-2t}$ satisfies the differential equation and has the same value of $x$ when $t = 0$. Sketch the graph of this function and compare the value of $x$ when $t = 1$ with that found in (a).

**7.** For the differential equation of Question 6, show that $\dfrac{dx}{dt} = 0$ when $x = 5\,e^{-t}$

and that $\dfrac{d^2x}{dt^2} = 0$ when $x = 7 \cdot 5\,e^{-t}$. Show this information on a sketch graph, and indicate the region in which the second derivative is positive.

Give a sketch of the family of solution curves.

## 34. MOMENTUM AND IMPULSE

**1.** (a) A ball of mass $0 \cdot 2$ kg travelling at 15 m/s is hit so as to give it a speed of 10 m/s in the opposite direction. Calculate the magnitude and direction of the impulse on the ball.

(b) If the ball had been deflected through $90°$ by an impulse of the same magnitude, show that the resultant speed would have been 20 m/s and find the direction of the impulse.

(c) If the deflection is to be only $60°$, find by how much the magnitude of the impulse may be reduced if the speed after impact is to be 20 m/s.

**2.** A pile-driver employs a block of mass 800 kg which strikes a pile of mass 100 kg. The velocity of the block immediately before impact is 8 m/s and it does not rebound.

Find how long the pile and block are moving before they come to rest if the resistance to penetration averages $8 \times 10^4$ N.

**3.** Two spherical satellites $A$ and $B$, of mass 100 kg and 200 kg respectively, collide in space. $A$ is originally travelling at 9000 m/s in a direction making an angle of $\tan^{-1}(\frac{4}{3})$ with the line of centres and $B$ at 8000 m/s at an angle of $\tan^{-1}(\frac{8}{15})$. Take $\mathbf{i}$ and $\mathbf{j}$ as unit vectors as shown in Figure 2, and find the final velocities of $A$ and $B$ if $A$ is deflected through an angle of $\tan^{-1}(\frac{24}{7})$. (The question should be answered by drawing *and* calculation.)

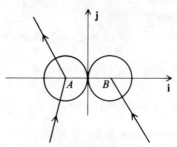

Fig. 2

**4.** A bullet, mass 25 g, is fired with velocity 800 m/s into a block of wood, mass 2 kg, lying on a smooth table. Find the velocity with which the block and bullet move after the bullet has become embedded in the block.

**5.** A ball $A$ of mass 40 g and velocity $\begin{pmatrix} 2 \\ 1 \end{pmatrix}$ m/s collides with a ball $B$ of mass 30 g and velocity $\begin{pmatrix} 1 \\ -2 \end{pmatrix}$ m/s. $\begin{pmatrix} 1 \\ 0 \end{pmatrix}$ is the unit vector along the line of centres. If the subsequent velocity of $B$ is $\begin{pmatrix} 2 \\ -2 \end{pmatrix}$ m/s, find the subsequent velocity of $A$. Find also the value of $e$ for the two balls. (The question should be answered by drawing *and* by calculation.)

**6.** A particle of mass $m$ moves so that its acceleration **a** at time $t$ is given by **a** $= -4t\mathbf{i}$. When $t = 0$ its velocity is **u** $= 32\mathbf{i}$. Find when it first comes to rest, and the impulse of the force from $t = 0$ until then.

## 35. PROBABILITY DISTRIBUTIONS

**1.** (*a*) Find (i) the expected score when one die is rolled; (ii) the expected value of the total score when two dice are rolled.
  (*b*) Find the theoretical standard deviation for each part of (*a*).

**2.** A game consists of rolling three dice. The stake is 10p. There is a prize of 10p for each six rolled (and the stake money back). If no six appears, the stake is lost. Does the game favour the player or the 'bank'?

**3.** Find the mean and variance of a population with a probability density function

$$\phi(x) = \tfrac{2}{3}x \text{ for } 0 \leqslant x \leqslant 1,$$

$$\phi(x) = \tfrac{1}{3}(3 - x) \text{ for } 1 < x \leqslant 3,$$

$$\phi(x) = 0 \text{ otherwise.}$$

Draw the graph of $\phi(x)$ and use it to find the probability of $x$ deviating from its mean by more than twice the standard deviation.

**4.** A mathematical model for the fraction $x$ of the sky covered with cloud $(0 < x < 1)$ assigns to this a probability density function

$$\phi(x) = k/\sqrt{\{x(1 - x)\}}.$$

974

Calculate:
  (i) the value of $k$;
  (ii) the expected fraction covered by cloud;
  (iii) the probability that not more than a quarter of the sky is covered.
[Hint: your integrations may be made easier by using the substitution $x = \sin^2 \theta$. You may assume this substitution is valid, even though the functions to be integrated may be discontinuous at the ends of the interval of integration.]   (OC)

**5.** In a type of skittles at a fair, there are three pins to be knocked down. Each pin knocked over scores 1 point. It is as easy to fell two pins as it is to miss altogether, but it is twice as hard as this to fell a single pin, as also to knock down all three. Write down the probability generator for one throw.

Use this to give, as fractions, the probabilities of the various possible scores after three throws (the pins being put up after each throw), and also the 'expected' total score. If it costs 5p for three throws, will it be more remunerative for the showman to offer a prize of $12\frac{1}{2}$p for a score of 6 or more, or a prize of 25p for a score of 7 or more?

**6.** It can be assumed that, for a binomial system with a large number of trials, 95% of the outcomes will lie within two standard deviations of the mean. If I throw a die 1000 times, how many sixes ought to make me suspicious that the die is biased, if my suspicions are aroused by events with a probability of less than 0·05?

## 36. WORK AND ENERGY

**1.** A railway truck of mass 5 tonnes runs freely from rest down an incline of 1 in 100, 100 metres in length. Find an expression for the work done by the forces and calculate the final velocity.

**2.** A car starts to climb a hill of 1 in 10 (along the road) at a speed of 100 km/h. After 0·8 km against the incline, and with the engine giving a constant force to the wheels, the speed has dropped to 50 km/h. If the car and contents weigh 750 kg and the resistance to motion (except that due to gravity) amounts to a constant 600 N, find the force exerted by the wheels.

**3.** A projectile is fired vertically upwards at an initial speed of 3000 km/h. Neglecting atmospheric resistance, find how high the projectile rises assuming that the force of gravity is inversely proportional to the distance from the earth's centre. (Take the radius of the earth to be 6400 km.)

**4.** A body moves in a plane with variable velocity **v** and under the action of a variable force **F**. Write down expressions for (i) the power and (ii) the work done by the force **F** between times $t = 0$ and $t = T$.

A particle of mass $m$ moves under the influence of a force **F** given by

$$\mathbf{F} = \lambda \begin{pmatrix} \sin kt \\ \cos kt \end{pmatrix}$$

at time $t$, where $\lambda$ and $k$ are constants. At time $t = 0$, the particle is at rest. Obtain $v$ in terms of $m$, $\lambda$, $k$ and $t$ and show that the power is given by

$$\frac{\lambda^2}{mk} \sin kt.$$

Write down an expression for the work done on the particle by the force from time $t = 0$ to $t = T$ and show that this cannot exceed

$$\frac{2\lambda^2}{mk^2}.$$ 

(OC)

**5.** A truck of mass 2 tonnes moving with speed $u$ m/s collides and couples with a truck of mass 5 tonnes moving in the same straight line with speed $v$ m/s. Prove that, for any values of $u$ and $v$ for which collision is possible, there is necessarily a loss of kinetic energy.   (OC)

**6.** A bus can develop 120 kW. If the total resistance to motion when the bus is fully loaded at a total mass of 14 tonnes is 3500 N, calculate the maximum speed of the bus ($a$) on the level, ($b$) up an incline of 1 in 80.

# 37

## ELECTRICITY

### 1. THE MATHEMATICAL MODEL

Electricity is now so fundamental to our way of life that we take it for granted. We need understand nothing of its nature or properties to use electrical appliances, but each time we switch on a light or turn on the television we initiate physical phenomena which can be described very precisely by simple mathematical models. All electrical devices consist of components which are joined by wires into closed *circuits*. Many modern devices contain large numbers of components joined in complex patterns but in principle the same circuit mathematics is used to design them as to describe how a single battery and bulb are connected in a pocket torch.

In this chapter we develop the model without going into any physical detail about components or their properties. First we set up the basic laws and definitions, and explain the symbols and conventions used in drawing circuit diagrams.

**1.1 Ohm's law.** Electrical devices operate when current flows through them. Figure 1 shows a simple circuit with a battery, a lamp, and a switch.

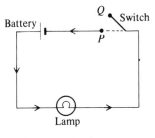

Fig. 1

Nothing happens until the two contacts $P$ and $Q$ of the switch are joined. Then, once the circuit is complete (i.e. closed), the battery pushes current $I$, measured in amperes (A), round the wires through the bulb. By convention, the current flows from the longer part of the battery symbol to the shorter. The electrical 'pushing force' (voltage) $V$ of a battery or any other source, such as the mains supply, is measured in

977

volts (V). All electrical devices resist the flow of current through them and this resistance $R$, a constant for each device, is measured in ohms ($\Omega$). In circuit diagrams, devices are represented by a standard *resistor* symbol —□—. It is assumed that all the resistance in the circuit is provided by such resistors and that the connecting wires have zero resistance.

There is an experimental law describing the relationship between the voltage $V$ V applied across a resistor of resistance $R$ $\Omega$ and the current $I$ A which flows. This is Ohm's law, which states that

$$V = IR$$

as long as the temperature of the resistor remains constant. Note that Ohm's law does not apply to all electrical devices; transistors, for example, do not obey it.

Using Ohm's law, the current $I_1$ flowing in the circuit of Figure 2($a$) is 1·5 A, while in the circuit of Figure 2($b$), where the resistance is halved, the current $I_2$ is twice as great (3 A).

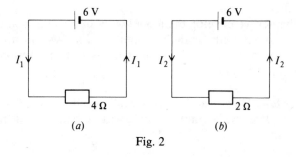

(a)                    (b)

Fig. 2

### Exercise A

**1.** ($a$) Find $I$ when $V = 12$ and (i) $R = 6$, (ii) $R = 2$, (iii) $R = 12$.

($b$) If $R = 20$, find $V$ to give a current of (i) 1 A, (ii) 5 A, (iii) 0·5 A. (See Figure 3.)

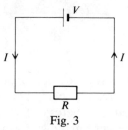

Fig. 3

**2.** When two light bulbs each of resistance 3 $\Omega$ are connected in series (see Figure 4), the light given by each is less than it would be if it was connected alone

978

to the same battery. In fact the combined resistance of resistors in series is the sum of their separate resistances. Find the current $I$ which flows through the two bulbs in Figure 4.

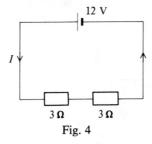

Fig. 4

**3.** Use the result for resistors in series quoted in Question 2 to find the currents in the circuits of Figure 5.

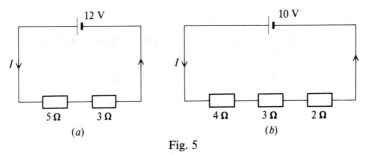

Fig. 5

**4.** What voltage would be required to 'push' 1·5 A through: (i) a resistor of 5 Ω (Figure 6(*a*)); (ii) a resistor of 3 Ω (Figure 6(*b*))?

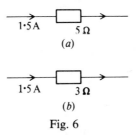

Fig. 6

How is the sum of your answers to parts (i) and (ii) related to the circuit in Figure 5(*a*)?

## 2. KIRCHHOFF'S LAWS

What happens when more than one resistor is connected to a battery? In Exercise A we used the fact (which can be checked experimentally) that two resistors in series behave as though they were a single equivalent

979

resistor, the resistance of which is the sum of the original resistors' resistances (Figure 7).

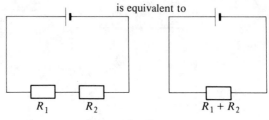

Fig. 7

A more complicated arrangement arises if two resistors are connected in parallel as in Figure 8.

*Example* 1

Calculate the currents $I$, $i_1$ and $i_2$ in the circuit shown in Figure 8.

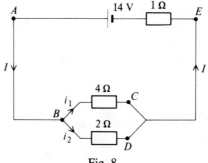

Fig. 8

If $I$ is the current flowing out of the battery, and $i_1$ and $i_2$ the currents in the branches, then we can verify experimentally that $I = i_1 + i_2$. This important rule is called *Kirchhoff's first law*: in words,

No current is lost at junctions.

To find the values of $i_1$ and $i_2$, we need another rule, namely *Kirchhoff's second law*:

The total battery voltage $V$ in any closed circuit is equal to the sum of the products of current and resistance $(I \times R)$ for each resistor in the circuit. That is,

$$V = \sum IR.$$

This is a generalization of Ohm's law: it applies to any closed circuit

980

within a larger circuit, and it deals with any number of resistors. It says in effect that Ohm's law can be applied additively to resistors in series in a closed circuit.

From Figure 8, consider the closed loop *ABCEA* (see Figure 9).

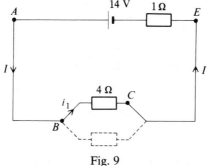

Fig. 9

In this loop the total battery voltage is 14 V, so by Kirchhoff's second law $14 = i_1 \times 4 + I \times 1$. Similarly, if we consider the closed loop *ABDEA*, the battery voltage is 14 V and the *IR* products total $i_2 \times 2 + I \times 1$, so $14 = 2i_2 + I$. Thus $i_1$, $i_2$ and $I$ satisfy the simultaneous equations

$$i_1 + i_2 = I,$$

$$14 = 4i_1 + I,$$

$$14 = 2i_2 + I.$$

Doubling the last equation and adding it to the middle one gives

$$42 = 4(i_1 + i_2) + 3I$$

$$\Rightarrow 42 = 7I \quad \text{or} \quad I = 6$$

whence                    $i_1 = 2 \quad \text{and} \quad i_2 = 4.$

The complete solution is illustrated in Figure 10.

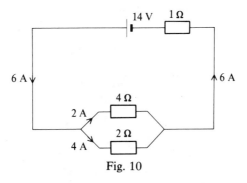

Fig. 10

We can also consider the closed loop *BCDB* (see Figure 11).

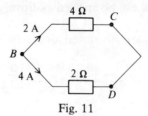

Fig. 11

If we follow the path *BCDB* clockwise, there are two *IR* terms:

$$2 \times 4 \quad \text{and} \quad -4 \times 2.$$

(The 4 A current is given a negative sign because it flows in the opposite direction.) By Kirchhoff's second law, $2 \times 4 + (-4 \times 2)$ should equal the total battery voltage $V$ in the circuit. Since there are no batteries in this circuit, $V$ is zero, and so our values for $i_1$ and $i_2$ have been confirmed.

### *Exercise B*

**1.** In the circuit of Figure 12, find the current through each resistor. What is the current flowing through the battery?

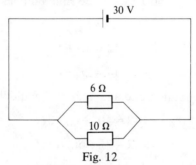

Fig. 12

**2.** If the pair of resistors in Question 1 is replaced by a single resistor, what must be its resistance if the same current flows through the battery?

**3.** (*a*) Find the total current *I* A flowing through the circuit in Figure 13.
(*b*) What single resistor will have the same effect as the set of three?

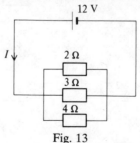

Fig. 13

982

**4.** (*a*) Find the current through each resistor in the circuit in Figure 14.
(*b*) What would happen if the switch at *A* were closed?

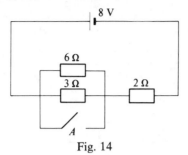

Fig. 14

**5.** Show that, if two resistors of $R_1 \, \Omega$ and $R_2 \, \Omega$ are connected in parallel, then they are equivalent to a single resistor $R\Omega$ where

$$\frac{1}{R} = \frac{1}{R_1} + \frac{1}{R_2}$$

(see Figure 15).

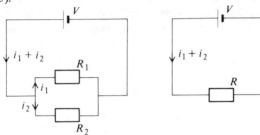

Fig. 15

**6.** Find the single resistor which is equivalent to each of the following sets of parallel resistors.
(*a*) 12 $\Omega$ and 36 $\Omega$;
(*b*) 0·5 $\Omega$ and 1 $\Omega$;
(*c*) 4 $\Omega$ and 6 $\Omega$;
(*d*) 5 $\Omega$, 10 $\Omega$ and 30 $\Omega$;
(*e*) 4 $\Omega$, 5 $\Omega$, 40 $\Omega$ and 40 $\Omega$.

**7.** Simplify the circuit in Figure 16 by finding the single resistor equivalent to the three resistors. Hence calculate the total current *I* A.

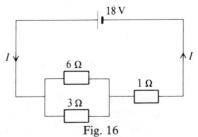

Fig. 16

983

**8.** Work out the total current $I$ A flowing in the circuit shown in Figure 17.

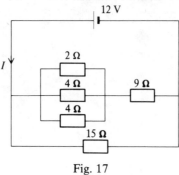

Fig. 17

## 3. MORE COMPLICATED CIRCUITS

**3.1**   It is not always the case that the resistors in a circuit are either in series or in parallel. In such situations, it is not possible to simplify the circuit, and we have to go back and work from first principles. The following examples illustrate such problems and their solution.

*Example* 2

Find the currents in each part of the circuit in Figure 18.

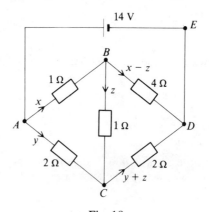

Fig. 18

Denote the currents in *AB*, *AC*, *BC* by $x$A, $y$A, $z$A respectively. Then, using Kirchhoff's first law at junctions *B* and *C*, the current in *BD* must be $x - z$ and that in *CD* must be $y + z$.

We have three unknown variables, and so require three independent equations for their solution. We shall obtain these equations from three

984

closed circuits: (i) clockwise round $ABCA$; (ii) clockwise round $BDCB$; (iii) anticlockwise round $ABDEA$. Applying Kirchhoff's second law:

(i)             $1x + 1z + 2(-y) = 0 \quad \Rightarrow \quad x - 2y + z = 0$;

(ii) $4(x - z) + 2[-(y + z)] + 1(-z) = 0 \quad \Rightarrow \quad 4x - 2y - 7z = 0$;

(iii)           $1x + 4(x - z) = 14 \quad \Rightarrow \quad 5x - 4z = 14$.

Subtracting equation (i) from (ii) we get ,

$$3x - 8z = 0,$$

which, with equation (iii), gives

$$x = 4 \quad \text{and} \quad z = 1\tfrac{1}{2}.$$

Substitution then gives $\qquad\qquad y = 2\tfrac{3}{4}.$

To solve this example, we used the three circuits $ABCA$, $BDCB$ and $ABDEA$. How many other closed circuits are there? Write down all those you can find, and use Kirchhoff's second law to write down the corresponding linear equations in $x$, $y$ and $z$. Explain why your equations are not all independent (consider for example $ABC$, $BDC$ and $ABDC$). How many independent equations are there?

**3.2 Potential difference.** So far our model of current electricity has been one where current flows round closed circuits, driven by a battery. We now need to focus on parts of a closed circuit rather than the whole.

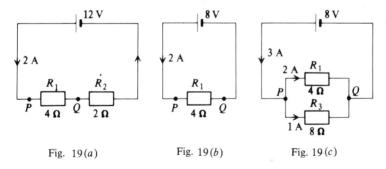

Fig. 19(a)          Fig. 19(b)          Fig. 19(c)

In Figure 19(a), (b) and (c) the resistor $R_1$ has been connected into three different circuits but in each, the same current flows through it. If we just focus on $R_1$, we see a current of 2 A

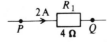

Fig. 19(d)

985

being driven through 4 Ω between the two terminals $P$ and $Q$. This current would be driven by 8 V in the simplest circuit with just a battery across $R_1$ (Figure 19($b$)). We say that the *potential difference* (p.d.) across $R_1$ is 8 V.

To generalize this idea, we restate Ohm's law.

The potential difference $V$ V across a resistor of resistance $R$ Ω when a current $I$ A flows through it is given by

$$V = IR.$$

Similarly, Kirchhoff's second law can be restated in terms of potential differences:

The algebraic sum of the potential differences round a closed circuit equals the total battery voltage in the circuit.

Notice that in Figure 19($a$) the potential difference across resistor $R_2$ is 4 V (as is required by Kirchhoff's second law), and in Figure 19($c$) the potential difference across $R_3$ is the same as that across $R_1$ because the resistors have common terminals.

**3.3 Potential differences within a circuit.** If the potential difference $V$ volts between two points in a circuit is known, the potential differences across each component along any path between those two points must add up to $V$ volts. For example, in Figure 20 (from Example 2), the potential difference between $E$ and $F$ is 14 V.

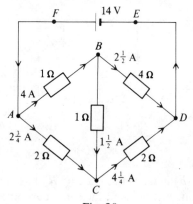

Fig. 20

Taking the path $FABDE$, there is a potential difference of $4 \times 1 = 4$ V across $AB$ and a further $4 \times 2\frac{1}{2} = 10$ V across $BD$; total 14 V. Again, taking the path $FABCDE$, there is a potential difference of 4 V across $AB$, $1\frac{1}{2}$ V across $BC$ and $8\frac{1}{2}$ V across $CD$; total 14 V.

986

**3.4 Potential.** It is not unusual to speak of the *potential at a point* of a circuit. This is the potential difference between that point and some arbitrary zero which is called *earth* whose circuit symbol is ⏚.

*Example* 3

In the electrical network in Figure 21, $A$, $B$ and $C$ are maintained at potentials 10 V, 7 V and 2 V respectively. Find the currents through the resistors.

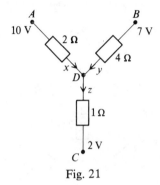

Fig. 21

Clearly this network is part of a much larger one, and the potentials at $A$, $B$ and $C$ are provided by batteries not shown. Connecting wires complete the circuits so that the currents flow.

Denote the currents in $AD$, $BD$ and $DC$ by $x$ A, $y$ A, $z$ A respectively. The potential difference between $A$ and $B$ is 3 V. Following the path $ADB$ we obtain

(i) $$2x + (-4)y = 3.$$

Similarly for $ADC$

(ii) $$2x + z = 8.$$

But for the currents at junction $D$

(iii) $$x + y = z.$$

Substituting for $z$ in (ii),

(iv) $$3x + y = 8.$$

Elimination between (i) and (iv) then gives

$$x = 2\tfrac{1}{2}, \quad y = \tfrac{1}{2}, \quad z = 3.$$

**3.5 Matrix methods.** We have seen that finding the currents flowing in various branches of an electrical network is a matter of applying

Kirchhoff's laws and then solving a set of linear equations. Clearly all the ideas of earlier chapters on linear equations will be relevant. In particular the matrix methods of Chapter 26 provide the basis for a routine which is essential for more complicated circuits.

Matrix methods of solution are developed fully in the SMP Further Mathematics course.

### *Exercise C*

**1.** Calculate the currents $x$ A, $y$ A and $z$ A shown in the circuit in Figure 22.

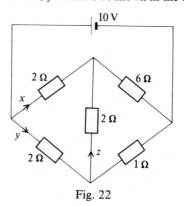

Fig. 22

**2.** Calculate the currents $x$ A, $y$ A and $z$ A shown in the circuit of Figure 23.

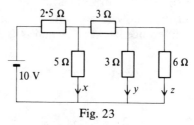

Fig. 23

**3.** In the circuit shown in Figure 24, a total current of 1 A flows in at $P$ and out at $Q$. Currents $x$ A, $y$ A and $z$ A flow through the resistors indicated. Work out the values of $x$, $y$ and $z$.

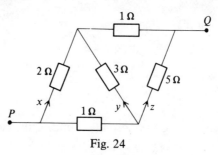

Fig. 24

**4.** In the electrical network in Figure 25 the terminals $A$, $B$, $C$ are maintained at potentials 6 V, 12 V, 0 V respectively. Calculate the currents $x$ A, $y$ A and $z$ A through the resistors.

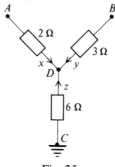

Fig. 25

**5.** A current of 10 A flows into the circuit of Figure 26 at $A$ and out at $B$. Find the currents $x$ A, $y$ A and $z$ A. Calculate the potential difference between $A$ and $B$ and hence find the resistance of the single resistor which is equivalent to the whole circuit.

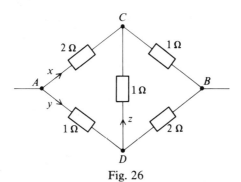

Fig. 26

**6.** Find the resistance $R$ Ω of the single resistor equivalent to the circuit of Figure 26 by carrying out these instructions: following the path $ACB$, write down the total potential difference between $A$ and $B$ in terms of $x$ and $z$. Now follow the paths $ADB$ and $ACDB$ to obtain two more expressions in terms of $x$, $y$ and $z$ for the potential difference between $A$ and $B$. By equating these expressions, express $y$ and $z$ in terms of $x$. Hence write down the potential difference across $AB$ and the total current $(x + y)$ A through the circuit in terms of $x$ alone. Then find $R$ using Ohm's law.

**7.** Find the currents $x$ A and $y$ A shown in Figure 27 when the switch $S$ is open. What is then the potential difference between $A$ and $B$? What is the effect of closing $S$?

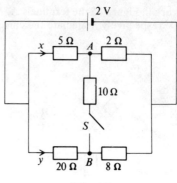

Fig. 27

**8.** Find $i_1$, $i_2$ and $i_3$ in Figure 28 by applying Kirchhoff's second law to circuits *ABEF* and *DCEF*.

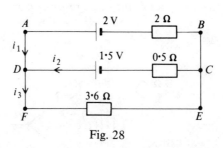

Fig. 28

**9.** Find the currents $x$ A, $y$ A and $z$ A in the circuit of Figure 29.

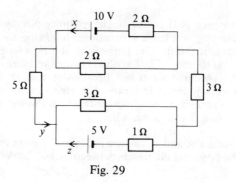

Fig. 29

990

**10.** Find the resistance of resistor $P$ if no current flows through $R$ (Figure 30).

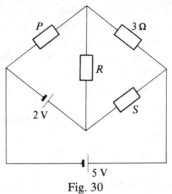

Fig. 30

## 4. THE MODEL EXTENDED

**4.1 Internal resistance.** We have assumed that the capability of a battery to drive current round a circuit is independent of the rest of the circuit. This turns out to be an oversimplification in practice because a battery always has a small *internal resistance* which we have previously ignored. It behaves like an ideal battery with a resistance $r\ \Omega$ in series (see Figure 31, where what we have previously shown by the single battery symbol —⊢ is enclosed by the dotted line). So when the battery is connected in a circuit with an external resistance $R\ \Omega$, the current it can drive through $R$ is reduced: i.e.

$$V = Ir + IR,$$

so

$$I = \frac{V}{R+r}.$$

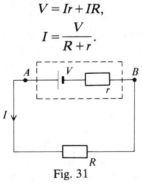

Fig. 31

In other words, the potential difference between the battery terminals $A$ and $B$, which is

$$IR = \frac{VR}{R+r},$$

will vary according to the value of the external resistance $R$ (and when $R$ is *small* compared with $r$, the potential difference will be very much less than the voltage written on the battery label).

991

**4.2 Electrical energy and power.** Energy comes in many forms, most of which are directly or indirectly interchangeable. Light and heat, kinetic, electrical, atomic and chemical energies are but a few forms. *Electrical energy* is important because of the ease with which it is carried; it is then changed into useful work when we switch on an electric fire, a washing machine, a refrigerator, or a light. Originally, this electrical energy may have been produced by a battery, which turns chemical energy directly into electrical energy, or at a power station, where chemical or atomic energy is transformed into heat, which is converted into kinetic and then into electrical energy. In hydroelectric systems, the kinetic energy of falling water is changed directly into electrical energy.

We measure the various kinds of energy in terms of their mechanical equivalents. Mechanical energy is easily measured: when a force moves the body to which it is applied, energy is expended which is proportional to the force, and to the distance the body moves in the direction in which the force is being applied. The energy expended when 1 newton moves through 1 metre is called 1 joule, as we saw in Chapter 36. However, electrical *energy* is not usually measured as such; we are more interested in *power*, which is the *rate of consuming energy*, or rate of doing work. The units of power are joules per second, or *watts* (W).

The units of electricity have been defined so that if a current of $I$ A flows through an appliance across which there is a potential difference of $V$ V, then the appliance consumes power $P = IV$ W.

In Example 1, the 14 V battery supplied a current of 6 A, thereby supplying power of 6 A × 14 V = 84 W. Of this total, the 1 Ω resistor was consuming 6 A × 6 V = 36 W. Work out the power consumed by the other two resistors, and check that the total power consumed is equal to the total power being supplied. This power would appear in the form of heat. The power consumed by an electric radiator is much greater (several kilowatts, i.e. thousands of watts), and the heat and light produced are evident.

Combination of the two formulae $V = IR$ and $P = IV$ gives two useful variations: $P = I^2R$ and $P = V^2/R$. With these formulae great care must be taken to use the appropriate currents and potential differences, i.e. those relevant to the component under consideration.

*Example* 4

A 12 V battery of internal resistance 2 Ω is connected to two resistors as in Figure 32. What power is consumed by the 24 Ω resistor if the switch at C is (*a*) open, and (*b*) closed?

992

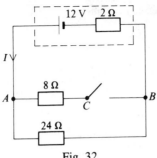

Fig. 32

(a)
$$I = \frac{12}{(2+24)} = 0 \cdot 46.$$

Power consumed in the 24 $\Omega$ resistor is $I^2 R$ watts

$$= (0 \cdot 46)^2 \times 24 = 5 \cdot 1 \text{ W}.$$

(b) The two resistors are equivalent to a single resistor of $R$ $\Omega$ where

$$\frac{1}{R} = \frac{1}{8} + \frac{1}{24} = \frac{1}{6} \Rightarrow R = 6.$$

The total current is now

$$I = \frac{12}{(2+6)} = 1 \cdot 5$$

and

$$V_{AB} = 1 \cdot 5 \times 6$$
$$= 9.$$

Power consumed in the 24 $\Omega$ resistor is $V^2/R$ watts

$$= 9^2/24$$
$$= 3 \cdot 4 \text{ W}.$$

This demonstrates (though the figures are not realistic) why car lights become dimmer while the self-starter is being operated. Note that if there were no internal resistance, the power in each case would be $12^2/24$ W, that is, 6 W.


### Exercise D

**1.** A 12 V battery of internal resistance 1 $\Omega$ is connected to a 5 $\Omega$ resistor as in Figure 31. What current flows and what is the potential difference across the battery terminals $A$ and $B$?

**2.** A 12 V battery of internal resistance 1 Ω is connected as shown in Figure 33. Calculate the current through each resistor and the potential difference across the battery terminals $A$ and $B$.

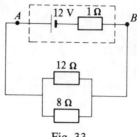

Fig. 33

**3.** When a battery is connected to a 7 Ω resistor, a current of 0·2 A flows. When a 5 Ω resistor is added in series, the current is reduced to 0·12 A. Find the voltage and internal resistance of the battery.

**4.** When a potential difference of $V$ V is applied to a resistor of $R$ Ω, a current of $I$ A flows. Find the power dissipated in the resistor if:

(a) $I = 5$, $V = 200$;  (b) $I = 3$, $R = 7$;  (c) $V = 230$, $R = 20$.

**5.** A 1 kW electric radiator is designed for use with 230 V mains. Find the resistance of the element. One day, the mains voltage drops, and the current through the element drops to 4 A. If the resistance of the element is then 5% less than before, what power does the fire now consume?

**6.** A 2 V battery with internal resistance 2 Ω is connected to two 30 Ω resistors in parallel. Find the power dissipated in each.

**7.** A battery of $E$ V and internal resistance $r$ Ω supplies current to an $R$ Ω resistor. Find expressions for the total power supplied by the battery, and the power dissipated in the external resistor.

**8.** If $P$ W is the power developed in the $R$ Ω resistor of the circuit shown in Figure 34, complete the following table, and draw the graph of $P$ against $R$.

$R$: 0  6  12  18  24  36
$P$:

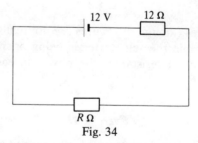

Fig. 34

**9.** In Question 8 find a formula for $P$ in terms of $R$, and then find by differentiation the value of $R$ for which $P$ is a maximum.

**10.** Two 2 V batteries of internal resistance 1 Ω are connected in parallel to a resistor of $R$ Ω (see Figure 35). What value of $R$ makes the power consumed in it a maximum?

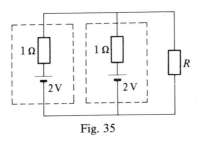

Fig. 35

## 5. ALTERNATING CURRENT

So far we have considered currents of constant magnitude flowing in one direction round a circuit. They are called *direct currents* (d.c.). The domestic electricity supply has a voltage which varies with time as shown in Figure 36(*a*). As a function of time,

$$v = V_0 \sin 100\pi t$$

where $V_0$ is the peak value of amplitude. This alternating voltage $v$ causes an *alternating current* (a.c.) $i$ which flows first in one direction and then in the other (see Figure 36(*b*)). The frequency is 50 cycles per second (or 50 hertz) which means that one complete cycle takes $\frac{1}{50}$ s; check that when $t = \frac{1}{50}$, $100\pi t = 2\pi$. In electronic circuits (in radio and television equipment, for instance), alternating voltages with much higher frequencies are used. In general, $v = V_0 \sin 2\pi ft$, where $f$ is the frequency.

Ohm's law still holds at any instant. As a result, when an alternating voltage is applied to a resistor, an alternating current flows, having the same frequency as the voltage and being *in phase* with it (see Figure 36). This means that the peaks occur simultaneously: $V_0 = I_0 R$.

It follows that an alternating voltage applied to the network of Figure 18, for instance, causes alternating currents of different strengths through the various resistors, and these are all in phase with the applied voltage. Their peak values are found by setting up and solving precisely the equations used in Example 2, since they are based on Kirchhoff's laws which apply *at any instant* in the alternating current case. When alternating voltages are applied to networks of resistors we can work out the currents in the various parts of the circuit by the same procedures as in the direct current problems.

995

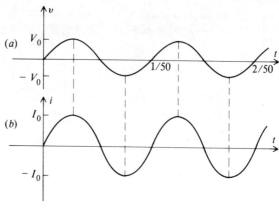

Fig. 36

**5.1  Inductance.** We must now consider another aspect of our network problems which has so far been ignored. All the components have been resistors, whereas in practice other types of component will usually feature as well. In this section we introduce inductors.

When a current flows in a coil of wire, a magnetic field is set up. The forces resulting from such a field make it possible to design an electric motor. Also, a *changing* magnetic field causes a voltage in the coil, called an *induced electro-motive force* (e.m.f.). Notice that when a constant current flows, there is no induced e.m.f.

The size of the induced e.m.f. $e_L$ is a function of the rate of change of current. We shall be concerned only with coils for which this function is linear. Then

$$e_L \propto \frac{di}{dt},$$

and we can write

$$e_L = -L\frac{di}{dt}.$$

$L$ is a positive constant and is called the *inductance* of the coil (an *inductor*). The minus sign indicates the fact that the induced e.m.f. opposes the change of current. If the current is increasing, $di/dt$ is positive, and the induced voltage opposes the applied voltage; when the current is falling, the situation is reversed. We use the symbol $e_L$ for the induced e.m.f. to avoid confusion with the constant $e$.

The value of $L$ depends upon the size and shape of the coil, and is approximately proportional to the number of turns of wire in the coil, provided it is closely wound.

996

The unit in which $L$ is measured (a henry) is determined by the defining equation, $e_L = -L\dfrac{di}{dt}$. So

$$1 \text{ henry} = 1 \text{ volt second/ampere}.$$

This is too large a unit to use in practice: most coils have inductance of a few millihenries (mH).

Figure 37 shows an alternating voltage $v$ volts applied to two separate components in series. The left-hand one (note the circuit symbol) is assumed to have inductance $L$ henries and negligible resistance; we call it an *inductor*. Similarly, it is assumed that the resistor is non-inductive.

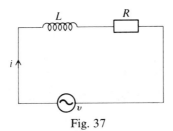

Fig. 37

Suppose that $L = 3$, $R = 5$ and there is a current of $i = 6 \sin 2t$. Then the induced e.m.f. will be

$$e_L = -L\frac{di}{dt} = -3 \times 12 \cos 2t = -36 \cos 2t.$$

This reduces the voltage available to drive current through the resistor to

$$v - 36 \cos 2t.$$

Ohm's law for the resistor gives

$$v - 36 \cos 2t = 5 \times 6 \sin 2t,$$

or
$$v = 30 \sin 2t + 36 \cos 2t.$$

Can you describe fully the graph of $v$, the applied voltage? We saw in Chapter 25 that it is a sine wave of amplitude $\sqrt{(30^2 + 36^2)}$, with the same period as the current wave but with its peaks at different instants. In fact the voltage wave is said to be *out of phase* with the current wave. Calculate the phase difference $\varepsilon$ marked in Figure 38.

Now we usually consider this circuit from the opposite point of view—given a particular applied alternating voltage, what will be the resulting current? Suppose the applied voltage is given by $v = 7 \sin 10t$, and $L = 3$ and $R = 5$ still. What will be the amplitude of the current?

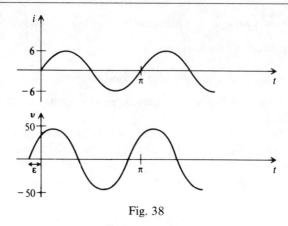

Fig. 38

Working as above, with $i = A \sin 10t + B \cos 10t$, we have

$$iR = 5A \sin 10t + 5B \cos 10t,$$

$$L\frac{di}{dt} = 30A \cos 10t - 30B \sin 10t,$$

and hence the applied voltage is

$$iR + L\frac{di}{dt} = (5A - 30B) \sin 10t + (30A + 5B) \cos 10t.$$

This comes to exactly $7 \sin 10t$ if

$$\begin{cases} 5A - 30B = 7, \\ 30A + 5B = 0. \end{cases}$$

Solve the simultaneous equations, and find the current $i$.

## 6. VECTOR AND COMPLEX NUMBER METHODS

We saw in Chapter 25 how vector ideas can be helpful with expressions of the form $a \sin \omega t + b \cos \omega t$, where $\omega$ is a fixed number, and in Chapter 32 how vectors in a plane and complex numbers have certain properties in common. We now link these two developments and find that complex numbers provide a useful vehicle for tackling some a.c. problems.

The idea is to set up one–one correspondences

$$a \sin \omega t + b \cos \omega t \iff \begin{pmatrix} a \\ b \end{pmatrix} \iff a + bj.$$

### Exercise E

**1.** Show that the one–one correspondence $a \sin \omega t + b \cos \omega t \Leftrightarrow a + bj$ is an isomorphism under addition.

**2.** What is the amplitude of $a \sin \omega t + b \cos \omega t$? What is the modulus of $a + bj$?

**3.** To what complex number does $r \sin(\omega t + \varepsilon)$ correspond? What is its modulus?

**4.** What is the name given to the property of a complex number corresponding to the phase angle of a wave?

**5.** If $i = a \sin \omega t + b \cos \omega t$ and $a = 2$, $b = 3$, $\omega = 1$, $R = 1 \cdot 5$, $L = 2 \cdot 5$, show on a single Argand diagram the complex numbers representing $i$, $di/dt$, $iR$, $L\, di/dt$.

**6.** Explain why rotation through $\frac{1}{2}\pi$ on the Argand diagram corresponds to multiplying by $j$, and hence why $L\, di/dt$ is represented by $L\omega jz$ if $i$ is represented by $z$.

**7.** Show that the modulus of the complex number coresponding to $iR + L\, di/dt$ is $\sqrt{(R^2 + L^2 \omega^2)}|z|$.

### 6.1 Summary and worked examples.

| *Waves* | *Complex numbers* |
|---|---|
| $i = a \sin \omega t + b \cos \omega t$ | $z = a + bj$ |
| $(a \sin \omega t + b \cos \omega t)$ $+ (c \sin \omega t + d \cos \omega t)$ $= (a + c)\sin \omega t + (b + d)\cos \omega t$ | $(a + bj) + (c + dj)$ $= (a + c) + (b + d)j$ |
| Amplitude $= \sqrt{(a^2 + b^2)}$ | Modulus $= \sqrt{(a^2 + b^2)}$ |
| $a \sin \omega t + b \cos \omega t$ $= r \sin(\omega t + \varepsilon)$ | $a + bj = r(\cos \theta + j \sin \theta)$ |
| where $r = \sqrt{(a^2 + b^2)}$, | where $r = \sqrt{(a^2 + b^2)}$, |
| $\sin \varepsilon = \dfrac{b}{\sqrt{(a^2 + b^2)}}$, | $\sin \theta = \dfrac{b}{\sqrt{(a^2 + b^2)}}$, |
| $\cos \varepsilon = \dfrac{a}{\sqrt{(a^2 + b^2)}}$, | $\cos \theta = \dfrac{a}{\sqrt{(a^2 + b^2)}}$, |
| $\varepsilon = $ phase of $i$, | $\theta = $ argument of $z$, |
| $\dfrac{di}{dt} = a\omega \cos \omega t - b\omega \sin \omega t.$ | $-b\omega + a\omega j = \omega j(a + bj) = \omega jz.$ |

Look carefully through the table above, which summarizes what you might have found while working through Exercise E. The reason why complex number methods prove so useful is indicated in the last line where differentiation is seen to correspond to an unexpectedly simple process—multiplication by $\omega j$.

We illustrate with the example started in Section 5.1 (see Figure 39).

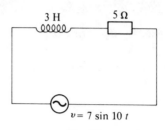

$$v = 7 \sin 10\,t$$

Fig. 39

Let the complex number $z$ correspond to the current (represented in Section 5.1 as $i = A \sin 10t + B \cos 10t$). Then the voltage across the resistor is represented by $5z$ and the voltage across the inductor is represented by $3 \times 10jz = 30jz$. The total voltage is then represented by $(5 + 30j)z$, and this is 7. Hence

$$z = \frac{7}{5+30j} = \frac{7(5-30j)}{(5+30j)(5-30j)} = \frac{7}{185} - \frac{42}{185}j,$$

corresponding to a current

$$\frac{7}{185} \sin 10t - \frac{42}{185} \cos 10t.$$

The amplitude of the current is

$$|z| = \frac{7}{|5+30j|} = \frac{7}{\sqrt{925}}.$$

Check with the values you found in Section 5.1.

Complex numbers here fulfil a role which we find repeated in diverse ways in many branches of applied mathematics. They are an artificial tool which acts as a catalyst in producing real solutions to real problems.

*Example 5*

Find the amplitudes of the alternating currents in each part of the circuit of Figure 40.

We can use Kirchhoff's laws much as in Example 2, treating the inductors as resistors with complex resistances (called *impedances*). For example, 2 henries is treated as $2\omega j$ ohms, here $8j$ ohms since $\omega = 4$, and similarly $v = 3 \cos 4t$ is treated as $3j$ volts.

1000

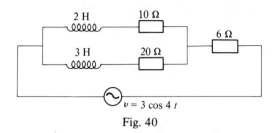

Fig. 40

It pays to show arrows with the currents (see Figure 41) although each current flows first in one direction and then in the other. If arrows are not shown, it is easy to make mistakes with Kirchhoff's first law in more complicated examples.

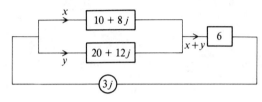

Fig. 41

From Kirchhoff's second law,

$$(10+8j)x+6(x+y)=3j,$$

$$(20+12j)y+6(x+y)=3j,$$

giving
$$(16+8j)x+6y=3j, \tag{1}$$

$$6x+(26+12j)y=3j. \tag{2}$$

Solve in the usual way; multiply (1) by $(13+6j)$ and (2) by 3.

$$(160+200j)x+(78+36j)y=-18+39j,$$

$$18x+(78+36j)y=9j.$$

Subtracting,

$$(142+200j)x=-18+30j,$$

thus
$$x=\frac{-18+30j}{142+200j}.$$

Start again, multiplying (1) by 3 and (2) by $(8+4j)$:

$$(48+24j)x+18y=9j,$$

$$(48+24j)x+(160+200j)y=-12+24j.$$

1001

Subtracting, $(142+200j)y = -12+15j$,

so
$$y = \frac{-12+15j}{142+200j}.$$

Finally,
$$|x| = \frac{|-18+30j|}{|142+200j|} \approx 0\cdot14$$

and
$$|y| = \frac{|-12j+15j|}{|142+200j|} \approx 0\cdot078.$$

**6.2 Capacitors.** We have seen complex numbers of the form $a+bj$ used for the impedance of a resistor and an inductor in series. It is also possible to use $a-bj$ for a series circuit; in such a case we should be dealing with a resistor and a third component called a *capacitor* (see also Chapter 38).

### *Exercise F*

**1.** An inductor has resistance 10 ohms and inductance 0·04 henries. Find its complex impedance when connected to a supply with voltage (*a*) $v = 50 \sin 40t$, (*b*) $v = 50 \sin 400t$. Find the current in each case.

**2.** A circuit contains two inductors in series with impedances $100+0\cdot1\omega j$, $50+0\cdot3\omega j$. Find the amplitude of the current and the potential difference for each component if the supply has 300 volt peak value and frequency 50 hertz.

**3.** Use the formula for resistors in parallel (see Exercise B, Question 5) to find the single impedance equivalent to impedances of $10+8j$ and $20+12j$ in parallel. Hence check Example 5.

**4.** (*a*) Solve
$$(4+j)x + (3-2j)y = 1+5j,$$
$$2jx + (5+6j)y = 3.$$

 (*b*) Solve
$$(2+j)x + (5+3j)y + jz = 2+4j,$$
$$x + (1+5j)y + (2+3j)z = 1+j,$$
$$3jy + (2+j)z = 4.$$

**5.** Find the amplitude of the current $I$ in the circuit shown in Figure 42.

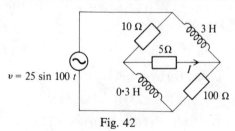

$v = 25 \sin 100\,t$

$10\,\Omega$  $3\,H$  $5\,\Omega$  $I$  $0\cdot3\,H$  $100\,\Omega$

Fig. 42

**6.** Find the applied voltage $v$ and the current $I$ in the circuit shown in Figure 43.

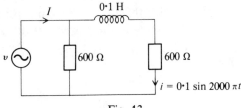

0·1 H

$v$    600 Ω    600 Ω

$i = 0{\cdot}1 \sin 2000\,\pi t$

Fig. 43

**7.** Find the potential difference across the terminals marked $A$, $B$ in Figure 44.

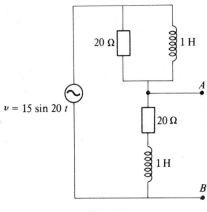

20 Ω    1 H

$v = 15 \sin 20\,t$

$A$

20 Ω

1 H

$B$

Fig. 44

# SUMMARY

*Potential difference*

The potential difference across a resistor is the product $IR$ of its resistance $R$ and the current $I$ flowing through it.

*Ohm's law*

$$V = IR.$$

*Kirchhoff's first law*

No current is lost or gained at junctions.

*Kirchhoff's second law*

The algebraic sum of the potential differences round a closed circuit equals the total battery voltage in the circuit.

*Power*

For a current $I$ amperes flowing through an $R$ ohm resistor which has a potential difference $V$ volts across it, the power $P$ watts is

$$P = IV = I^2R = V^2/R.$$

*Inductance*

$$e_L = -L\frac{di}{dt}.$$

# 38

# DIFFERENTIAL EQUATIONS: METHODS AND APPLICATIONS

## 1. INTRODUCTION

In Chapter 33 we saw how to sketch the family of solution curves for any differential equation of the first order. We also saw how to solve such equations numerically.

Sometimes we can go further. In this chapter we concentrate on a few categories of differential equations for each of which we can find a *complete* solution in the form of an equation for the whole family of solution curves.

In essence, all the methods of this chapter involve integration carried out on the basis of our experience of differentiation. Sketching the family of solution curves is often a great help in recognizing the equation for the family.

*Example* 1

Sketch some members of the family of solution curves for the differential equation $dy/dx = -x/y$ $(y>0)$. Verify by differentiation that the equation for the family is $x^2 + y^2 = a^2$ $(y>0)$.

From the differential equation, we can see that the gradient is zero when $x$ is zero, negative in the quadrant where $x$ and $y$ have the same sign, and positive in the other quadrant.

Calculation of some compass-needle gradients and consideration of symmetry gives us the sketch shown in Figure 1. Do you recognize this family?

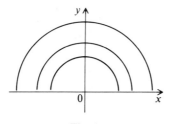

Fig. 1

If $x^2 + y^2 = a^2$, and $y > 0$, then $y = +\sqrt{(a^2 - x^2)} = +(a^2 - x^2)^{\frac{1}{2}}$. So

$$\frac{dy}{dx} = -2x \cdot \tfrac{1}{2}(a^2 - x^2)^{-\frac{1}{2}}$$

$$= \frac{-x}{\sqrt{(a^2 - x^2)}} = \frac{-x}{y}.$$

Show that the family of semicircles given by $x^2 + y^2 = a^2$ ($y < 0$) also gives rise to the same differential equation.

### Exercise A

Sketch the family of solution curves for each of the following differential equations (in some cases you will need to use the compass-needle method, in others the general shape is clear). Write down the equation of any family which you recognise and check your answers by differentiation.

1. $\dfrac{dy}{dx} = 2x$.  2. $\dfrac{dy}{dx} = \dfrac{3}{y}$.  3. $\dfrac{dy}{dx} = y$.

4. $\dfrac{dy}{dx} = \dfrac{2}{x}$.  5. $\dfrac{dy}{dx} = x^2$.  6. $\dfrac{dy}{dx} = y - 2$.

7. $\dfrac{dy}{dx} = \dfrac{-y}{x}$.  8. $\dfrac{dy}{dx} = \dfrac{-1}{x^2}$.  9. $\dfrac{dy}{dx} = \dfrac{2}{1 + x^2}$.

10. $\dfrac{dy}{dx} = \dfrac{y}{x}$.

## 2. SOLUTION BY INTEGRATION

**2.1 Equations of the form $dy/dx = f(x)$.** In Figure 2 we show the family given by $dy/dx = 2x$ (see Exercise A, Question 1). It is easy to see by direct integration that the equation of this family is $y = x^2 + c$.

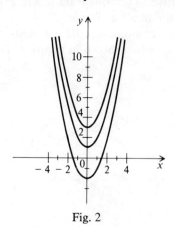

Fig. 2

Similarly the family given by $dy/dx = 2/x$ (Exercise A, Question 4) is found by integration to be $y = 2 \ln |x| + c$.

Clearly when $dy/dx$ is expressed as a function of $x$ only, as in these examples, the family can be obtained by direct integration of that function. Which of the other questions in Exercise A come into this category? To carry out the integration it may be necessary to use some of the techniques summarized in Chapter 20 or Chapter 29.

**2.2   Boundary conditions.** We saw in Chapter 33 that for first-order equations there will be exactly one member of a family of solution curves through any given point of the plane (unless the value of $dy/dx$ is undefined). So far we have been concerned with *general solutions*: equations with no definite value for the constant of integration $c$. But each value of $c$ specifies a distinct member of the family; by choosing the appropriate value we can find the curve (which is then called the *particular solution*) through any particular point.

For example, the member of the family of parabolas in Figure 2 which passes through the point (2, 3) is $y = x^2 - 1$, given by $c = -1$. Write down the equation of the member through $(-2, -1)$.

The condition that a solution should pass through a particular point is often called a *boundary condition* (or *initial condition* when it involves $t = 0$).

Notice that each member of the family of solution curves for a differential equation of the form $dy/dx = f(x)$ can be mapped onto any other by a translation parallel to the $y$-axis.

### Exercise B

**1.** Give the general solution for each of the following:

(a) $\dfrac{dy}{dx} = \cos x$;        (b) $\dfrac{dy}{dx} = x\sqrt{(x^2 + 7)}$;        (c) $\dfrac{dy}{dx} = \dfrac{1}{(9 + x^2)}$;

(d) $\dfrac{dy}{dx} = x^2(x^3 + 5)^4$;        (e) $\dfrac{dx}{dt} = \dfrac{1}{\sqrt{t}}$;        (f) $\dfrac{dv}{dt} = \sec^2 t$.

**2.** Give the general solution for each of the following differential equations:
  (a) $dy/dt = 2t/(t^2 + 3)$;        (b) $dy/dx = x^2/(x^3 + 5)$;
  (c) $(x + 3) dy/dx = 2x$;        (d) $(t + 3/t) dx/dt - 2 = 0$.

**3.** Solve the following differential equations and sketch the family:
  (a) $dy/dx = e^x$;        (b) $x^2 dy/dx + 1 = 0$;
  (c) $dy/dx = 1/x$.

**4.** For each of the following, find (i) the general solution and (ii) the particular solution satisfying the given boundary condition:
  (a) $dy/dx = 4x + 1$, for $y = 5$ when $x = 1$;
  (b) $dy/dx = x + \sin x$, for $y = 4$ when $x = 0$.

**5.** Find the solution of $dy/dt = (4+t)/5t^2$ if $y = 3$ when $t = 1$.

**6.** Given that $dy/dx + 7x = x^4$ and that $y = 2$ when $x = 3$, find the value of $y$ when $x = 5$.

**7.** A can of water is being heated at a rate which is decreasing steadily with time. The temperature $\theta$ °C after $t$ min satisfies the differential equation

$$d\theta/dt = 8 - 4t/3.$$

Find $\theta$ when $t = 4$ if $\theta = 32$ initially.
   Do you think the model will still be valid at time $t = 10$?

**8.** Here are some ways in which the depth $y$ cm of water in a swimming bath might vary with time $t$ hours. In each case take the initial depth to be 150 cm ($y = 150$ when $t = 0$). Sketch the $t \to y$ graph, solve the differential equation and compare the depths after 5 days ($t = 120$).
   (*a*) $dy/dt = 50/(t+10)^2$;     (*b*) $dy/dt = 0.3 + 0.2 \cos(\pi t/60)$;
   (*c*) $dy/dt = 1 - 0.5\, e^{t/200}$.

**9.** Find the general solutions to (*a*) $dy/dx = 1/x$, and (*b*) $dy/dx = -x$. Sketch some members of both families on the same graph. At what angle do the members of one family meet members of the other?

**2.3   Equations of the form $dy/dx = g(y)$.** In Figure 3 we show the family given by $dy/dx = 3/y$ which you will have sketched in Exercise A, Question 2.

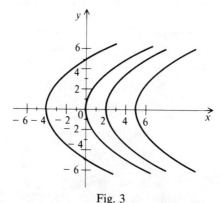

Fig. 3

Here the derivative is a function of $y$, not $x$, so it is not so easy to see how to carry out an integration to find the equation of the family.
   What simple transformation maps one member of this family onto another?
   We saw in Section 2.2 that translations parallel to the $y$-axis mapped solutions of $dy/dx = f(x)$ onto each other. For $dy/dx = g(y)$ the translation is parallel to the $x$-axis.
   Further, the solution curves in Figure 3 look like parabolas symmetrical about the $x$-axis; a reflection in the line $y = x$ of the familiar

1008

family $y = kx^2 + c$. Check, by calculating the gradients of half-a-dozen compass needles, that the sketch of Figure 3 seems to be a reflection of the solution family of $dy/dx = \frac{1}{3}x$. This suggests that the equation of the family in Figure 3 is of the form $x = ky^2 + c$.

For equations of the form $dy/dx = g(y)$ we need to interchange the roles of $x$ and $y$, and *regard x as a function of y*.

Rewriting $dy/dx = 3/y$ as $dx/dy = \frac{1}{3}y$ (see Chapter 13, p. 307), we can now integrate at once to give

$$x = \tfrac{1}{6}y^2 + c$$

as the equation of the family. The next example further illustrates the process.

*Example 2*

Find the general solution of the differential equation $dy/dx = y + 1$ and sketch the family of solution curves.

Rewriting $dy/dx = y + 1$ as

$$\frac{dx}{dy} = \frac{1}{y+1}$$

and integrating, we obtain $x = \ln|y + 1| + c$.

Once again, a translation parallel to the $x$-axis maps one solution curve onto another (see Figure 4), but in this example the line $y = -1$ (which is itself a solution) divides the family into two distinct 'sub-families', according to whether $(y + 1)$ is positive or negative.

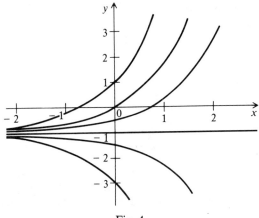

Fig. 4

We can recast the equation of the family into a form with $y$ as subject:

$$x = \ln|y + 1| + c \Rightarrow |y + 1| = e^{x-c},$$

or
$$|y+1| = A\,e^x$$

where $A = e^{-c}$, and finally $y = B e^x - 1$ where $B$ can be positive or negative.

Check by differentiation that this general solution satisfies the differential equation.

## Exercise C

**1.** Find the general solution for each of the following. Check your answers by differentiation.

(a) $\dfrac{dx}{dy} = \dfrac{1}{5y}$;  (b) $\dfrac{dy}{dx} = -3y$;

(c) $\dfrac{dy}{dx} = \dfrac{1}{(y+2)}$;  (d) $\dfrac{dx}{dy} = \dfrac{1}{(8-y)}$;

(e) $\dfrac{dv}{dt} = \dfrac{4}{v^2}$;  (f) $\dfrac{dx}{dt} = -10x^2$.

**2.** Find the general solutions of these differential equations:

(a) $\dfrac{dy}{dx} = -2y$;  (b) $\dfrac{dy}{dx} = 60 - 2y$.

Sketch the family of solution curves for each. For each equation, find the particular solution with the initial condition $y = 25$ when $x = 0$, and show it on your sketch.

**3.** Find the general solution of the differential equation
$$\frac{dy}{dx} = 1 + y^2.$$

Sketch the family of solution curves.

**4.** Solve the differential equation
$$\frac{dp}{dt} = \sqrt{(4 - p^2)},$$

given that $p = 0$ when $t = \tfrac{1}{3}\pi$.

**5.** Find the general solutions of:

(a) $\dfrac{dy}{dx} = (y+1)(y-3)$;  (b) $\dfrac{dp}{dt} = \dfrac{(50-p)(60-2p)}{1000}$;

(c) $\dfrac{dt}{dy} = \dfrac{1}{t} - t$;  (d) $\dfrac{dy}{dx} = \dfrac{y^2}{3y+5}$.

**6.** In a chemical reaction, a chemical $Z$ is formed. When the concentration of chemical $Z$ is $z$ moles per litre, $z$ is known to satisfy the differential equation
$$\frac{dz}{dt} = k(c - z)^2$$

where $k$ and $c$ are constants. Find a formula for $z$ at time $t$ (including $c$ and $k$). Sketch the family of solution curves.

1010

**7.** (*a*) A possible model for the way in which the speed $v$ m/s of a parachutist in free fall varies with time (taking air resistance into account) was given in Chapter 33 to be

$$\frac{dv}{dt} = 10 - 0 \cdot 2v.$$

Find the speed at time $t = 8$, given that $v = 0$ when $t = 0$.

(*b*) Another possible model for the same situation was

$$\frac{dv}{dt} = 10 - 0 \cdot 1v^2.$$

Find the solution of this equation with initial conditions $(0, 0)$ and compare the speed at $t = 8$ with part (*a*).

# 3. FORMULATION

Solving a differential equation is often a straightforward process. The difficult stage in creating and using a mathematical model is usually setting up the model in the first place. In this section we consider how to obtain differential equations from descriptions of situations in words; how to choose notation and make appropriate assumptions. The examples which follow illustrate the general method.

*Example* 3

A child makes his way to school at a speed which is proportional to the distance he still has to cover. He leaves home, 2 km from school, running at 10 km/h. How long will it be before he has gone nine-tenths of the way?

Let $x$ km be the distance from *home* that he has travelled at time $t$ hours. At that instant he will be $(2 - x)$ km from school.

First we record the boundary conditions:

$$x = 0 \quad \text{and} \quad \frac{dx}{dt} = 10 \quad \text{when } t = 0.$$

Next we write down the differential equation which translates into symbols the statement 'the rate of change of distance from home equals a constant multiplied by the distance from school':

$$\frac{dx}{dt} = k(2 - x).$$

Then we use the boundary condition to find the constant of proportionality, $k$. Substitution into the differential equation gives

$$10 = 2k \Rightarrow k = 5$$

1011

and the differential equation becomes

$$\frac{dx}{dt} = 5(2-x),$$

or

$$\frac{dt}{dx} = \frac{1}{5(2-x)}.$$

The general solution of this equation is

$$t = -\tfrac{1}{5}\ln|2-x| + c.$$

Using the boundary condition we find the particular solution which fits the problem: $x = 0$ when $t = 0$ gives

$$0 = -\tfrac{1}{5}\ln 2 + c$$

so

$$c = \tfrac{1}{5}\ln 2,$$

and

$$t = \tfrac{1}{5}[\ln 2 - \ln|2-x|].$$

When the child has travelled nine-tenths of the way, $x = 1\cdot 8$ and

$$t = \tfrac{1}{5}[\ln 2 - \ln 0\cdot 2]$$

$$= \tfrac{1}{5}\ln 10$$

$$\approx 0\cdot 46.$$

That is, he has gone nine-tenths of the way about 28 minutes after he leaves home.

Although the model we have been using is plausible enough for the part of the journey we have been concerned with, why is it unsuitable for the whole journey to school?

*Example* 4: *Acceleration*

A bullet is fired from a rifle at 1000 m/s and experiences a retardation due to air resistance of $0\cdot 002v^2$ m/s$^2$, where $v$ m/s is the speed of the bullet. How fast is it travelling when it has gone 500 metres?

Here, *retardation* is negative acceleration. Acceleration is rate of change of velocity, written either as $dv/dt$ or, using the chain rule, as

$$\frac{dx}{dt} \times \frac{dv}{dx} \quad \text{which is} \quad v\frac{dv}{dx}.$$

We use whichever form is appropriate.

The initial conditions are $x = 0$ and $v = 1000$ at $t = 0$.

1012

Now we find the differential equation:

$$\text{retardation} = 0 \cdot 002v^2 \Rightarrow \text{acceleration} = -0 \cdot 002v^2$$

$$\Rightarrow \frac{dv}{dt} = -0 \cdot 002v^2,$$

or

$$v\frac{dv}{dx} = -0 \cdot 002v^2.$$

Since our question is about speed and *distance*, we use the second equation.

$$v\frac{dv}{dx} = -0 \cdot 002v^2 \Rightarrow \frac{dv}{dx} = -0.002v = \frac{-v}{500},$$

or

$$\frac{dx}{dv} = \frac{-500}{v}.$$

Integration gives the general solution

$$x = -500 \ln v + c$$

and the initial condition $x = 0$ when $v = 1000$ gives

$$c = 500 \ln 1000.$$

Hence the particular solution is

$$x = 500 \ln \left(\frac{1000}{v}\right).$$

When $x = 500$,

$$500 = 500 \ln \left(\frac{1000}{v}\right) \Rightarrow \frac{1000}{v} = e$$

$$\Rightarrow v \approx 368.$$

So the speed is about 368 m/s when the bullet has travelled 500 m.

*Example 5*

Boiling water left for 5 minutes in a room kept at 20°C cools to 90°C. When will it be at 60°C?

The assumption we shall make is that the water cools at a rate proportional to the amount by which its temperature exceeds that of the room. If $\theta$°C is the temperature of the water, we obtain

$$\frac{d\theta}{dt} = k(\theta - 20).$$

1013

However, it is simpler to take $x$ to be the temperature above that of the room, i.e. $x = \theta - 20$, giving $dx/dt = kx$

$$\Rightarrow x = a\,e^{kt}.$$

When $t = 0$, $x = 80$, so

$$x = 80\,e^{kt},$$

and substituting $t = 5$, $x = 70$ gives

$$k = \tfrac{1}{5} \ln \tfrac{7}{8} \approx -0.0267.$$

When $x = 40$, $\qquad t = \dfrac{1}{k} \ln \tfrac{1}{2} \approx 25.95,$

which means that the water reaches 60°C after 26 minutes.

*Example* 6: *Mixing*

In this example, the word 'acid' will be used to describe a mixture of acid and water. Acid at 20% concentration, for example, contains 80% water.

A large tank contains 450 litres of acid at 50% concentration. Water (which we shall assume mixes instantaneously with acid) is pumped in at the rate of 9 litres per minute, and acid is pumped out at the same rate. How long will it be before the concentration drops to 20%?

Let $z$ be the number of litres of water in the tank after $t$ minutes. Assuming that water and acid mix instantaneously, 9 litres of acid will contain $9z/450$ litres of water. Thus in 1 minute the amount of water in the tank will increase by 9 and decrease by $9z/450$, equivalent to a net increase of $9 - 9z/450$. This is symbolized by the differential equation

$$\frac{dz}{dt} = 9 - \frac{9z}{450}$$

$$= \frac{9}{450}(450 - z).$$

Then $\qquad \dfrac{dt}{dz} = \dfrac{50}{450 - z}.$

Integrating, we obtain $t = -50 \ln |450 - z| + c$. The initial 50% concentration means that $z = 225$ when $t = 0$, giving $c = 50 \ln 225$. Hence the required solution is

$$t = 50(\ln 225 - \ln |450 - z|) = 50 \ln \left| \frac{225}{450 - z} \right|.$$

1014

For 20% acid, 80% water we substitute $z = 360$, giving

$$t = 50 \ln (225/90) \approx 45 \cdot 8.$$

So the concentration drops to 20% after about 46 minutes.

### Exercise D

**1.** The rate of increase of the population of a colony of insects $t$ days after the beginning of an experiment is proportional to the population $P$ at that time. If the colony initially contains 100 insects and at that time is growing at a rate of 50 insects per day, find how many there are after ten days.

**2.** A bicycle wheel is set spinning at a rate of 40 revolutions per minute, and slows down under the action of the friction at the bearings. The effect of this is to produce a retardation of $2z$ revolutions per minute per minute, where $z$ is the rate of rotation in revolutions per minute. At what rate is it rotating one minute after it is set in motion?

**3.** A radioactive substance decays at a rate proportional to its mass. When the mass of a sample is $0 \cdot 020$ g, the decay rate is $0 \cdot 001$ g per day.

(a) $t$ days later the mass is $m$ g. Write down a differential equation and solve it to give $m$ in terms of $t$ for these initial conditions.

(b) How long does the sample take to decay to $0 \cdot 010$ g?

(c) How long does it take to decay from $0 \cdot 012$ g to $0 \cdot 003$ g?

(d) What is the rate of decay after 10 days?

**4.** A body which has moved $x$ metres after $t$ seconds has a constant acceleration of $3$ m/s$^2$. If the velocity $v = 1$ when $x = 0$, calculate the value of $x$ when $v = 5$ (use acceleration $= v \, dv/dx$).

**5.** The volume of a large spherical snowball decreases as it melts at a rate proportional to its surface area at any instant. Express this statement in symbols. What is the constant of proportionality if a snowball of radius 30 cm takes 10 days to melt? After how many days will (a) the radius be halved, and (b) the volume be halved?

**6.** A tank with capacity 50 litres is full of a liquid chemical, and it is desired to flush the chemical out with water. The water is fed into the tank through a pipe at a rate of 100 litres per minute, mixes (we suppose instantaneously) with the chemical, and the mixture is drained off through another pipe at the same rate. If there are $x$ litres of liquid chemical in the tank after $t$ minutes, show that $x$ satisfies the differential equation

$$\frac{dx}{dt} = -2x.$$

Find a formula for the amount of chemical remaining in the tank after $t$ minutes, and find the time that must elapse before this amount drops to (i) $0 \cdot 5$ litres, (ii) $0 \cdot 005$ litres. How long does it take for the concentration to be halved? Where is the assumption of instantaneous mixing introduced into the mathematical formulation?

**7.** The rate at which the temperature of the bath water drops is proportional to the amount by which this temperature exceeds that of the surrounding atmosphere, which may be taken to remain constant at 15 degrees. If it takes 10 minutes for the temperature to fall from 40 to 35 degrees, calculate the constant of proportion, and find how long it would take for the temperature to fall from 55 to 45 degrees.

**8.** A motor boat is travelling at 30 knots in still water when the engine cuts out. It is known that when moving at $v$ knots, the boat experiences a retardation due to water resistance of $\lambda v^2$ knots per second. Write a differential equation for the speed at a time $t$ seconds after the engine cuts out, and solve it.

It is observed that the speed drops to 10 knots in 15 seconds. Use this information to find the value of $\lambda$, and hence find how long it takes for the speed to drop to 5 knots.

**9.** A car initially travelling at 15 m/s freewheels to rest. The retardation of the car has two components: one a constant $0{\cdot}08$ m/s$^2$ due to friction in the working parts and road resistance, and the other due to air resistance, of $0{\cdot}02\ v^2$ m/s$^2$, where $v$ is the speed in m/s. Find how long it takes for the car to freewheel to rest.

**10.** A 50 litre tank contains a mixture of 30 litres of blue paint and 20 litres of yellow paint. 2 litres of blue paint and 3 litres of yellow paint are pumped in each minute while 5 litres of the mixture are pumped out.

(*a*) After how long would you expect there to be 25 litres of each paint in the tank?

(*b*) If it was found in practice to take a shorter or a longer time, what would be possible explanations?

(*c*) Would the 100th and the 200th litre pumped out be significantly different in colour?

**11.** A tank has a square base of side $a$ and vertical sides. It initially contains liquid to a depth $b$. There is a small pipe leading from the bottom of the tank and when a tap in this is opened, the tank empties. Find the time taken for the tank to empty in terms of $b$ and $\lambda$, where $\lambda$ is the rate at which the height $h$ of the liquid decreases initially, assuming:

(*a*) that $dh/dt$ is proportional to $h$;

(*b*) that $dh/dt$ is proportional to $\sqrt{h}$.

Which assumption is more likely to be correct?

**12.** In a pathological investigation of the spread of infection in a culture, it is found that the rate of increase of the area of the infected part is directly proportional to the product of the infected area and the uninfected area. Initially one half of the total area is infected, and it is found that the initial rate of growth is such that, if it remained constant, the culture would be completely infected in 24 hours. Set up a differential equation relating $x$, the infected proportion of the total area, to time $t$ and deduce that after 12 hours about 73% of the culture is infected.

**13.** Detectives discover a murder victim at 6 a.m. and the body temperature of the victim is then 25 °C. Thirty minutes later the police surgeon arrives, and the body temperature is then 22 °C. If the room temperature is a constant 15 °C, and normal body temperature is 37 °C, at what time did the surgeon estimate that the crime was committed? State your assumptions. (See Question 7.)

**14.** A mass of 5 kg experiences a constant force of $\begin{pmatrix} 15 \\ 8 \end{pmatrix}$ N. If its velocity is $v$ m/s after time $t$ s, use Newton's second law to write down a differential equation satisfied by $v$. Show that the solution is $\mathbf{v} = \mathbf{u} + \begin{pmatrix} 3 \\ 1 \cdot 6 \end{pmatrix} t$. What is the significance of $\mathbf{u}$?

If the velocity is $\begin{pmatrix} 8 \\ 7 \cdot 2 \end{pmatrix}$ m/s when $t = 2$, find $\mathbf{u}$ and the velocity when $t = 4$.

# 4. SEPARATION OF VARIABLES

**4.1 Implicit differentiation.** The methods we have used to solve the types of differential equation we met in Sections 1 and 2 depend on rearranging the equations so that a single integration can be carried out. The method we introduce now makes use of our experience of implicit differentiation (which we met in Section 4 of Chapter 20).

*Example* 7

Differentiate $y^2 = 3x^2 + c$ with respect to $x$. Deduce the general solution of

$$\frac{dy}{dx} = \frac{x}{y} \quad (y \neq 0)$$

and check your answer by differentiation.

In Example 1 on p. 1005 we differentiated a very similar expression by first making $y$ the subject; here we use the alternative method of Chapter 20. We have

$$\frac{d}{dx}(y^2) = \frac{d}{dx}(3x^2 + c).$$

Using the chain rule

$$\frac{d}{dx}(y^2) = \frac{d}{dy}(y^2) \times \frac{dy}{dx} = 2y\frac{dy}{dx}.$$

So

$$2y\frac{dy}{dx} = 6x$$

or

$$\frac{dy}{dx} = \frac{3x}{y} \quad (y \neq 0).$$

To find the solution of $\dfrac{dy}{dx} = \dfrac{x}{y}$ we reverse the process:

$$\frac{dy}{dx} = \frac{x}{y} \Rightarrow 2y\frac{dy}{dx} = 2x$$

$$\Rightarrow \int \left(2y\frac{dy}{dx}\right) dx = \int 2x\, dx$$

$$\Rightarrow \int 2y\, dy = \int 2x\, dx$$

$$\Rightarrow y^2 = x^2 + c.$$

Carry out the check for yourself.

### Exercise E

**1.** Differentiate the following with respect to $x$:

(a) $y^2 = x^3 + 4$;     (b) $\sin y = x^2 + 5$;     (c) $y^3 = \dfrac{1}{x} - 7$;

(d) $\ln y = x^3 + 6$;     (e) $(y-1)^3 = \sin x$.

**2.** Reverse the steps of Question 1 (as in Example 7) to find the general solutions of the following differential equations:

(a) $\dfrac{dy}{dx} = \dfrac{x^2}{y}$;     (b) $\dfrac{dy}{dx} = \dfrac{x}{\cos y}$;     (c) $\dfrac{dy}{dx} = \left(\dfrac{1}{xy}\right)^2$;

(d) $\dfrac{dy}{dx} = x^2 y$;     (e) $\dfrac{dy}{dx} = \dfrac{\cos x}{(y-1)^2}$.

**4.2  Formalizing the method.** The technique illustrated in Example 7 depends on our being able to 'separate' the two variables (here $x$ and $y$) so that one side of the equation consists of a function of $x$ alone, and the other side has a product of $dy/dx$ and a function of $y$.

In other words we must have an equation which can be rearranged in the form

$$f(y)\frac{dy}{dx} = g(x) \tag{1}$$

and then, integrating with respect to $x$, we obtain

$$\int f(y)\frac{dy}{dx}\, dx = \int g(x)\, dx \tag{2}$$

or     $$\int f(y)\, dy = \int g(x)\, dx. \tag{3}$$

1018

Provided the two integrations can be performed, the differential equation has then been solved. The method is called *separating the variables*.

In practice we usually omit line (2) and proceed directly from line (1) to line (3). But we should bear in mind that it is integrating both sides of line (1) with respect to $x$ which leads to line (3), in which one integral is with respect to $x$ and the other with respect to $y$.

*Example 8*

Solve
$$\frac{dv}{dt} = 6vt.$$

Here
$$\frac{1}{v}\frac{dv}{dt} = 6t$$

$$\Rightarrow \int \frac{1}{v}\,dv = \int 6t\,dt$$

$$\Rightarrow \ln|v| = 3t^2 + c.$$

## *Exercise F*

1. Find the general solutions of:

(a). $\dfrac{ds}{dt} = \dfrac{s}{t}$;
    (b) $y^2\dfrac{dy}{dx} = x$;
    (c) $\dfrac{dx}{dt} = x^2 t$;

(d) $t\dfrac{dv}{dt} = \sqrt{(v+1)}$;
    (e) $\dfrac{dy}{dx} = y - y\sin x$;
    (f) $\dfrac{dy}{dx} = \dfrac{1}{\sqrt{(xy)}}$.

2. (a) Find the solution of the differential equation $dy/dx = \sqrt{(xy)}$ which passes through the point $(4, 1)$.

(b) Find the solution of $x\,(dy/dx) = 1/\cos y$ which passes through the point $(1, \frac{3}{4}\pi)$.

3. Which of the following differential equations can be solved using the method of separation of variables? Solve those to which the method does apply and explain why it cannot be used with the others.

(a) $\dfrac{dy}{dx} = 2x - y$;
    (b) $\dfrac{dy}{dx} = 7 - 5y$;
    (c) $\dfrac{dy}{dx} = x + xy^2$;

(d) $\dfrac{dy}{dx} = xy + 4$;
    (e) $x + y\dfrac{dy}{dx} = 10$.

4. Find the solution of the differential equation $dy/dx = -xy$ which passes through the point $(0, 1/\sqrt{(2\pi)})$. Make $y$ the subject of your solution.

5. During a fermentation process, the rate of decomposition of the fermenting 'must' is given by $dm/dt = -m/(1+t)^2$, where $m$ kg is the mass of the must present at time $t$ hours after the process begins. Show that if $m = 10$ when $t = 0$, after a very long time there will be about $3\cdot7$ kg of must left.

**6.** A tank contains 20 litres of a solution of a dangerous chemical in water. The concentration of the chemical is reduced by running in pure water at a rate of 2 litres per minute and allowing 3 litres per minute of the solution to run out of the tank.

If there are $x$ kg of chemical in the tank at time $t$ minutes after the dilution starts, show that

$$\frac{dx}{dt} = \frac{-3x}{20 - t}.$$

Find the general solution of this differential equation. Find the percentage change in the concentration of the chemical solution in 10 minutes and explain why it is independent of the initial conditions.

**7.** Bacteria in a tank of water increase at a rate proportional to the number present. Water is drained out of the tank, initially containing 100 litres, at a steady rate of 2 litres per hour. Show that if $N$ is the number of bacteria present at time $t$ hours after the time at which the draining starts, then

$$\frac{dN}{dt} = kN - \frac{2N}{100 - 2t}.$$

If $k = 0.7$ and, at $t = 0$, $N = N_0$, find in terms of $N_0$ the number of bacteria after 24 hours.

**8.** A country has 200 million notes in circulation at any time. It mints new currency at a rate of 3 million notes a year and exports currency at the same rate. If this process has been going on for some time, how much of the currency in circulation now would you expect to have been minted in the last five years? (Assume that the money coming back from abroad does not return to circulation.)

## 5. LINEAR DIFFERENTIAL EQUATIONS

**5.1 Particular solutions.** When a hot coffee percolator is left, it cools so that

$$\frac{dy}{dt} = -4y,$$

where $y$ is the number of degrees above room temperature, and the time is measured in hours. By what percentage will its temperature drop in 5 minutes?

At any time $t$ its temperature will be given by

$$y = a\,e^{-4t},$$

so $t = \frac{5}{60}$ gives $y \approx 0.72a$, 28% down.

When the percolator is switched to low, heat is applied at a rate which, in the absence of cooling, would raise the temperature by 4 °C per minute, so now

$$\frac{dy}{dt} = 240 - 4y \quad \text{or} \quad \frac{dy}{dt} + 4y = 240,$$

and by previous methods we obtain

$$y = a\,e^{-4t} + 60.$$

The solution family (see Figure 5) shows what happens. If $y$ is 60, the coffee remains at this temperature, the loss of heat being exactly balanced by the gain. Otherwise, depending on its initial condition, it warms up or cools down towards this temperature. Notice that $y$ is the sum of two parts, the particular value 60 and a general term $a\,e^{-4t}$. The general term satisfies $dy/dt = -4y$, or makes $dy/dt + 4y$ equal to zero, while the particular value modifies this to make $dy/dt + 4y$ come to 240 instead of zero.

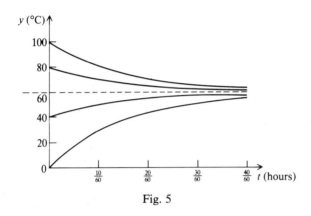

Fig. 5

Finally, suppose the percolator is turned up to a setting which, in the absence of cooling, would raise the temperature at a rate $220 + 240t$, so that now

$$\frac{dy}{dt} = -4y + 220 + 240t \quad \text{or} \quad \frac{dy}{dt} + 4y = 220 + 240t.$$

A sketch of the solution family (see Figure 6) shows a similar situation except that the trend is towards the line $y = 60t + 40$. Depending on its initial condition, it warms up or cools down so that eventually it approaches the temperature $60t + 40$. As you probably guessed, the complete family is given by

$$y = a\,e^{-4t} + 60t + 40,$$

usually called the *complete solution*. Once again this is the sum of two parts, the particular function $60t + 40$ called the *particular integral* and the general term $a\,e^{-4t}$ called the *complementary function*. The general term satisfies $dy/dt = -4y$, or makes $dy/dt + 4y$ equal to zero. The

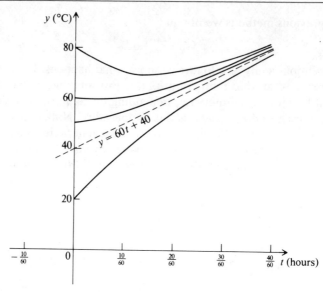

Fig. 6

particular integral modifies this to make $dy/dt + 4y$ come to $220 + 240t$ instead of zero.

**5.2  Particular integral.** A similar situation holds however the heat provided by the pot varies with time. But sketching the solution family is a rather cumbersome approach, when all we really need to discover is a particular integral which satisfies the circumstances. This is best done by enlightened trial and error.

*Example* 9

Solve
$$\frac{dy}{dt} + 3y = 10 + 9t^2.$$

The complementary function is $y = a\, e^{-3t}$, which makes $dy/dt + 3y$ zero. To modify this and make it come to $10 + 9t^2$ instead of zero we shall need a particular integral which is a quadratic in $t$. So we try $y = At^2 + Bt + C$ and look for suitable values for $A, B, C$. Often this can be done by observation, but we shall work methodically. Now,

$$y = At^2 + Bt + C \text{ implies that } \frac{dy}{dt} = 2At + B.$$

So
$$\frac{dy}{dt} + 3y = 2At + B + 3At^2 + 3Bt + 3C$$

$$= 3At^2 + (2A + 3B)t + (B + 3C).$$

1022

If this is to be the same as $9t^2+0t+10$, then by comparison $A=3$, so $B=-2$ and $C=4$. So the particular integral is $3t^2-2t+4$, giving the complete solution

$$y = a e^{-3t} + 3t^2 - 2t + 4.$$

We have so far restricted our attention to particular integrals which are polynomials. But the same principles apply to other functions, as will be seen by working through the first few questions in Exercise G.

We are now in a position to solve any linear differential equation of the form $dy/dt - ky = f(t)$. First we find a particular integral $p(t)$ which makes $dy/dt - ky$ come to $f(t)$, then we add to it the complementary function $a e^{kt}$ to get the complete solution $y = a e^{kt} + p(t)$.

Finally, for any specific problem, the value of the constant $a$ can be found from the boundary conditions.

**5.3 Linearity.** Solve $dy/dt + y^2 = 3 + 9t^2$.

Here the complementary function, which makes $dy/dt + y^2$ zero, is found to be $1/(t+c)$. A particular integral, which makes $dy/dt + y^2$ come to $3 + 9t^2$ instead of zero, is easily observed to be $3t$. So the complete solution appears to be $y = 1/(t+c) + 3t$. But is this the solution? Does $dy/dt + y^2$ come to $3 + 9t^2$?

The fact that this method breaks down here is because the $y$ is squared. All would be well if $y^2 = [1/(t+c)]^2 + [3t]^2$. It is not hard to see that the method will work only so long as all the operations $L$ on $y$ have the property called *linearity* which requires

$$L(f+g) = L(f) + L(g)$$

for any functions $f$, $g$ of $t$ (see Chapter 19). The operation 'times three' does have the linearity property, as does the operation 'differentiate'; but 'square' does not. This is why we could be sure the method would work in section 5.2, but not in section 5.3.

**\*5.4 Proof.** If $L$ is a linear operator and $p(t)$ is a particular solution for $y$ of $L(y) = f(t)$, we need to prove that all solutions are given by $y = g(t) + p(t)$, where $g(t)$ is the general set of solutions of $L(y) = 0$.

First, $g(t) + p(t)$ does satisfy $L(y) = f(t)$, because

$$L[g(t) + p(t)] = L[g(t)] + L[p(t)]$$
$$= 0 + f(t) = f(t).$$

But might there not be other solutions as well? If $q(t)$ is a solution of $L(y) = f(t)$, then

$$L[q(t) - p(t)] = L[q(t)] - L[p(t)] = f(t) - f(t) = 0.$$

So $q(t) - p(t)$ satisfies $L(y) = 0$ and is thus one of the set $g(t)$. Hence

$$q(t) = g(t) + p(t).$$

This means that the method does give all the possible solutions.

### Exercise G

**1.** Find the values of $A$, $B$, and $C$ for which:
   (a) $y = A$ is a solution for $dy/dx + 4y = 12$;
   (b) $y = Ax + B$ is a solution for $dy/dx + 4y = 4x + 9$;
   (c) $y = Ce^t$ is a solution for $dy/dt + 2y = 12 e^t$.

**2.** (a) Show that if $y = Ax^2 + Bx + C$ is a particular integral for the equation $dy/dx - y = 2x - 3x^2$, then

$$-Ax^2 + (2A - B)x + B - C = 2x - 3x^2,$$

and find $A$, $B$, $C$ by comparing coefficients of $x^2$, $x^1$ and $x^0$.

   (b) Show that if $y = A \sin 2x + B \cos 2x$ is to be a particular integral for $dy/dx + y = 5 \sin 2x$ then

$$(A - 2B) \sin 2x + (2A + B) \cos 2x = 5 \sin 2x.$$

Show further, by equating the coefficients of $\sin 2x$ and $\cos 2x$ in this equation that $A - 2B = 5$ and $2A + B = 0$. Find $A$ and $B$. Check your particular integral by substituting back in the differential equation.

**3.** Find the complete solutions of these differential equations. In each case sketch the family of solutions and write down the equation of the solution that passes through the origin.
   (a) $dy/dx + 3y = 24$;　　　(b) $dy/dx + 2y = 2x - 7$.

**4.** Write down the general solution of each of the following:
   (a) $dy/dx - 2y = 12$;　　　(b) $dy/dt + 8y = 10$;
   (c) $dP/dt + 3P = 0$;　　　(d) $dV/dh - V = 5 - 5h$.

**5.** Solve:
   (a) $dy/dx + 5y = 2$;　　　(b) $2 \, dy/dx + 5y = 4 e^{-3x}$;
   (c) $dy/dx + y = \sin 3x$;　　　(d) $dy/dx + 2y = x^2$;
   (e) $dy/dx = 0 \cdot 1 - 0 \cdot 5y$.

**6.** (a) Try $y = A e^{4x}$ as a particular integral for $dy/dx - 4y = 3 e^{4x}$. Explain why the method breaks down.

   (b) Try $y = Ax e^{4x}$ instead. Write down the complete solution.

   (c) Find the general solution of:

   　　(i) $dy/dx + 2y = e^{-2x}$;　　　(ii) $dy/dx - 6y = 3 e^{6x}$.

**7.** If $y = z e^{4x}$, express $dy/dx$ in terms of $x$, $z$, $dz/dx$. Use this substitution to solve $dy/dx - 4y = 3 e^{4x}$ and compare your answer with Question 6(b).

**8.** When a kettle is $\theta \, ^\circ C$ above (constant) room temperature its temperature is falling at a rate of $0 \cdot 01\theta^\circ C/\min$. If it is then heated by an element which can deliver heat at a steady rate sufficient to raise the temperature of the kettle by $0 \cdot 5^\circ C/\min$ in the absence of cooling, then $\theta$ will satisfy approximately the differential equation $d\theta/dt = 0 \cdot 5 - 0 \cdot 01\theta$. If $t = 0$ when $\theta = 12$, find $\theta$ in terms of $t$. Sketch the $t \to \theta$ graph.

**9.** The population $P$ of a town after $t$ years is growing in such a way that it satisfies the differential equation

$$\frac{dP}{dt} = 0 \cdot 0468P + 10\,000.$$

Can you explain why this should be so?

Solve the equation, given that the initial population is 200 000, and calculate the population after 2 years.

**10.** A culture of bacteria (initial number $N_0 = 2$ million) is growing. But bacteria are being removed at a constant rate equivalent to 800 000 per hour, so that the number $N$ at time $t$ satisfies the differential equation

$$\frac{dN}{dt} = 1 \cdot 6N - 800\,000.$$

Solve this equation, and calculate $N$ ($a$) when $t = 1$, ($b$) when $t = 2$.

**11.** The acceleration of a sphere falling through a liquid is $(30 - 3v)$ cm/s², where $v$ is its speed in cm/s.

($a$) Sketch the graph of $v$ against $t$.

($b$) If the sphere starts from rest, how fast will it be travelling at time $t$, and how far will it then have fallen?

($c$) What is the maximum possible velocity? Is this ever reached?

**12.** A car is started from rest under a force which is proportional to the time against a resistance proportional to the velocity.

($a$) Show that the differential equation is of the form $dv/dt + kv = \lambda t$.

($b$) Integrate this equation.

($c$) Show that $v = \frac{1}{2}\lambda t^2$ for small values of $t$.

## *6. APPLICATIONS TO ELECTRICITY

**6.1  Inductance.** We saw in Chapter 37 that when a changing current $i$ flows through the inductor $L$ in the circuit of Figure 7, an induced e.m.f.

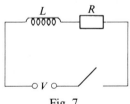

Fig. 7

is produced of magnitude $L(di/dt)$, which opposes the applied voltage $V$, reducing the potential difference across the resistor $R$. We have (using Ohm's law for the resistor)

$$V - L\frac{di}{dt} = iR$$

or

$$L\frac{di}{dt} + iR = V.$$

1025

This is a linear first-order differential equation which can be solved for any applied voltage $V$ (whether constant or alternating) using the methods of Section 5.

If $V$ is constant and a current $i$ amperes is flowing $t$ seconds after the switch is closed, $L(di/dt)+iR = V$ can be written

$$\frac{di}{dt}+\frac{R}{L}i=\frac{V}{L},$$

which has a particular integral $i = V/R$ and complementary function $i = A\,e^{-Rt/L}$. So the complete solution is

$$i = \frac{V}{R}+A\,e^{-Rt/L}.$$

If we take $i = 0$ when $t = 0$, $A = -V/R$, so finally

$$i = \frac{V}{R}(1-e^{-Rt/L}).$$

Figure 8 shows the graph of this solution. Notice that when $t$ becomes large, the complementary function is very small and the particular integral term gives the *steady-state* current. In the steady-state, $L$ has no effect and it is as if the battery were connected to the resistor alone.

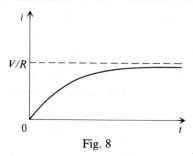

Fig. 8

**6.2 Capacitance.** The simplest sort of capacitor consists of two metal plates with a gap between them. A charge $+q$ on one plate sets up a charge $-q$ on the other, causing a potential difference between the plates which is proportional to $q$:

$$V = \frac{1}{C}q$$

where the constant $C$ (called the *capacitance*) depends on the construction of the capacitor.

When a capacitor with no charge on its plates is connected to a source of voltage, current flows in the circuit (see Figure 9) until the charge stored on the plates produces a potential difference large enough to balance the potential differences round the circuit (satisfying Kirchhoff's second law). If the source of voltage is removed and the capacitor is put in series with a resistor, it will *discharge*, causing a current to flow until the charge is exhausted.

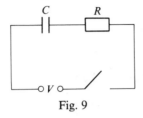

Fig. 9

The current $i$ is the rate of flow of charge or the rate of change of charge stored on the capacitor, i.e.

$$i = \frac{dq}{dt}.$$

The units of charge are *coulombs*: 1 coulomb/second is a current of 1 ampere.

Capacitance is measured in farads: 1 volt = 1 coulomb/farad.
(Note: farads are very large units; common capacitances are measured in microfarads: $1 \ \mu F = 10^{-6} \ F$.)

*Example* 10

A 9 V battery is connected in series with a resistor $R$ $(2 \times 10^4 \ \Omega)$ and a capacitor $C$ $(10^3 \ \mu F)$ when switch $S_1$ is closed (see Figure 10). Find the charge on the capacitor after 60 seconds. (Assume $q = 0$ when $t = 0$.)

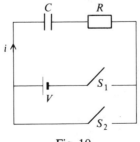

Fig. 10

It is easiest to write down and solve the differential equation in general terms and then substitute the appropriate numerical values.

1027

Applying Kirchhoff's second law we have

$$\frac{q}{C} + iR = V,$$

or

$$\frac{q}{C} + R\frac{dq}{dt} = V.$$

The complete solution is

$$q = A\, e^{-t/CR} + CV.$$

Using the initial values, $q = 0$ when $t = 0$, we obtain

$$q = CV(1 - e^{-t/CR}).$$

(See Figure 11.)

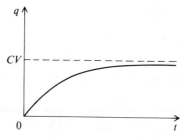

Fig. 11

Substituting the numerical values of voltage, capacitance and resistance into this solution we have, for $t = 60$,

$$10^{-3} \times 9(1 - e^{-60/20}) \approx 9 \times 10^{-3} \times 0.95$$

$$= 8.55 \times 10^{-3} \text{ coulombs},$$

i.e. 95% of the steady-state value $CV$.

### Exercise H

**1.** Using the equations of Section 6.1, find how long it will be before the current in the circuit of Figure 7 reaches 90% of its steady-state value if $V = 20$ volts, $L = 0.2$ henries, $R = 40$ ohms.

**2.** Show that if switch $S_1$ is opened when $C$ is fully charged (see Figure 10) and then switch $S_2$ is closed, the charge $q$ on $C$ after $t$ seconds will satisfy

$$R\frac{dq}{dt} + \frac{q}{C} = 0.$$

Find the solution of this equation, using the initial conditions $q = CV$ when

1028

$t = 0$. Sketch the solution curve. How long will it take for the charge to fall to 50% of its initial value?

**3.** A capacitor of $0 \cdot 1$ microfarad is holding a charge of $10^{-6}$ coulomb. A switch is closed to put it in circuit with a resistor of $2 \times 10^6$ ohms. Find: $(a)$ the initial potential difference across the capacitor; $(b)$ the initial current in the circuit; $(c)$ to what value the charge has fallen after $0 \cdot 3$ second.

**4.** Verify that in the charging process of Section 6.2 the capacitor is about 95% charged when $t = 3CR$. How long, in terms of $CR$, does it take to be 50% charged?

**5.** With the notation of Section 6.1, and a constant voltage $V$, calculate in terms of $L$ and $R$ the time needed for the current to reach half its steady-state value.

**6.** An alternating voltage $V = 7 \sin 10t$ is applied to an inductance of 3 henries in series with a resistance of $5\Omega$. Calculate the amplitude of the resulting current by solving the appropriate differential equation. Compare the answer and the method of solution with the work of Section 6.1 in Chapter 37.

**7.** An alternating voltage $V = 2 \sin 3t$ is applied across a capacitance of $500 \ \mu F$ in series with a resistor of $10^3 \ \Omega$. Show that the current $i$ in the circuit satisfies

$$10^3 \frac{di}{dt} + \frac{1}{5 \times 10^{-4}} i = 6 \cos 3t.$$

Find the amplitude of the steady-state current.

### Miscellaneous Exercise

**1.** Solve:

$(a)$ $\dfrac{dx}{dt} + 3x = 15$;   $(b)$ $3\dfrac{dx}{dt} + x = 10 \ e^{-2t}$;   $(c)$ $\dfrac{dx}{dt} + 4x = 5t^2$;

$(d)$ $\dfrac{dx}{dt} + 5x = x^2$;   $(e)$ $\dfrac{dx}{dt} + 5x = \cos 2t$;   $(f)$ $\dfrac{dx}{dt} - 4x = 6 \ e^{4t}$;

$(g)$ $\dfrac{dx}{dt} + x = \dfrac{1}{x}$;   $(h)$ $3\dfrac{dx}{dt} - x = t + e^t$;   $(i)$ $\dfrac{dx}{dt} - x = t \ e^t$;

$(j)$ $\dfrac{dx}{dt} + 3x = tx$;   $(k)$ $\dfrac{dx}{dt} = x - t + 4$.

**2.** One of the products of fission of a radioactive substance $A$ is another radioactive substance $B$. 1 unit of mass of $B$ results from the fission of 2 units of mass of $A$. The decay rates are $m_1/100$, $m_2/500$ mg per day where $m_1$ and $m_2$ are the masses of $A$, $B$ in mg.

$(a)$ Use this data to form two differential equations.

$(b)$ Start with 20 mg of A. Find $m_1$ and hence $m_2$ in terms of $t$.

$(c)$ Draw rough sketches of the graphs of $m_1$ and $m_2$ against $t$, and show that $m_2$ has a maximum value when $m_2 = 2 \cdot 5 m_1$.

**3.** Describe the solution curves of the differential equation

$$\left(\frac{dy}{dx}\right)^2 - \frac{dy}{dx} = 0.$$

1029

**4.** The height $y$ m of a tree at age $t$ years satisfies the differential equation

$$\frac{dy}{dt} + ay = b$$

where $a$ and $b$ are positive constants for a given species.

Show that the tree grows towards a maximum height.

A tree planted when it is 2 m high has an initial rate of growth of 0·4 m per year. If its maximum height is 22 m, find how long it takes to reach half that height.

**5.** Show that $y = A \sin kt + B \cos kt$ is a solution of

$$\frac{d^2y}{dt^2} = -k^2y,$$

for all $A$, $B$.

**6.** Find by trial two independent solutions of $d^2y/dt^2 = k^2y$. Hence write down a solution containing two undetermined constants.

**7.** If $x = z e^{-at}$, write down an expression for $dx/dt$ in terms of $t, z$ and $dz/dt$ and show that

$$\frac{d^2x}{dt^2} = \left(\frac{d^2z}{dt^2} - 2a\frac{dz}{dt} + a^2z\right) e^{-at}.$$

Use this substitution to eliminate $x$ in each of the following equations and hence find solutions to each containing two undetermined constants.

(a) $\dfrac{d^2x}{dt^2} + 2a\dfrac{dx}{dt} + a^2x = 0$;     (b) $\dfrac{d^2x}{dt^2} + 2a\dfrac{dx}{dt} + (a^2+b^2)x = 0$;

(c) $\dfrac{d^2x}{dt^2} + 2a\dfrac{dx}{dt} + (a^2-b^2)x = 0$.

**8.** Use Question 7 to write down or derive the complete solution of

$$p\frac{d^2x}{dt^2} + q\frac{dx}{dt} + rx = 0.$$

Distinguish between the different cases that may arise.

**9.** Use a simple step-by-step method, proceeding by intervals $\delta x = 0 \cdot 2$, to construct a table of values over the interval $1 \leqslant x \leqslant 2$ for the solution of the differential equation

$$\frac{dy}{dx} + y = \frac{1}{x},$$

satisfying the condition that $y = 0$ when $x = 1$.

What is the complementary function for this differential equation?

Another solution curve of this differential equation passes through the point $(1\cdot6, 2\cdot3)$. Use the result of the first part, together with your knowledge of the complementary function, to find the points of this curve corresponding to $x = 1$ and $x = 2$.

**10.** A tank $A$ contains a mixture of 250 litres of blue paint and 250 litres of yellow paint. Blue paint is pumped into $A$ at 15 litres/min, and paint is pumped

1030

out at the same rate into a tank $B$, which initially contains a mixture of 300 litres of blue paint and 200 litres of yellow paint. Paint is pumped out of $B$ at the same rate. Assuming perfect mixing in each tank, when will the paint in $B$ be yellower than that in $A$?

# SUMMARY

In differential equations of the first order and first degree there is exactly one member of the solution family through any point (provided $dy/dx$ is defined at that point). This chapter is about these equations only.

The solution family contains one arbitrary constant which, for a specific member, may be determined by a boundary or initial condition.

Differential equations of the form $dy/dx = f(x)$ are solved by integrating:

$$y = \int f(x)\,dx + c.$$

Differential equations of the form $dy/dx = g(y)$ are solved by rearranging as

$$\frac{dx}{dy} = \frac{1}{g(y)}$$

and integrating:

$$x = \int \frac{1}{g(y)}\,dy + c.$$

The differential equation $dy/dt = ky$ has the general solution

$$y = A\,e^{kt}.$$

The solution of the differential equation $dy/dx - g(x)/f(y)$ is obtained by separating the variables to give $f(y)\,dy/dx = g(x)$ and integrating:

$$\int f(y)\,dy = \int g(x)\,dx.$$

A differential equation of the form $dy/dt + ky = f(t)$ has a *complete solution* obtained by adding a *particular integral* to the *complementary function*. This is because the operators on $y$ are *linear*.

A *particular integral* is a specific function $p(t)$ which satisfies the differential equation. We try a function $p(t)$ which is of the same form as the function $f(t)$.

The *complementary function* is the general solution of the reduced equation $dy/dt + ky = 0$, namely $y = a\,e^{-kt}$.

1031

If operator $L$ has the property called *linearity* then

$$L[f(t)+g(t)] = L[f(t)]+L[g(t)]$$

for any functions $f$ and $g$.

# 39

# THE NORMAL DISTRIBUTION: SAMPLES AND SIGNIFICANCE

## 1. INTRODUCTION

Following the general discussion of probability models, discrete and continuous, in Chapter 35, we now need to look closely at one particular model. This model has several important uses in probability theory, of which we develop two in detail.

**1.1 An approximation to the binomial model.** Figure 1 is a typical probability histogram from a binomial model. You will have produced some like this in Chapter 30 and have found that for large enough $n$ all binomial histograms have the same bell shape, symmetrical about the mean. You have seen that it is tedious to calculate binomial probabilities when $n$ is large; the model developed in this chapter provides an alternative which makes the work easier.

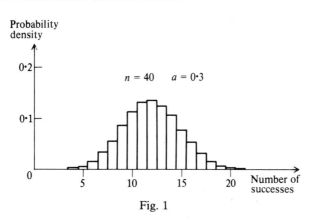

Fig. 1

**1.2 A model for some statistical histograms.** Figure 2 is a statistical histogram arising from an investigation of the resistance of 300 elements for 1 kW electric fires. In contrast to Figure 1, the domain (the resistance) is a continuous variable and the width of the rectangles depends upon an arbitrary decision about the grouping of the measurements made by the tester. Many statistical histograms illustrating measure-

1033

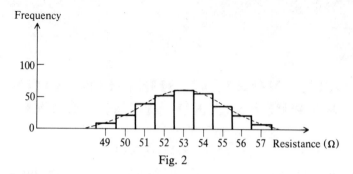

Fig. 2

ments of this sort (for instance, heights or masses of adult animals, lifetimes of insects, etc.) have the same symmetrical bell shape.

**1.3  Setting up the model.** We wish to set up a continuous model with a bell-shaped graph suitable for use in these and other equivalent situations. From the symmetry of the histograms above, the mean values are at the humps. The main differences are in the position of these humps and the spread. So, in looking for appropriate models, we shall follow Chapter 35, Section 7, and use mean and standard deviation to help us find a satisfactory fit. Initially, it is sensible to develop a model centred on $x = 0$ (see Figure 3). This can then be stretched and translated to fit Figures 1 and 2.

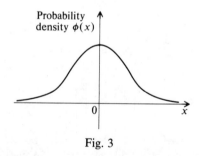

Fig. 3

We need a simple formula giving the right shape and properties. Because of the symmetry, an even function is necessary. This condition still leaves us with a wide choice, for example,

$(a)$ $y = \dfrac{1}{1+x^2}$,        $(b)$ $y = \dfrac{1}{1+x^4}$,

$(c)$ $y = \exp(-x^2)$,        $(d)$ $y = 1 + \cos x, \; -\pi \leqslant x \leqslant \pi$.

To make each of these a probability density function, a constant factor must be introduced to make the total area 1 (see p. 918).

### Exercise A

**1.** Draw the graphs of the four functions suggested in Section 1 and compare their shapes with Figures 1 and 2.

**2.** Which of the four functions can you integrate?

**3.** Find the $x$-coordinates of the points of inflexion of each of the graphs.

## 2. NORMAL PROBABILITY DENSITY

For various reasons which will emerge, the model we intend to follow up is

$$\phi(x) = k \exp(-x^2),$$

taking the domain from $-\infty$ to $\infty$. When drawing the graph, you will have found that beyond values of $x$ of $\pm 3$ or $\pm 4$ the values of $\exp(-x^2)$ are negligible, so the further extent of the domain is of little practical importance. In Figure 1, similarly, the domain is $\{0, 1, 2, \dots, 40\}$ but the probability of getting any number greater than 25 is minute.

This model was originally propounded by Gauss in connection with the analysis of measurement errors. The graph is consequently some-times called the *error curve* or *Gaussian curve*; more often it is called a *Normal curve*, the capital *N* indicating that Normal is not being employed in its usual sense as an adjective.

To use it as a probability model, we need to be able to calculate areas under the graph and to find the mean and standard deviation. The mean is obviously 0, but the other tasks are more difficult since $\exp(-x^2)$ cannot be integrated. However, our approximate methods (Simpson's rule, Taylor approximations) enable us to obtain values with sufficient accuracy.

It can be shown (Exercise B, Question 3) that the model has standard deviation equal to $1/\sqrt{2}$. Accordingly we apply a stretch in the $x$-direction with scale factor $\sqrt{2}$ to give a model with standard deviation 1. We then have the *standardized* Normal probability density function

$$\phi(x) = k \exp[-(x/\sqrt{2})^2]$$

i.e.                  $\phi(x) = k \exp(-\tfrac{1}{2}x^2).$

To complete the model we must find the appropriate value for $k$; this turns out to be $1/\sqrt{(2\pi)}$, though the proof is too difficult to include here (but see Project Exercise 2).

### Exercise B

**1.** Use Simpson's rule with eight intervals to estimate $\displaystyle\int_{-4}^{4} \exp(-\tfrac{1}{2}x^2)\,dx.$ Compare with the value of $\sqrt{(2\pi)}$.

**2.** Deduce from Exercise A, Question 3, or prove independently that the points of inflexion of

$$\phi(x) = \frac{1}{\sqrt{(2\pi)}} \exp\left(-\tfrac{1}{2}x^2\right)$$

occur where $x = \pm 1$.

**3.** Write down the integral of $x \exp(-x^2)$. Use the formula for integration by parts to show that

$$\int_{-\infty}^{\infty} x^2 \exp(-x^2)\, dx = \tfrac{1}{2} \int_{-\infty}^{\infty} \exp(-x^2)\, dx.$$

[Hint: take $u = x$, $dv/dx = x \exp(-x^2)$.]

Deduce that, for the probability density function $\phi(x) = k \exp(-x^2)$, $\sigma = 1/\sqrt{2}$.

## 2.1 Use of tables.

In order to use the Normal model, we need values of the Normal probability density function and its associated cumulative probability. These have been tabulated (see, for example, SMP *Advanced Tables*). It is not, however, necessary to tabulate the function for different values of $\mu$ and $\sigma$, any more than we need separate tables for $\sin x$, $\sin 2x$, $\sin 3x$; instead we choose a standardized form of the function, and then apply suitable transformations to this to obtain the general function.

The standardized form used is the one with mean 0 and standard deviation 1. The units along the $x$-axis of the standardized graph are therefore standard deviations from the mean.

We can illustrate the use of these tables with the example about electrical resistances from Section 1. Suppose the mean and standard deviation of the 300 elements are 53 ohms and 2 ohms respectively, and assume that the resistances fit a Normal density function with these parameters. What is the probability that a given element will have a resistance less than 54 ohms?

The probability of a resistance less than 54 ohms is represented by the shaded area in Figure 4. This is equal to the shaded area under the standardized Normal curve of Figure 5.

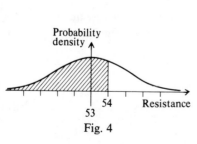

Fig. 4

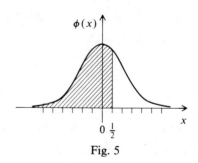

Fig. 5

1036

To map the curve of Figure 4 onto the other requires a translation of 53 to the left and a stretch with scale factor $\frac{1}{2}$ in the $x$-direction. To retain the total area of 1, we double the probability densities (that is, apply a stretch in the $y$-direction, scale factor 2). Since 54 ohms is $\frac{1}{2}$ standard deviation above the mean, we want the area under the standardized graph to the left of $x = \frac{1}{2}$.

For the standardized graph, we have tables of $\phi(x)$ and also the cumulative probability $\Phi(X) = \int_{-\infty}^{X} \phi(x)\, dx$ (see Figure 6).

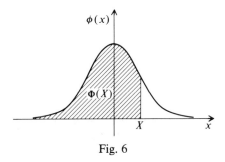

Fig. 6

We want $\Phi(\frac{1}{2})$, and the tables give this as $0\cdot691$.

The tables cover only positive values of $X$, and we must use symmetry to cope with negative values. Explain why

$$\Phi(-X) = 1 - \Phi(X).$$

*Example* 1

Observations suggest that the heights of adult males in Ruritania fit a Normal function with mean 175 cm and a standard deviation 7 cm. What proportion of the population has a height between 160 and 180 cm?

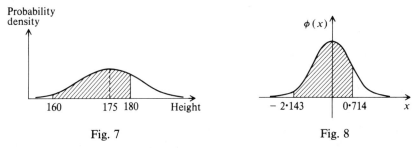

Fig. 7                                    Fig. 8

The probability that a man chosen at random has the required height is given by the area under the graph of Figure 7 for the interval from 160 to 180. This can be found as the difference between values of $\Phi$ corresponding to the two ends of the interval. Now, we find that 180 is $\frac{180-175}{7} \approx 0 \cdot 714$ standard deviations above the mean; and 160 is $\frac{175-160}{7} \approx 2 \cdot 143$ standard deviations below (see Figure 8). The required probability is therefore

$$\Phi(0 \cdot 714) - \Phi(-2.143) = \Phi(0 \cdot 714) - [1 - \Phi(2 \cdot 143)]$$
$$\approx 0 \cdot 762 - 1 + 0 \cdot 984$$
$$= 0 \cdot 746.$$

So we expect about 75% of men in Ruritania to have heights between 160 cm and 180 cm.

## Example 2

Tests carried out on Scimitar razor blades over a long period of time have shown that the number of satisfactory shaves obtained from each blade approximates very closely to a Normal distribution, with mean $8 \cdot 1$ and standard deviation $2 \cdot 0$. Estimate the percentage of blades that will give ten or more satisfactory shaves.

Here we are using the continuous Normal distribution as a model for a *discrete* statistical situation (counting rather than measuring) and we have to remember that the lower boundary for 'ten or more' will be $9 \cdot 5$, which is $\frac{9 \cdot 5 - 8 \cdot 1}{2} = 0 \cdot 7$ standard deviations above the mean.

So the probability that a blade will give ten or more shaves is given by

$$1 - \Phi(0 \cdot 7) \approx 1 - 0 \cdot 758 = 0 \cdot 242,$$

i.e. about 24% of the blades will give ten or more shaves.

### Exercise C

**1.** On the same axes, sketch the Normal probability density functions with:
(a) $\mu = 0$, $\sigma = 1$; (b) $\mu = 0$, $\sigma = 2$; (c) $\mu = 3$, $\sigma = 2$.

**2.** Estimate $\int_0^{0 \cdot 4} \frac{1}{\sqrt{(2\pi)}} \exp(-\tfrac{1}{2}x^2)\,dx$ using Simpson's rule with two strips. Compare with the value given from the tables. [Take $1/\sqrt{(2\pi)}$ as $0 \cdot 3989$.]

**3.** From the quadratic polynomial approximation for $e^h$, i.e. $1 + h + \tfrac{1}{2}h^2$, write down a fourth-degree approximation for $\exp(-\tfrac{1}{2}x^2)$. Hence estimate $\int_0^{0 \cdot 4} \frac{1}{\sqrt{(2\pi)}} \exp(-\tfrac{1}{2}x^2)\,dx$.

1038

**4.** Find an approximate value for $\Phi(1)$ by the method of Question 3, starting with a *cubic* polynomial approximation for $e^h$.

**5.** Show that the general Normal probability density function (with mean $\mu$ and standard deviation $\sigma$) has equation

$$\phi(x) = \frac{1}{\sigma\sqrt{(2\pi)}} \exp\left[-(x-\mu)^2/2\sigma^2\right].$$

**6.** Given $y = k \exp\left(-\frac{1}{2}x^2\right)$, show that $dy/dx = -xy$. Solve this differential equation by the step-by-step method of Chapter 33, starting with $x = 0$, $y = 0\cdot4$ and taking values of $x$ up to 2 in steps of $0\cdot2$.

**7.** At a weather station, the mean annual rainfall is 850 mm with standard deviation 100 mm. If the rainfall records over a large number of years fit the Normal model closely, what is the probability that in a particular year the rainfall will not exceed 1000 mm?

**8.** The times taken by a skilled craftsman to make the delicate suspension unit for a galvanometer fit the Normal probability model, with mean 54 minutes and standard deviation 5 minutes. What is the probability that it will take him longer than an hour to make one? What is the probability that none of the four units he makes in a morning takes longer than 50 minutes?

**9.** The blood pressure of adult males in England is Normally distributed, with mean 125 and standard deviation 8. What proportion of the male population has dangerously high blood pressure if the danger level is 140?

**10.** The IQ for students in a fixed age-group is reputed to have a mean of 100 and a standard deviation of 15, with a Normal probability density.
    (*a*) What is the probability that a student chosen at random will have an IQ between 80 and 110?
    (*b*) What is the lowest IQ of the top 3%?
    (*c*) What is the probability that, of three students selected at random, none will have an IQ below 120?

**11.** The mean life of the African locust is 28 days. If the probability of a locust surviving longer than 31 days is $0\cdot25$, estimate the standard deviation of the lifetime (assuming a Normal distribution).

**12.** Steel rods are required to be of length 10 cm, and a machine cuts them with a mean length of $10\cdot02$ cm and a standard deviation of $0\cdot015$ cm. Assuming a Normal probability density, what proportion of the rods will be rejected for being too short?
    If the spread of the measurements is unaltered by adjusting the position of the cut, how large should the mean be made if only a 1% rejection rate can be tolerated?
    Alternatively, to what would the standard deviation have to be reduced if the mean length was to be unaltered and the 1% rejection rate achieved?

**13.** A certain make of car battery has a mean life of 26 months, and the makers guarantee to pay compensation to anyone whose battery does not last two years. The firm in fact pays compensation for $\frac{1}{2}$% of the batteries sold. Assuming that the battery life has Normal probability density, find the standard deviation of the battery life. How many batteries per thousand will last longer than 27 months?

THE NORMAL DISTRIBUTION [39

**14.** Several hundred eight-year-old children were asked how much pocket money they were given. The replies gave a distribution that was approximately Normal, with mean 40p and standard deviation 15p. Estimate the proportion of the children who received (a) more than 50p, (b) less than 10p.

**15.** An author averages 500 words to a page. If the frequency function for the number of words per page is approximately Normal, with standard deviation 30 words, estimate the number of pages in a 200 page book on which you would expect to find (a) more than 520 words, (b) between 500 and 520 words, (c) less than 450 words.

**16.** The masses in kilograms of the babies born in one hospital during a given month were as follows:

| Mass (kg) | Frequency |
|-----------|-----------|
| 1·0–1·5 | 1 |
| 1·5–2·0 | 8 |
| 2·0–2·5 | 23 |
| 2·5–3·0 | 37 |
| 3·0–3·5 | 31 |
| 3·5–4·0 | 16 |
| 4·0–4·5 | 4 |

Show this information on a histogram and calculate the mean $m$ and standard deviation $s$.

It is suggested that the masses of new-born babies are Normally distributed. Use your tables, with the values of $\mu$ and $\sigma$ set equal to $m$ and $s$ calculated from the data, to find the probabilities for each of the seven intervals in the table. Compile a similar table of frequencies predicted by the Normal model and compare it with the data.

**17.** A firm decides to enter the export market to sell shoes to the Happy Isles. They find 26 islanders living in London and measure their feet, with these results:

| Shoe size | 7 | 8 | 9 | 10 | 11 |
|-----------|---|---|---|----|----|
| Frequency | 4 | 5 | 8 | 6 | 3 |

They decide to fit these figures to a Normal curve, and to base the proportions of different sizes in their first consignment of 5000 pairs of shoes on this. How many pairs of size 9 and how many pairs of size 12 should they include?

# 3. THE NORMAL MODEL AS AN APPROXIMATION TO THE BINOMIAL

Suppose that there is an outbreak of mumps in a large city. If a certain proportion—say, 60%— of the population has already had the disease, the outbreak is likely to die down quickly; if not, it is likely to become an epidemic.

To help decide whether special precautions are necessary, 500 people are asked whether they have had mumps; 320 say 'yes'. How far should we be convinced by this evidence that an epidemic is unlikely? At first sight, we might suggest that since 64% have had mumps, we are all right. But this is only 64% of the *sample*; we really know very little about the population as a whole. If we had asked three, and two said 'yes'—or even if it were six out of six—the sample would be too small to affect our decision. Can we be sure, on this evidence, that the proportion is not as low as 60%?

Now we know enough about the binomial probabilities to give some sort of answer to this question; if we rephrase it:

'Suppose that in a large population 60% have had mumps. If 500 are chosen independently and at random, what is the probability that 320 or more will have had it?'

The answer can be expressed as a sum of binomial probabilities:

$$\sum_{320}^{500} \frac{500!}{i!(500-i)!}(0\cdot6)^i(0\cdot4)^{500-i}.$$

As we saw in Chapter 30, the difficulties of calculating even one term of this series are formidable. Fortunately, we can use a Normal model with the same $\mu$ and $\sigma$ instead. The answer will then be approximate but quite good enough for all practical purposes. (The full justification follows in Section 4.)

For the binomial model,

$$\mu = na = 500 \times 0\cdot6 = 300,$$

$$\sigma = \sqrt{(nab)} \approx 10\cdot95.$$

We want the sum of the areas of the rectangles in Figure 9 centred on 320, 321, 322, ... This corresponds to the area in Figure 10 to the right of 319·5, which is $\dfrac{319\cdot5 - 300}{10\cdot95}$ standard deviations to the right of the mean.

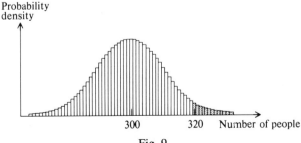

Fig. 9

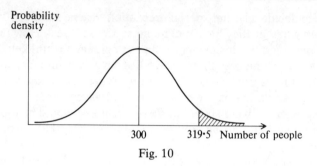

Fig. 10

The probability is

$$1 - \Phi\left(\frac{319 \cdot 5 - 300}{10 \cdot 95}\right) \approx 0 \cdot 04.$$

So if a sample of 500 contains 320 who have had mumps, this provides good evidence (though not conclusive) that the proportion in the population at large is not as low as 60%.

**3.1   How good is the Normal approximation to the binomial?**  We have seen in Chapter 30 that for values of $a$ close to $0 \cdot 5$, the outline of a binomial histogram has the characteristic Normal bell shape even for quite small values of $n$. We also saw that, for other values of $a$, binomial histograms have this shape provided $n$ is large enough.

Figure 11 displays the binomial probabilities with $n = 6$, $a = 0 \cdot 4$ and superimposed is the Normal curve with the same expected value and standard deviation. One can see by eye that the area of each rectangle is approximately equal to the area under the curve over the same interval.

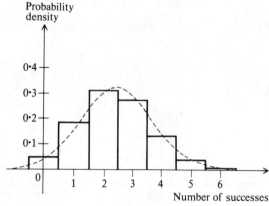

Fig. 11

Let us take one specific example. From the binomial model, $p_4 = \binom{6}{4}(0·4)^4(0·6)^2 \approx 0·138$. Also $\mu = na = 2·4$, $\sigma = \sqrt{(nab)} = 1·2$.

Now the area under the Normal curve with these parameters between 3·5 and 4·5 is

$$\Phi\left(\frac{4·5-2·4}{1·2}\right) - \Phi\left(\frac{3·5-2·4}{1·2}\right) = \Phi(1·75) - \Phi(0·92)$$

$$= 0·960 - 0·821$$

$$= 0·139.$$

Our later proof (p. 1046) will show that as $n$ is increased, even for values of $a$ well away from 0·5, the fit gets better and better.

We see then that the *continuous* Normal model can be used to calculate quickly values for the *discrete* binomial model. The routine is invariable:

(*a*) visualize the question in terms of the original histogram;

(*b*) approximate by means of areas under a Normal curve, taking care to get the correct $x$-interval;

(*c*) calculate $\mu$ and $\sigma$ and obtain the relevant interval for the standardized Normal curve;

(*d*) find the required areas with the help of the tables.

### Exercise D

**1.** A coin is tossed 100 times. Use the Normal approximation to the binomial probability function to find the probability of getting more than 54 heads. Repeat the calculation to find the probabilities of (*a*) more than 540 heads in 1000 tosses, (*b*) more than 5400 heads in 10 000 tosses.

**2.** In the course of a game, a fair die is thrown 180 times. What is the probability that there will be fewer than 24 sixes?

**3.** An airline regularly books 80 passengers for an aeroplane with 75 seats. If the probability that any particular passenger will not turn up is $\frac{1}{10}$, what is the probability that (*a*) just 75, (*b*) more than 75 passengers actually arrive? If it offers 100 such flights in a year, on average how many times will it be overbooked?

**4.** A school makes 500 entries for a particular examination, and usually has a 90% pass rate. Assuming that each entry has a $\frac{9}{10}$ chance of a pass, what is the probability that fewer than 440 passes are recorded?

**5.** 30% of the population of Ruritania are left-handed. If a random sample of 200 people is taken, what is the probability that less than 50 will be left-handed?

**6.** A small hall holds 244 people. The booking agents reckon that on average 4% of those who buy tickets fail to use them. If they regularly sell 250 tickets for a show, how often will they have to provide extra chairs?

**7.** In a particular constituency, 23 000 people propose to vote Labour and 17 000 Conservative, in a straight fight. On the eve of the poll, 200 voters chosen at random are asked their intentions, and answer truthfully. What is the probability that the sample will indicate. (*a*) a tie, (*b*) a Conservative victory?

**8.** Repeat Question 7 for a sample of 40, and for a sample of 400.

**9.** A playing card is drawn from a standard pack of 52 (with no jokers). Its suit is noted and it is replaced. The pack is shuffled and a card is again drawn. If in all 50 cards are drawn, find the probability that (*a*) more than 30 are black, (*b*) fewer than 9 clubs are drawn.

**10.** 1000 people, chosen at random within a region, are asked whether they were watching a particular television programme at 8.30 p.m. last Tuesday. If in fact 29% of the population of the region were watching, what is the probability that 300 or more of the sample were doing so? Repeat for 28%, 27%. Can you find by trial and error the true percentage which will make this probability just about 0·025?

## *4. LIMITING FORM OF THE BINOMIAL FUNCTION

**4.1 Standardizing the histogram.** Figure 12 shows the histogram of the last Section ($a = 0·4$, $n = 6$), transformed so that the mean is 0 and the standard deviation 1. Figure 13 shows the histogram of Figure 1 similarly standardized.

The calculations to transform Figure 11 to Figure 12 are set out in the table below:

$n = 6$,  $a = 0·4$;  $\mu = na = 2·4$;  $\sigma = \sqrt{(nab)} = 1·2$.

| $i$ | $p_i$ | $x = (i - \mu)/\sigma$ | $y = p_i\sigma$ |
|---|---|---|---|
| 0 | 0·047 | −2 | 0·056 |
| 1 | 0·187 | −1·17 | 0·224 |
| 2 | 0·311 | −0·33 | 0·373 |
| 3 | 0·276 | 0·5 | 0·331 |
| 4 | 0·138 | 1·33 | 0·166 |
| 5 | 0·037 | 2·17 | 0·044 |
| 6 | 0·004 | 3 | 0·005 |

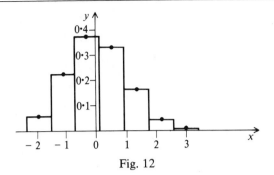

Fig. 12

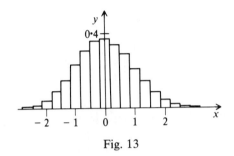

Fig. 13

The procedure is:

(i) calculate the probabilities, remembering (see Chapter 30) to use the ratio of consecutive probabilities

$$\frac{p(i+1)}{p(i)} = \frac{n-i}{i+1} \times \frac{a}{b};$$

(ii) calculate $\mu$ and $\sigma$;

(iii) obtain the $x$-values by subtracting $\mu$ from each $i$ (that is, translating to the left) and dividing by $\sigma$ (a stretch);

(iv) obtain the $y$-values by multiplying the probabilities by $\sigma$ (to keep the total area 1).

Before reading on, you should make the calculations and plot the histogram yourself for one similar example; with a calculator this should not be too lengthy. It would be an advantage if the class as a whole covered most of the following.

(a) $n = 8, a = 0.7$;  (b) $n = 10, a = 0.2$;
(c) $n = 10, a = 0.5$;  (d) $n = 10, a = 0.9$;
(e) $n = 16, a = 0.7$;  (f) $n = 20, a = 0.2$;
(g) $n = 25, a = 0.2$.

Figure 14 shows the transformed histograms for $a = 0.2$ with $n = 5, 10, 20$, and we can see clearly how the outlines approach the symmetrical Normal shape as $n$ is increased.

1045

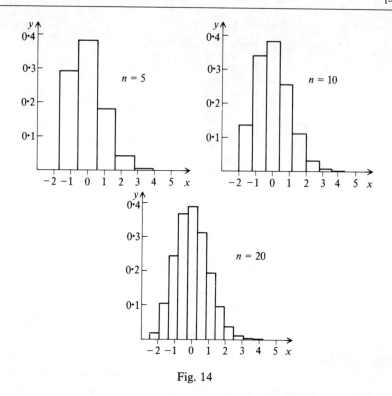

Fig. 14

**4.2   The Normal probability function.** We can now derive the equation for the Normal curve which we quoted in Section 2. We concentrate on the midpoints of the top edges of the rectangles (see Figure 12). The larger $n$ is, the closer together these points are. If we write the displacement vector from one to the next as

$$\binom{\delta x}{\delta y},$$

then the limit of $\delta y/\delta x$ will give us a differential equation from which, hopefully, the equation of the standardized Normal curve will emerge as a solution.

Now $\delta x = 1/\sigma$, since consecutive $i$-values differ by 1 and hence consecutive $x$-values differ by $1/\sigma$. Also $\delta y = \sigma p(i+1) - \sigma p(i)$, the difference between the heights of two consecutive rectangles. Then

$$\frac{\delta y}{\delta x} = \sigma^2[p(i+1) - p(i)].$$

The ratio of consecutive probabilities is much simpler than the expressions for the probabilities themselves, so we proceed as follows.

$$\frac{1}{y}\frac{\delta y}{\delta x} = \frac{\sigma^2[p(i+1)-p(i)]}{\sigma p(i)}$$

$$= \sigma\left[\frac{p(i+1)}{p(i)}-1\right]$$

$$= \sigma\left[\frac{n-i}{i+1}\times\frac{a}{b}-1\right].$$

Show that this simplifies to

$$\sigma\left(\frac{na-i-b}{(i+1)b}\right)$$

and then to

$$\frac{-xnab-b\sqrt{(nab)}}{nab+xb\sqrt{(nab)}+b},$$

using $x = (i-na)/\sigma$ and $\sigma = \sqrt{(nab)}$.

As $n$ tends to infinity, this fraction tends to $-x$, the first term in the numerator and denominator becoming more and more dominant. In the limit, we have then

$$\frac{1}{y}\frac{dy}{dx} = -x.$$

The methods of the last chapter now give

$$\ln y = -\tfrac{1}{2}x^2 + k,$$

i.e.

$$y = A\exp(-\tfrac{1}{2}x^2).$$

The value of the constant of integration must be chosen, as we have observed earlier, to give a total area of 1.

## 5. HYPOTHESIS TESTING

In Section 3 we discussed the possibility of a mumps epidemic occurring on the evidence from a sample of 500 people.

Such a process of investigating the nature of a population by examining a sample drawn from it is one of the central problems of statistics. For example, food manufacturers employ market researchers to select and question samples of housewives to try to find out how acceptable their product is to the population at large; political opinion polls are taken to try to predict who will win an election.

The difficulty with sampling is that the problem is usually back-to-front. If we *knew* that in a constituency of 20 000 people, 12 000 proposed to vote Conservative and 8000 Labour, and we were about to ask a sample of 200 people how they were going to vote, we could easily answer questions about the *sample* such as 'what is the probability that the sample will contain less than 50 Conservatives?' or 'what is the probability that the sample will predict a Labour victory?'.

But in fact what we want to do is make predictions about the *whole* constituency from the results of the sample. The real problem is almost always not 'What samples might I reasonably expect to draw from a given population?', but 'What parent populations might a given sample reasonably have been drawn from?'. To see how this problem is tackled, we return to the mumps example. How can we estimate the true proportion of the population who have had mumps?

What we did in Section 3 was to say 'If 60% of the population have had mumps, what is the probability that 320 or more of a sample of 500 will have had it?'. In other words we used the sample result, 320 out of 500, to *test the 60% hypothesis*.

We might similarly have tested a variety of other hypotheses; here is a table showing five other results:

| Hypothetical proportion | Probability of 320 or more |
|---|---|
| 66% | 0·839 |
| 64% | 0·519 |
| 62% | 0·191 |
| 60% | 0·038 |
| 58% | 0·004 |
| 56% | 0·0002 |

**5.1  Significance levels.** When we come to consider the question 'what parent populations might reasonably have led to the sample which was actually obtained?', we have to define what we mean by 'reasonable'. The usual way is to decide in advance to *reject* any hypothesis giving rise to a probability *below* a certain *significance level*. For example rejecting at the 5% significance level means rejecting a hypothesis which would give the observed sample result (or more) with probability *less than* 0·05.

So, from the table above, we should reject the 56%, 58% and 60% hypotheses at the 5% significance level, and we are reasonably confident that the parent population contains more than 60% who have had mumps.

Other significance levels which are used are 1% and 0·1%.

**5.2   The null hypothesis.** One common situation is illustrated by the next example. If a new technique or product is being tested, we want to compare the results of a sample with probabilities calculated using a model which assumes the new is *no better or worse* than the old. This 'no change' hypothesis is called the *null hypothesis*.

*Example 3*

According to audience research results, $\frac{1}{3}$ of all TV viewers who watch the evening news watch it on Channel X. In an attempt to boost their audience, Channel X introduce a new and glamorous newsreader. A survey of 1000 viewers taken at the end of the first week revealed that now only 306 were watching the news on Channel X. Should the new reader be kept on?

We use the null hypothesis that the proportion is still $\frac{1}{3}$, i.e. that the new reader is no better or worse than the old. On this hypothesis we calculate the probability of obtaining 306 or fewer viewers who watched Channel X in a sample of 1000.

For

$$n = 1000 \quad \text{and} \quad a = \tfrac{1}{3}$$

we have

$$\mu = na \approx 333$$

and

$$\sigma = \sqrt{(nab)} \approx 15.$$

Using the Normal approximation to the binomial, the required probability is given by

$$1 - \Phi\left(\frac{333 - 306 \cdot 5}{15}\right) \approx 1 - \Phi(1 \cdot 77) \approx 0 \cdot 038.$$

So we should reject the null hypothesis on the 5% level and say that this sample *suggests* that the new reader is *less* popular than the old one. Of course a longer trial period and further samples would be needed before any further action was taken.

### Exercise E

**1.** On the hypothesis that 70% of the people over 21 in your region can drive a car, what is the probability that if you approach 100 such people, chosen at random, you will find that 65 or fewer of them can actually do so? Does this sample result cast doubt on the hypothesis?

**2.** On the hypothesis that 80% of cat-owners use Purrfecta, what is the probability that of a sample of 20 owners chosen at random fewer than 12 use it? Would this sample result cast doubt on the hypothesis?

**3.** A demologist is investigating the theory that at least 25% of people over 40 in this country have their home in the town in which they were born. What conclusion do you draw if only 40 out of a sample of 200 do so?

**4.** Not more than 20% of households in this country are thought to run a freezer. A sample of 2000 households reveals 440 freezers. Comment.

**5.** You are testing the hypothesis that not more than 25% of the cars on British roads are blue. What number of cars in a count of 200 would convince you that the hypothesis is false?

**6.** There is a theory that 4% more male babies than female are born in this country; show that this implies that about 49% of births are of girls. You are going to collect data on 2000 consecutive births in a hospital; what would convince you that the '49% or fewer' hypothesis was false?

**7.** In a population of about 8000, you expect about 40% to be non-smokers. You want to be able to rule out the hypothesis 'two-thirds or more smoke'. What size of sample should you take?

**8.** A gardener usually finds that 75% of his lettuce seeds germinate. Last year he used a new variety of seed, and out of 200 seeds sown, 140 germinated. Would you recommend him to try the new variety again?

**9.** 30 out of a sample of 50 beer-drinkers preferred Real Ale to keg beer. Does this sample result provide reasonable evidence that such a preference exists in the beer-drinking population as a whole?

**10.** Before an intensive anti-smoking advertising campaign it was estimated that 60% of the adult population of Britain smoked cigarettes to some extent. Afterwards a survey found 164 smokers out of 300 people asked. Does this result provide significant evidence that the campaign was successful?

# 6. ESTIMATION OF PARAMETERS

So far, we have only been concerned with cases where we want to know whether a population parameter is above or below a certain level. Sometimes we want to make as good an estimate as we can of what the parameter is, and a slightly different procedure is necessary.

If we want to say as much as we can about the population on the evidence of our single sample of 320 out of 500, we shall want not only to reject a 58% hypothesis because it is too low, but also a 70% hypothesis because it is too high. We therefore need to consider how each hypothesis in turn would have doubt cast on it by particular samples.

1050

Thus, if we work at the 5% level of significance, the 60% hypothesis will give us samples with mean 300 and standard deviation $\sqrt{120}$ for the number who have already had mumps, as shown in Figure 15.

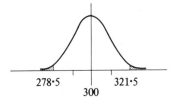

$$278\cdot5 \qquad \begin{array}{c}300\end{array} \qquad 321\cdot5$$

Fig.15

If the number is over 321 or under 279, it falls in the shaded region, whose *total* area if 0.05, and therefore provides evidence against the 60% hypothesis at the 5% level. The reason for this is that $\Phi(1\cdot96) \approx 0\cdot975$, so that 95% of the area lies between $\mu + 1\cdot96\,\sigma$ and $\mu - 1\cdot96\,\sigma$; in this case, the dividing lines fall at $300 \pm 1\cdot96\sqrt{120}$, that is, at $278\cdot5$ and $321\cdot5$. We are now using a *two-tail test*, whereas we have used only a *one-tail test* before.

There are no hard-and-fast rules about which is correct; a two-tail test is more often used, especially in estimation problems, but, as in the problem originally posed, a one-tail test may be more appropriate.

**6.1   A 95% confidence interval.** If we had to suggest a single estimate based on our sample, 64% would probably be the best we could do. But this is not very useful without some indication of how accurate it is, and we usually provide this by saying which hypotheses do not have evidence against them at the 5% level. Thus, we can make a new table:

| Hypothetical proportion | Standard deviation | 95% of observations will lie between |
|:---:|:---:|:---:|
| 60% | 10·95 | 278·5 and 321·5 |
| 62% | 10·85 | 288·7 and 331·3 |
| 64% | 10·73 | 299·0 and 341·0 |
| 66% | 10·59 | 309·2 and 350·8 |
| 68% | 10·43 | 319·6 and 360·4 |

To the nearest whole number, our confidence limits are from 60% to 68%; any higher or lower percentage would be rejected at the 5% level on the evidence of this sample.

Notice that with the low, 60% proportion, the observed sample number of 320 is just inside the upper limit; while with the high, 68% proportion, 320 is just inside the lower limit.

The working is illustrated by Figure 16, which shows where 95% of observations will lie for each of the hypotheses listed.

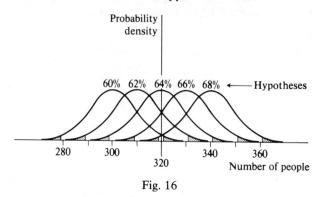

Fig. 16

**6.2   Finding the confidence interval.** Clearly we do not always want to go to the trouble of drawing up tables like the one in Section 6.1.

A direct method is as follows. If the proportion who have had mumps is $a\%$, then the mean of a sample of 500 will be $500a$, and the standard deviation $\sqrt{(500a(1-a))}$. We wish to find $a$ so that

$$500a \pm 1{\cdot}96\sqrt{(500a(1-a))} = 320.$$

This involves solving a rather unpleasant quadratic equation. A perfectly adequate approximation can be made using the following alternative approach. Since $\sigma$ does not vary much with $a$ (see the table above), we can take the value $\sigma \approx 10{\cdot}73$ from our sample proportion (320 out of 500, or 64%). So our confidence interval for $a$ is approximately

$$0{\cdot}64 \pm 2 \times \frac{10{\cdot}73}{500},$$

or 60% to 68%. (Note that it is good enough to round off $1{\cdot}96\,\sigma$ to $2\,\sigma$ to give an answer to the nearest whole number.)

These limits can then be confirmed using the correct standard deviations (as in Section 6.1).

### Exercise F

**1.** 65 out of a sample of 100 people interviewed were able to drive. Assuming that the conditions of the experiment justify a binomial model, give a 95% confidence interval for the proportion in the population.

**2.** 12 cat-owners out of 20 interviewed use Purrfecta. Give a 95% confidence interval for the proportion in the population at large who use it, stating any assumptions you make about the experiment.

1052

**3.** 61 blue cars are observed in a count of 200 passing a certain point on a country road. Give 95% confidence limits for the proportion of blue cars passing that point.

**4.** A sample of 2000 households, chosen at random from the whole population of Bristol, showed that 440 of them run a freezer. Give a 99% confidence interval for the proportion of Bristol households with a freezer; say clearly what the numbers you quote indicate.

**5.** 40 people out of 200 interviewed have their home in the town in which they were born. They were drawn by a random process from the electoral register of a town of 20 000. What conclusion can you draw?

**6.** 980 out of 2000 babies born in a particular hospital are girls. Give 99% confidence limits for the proportion of births of girls among all births, and for the ratio of boys born to girls.

**7.** A survey showed that, out of a sample of 250 viewers, 75 watched the Cup Final on television last year. Estimate 95% confidence limits for the proportion of TV viewers in the whole country who watched the Cup Final.

**8.** Repeat Question 7 for a sample result of 150 out of 500.

**9.** What do we have to do to the sample size to halve the length of the confidence interval?

**10.** Write a program to read $n$, the sample size, and $i$, the number of 'successes' in the sample, and to output a 95% confidence interval.

## *7. SAMPLING FROM MORE GENERAL POPULATIONS

Up to now, we have only considered samples from populations of attributes—the question asked is answered 'yes' or 'no', rather than '7' or '14·3 kg'; we have simply counted how many times we get the answer 'yes'. The Normal curve can however give a good deal of help in a more general sampling problem, because of a remarkable result, which we shall illustrate but not prove, called the *central limit theorem*.

**7.1 The central limit theorem.** Under certain very general conditions, the central limit theorem says:

If we take a parent population of any description, with mean $\mu$ and standard deviation $\sigma$, and draw samples of $n$ members (independently and with replacement), then the means of these samples form a population with mean $\mu$ and standard deviation $\sigma/\sqrt{n}$; and for large $n$ the probability density function approximates to the Normal curve.

We illustrate this with three examples.

*Example* 4

Throw four dice 100 times, recording the total number of 'pips' showing in each throw (the score). What are the mean and standard deviation of your scores?

The sample is a sample of size 4 from a population in which 1, 2, 3, 4, 5, 6 are equally likely, and the scores range from 4 to 24. The 100 repetitions give a population whose mean and standard deviation should not be too far from the theoretical values suggested here. We can turn the population of scores into a population of means by simply dividing by 4. An advantage of taking an artificial example like this is that we can easily analyse all possible samples; the generator

$$(\tfrac{1}{6}(t + t^2 + t^3 + t^4 + t^5 + t^6))^4$$

(or direct counting methods) will show that the probabilities of the various possible scores (and means) are:

| Score | Mean | Probability | Score | Mean | Probability |
|-------|------|-------------|-------|------|-------------|
| 4 | 1 | $1/6^4$ | 15 | 3·75 | $140/6^4$ |
| 5 | 1·25 | $4/6^4$ | 16 | 4 | $125/6^4$ |
| 6 | 1·5 | $10/6^4$ | 17 | 4·25 | $104/6^4$ |
| 7 | 1·75 | $20/6^4$ | 18 | 4·5 | $80/6^4$ |
| 8 | 2 | $35/6^4$ | 19 | 4·75 | $56/6^4$ |
| 9 | 2·25 | $56/6^4$ | 20 | 5 | $35/6^4$ |
| 10 | 2·5 | $80/6^4$ | 21 | 5·25 | $20/6^4$ |
| 11 | 2·75 | $104/6^4$ | 22 | 5·5 | $10/6^4$ |
| 12 | 3 | $125/6^4$ | 23 | 5·75 | $4/6^4$ |
| 13 | 3·25 | $140/6^4$ | 24 | 6 | $1/6^4$ |
| 14 | 3·5 | $146/6^4$ | | | |

The histograms of the parent population, and of the population of means of samples, are drawn on the same scale in Figure 17.

The Normal tendency is already marked, though the sample is of size 4 only; the other results are always exact, not approximate, as detailed calculation (or work with generators) will show. They are:

| | Mean | Standard deviation |
|---|------|--------------------|
| Parent population | 3·5 | $\sqrt{(35/12)}$ |
| Population of scores | 14 | $\sqrt{(35/3)}$ |
| Population of means | 3·5 | $\sqrt{(35/48)}$ |

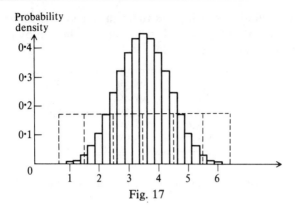

Fig. 17

## Example 5

Six distances, given to the nearest km, are added; what is the distribution of possible errors in the total?

Here, the parent population is continuous, all errors between $-0.5$ km and $+0.5$ km being equally likely; the mean is 0, and the standard deviation can be shown to be $\sqrt{(1/12)}$, or about $0.289$. The mean of the population of sums of errors is clearly 0; the maximum and minimum are $\pm 3$ km, but the standard deviation is only $\sqrt{(1/2)}$, about $0.707$. We could use the Normal tables to work out how often the total would be correct to the nearest km, and so on.

The sum of three such errors is considered in Chapter 35 (Exercise G), a complete distribution being given; already the Normal tendency is quite marked. It would be interesting to do a simulation of this problem—using two-digit random numbers, say, and interpreting 00 to 49 as positive and 50 to 99 as negative (e.g. 23, 84 would be $+0.23$, $-0.34$).

## Example 6

100 airline passengers board a particular flight daily, and their baggage has mean weight 13·8 kg with standard deviation 5·47 kg. How often will the airline have to handle more than 1500 kg of baggage?

Oddly enough, we do not need to know the shape of the parent population at all. We can deduce at once from the central limit theorem that the mean weight of baggage per passenger is approximately Normally distributed, with mean 13·8 and standard deviation $5.47/\sqrt{100} = 0.547$. Standardizing, the probability that the mean is over 15 kg is

$$1 - \Phi\left(\frac{1.2}{0.547}\right) \approx 0.014.$$

Again, a simulation which gives the right mean and standard deviation, and indicates a very skew distribution, can be run by interpreting two-digit random numbers as follows:

| | | | |
|---|---|---|---|
| 00–04 | 2 kg | 30–39 | 12 kg |
| 05–09 | 4 kg | 40–49 | 14 kg |
| 10–14 | 6 kg | 50–59 | 16 kg |
| 15–19 | 8 kg | 60–79 | 18 kg |
| 20–29 | 10 kg | 80–99 | 20 kg |

## 7.2  Variance of the sum of two independent variables.

*Example 7*

A journey is made up of two parts—a bus ride, which takes 16 minutes on average, with a standard deviation of 3 minutes; and a car drive, which takes 24 minutes with standard deviation 2 minutes. The two parts are independent of one another. What can you say about the total journey time?

Nothing is said about the distributions here, but the answer is always the same. We shall not prove it here, though a partial proof is suggested in Question 10 below. If we take the simplest possible distribution fitting the data—13 min or 19 min plus 22 min or 26 min—then the four equally likely totals are 35, 39, 41, 45 minutes, and a brief calculation shows that the expected value is 40 minutes with standard deviation $\sqrt{13}$ minutes.

This illustrates the fact that if $x_1$ is distributed with mean $\mu_1$ and variance $\sigma_1^2$, and $x_2$ with mean $\mu_2$ and variance $\sigma_2^2$, then, provided that the two are independent, $x_1 + x_2$ is distributed with mean $\mu_1 + \mu_2$ and variance $\sigma_1^2 + \sigma_2^2$.

We can at once extend this to show that if we take a sample of $n$ independent readings from a population with mean $\mu$ and variance $\sigma^2$, then their sum is distributed with mean $n\mu$ and variance $n\sigma^2$, and therefore their mean is distributed with mean $\mu$ and variance $\sigma^2/n$, as quoted in the central limit theorem above.

## *Exercise G*

**1.** A grocer sells raisins and currants in packets with mean net weights 500 g and 250 g, and standard deviations of 20 g and 15 g respectively. Housewives shopping at this grocer's use one packet each in their Christmas cakes. Find the expected value and variance of the total weight of fruit used in their cakes.

**2.** Lengths of fire hose are joined by fitting the 'arm' end of one into the 'sleeve' end of the other. The arms have mean external diameter 89 mm, and the sleeves mean internal diameter 94 mm; each has variance 8 mm$^2$. Find the probability that the difference in diameter of a pair chosen at random will be less than 1 mm or more than 7 mm. (The variance of $x_1 - x_2$ is $\sigma_1^2 + \sigma_2^2$; can you see why?)

**3.** Throw five dice 100 times, recording the total score, and verify that the mean is about 17·5 and the variance about 175/12.

**4.** A map shows the distances between the centres of towns to the nearest km. In planning a long journey I add up 25 such distances in order to find the total distance. What is the probability that this gives the total correct to the nearest km? (See Example 5.)

**5.** Samples of size 50 are taken from a population with mean 17 and standard deviation 4. Draw a graph showing the approximate probability density function for the means of the samples, and calculate the probability of obtaining a sample whose mean is less than 16.

**6.** Packets of butter of nominal weight 250 g are turned out by a machine which produces a mean weight of 253 g and standard deviation of 5 g. What is the probability of buying an underweight package? If the butter is packed in boxes of 36 packets, what is the probability of getting a box for which the mean weight is less than 250 g?

**7.** In a game of Ludo a player is within one throw of home when he has scored a total of 64 on his die. Find the probability that he will achieve this within 16 throws. (Find the probability of getting 64 or more in exactly 16 throws.)

**8.** Wire cables are formed from 10 separate wires, the strength of each wire being Normally distributed with a mean of 2500 N and a standard deviation of 98 N. Assuming that the strength of a cable is the sum of that of its separate wires, what proportion of cables will have a breaking strain of less than 24 600 N? If this proportion is to be reduced to 1 in 1000, and the variance of the strength of the individual wires cannot be changed, what mean strength of wire must be demanded?

**9.** Tent-poles for a frame tent are in three sections, supposedly of length (from foot to shoulder in each case) 70 cm, 62 cm, 55 cm. A batch of 50 long sections shows a mean of 70 cm and a standard deviation of 0·4 cm; a batch of 60 mid-sections also has the correct mean, with a standard deviation of 0·35 cm; but a sample of 50 short sections proves to have a mean of only 54·4 cm and a standard deviation of 0·6 cm. How likely is it that a complete pole as sent out by the manufacturers will be more than 2 cm too short?

**10.** (*a*) If $G(t) = p_0 + p_1 t + p_2 t^2 + p_3 t^3$, $H(t) = q_0 + q_1 t + q_2 t^2$, and $G$, $H$ generate the independent variables $x$, $y$, show that $x + y$ is generated by $G(t) . H(t)$.

(*b*) Assuming that the result in (*a*) is generally true, and writing $K(t) = G(t) . H(t)$, prove that

$$K'(1) = G'(1) + H'(1),$$

$$K''(1) + K'(1) - (K'(1))^2 = G''(1) + G'(1) - (G'(1))^2 + H''(1) + H'(1) - (H'(1))^2;$$

hence prove the result of Section 7.2 for the discrete case.

(*c*) Writing $L(t) = (G(t))^n$, prove the other result of Section 7.2 directly.

# SUMMARY

*Normal model*

$$\phi(x) = \frac{1}{\sqrt{(2\pi)}} \exp\left(-\tfrac{1}{2}x^2\right)$$

is the standardized Normal probability density function. It has expected value 0 and standard deviation 1.

With the use of tables and suitable transformations, the model may be used in many practical situations involving continuous variables.

*Normal approximation to binomial models*

Normal models provide good approximations to some roughly symmetrical histograms from discrete models, e.g. binomial histograms with large $n$. In such cases one must remember to use a 'continuity correction'; for example, $p(10$ or more$)$ is approximated by the area under a Normal curve to the right of $9\cdot5$.

*Hypothesis testing, confidence intervals*

A binomial hypothesis can be tested using a one-tail or a two-tail test and approximating by the Normal curve; if the probability of obtaining the sample we have observed, or a less likely one, is less than $0\cdot05$, we say that the evidence against the hypothesis is significant at the 95% level. The set of hypotheses against which the sample does not provide evidence at the 95% level is called a 95% confidence interval.

*Central limit theorem*

For a parent population with mean $\mu$ and standard deviation $\sigma$, if we draw samples of size $n$, independently and with replacement, then the means of such samples form a population with mean $\mu$ and standard deviation $\sigma/\sqrt{n}$; and, for large $n$, the probability density function for these means is approximately Normal.

# 40

# LINEAR ALGEBRA AND GEOMETRY REVIEW

## 1. INTRODUCTION

In Chapter 21 we used one geometrical interpretation of three linear equations in three unknowns—each equation being regarded as a plane—while in Chapter 26 an entirely different interpretation in terms of transformations was used for the same situation. In this chapter we introduce $3 \times 3$ determinants and use them to provide a link between the two previous approaches.

The first exercise reviews elementary work in two dimensions.

### Exercise A

**1.** Find the matrix of the shear which maps the vector $\mathbf{i} + 2\mathbf{j}$ onto $\mathbf{i}$, leaving the line $x = 0$ invariant. Find the image under this shear of the vector $\mathbf{i} + 4\mathbf{j}$. Sketch the image vectors on a rectangular grid, and find the area of the parallelogram with these two image vectors as sides. What is the area of the parallelogram with vertices $(0, 0)$, $(1, 2)$, $(2, 6)$ and $(1, 4)$?

**2.** (*a*) Find the matrix of a shear which leaves $x = 0$ invariant, and maps the vector $2\mathbf{i} + \mathbf{j}$ onto a vector parallel to $\mathbf{i}$. Find also the image under this shear of the vector $4\mathbf{i} + 3\mathbf{j}$. What is the area of the parallelogram with $2\mathbf{i} + \mathbf{j}$ and $4\mathbf{i} + 3\mathbf{j}$ as sides?

(*b*) Show that the unit square is mapped onto the parallelogram of part (*a*) by the transformation with matrix

$$\begin{pmatrix} 2 & 4 \\ 1 & 3 \end{pmatrix}.$$

What is the connection between the numbers in this matrix and the area of the parallelogram?

**3.** Use the methods suggested by Questions 1 and 2 to find the areas of parallelograms which are the images of the unit square under transformations with matrices

(i) $\begin{pmatrix} 6 & 2 \\ 3 & 4 \end{pmatrix}$,    (ii) $\begin{pmatrix} a & b \\ c & d \end{pmatrix}$   $(a \neq 0)$.

**4.** Repeat Question 3 with the matrix $\begin{pmatrix} 2 & 6 \\ 4 & 3 \end{pmatrix}$. Do you need to modify your answer to 3(ii)?

**5.** What is the area of the parallelogram with $\begin{pmatrix} 0 \\ c \end{pmatrix}$ and $\begin{pmatrix} b \\ d \end{pmatrix}$ as two of its sides? Does this agree with the value obtained from your answer to 3(ii) when you substitute $a = 0$?

**6.** If $a$ and $b$ are positive, show that $\begin{pmatrix} a \\ c \end{pmatrix}$ is anticlockwise of $\begin{pmatrix} b \\ d \end{pmatrix} \Leftrightarrow ad - bc < 0$. What is the significance of this result in terms of the transformation with matrix $\begin{pmatrix} a & b \\ c & d \end{pmatrix}$?

## 2. DETERMINANTS

**2.1 Determinants and scale factors.** In Question 3 of Exercise A, you showed that the area of the parallelogram onto which the unit square is mapped by the transformation with matrix $\mathbf{M} = \begin{pmatrix} a & b \\ c & d \end{pmatrix}$ is $|ad - bc|$, or $|\det \mathbf{M}|$ using the notation $\det \mathbf{M} = ad - bc$. The significance of the sign of $\det \mathbf{M}$ is illustrated by Question 4. As shown in Figure 1, $\begin{pmatrix} 2 \\ 4 \end{pmatrix}$, the image of **i**, is anticlockwise of $\begin{pmatrix} 6 \\ 3 \end{pmatrix}$, the image of **j**. So the unit square has been 'turned over' by the transformation. The condition for this to happen is precisely that $\det \mathbf{M} < 0$.

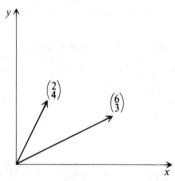

Fig. 1

If the whole plane is divided by sets of lines parallel to the coordinate axes into squares congruent to the unit square, these squares will all be mapped onto parallelograms congruent to each other. This suggests that the area of any region of the plane is multiplied by $\det \mathbf{M}$ under the transformation. We call $\det \mathbf{M}$ the *area scale factor* of the transformation, negative determinants indicating that an 'opposite' transformation has taken place, i.e. that the unit square has been 'turned over'.

1060

In a similar way, we could define the *volume scale factor*, or *determinant*, of a $3 \times 3$ matrix to be the volume of the parallelepiped onto which the unit cube is mapped, or $-1 \times$ this volume, if the transformation turns the unit cube 'inside out'.

**2.2  Volume of a parallelepiped.** Figure 2 shows a parallelepiped which is the image of the unit cube under a transformation mapping $\mathbf{i} \to \mathbf{a}$, $\mathbf{j} \to \mathbf{b}$ and $\mathbf{k} \to \mathbf{c}$.

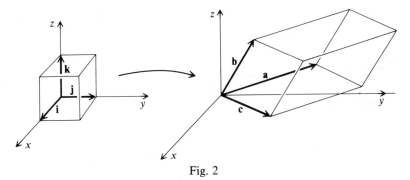

Fig. 2

To find the volume of the parallelepiped, it is convenient to represent the parallelepiped by the matrix

$$\mathbf{M} = \begin{pmatrix} a_1 & b_1 & c_1 \\ a_2 & b_2 & c_2 \\ a_3 & b_3 & c_3 \end{pmatrix}$$

of the transformation in question.

Its volume will be the same as that of any parallelepiped obtained from it by shearing—that is, represented by a matrix obtained from $\mathbf{M}$ by pre-multiplication by elementary matrices of type $\begin{pmatrix} 1 & 0 & 0 \\ k & 1 & 0 \\ 0 & 0 & 1 \end{pmatrix}$ etc.

Pre-multiplication by such a matrix is equivalent to performing *elementary row-operations* (see Chapter 26, p. 655).

We now proceed to apply such row-operations. Let $R_i$ denote the $i$th row. The operations

'Replace $\quad R_2$ by $\left(R_2 - \dfrac{a_2}{a_1} R_1\right)$ and $R_3$ by $\left(R_3 - \dfrac{a_3}{a_1} R_1\right)$',

transform $\begin{vmatrix} a_1 & b_1 & c_1 \\ a_2 & b_2 & c_2 \\ a_3 & b_3 & c_3 \end{vmatrix}$ into $\begin{vmatrix} a_1 & b_1 & c_1 \\ 0 & b_2' & c_2' \\ 0 & b_3' & c_3' \end{vmatrix}$,

where
$$b_2' = b_2 - \frac{a_2 b_1}{a_1}, \quad c_2' = c_2 - \frac{a_2 c_1}{a_1},$$

$$b_3' = b_3 - \frac{a_3 b_1}{a_1}, \quad c_3' = c_3 - \frac{a_3 c_1}{a_1}$$

and we assume $a_1 \neq 0$. Next replace the new $R_3$ by $\left(R_3 - \frac{b_3'}{b_2'} R_2\right)$, to

transform $\begin{vmatrix} a_1 & b_1 & c_1 \\ 0 & b_2' & c_2' \\ 0 & b_3' & c_3' \end{vmatrix}$ into $\begin{vmatrix} a_1 & b_1 & c_1 \\ 0 & b_2' & c_2' \\ 0 & 0 & c_3'' \end{vmatrix}$, where $c_3'' = c_3' - \frac{b_3'}{b_2'} c_2'$, and

we assume $b_2' \neq 0$. Thus the parallelepiped with sides $\begin{pmatrix} a_1 \\ 0 \\ 0 \end{pmatrix}$, $\begin{pmatrix} b_1 \\ b_2' \\ 0 \end{pmatrix}$, $\begin{pmatrix} c_1 \\ c_2' \\ c_3'' \end{pmatrix}$

has the same volume as the original parallelepiped.

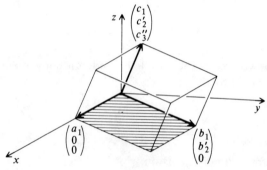

Fig. 3

Figure 3 shows the transformed parallelepiped. Note that one of its faces (shaded) lies in the plane $z = 0$. The area of this face is $|a_1 \times b_2'|$, and hence the volume of the parallelepiped is $|a_1 \times b_2' \times c_3''|$. Now

$$a_1 \times b_2' \times c_3'' = a_1 b_2' \left(c_3' - \frac{b_3'}{b_2'} c_2'\right)$$

$$= a_1 (b_2' c_3' - b_3' c_2')$$

$$= a_1 \left[\left(b_2 - \frac{a_2 b_1}{a_1}\right)\left(c_3 - \frac{a_3 c_1}{a_1}\right) - \left(b_3 - \frac{a_3 b_1}{a_1}\right)\left(c_2 - \frac{a_2 c_1}{a_1}\right)\right]$$

In the expansion of this last expression, the two terms having non-trivial denominators cancel, leaving six terms expressible as

$$a_1(b_2 c_3 - b_3 c_2) - a_2(b_1 c_3 - b_3 c_1) + a_3(b_1 c_2 - b_2 c_1) \tag{1}$$

1062

This expression is the volume of the parallelepiped, or $-1 \times$ this volume if the transformation has turned the unit cube inside out. In any event, the expression gives the volume scale factor, or determinant, of the matrix $\mathbf{M}$, written $\det \mathbf{M}$. We often denote $\det \mathbf{M}$ by $\begin{vmatrix} a_1 & b_1 & c_1 \\ a_2 & b_2 & c_2 \\ a_3 & b_3 & c_3 \end{vmatrix}$.

Similar notation is used for the determinant of a $2 \times 2$ matrix, and an alternative way of writing expression (1) is

$$a_1 \begin{vmatrix} b_2 & c_2 \\ b_3 & c_3 \end{vmatrix} - a_2 \begin{vmatrix} b_1 & c_1 \\ b_3 & c_2 \end{vmatrix} + a_3 \begin{vmatrix} b_1 & c_1 \\ b_2 & c_2 \end{vmatrix}.$$

The special cases which we avoided in the derivation of $\det \mathbf{M}$ are easily dealt with, giving the same result.

For example, if $a_1 = 0$, simply change $b_2$ or $c_2$ to zero (if possible) instead of $a_2$. The details are left as an exercise.

**2.3  Simplifying determinants.** Expression (1) for the determinant given in Section 2.2 is unwieldy and in practice it is more convenient to make use of the methods used in the derivation of $\det \mathbf{M}$ to simplify the working.

*Example* 1

Evaluate the determinant

$$\begin{vmatrix} 1 & 2 & 3 \\ 1 & 3 & 5 \\ 2 & 2 & 5 \end{vmatrix}.$$

Using the method of row-operations of Section 2.2

$$\begin{vmatrix} 1 & 2 & 3 \\ 1 & 3 & 5 \\ 2 & 2 & 5 \end{vmatrix} = \begin{vmatrix} 1 & 2 & 3 \\ 0 & 1 & 2 \\ 0 & -2 & -1 \end{vmatrix} \qquad \text{(Replace } R_2 \text{ by } R_2 - R_1 \text{ and replace } R_3 \text{ by } R_3 - 2R_1.)$$

$$= \begin{vmatrix} 1 & 2 & 3 \\ 0 & 1 & 2 \\ 0 & 0 & 3 \end{vmatrix}. \qquad \text{(Replace } R_3 \text{ by } R_3 + 2R_2.)$$

We can now evaluate the determinant directly as

$$a_1 b_2' c_3'' = 1 \times 1 \times 3 = 3.$$

1063

### Exercise B

**1.** Evaluate the determinants:

(i) $\begin{vmatrix} 1 & 1 & 1 \\ 1 & 2 & 3 \\ 1 & 4 & 5 \end{vmatrix}$;    (ii) $\begin{vmatrix} 1 & 1 & 1 \\ 1 & 2 & 3 \\ 1 & 3 & 5 \end{vmatrix}$;    (iii) $\begin{vmatrix} 1 & 2 & 3 \\ 4 & 5 & 6 \\ 7 & 8 & 9 \end{vmatrix}$.

**2.** Find the volume of a parallelepiped with one vertex at the origin, and $(1, 4, 7)$, $(2, 5, 8)$, and $(3, 6, 10)$ as vertices adjoining $O$ (that is, joined to $O$ by an edge.)

**3.** Find the volume of the parallelepiped $ABCDA'B'C'D'$ in Figure 4, where $A$ is $(2, 4, 3)$, $B$ is $(3, 3, 4)$, $C$ is $(2, 4, 5)$ and $A'$ is $(3, 5, 2)$.

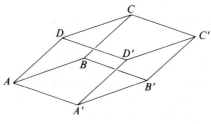

Fig. 4

**4.** If **M** maps the unit cube onto parallelepiped $P$, and **L** maps $P$ onto parallelepiped $Q$, what is the ratio of the volume of the unit cube to that of $Q$? Use your answer to express det $(\mathbf{LM})$ in terms of det **L** and det **M**.

**5.** If **M** maps the unit cube onto $P$, $\mathbf{M}^{-1}$ (if it exists) will map $P$ back onto the unit cube. What does this tell you about det $(\mathbf{M}^{-1})$?

**6.** If **M** is as in Section 2.2, and det $\mathbf{M} = 0$, what must be true about the column vectors **a**, **b**, **c**? Illustrate, with reference to Question 1(ii). What kind of transformation does **M** represent, and what is the image of three-dimensional space under **M**? Comment, with reference to Question 5.

**7.** If **M** is as in Section 2.2, we define $\tilde{\mathbf{M}}$ to be the matrix

$$\begin{pmatrix} a_1 & a_2 & a_3 \\ b_1 & b_2 & b_3 \\ c_1 & c_2 & c_3 \end{pmatrix}$$

Show directly, by expanding the determinant of $\tilde{\mathbf{M}}$, that det $\tilde{\mathbf{M}} = $ det **M**. ($\tilde{\mathbf{M}}$ is called the *transpose* of **M**, obtained by interchanging the rows and columns of **M**, or by reflecting the positions of the entries of **M** in the leading diagonal.)

## 3. LINEAR EQUATIONS
## AND TRANSFORMATIONS

**3.1 Matrices and transformations.** We saw in Chapter 26 that if we represent a set of linear equations, such as

$$\left.\begin{array}{l} x+y+z=3 \\ x+2y+3z=5 \\ x+4y+5z=7 \end{array}\right\},$$

in its matrix form, which in this case is

$$\begin{pmatrix} 1 & 1 & 1 \\ 1 & 2 & 3 \\ 1 & 4 & 5 \end{pmatrix} \begin{pmatrix} x \\ y \\ z \end{pmatrix} = \begin{pmatrix} 3 \\ 5 \\ 7 \end{pmatrix},$$

solving the equations means finding a vector $\begin{pmatrix} x \\ y \\ z \end{pmatrix}$ which maps onto $\begin{pmatrix} 3 \\ 5 \\ 7 \end{pmatrix}$

under the transformation with matrix $\begin{pmatrix} 1 & 1 & 1 \\ 1 & 2 & 3 \\ 1 & 4 & 5 \end{pmatrix}$.

We can express such a set of linear equations symbolically by the single equation

$$\mathbf{Mr} = \mathbf{d}. \tag{2}$$

We saw in Chapter 26 that if the *columns* **a**, **b** and **c** of **M** are linearly independent then **M** represents a one–one transformation and equation (2) will have a unique solution. If, however, **a**, **b** and **c** are *dependent*, then **M** represents a squashing transformation and we have either no solution or an infinite number of solutions.

In this chapter we have seen that if **a**, **b** and **c** are dependent (i.e. coplanar; see Exercise B, Question 6), then **M** maps the unit cube onto a parallelepiped of zero volume, that is, $\det \mathbf{M} = 0$. This gives us a rapid way of testing whether **M** is a squash or not; if $\det \mathbf{M} = 0$ we have an infinite number of solutions or none at all. The condition for a unique solution is $\det \mathbf{M} \neq 0$.

*Example* 2

Solve

$$\left.\begin{array}{l} x+y+z=3 \\ x+2y+3z=5 \\ x+4y+7z=9 \end{array}\right\}.$$

Direct evaluation of the determinant gives

$$1 \times (14-12) - 1 \times (7-4) + 1 \times (3-2) = 0,$$

which warns us to expect either no solution or an infinite number.

Using the row-operation method of Chapter 26,

$$\begin{pmatrix} 1 & 1 & 1 \\ 1 & 2 & 3 \\ 1 & 4 & 7 \end{pmatrix} \begin{pmatrix} x \\ y \\ z \end{pmatrix} = \begin{pmatrix} 3 \\ 5 \\ 9 \end{pmatrix}$$

becomes in turn $\begin{pmatrix} 1 & 1 & 1 \\ 0 & 1 & 2 \\ 0 & 3 & 6 \end{pmatrix} \begin{pmatrix} x \\ y \\ z \end{pmatrix} = \begin{pmatrix} 3 \\ 2 \\ 6 \end{pmatrix}$   (Replace $R_2$ by $R_2 - R_1$ and $R_3$ by $R_3 - R_1$.)

and then $\begin{pmatrix} 1 & 1 & 1 \\ 0 & 1 & 2 \\ 0 & 0 & 0 \end{pmatrix} \begin{pmatrix} x \\ y \\ z \end{pmatrix} = \begin{pmatrix} 3 \\ 2 \\ 0 \end{pmatrix}$.   (Replace $R_3$ by $R_3 - 3R_2$.)

This matrix equation corresponds to the simultaneous set of equations

$$\left. \begin{aligned} x + y + z &= 3 \\ y + 2z &= 2 \\ 0z &= 0 \end{aligned} \right\}.$$

The last of these is satisfied by *any* value of $z$. Putting $z = \lambda$, we obtain

$$y = 2 - 2\lambda$$

from the second equation and

$$\begin{aligned} x &= 3 - (2 - 2\lambda) - \lambda \\ &= 1 + \lambda \end{aligned}$$

from the first. So the original set of equations is satisfied by the *line* of solutions

$$\begin{pmatrix} x \\ y \\ z \end{pmatrix} = \begin{pmatrix} 1 + \lambda \\ 2 - 2\lambda \\ \lambda \end{pmatrix} = \begin{pmatrix} 1 \\ 2 \\ 0 \end{pmatrix} + \lambda \begin{pmatrix} 1 \\ -2 \\ 1 \end{pmatrix}.$$

In other words, a whole *line* of points is mapped on to $(3, 5, 9)$ by the transformation whose matrix is $\begin{pmatrix} 1 & 1 & 1 \\ 1 & 2 & 3 \\ 1 & 4 & 7 \end{pmatrix}$.

Do all points in three-dimensional space have lines as their inverse images under this transformation? Find the inverse images of $(0, 0, 0)$

1066

and $(2, 1, -1)$. Have the three inverse image lines we have found so far anything in common? Why is it not possible to find an inverse image for $(1, 2, 3)$?

## Exercise C

**1.** (a) Find $x$, $y$ and $z$ so that $x\begin{pmatrix}1\\2\\1\end{pmatrix} + y\begin{pmatrix}-1\\1\\0\end{pmatrix} + z\begin{pmatrix}1\\5\\2\end{pmatrix} = \begin{pmatrix}0\\0\\0\end{pmatrix}$.

(b) Solve the equation $\begin{pmatrix}1 & -1 & 1\\2 & 1 & 5\\1 & 0 & 2\end{pmatrix}\begin{pmatrix}x\\y\\z\end{pmatrix} = \begin{pmatrix}4\\-1\\1\end{pmatrix}$.

(c) Show that the line $\begin{pmatrix}x\\y\\z\end{pmatrix} = \begin{pmatrix}p\\q\\r\end{pmatrix} + \lambda\begin{pmatrix}-2\\-1\\1\end{pmatrix}$ is mapped onto a single point by

the transformation whose matrix is $\begin{pmatrix}1 & -1 & 1\\2 & 1 & 5\\1 & 0 & 2\end{pmatrix}$.

(d) Show that the image point you have found in part (c) lies on the plane $x + y - 3z = 0$. Hence show that this plane is the range of the transformation.

(e) Explain why $\begin{pmatrix}1 & -1 & 1\\2 & 1 & 5\\1 & 0 & 2\end{pmatrix}\begin{pmatrix}x\\y\\z\end{pmatrix} = \begin{pmatrix}3\\1\\0\end{pmatrix}$ has no solution.

**2.** (a) Solve the equations

$$\left.\begin{array}{r}x + 2y - z = 0\\x - y + 2z = 0\\2x + y + z = 0\end{array}\right\}.$$

(b) Find scalars $x$, $y$ and $z$ so that

$$x\begin{pmatrix}1\\1\\2\end{pmatrix} + y\begin{pmatrix}2\\-1\\1\end{pmatrix} + z\begin{pmatrix}-1\\2\\1\end{pmatrix} = \begin{pmatrix}0\\0\\0\end{pmatrix}.$$

(c) Evaluate $\begin{pmatrix}1 & 2 & -1\\1 & -1 & 2\\2 & 1 & 1\end{pmatrix}\begin{pmatrix}3\\0\\-1\end{pmatrix}$ and hence write down the full solution set of

the equation

$$\begin{pmatrix}1 & 2 & -1\\1 & -1 & 2\\2 & 1 & 1\end{pmatrix}\begin{pmatrix}x\\y\\z\end{pmatrix} = \begin{pmatrix}4\\1\\5\end{pmatrix}.$$

(d) Show that the range of the transformation whose matrix is $\begin{pmatrix} 1 & 2 & -1 \\ 1 & -1 & 2 \\ 2 & 1 & 1 \end{pmatrix}$

is the plane $x + y - z = 0$. Find a relation connecting the *rows* of this matrix. What is the link between this relation and the range?

**3.** (a) Show that the solution set of the equations

$$\left. \begin{array}{l} x + 2y - z = 7 \\ 2x + 4y - 2z = 14 \\ 5x + 10y - 5z = 35 \end{array} \right\}$$

is a plane of points. Give the equation of this plane (i) in Cartesian form, (ii) in parametric form.

(b) Show that the transformation described by $\begin{pmatrix} 1 & 2 & -1 \\ 2 & 4 & -2 \\ 5 & 10 & -5 \end{pmatrix}$ maps parallel

planes $x + 2y - z = d$ onto points on a certain line. Find the equation of this image line.

(c) Explain why $\begin{pmatrix} 1 & 2 & -1 \\ 2 & 4 & -2 \\ 5 & 10 & -5 \end{pmatrix} \begin{pmatrix} x \\ y \\ z \end{pmatrix} = \begin{pmatrix} 2 \\ 4 \\ 9 \end{pmatrix}$ has no solution.

(d) Explain the connection in part (b) between the linear-dependence relation of the rows of the matrix and the equation of the image line.

**4.** Solve the equation $\begin{pmatrix} 2 & 1 & 9 \\ 3 & 1 & 16 \\ -1 & 2 & -17 \end{pmatrix} \begin{pmatrix} x \\ y \\ z \end{pmatrix} = \begin{pmatrix} 0 \\ 0 \\ 0 \end{pmatrix}$. Find the equation of the plane

onto which the transformation maps three-dimensional space.

**5.** Express

$$\left. \begin{array}{l} x + y - z = 2 \\ 3x - 5y + z = -2 \\ 4x - 2y - z = 2 \end{array} \right\}$$

in the form $x\mathbf{a} + y\mathbf{b} + z\mathbf{c} = \mathbf{d}$. Which sets of three vectors selected from $\mathbf{a}$, $\mathbf{b}$, $\mathbf{c}$ and $\mathbf{d}$ are dependent? What does this imply about the types of solutions to the equations? Confirm this by solving the equations. Find the linear relation connecting the three equations.

**6.** Without solving the equations, find the values of $p$ and $q$ for which

$$\left. \begin{array}{l} x + y + z = 5 \\ 2x - y + 3z = p \\ qx + 5y + z = 0 \end{array} \right\}$$

have (a) an infinity of solutions, (b) no solution. In case (a), find the linear relation connecting the three equations.

1068

**3.2  Summary.** The results of Section 3.1 and Exercise C suggest the following conclusions:

In general, if

$$\mathbf{M} = \begin{vmatrix} a_1 & b_1 & c_1 \\ a_2 & b_2 & c_2 \\ a_3 & b_3 & c_3 \end{vmatrix}, \quad \text{where } \begin{vmatrix} a_1 \\ a_2 \\ a_3 \end{vmatrix} = \mathbf{a}, \text{ etc.,}$$

then $\mathbf{M}$ is a squash $\Leftrightarrow \det \mathbf{M} = 0$

$\Leftrightarrow$ the image of the unit cube under $\mathbf{M}$ has zero volume

$\Leftrightarrow$ the vectors $\mathbf{a}, \mathbf{b}, \mathbf{c}$ are coplanar

$\Leftrightarrow \mathbf{a}, \mathbf{b}, \mathbf{c}$ are linearly dependent

$\Leftrightarrow$ we can find $p, q, r$ not all zero, such that $p\mathbf{a} + q\mathbf{b} + r\mathbf{c} = \mathbf{0}$

$$\Leftrightarrow \begin{vmatrix} a_1 & b_1 & c_1 \\ a_2 & b_2 & c_2 \\ a_3 & b_3 & c_3 \end{vmatrix} \begin{vmatrix} x \\ y \\ z \end{vmatrix} = \begin{vmatrix} 0 \\ 0 \\ 0 \end{vmatrix} \text{ has an infinite number}$$

of solutions, of two kinds:

(i) If two of $\mathbf{a}, \mathbf{b}$ and $\mathbf{c}$ are independent, but $\mathbf{a}, \mathbf{b}$ and $\mathbf{c}$ are dependent, the range of $\mathbf{M}$ is a plane, and the solution of $\mathbf{Mr} = \mathbf{0}$ is a line through the origin $\mathbf{r} = \lambda \begin{vmatrix} p \\ q \\ r \end{vmatrix}$; i.e. the components of the direction vector of the line are the coefficients of the linear relation between the columns.

(ii) If $\mathbf{b}$ and $\mathbf{c}$ are scalar multiples of $\mathbf{a}$, the range of $\mathbf{M}$ is the line $\mathbf{r} = \lambda \mathbf{a}$ and the solution of $\mathbf{Mr} = \mathbf{0}$ is the plane $a_1 x + b_1 y + c_1 z = 0$.

Further, solutions to $\mathbf{Mr} = \mathbf{d}$, when $\mathbf{M}$ is a squash, exist only when $\mathbf{d}$ lies in the plane (or line) of $\mathbf{a}, \mathbf{b}$ and $\mathbf{c}$. Referring to the categories above we have either:

(i) $\mathbf{M}$ maps lines parallel to $\mathbf{r} = \lambda \begin{vmatrix} p \\ q \\ r \end{vmatrix}$ onto points on a plane i.e.

solutions of $\mathbf{Mr} = \mathbf{d}$ are lines $\mathbf{r} = \begin{vmatrix} p_1 \\ p_2 \\ p_3 \end{vmatrix} + \lambda \begin{vmatrix} p \\ q \\ r \end{vmatrix}$, or (ii) $\mathbf{M}$ maps planes

parallel to $a_1 x + b_1 y + c_1 z = 0$ onto points on a line.

## 4. PLANES, LINES AND LINEAR EQUATIONS

**4.1** In the last section we were chiefly concerned with the transformation represented by $\mathbf{M}$; now we turn to the geometry of the planes represented by the equations

$$\left.\begin{array}{l} a_1x + b_1y + c_1z = d_1 \\ a_2x + b_2y + c_2z = d_2 \\ a_3x + b_3y + c_3z = d_3 \end{array}\right\}.$$

In Exercise B, Question 7, we found that $\det \mathbf{M} = \det \tilde{\mathbf{M}}$. So

$$\det \mathbf{M} = 0 \Leftrightarrow \det \tilde{\mathbf{M}} = 0$$

$$\Leftrightarrow \text{the rows of } \mathbf{M} \text{ are linearly dependent.}$$

But we saw in Chapter 21 that the rows of $\mathbf{M}$ are the normal vectors of the three planes. The geometrical significance of these three normal vectors being dependent is that the planes form either a sheaf or a prism (or two or three planes are parallel—how could you tell this quickly from the equations?).

Thus, in Example 2, the three planes meet in a sheaf whose axis is the

line $\begin{pmatrix} x \\ y \\ z \end{pmatrix} = \begin{pmatrix} 1 \\ 2 \\ 0 \end{pmatrix} + \lambda \begin{pmatrix} 1 \\ -2 \\ 1 \end{pmatrix}$.

### Exercise D

**1.** (*a*) Find the equation of the line in which these planes meet:

$$x - y + z = 0$$
$$2x + y + 5z = 3$$
$$x + 2z = 1.$$

(*b*) Show that these planes form a prism:

$$x - y + z = 3$$
$$2x + y + 5z = 1$$
$$x + 2z = 0.$$

**2.** Find the value of $q$ if these planes form a sheaf:

$$x + 2y - z = 6$$
$$x - y + 2z = q$$
$$2x + y + z = -1.$$

**3.** Describe the geometrical configuration of the planes

$$x + y + z = 4$$
$$x + 2y + 3z = 2$$
$$x + 4y + 7z = 1.$$

**4.** (*a*) Find the linear relation between the rows of the matrix

$$\mathbf{M} = \begin{pmatrix} 2 & 1 & -1 \\ -1 & 0 & 3 \\ 2 & 2 & 4 \end{pmatrix}.$$

(*b*) Show that the transformation described by $\mathbf{M}$ maps three-dimensional space onto a plane, and find the Cartesian equation of this plane. Compare your equation with the relation in part (*a*).

(*c*) Describe the geometrical configuration of the planes

(i)    $2x + y - z = 5$     (ii)    $2x + y - z = 5$

      $-x + 3z = 2$             $-x + 3z = 2$

  $2x + 2y + 4z = 6$      $2x + 2y + 4z = 14.$

**5.** (*a*) Describe the geometrical configuration of the planes

$$2x - y + 3z = 1$$
$$x + 4y - z = 6$$
$$4x - 2y + 6z = 3.$$

(*b*) Find the range of the transformation described by

$$\begin{pmatrix} 2 & -1 & 3 \\ 1 & 4 & -1 \\ 4 & -2 & 6 \end{pmatrix}.$$

(*c*) Explain, in two different ways, why

$$\begin{pmatrix} 2 & -1 & 3 \\ 1 & 4 & -1 \\ 4 & -2 & 6 \end{pmatrix} \begin{pmatrix} x \\ y \\ z \end{pmatrix} = \begin{pmatrix} 1 \\ 6 \\ 3 \end{pmatrix}$$

has no solution.

**4.2 Prisms and sheafs.** Why is it that the equations

$$x + y + z = 3$$
$$x + 2y + 3z = 5$$
$$x + 4y + 7z = 9$$

represent a sheaf, and have an infinity of solutions, whereas the equations

$$x + y + z = 4$$

$$x + 2y + 3z = 2$$

$$x + 4y + 7z = 1$$

represent a prism, and have no solution? If **M** is a squash, when does **Mr** = **d** have a solution? Any squashing matrix may be reduced by row-operations to a matrix whose third row consists of zeros. This means that the rows of a squashing matrix are dependent: for the matrix

$$\begin{pmatrix} 1 & 1 & 1 \\ 1 & 2 & 3 \\ 1 & 4 & 7 \end{pmatrix}$$

of Example 2, check that $2R_1 - 3R_2 + R_3$ is a row of zeros. Reducing the third row of this matrix to zero is equivalent to the row-operation 'Replace $R_3$ by $2R_1 - 3R_2 + R_3$'. The equation **Mr** = **d** will have solutions if these row-operations reduce the vector **d** to one of form $\begin{pmatrix} d_1 \\ d_2 \\ 0 \end{pmatrix}$. So

for the matrix in question, there will be solutions if **d** satisfies

$$2d_1 - 3d_2 + d_3 = 0;$$

i.e. $$2x - 3y + z = 0$$

is the equation of the range of the transformation in question.

This argument can be generalized, and so *dependence relations between the rows of* **M** *give equations satisfied by the range of* **M**.

### Miscellaneous Exercise

**1.** By evaluating $\begin{vmatrix} 2 & 4 & 3 \\ 3 & 2 & 7 \\ 1 & 0 & 1 \end{vmatrix}$, determine whether or not $\begin{pmatrix} 2 \\ 3 \\ 1 \end{pmatrix}$, $\begin{pmatrix} 4 \\ 2 \\ 0 \end{pmatrix}$ and $\begin{pmatrix} 3 \\ 7 \\ 1 \end{pmatrix}$ are dependent vectors. Are the vectors $\begin{pmatrix} 2 \\ 4 \\ 3 \end{pmatrix}$, $\begin{pmatrix} 3 \\ 2 \\ 7 \end{pmatrix}$, $\begin{pmatrix} 1 \\ 0 \\ 1 \end{pmatrix}$ dependent?

**2.** Use a determinant to find the value of $k$ for which the vectors $\begin{pmatrix} k \\ 0 \\ 1 \end{pmatrix}$, $\begin{pmatrix} 3 \\ 2 \\ 2 \end{pmatrix}$, $\begin{pmatrix} 1 \\ 4 \\ 3 \end{pmatrix}$ are linearly dependent.

1072

**3.** What vectors are mapped onto the origin by the matrix

$$\begin{pmatrix} 2 & 1 & 3 \\ 3 & 1 & 4 \\ 1 & -2 & -1 \end{pmatrix}?$$

Find a solution of

$$\left. \begin{array}{r} 2x + y + 3z = 6 \\ 3x + y + 4z = 9 \\ x - 2y - z = 3 \end{array} \right\}$$

having $y = z = 0$, and hence write down the general solution of these equations.

**4.** Adapt the method of Example 2 to solve the equation

$$\begin{pmatrix} 1 & 2 & -3 \\ -2 & -4 & 6 \\ 4 & 8 & -12 \end{pmatrix} \begin{pmatrix} x \\ y \\ z \end{pmatrix} = \begin{pmatrix} 5 \\ -10 \\ 20 \end{pmatrix}.$$

What is the image of three-dimensional space under the transformation in this equation?

**5.** Write down two distinct dependence relations between the vectors

$$\begin{pmatrix} 1 \\ -2 \\ 4 \end{pmatrix}, \begin{pmatrix} 2 \\ -4 \\ 8 \end{pmatrix}, \begin{pmatrix} -3 \\ 6 \\ -12 \end{pmatrix}.$$

Hence find two independent solutions of $\mathbf{Mr} = \mathbf{0}$, where $\mathbf{M}$ is the matrix of Question 4. How is your answer related to the solution found in Question 4?

**6.** Show that $\mathbf{a}, \mathbf{b}, \mathbf{c}$ linearly dependent and $\mathbf{a}, \mathbf{b}, \mathbf{d}$ linearly dependent does not imply $\mathbf{a}, \mathbf{c}, \mathbf{d}$ linearly dependent. Invent a set of three equations in three unknowns to which these conditions apply. Have they a solution?

**7.** Show that there are three values of $a$ for which the equations

$$\left. \begin{array}{r} ax + y + 2z = 0 \\ x - ay = 0 \\ 4x - 3y + az = 0 \end{array} \right\}$$

have a non-trivial solution, and find them.

**8.** By considering the determinant

$$\begin{vmatrix} a_1 & b_1 & c_1 \\ a_1 & b_1 & c_1 \\ a_2 & b_2 & c_2 \end{vmatrix}$$

and another one like it, show that

$$(x, y, z) = \left( \begin{vmatrix} b_1 & c_1 \\ b_2 & c_2 \end{vmatrix}, -\begin{vmatrix} a_1 & c_1 \\ a_2 & c_2 \end{vmatrix}, \begin{vmatrix} a_1 & b_1 \\ a_2 & b_2 \end{vmatrix} \right)$$

is a solution of the equations

$$a_1 x + b_1 y + c_1 z = 0$$
$$a_2 x + b_2 y + c_2 z = 0.$$

**9.** Use a determinant to find the two values of $k$ for which

$$\begin{pmatrix} 3 & 1 \\ 1 & 3 \end{pmatrix}\begin{pmatrix} x \\ y \end{pmatrix} = k\begin{pmatrix} x \\ y \end{pmatrix}$$

has a non-trivial solution. Find vectors $\begin{pmatrix} x \\ y \end{pmatrix}$ corresponding to these values of $k$. If these vectors are **u** and **v**, what is the image of $a\mathbf{u} + b\mathbf{v}$ under the transformation described by this matrix? Illustrate with a diagram, and describe the transformation in terms of these invariant directions.

## SUMMARY

With the notation $\mathbf{M} = \begin{pmatrix} a_1 & b_1 & c_1 \\ a_2 & b_2 & c_2 \\ a_3 & b_3 & c_3 \end{pmatrix}$ and $\mathbf{a} = \begin{pmatrix} a_1 \\ a_2 \\ a_3 \end{pmatrix}$, $\mathbf{b} = \begin{pmatrix} b_1 \\ b_2 \\ b_3 \end{pmatrix}$, $\mathbf{c} = \begin{pmatrix} c_1 \\ c_2 \\ c_3 \end{pmatrix}$

and $\mathbf{n}_1 = \begin{pmatrix} a_1 \\ b_1 \\ c_1 \end{pmatrix}$ which is normal to $a_1 x + b_1 y + c_1 z = d$, etc., we can sum

up by linking the six equivalent statements in Figure 5.

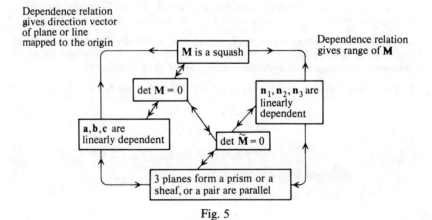

Fig. 5

# REVISION EXERCISES

## 37. ELECTRICITY

**1.** Find the potential difference across the terminals $A$ and $B$ in Figure 1.

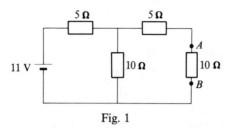

Fig. 1

**2.** For the circuit shown in Figure 2, calculate the equivalent single resistance when current flows between $A$ and $B$.

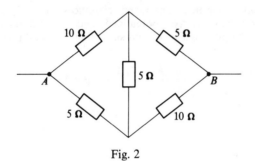

Fig. 2

**3.** State Kirchhoff's laws.

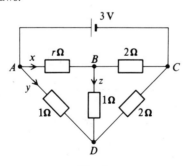

Fig. 3

In the circuit shown in Figure 3, arm $AB$ contains a variable resistance $r$ Ω. If $x$, $y$ and $z$ are respectively the currents (in amperes) in $AB$, $AD$ and $BD$, write down in terms of $x$, $y$ and $z$ the currents in $BC$ and $DC$.

1075

By considering the changes in potential around path $ABDA$ and across paths $ABC$, $ADC$, obtain the equation

$$\begin{pmatrix} r & -1 & 1 \\ r+2 & 0 & -2 \\ 0 & 3 & 2 \end{pmatrix} \begin{pmatrix} x \\ y \\ z \end{pmatrix} = 3 \begin{pmatrix} 0 \\ 1 \\ 1 \end{pmatrix},$$

and (by reduction to lower triangular form or otherwise) show that

$$x = \frac{21}{11r+10}.$$

Show that the current drawn from the battery is

$$\frac{3(5r+9)}{11r+10} \text{ amperes,}$$

and that this decreases as $r$ is increased.

Deduce the current that would be drawn if $AB$ were completely disconnected from the circuit.

Show that $r$ consumes maximum power when it is set at $\frac{10}{11}$.   (OC)

**4.** In the circuit shown in Figure 4, the resistances are $1/K_1$, $1/K_2$ and $1/K_3$. The terminal $A$ is held at a fixed potential $V$, and $C$ is at zero potential. Find an expression for the potential at $B$, and show that the total power consumed is given by

$$\frac{K_1(K_2+K_3)V^2}{K_1+K_2+K_3}.   \text{(OC)}$$

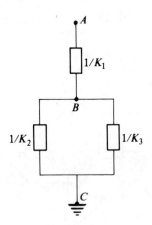

Fig. 4

**5.** A 12 V car battery, with internal resistance 1 $\Omega$, has a lighting circuit of total resistance 6 $\Omega$ permanently connected across its terminals. It is required to connect an additional resistance $R$ $\Omega$ temporarily across the terminals, without disconnecting the lights, to take maximum power through $R$. Find $R$, and the resulting loss of power in the lighting circuit.

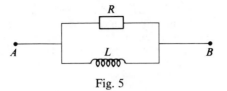

Fig. 5

**6.** What is the complex impedance of the circuit in Figure 5, in which a resistance of $R\,\Omega$ is in parallel with an impedance of $L$ H, when the voltage applied across $AB$ is $V\cos\omega t$?

If $V$ and $I$ are the complex voltage and current, show that

$$I = \left(\frac{1}{R} - \frac{1}{\omega L}j\right)V,$$

and hence, or otherwise, find the steady-state current in the circuit in the form $i = A\cos(\omega t - \alpha)$. Give $A$ and $\alpha$ in terms of $V$, $R$, $L$ and $\omega$.

## 38. DIFFERENTIAL EQUATIONS: METHODS AND APPLICATIONS

**1.** Give the general solutions of the following differential equations:

(a) $\dfrac{dy}{dx} = 5x$;   (b) $\dfrac{dy}{dx} = \dfrac{-y}{2}$;   (c) $\dfrac{dv}{dt} = 3v^2$;

(d) $\dfrac{dn}{dt} = \dfrac{-t}{n}$;   (e) $\dfrac{dQ}{dt} + \dfrac{Q}{10} = 2$.

**2.** Sketch the families of solution curves for each of the following differential equations and pick out the particular solution satisfying $y = 1$ when $x = 0$ for each.

(a) $\dfrac{dy}{dx} + 2y = 6$;   (b) $\dfrac{dy}{dx} + 2y = 4x + 4$;   (c) $\dfrac{dy}{dx} = \dfrac{y-2}{x-1}$.

**3.** Prove that, if $y = f(x)$ satisfies the differential equation

$$\frac{dy}{dx} = -2xy,$$

then so does $y = kf(x)$ where $k$ is any real number.

Find the equation of the solution curve through the point $(0, 1)$, and sketch a graph showing several curves of the family of solutions. (OC)

**4.** Find the solution of the differential equation

$$\frac{dy}{dt} = y e^{-t}$$

for which $y = 1$ when $t = 0$.

Prove that, for this solution, $y$ increases with $t$. Give the limit of $y$ as $t$ tends to infinity. (OC)

1077

**5.** A radioactive substance $P$ decays and changes (without loss of mass) into a substance $Q$, which itself similarly changes into a third substance $R$. $R$ suffers no further change. The masses of $P$, $Q$ and $R$ present at time $t$ are given by $p$, $q$ and $r$ grams respectively. The rates of change are such that

$$\frac{dp}{dt} = -2p \qquad (1)$$

and

$$\frac{dr}{dt} = q.$$

Show that

$$\frac{dq}{dt} = 2p - q.$$

Initially (at time $t = 0$) there is 1 gram of substance $P$ and none of substance $Q$. Integrate equation (1) and hence show that $q$ satisfies the differential equation

$$\frac{dq}{dt} + q = 2 e^{-2t}. \qquad (2)$$

Show that (2) may be written in the form

$$\frac{d}{dt}(q e^t) = 2 e^{-t},$$

and integrate to find $q$ as a function of $t$. Hence prove that at any subsequent time there is never more than $\frac{1}{2}$ gram of $Q$ present.   (OC)

**6.** A particle $P$ of mass $m$ is in motion along a straight path through $O$. It is subject to a force of repulsion from $O$ of magnitude $k/x^2$ (where $x$ is its displacement from $O$ at time $t$ and $k$ is a positive constant). Show that $x$ satisfies the differential equation

$$v \frac{dv}{dx} = \frac{k}{mx^2}.$$

Show that, if $P$ is initially projected towards $O$ with speed $u$ from a point with displacement $a$ ($>0$) from $O$, then $x$ will decrease to a value

$$\frac{2ka}{2k + mau^2}.$$

What can you say about the sign of $dv/dt$? Deduce that in the subsequent motion $x$ will increase without limit. Show also that $v$ will increase, but to a limiting value, and find this value.   (OC)

## 39. THE NORMAL DISTRIBUTION: SAMPLES AND HYPOTHESES

**1.** At a small country Fire Station, the time intervals between the answering of an emergency telephone call and the fire-engine departing are Normally distributed, with mean 130 seconds and standard deviation 20 seconds.

(a) In what proportion of alarms does the fire-engine leave in less than $1\frac{1}{2}$ minutes?

(b) What is the probability that, of three calls answered in a day, in only one did it take longer than $2\frac{1}{2}$ minutes for the engine to leave?

**2.** The intelligence of an individual is frequently described by a positive integer known as an IQ (intelligence quotient). The distribution of IQs amongst children of a certain age-group can be approximated by a Normal probability model with mean 100 and standard deviation 15. Write a sentence stating what you under-stand about the age-group from the fact that $\Phi(2\cdot5) = 0\cdot994$.

A class of 30 children is selected at random from the age-group. Calculate (to 2 significant figures) the probability that at least one member of the class has an IQ of 138 or more. (OC)

**3.** An inter-city telephone exchange has 100 lines and on average 80 are in use at any moment (on a typical business-day morning). Calculate:

(i) the probability that all lines are engaged;

(ii) the probability that more than 30 lines are free.

We say that a number $x$ of lines is the 'effective minimum level' if the number of lines in use exceeds $x$ for 95% of the time. Find $x$. (You may assume that for large $n$ the binomial probability may be approximated by a Normal probability with mean $na$ and variance $nab$.) (OC)

**4.** It is estimated that 1400 commuters regularly aim to catch the 5.30 p.m. train at a certain London terminus, that 50 will have arrived before the platform gate is opened at 5.20 p.m., and that when the train leaves on time 70 arrive too late. Assuming the distribution of arrival times to be Normal, use tables to obtain the mean and standard deviation. Hence estimate:

(i) at what time the platform gate should be opened if not more than 20 passengers are to be kept waiting at the gate;

(ii) how many of the commuters will miss the train on a day when (unexpec-tedly) it leaves two minutes late. (OC)

**5.** Two types of seed $X$ and $Y$, difficult to distinguish, are such that in the long run under given conditions 80% of type $X$ but only 60% of type $Y$ will germinate. Samples of 100 seeds of type $X$ are selected at random. Find the mean and standard deviation of the number germinating.

A package arrives at a nursery without its label. It contains just one type of seed done up in packets each containing 100 seeds. The nurseryman knows that the seed is either of type $X$ or of type $Y$, and thinks that it is more likely to be the former. He decides to plant a packet and to accept the seed as type $X$ provided that at least 68 germinate, but otherwise to regard it as type $Y$. Using the Normal approximation, find the probability that the nurseryman will wrongly label type $X$ seed as type $Y$.

What is the probability that he will wrongly label type $Y$ seed as type $X$?

**6.** 60% of the population prefer plain chocolate to milk chocolate. A person organizing a party for 100 guests, each of whom is to be given a box of chocolates as a present, lays in a stock of 70 boxes of plain and 45 boxes of milk. What is the probability that every guest will be able to have the kind they prefer?

## 40. LINEAR ALGEBRA AND GEOMETRY REVIEW

**1.** (*a*) Find the solution set of the equations

$$\left.\begin{aligned} x - 3y + 7z &= -7 \\ 4x + 3y + z &= 2 \\ 5x + 5y - z &= 5 \end{aligned}\right\}$$

and interpret your result geometrically. Find a dependence relation between the vectors

$$\begin{pmatrix} 1 \\ -3 \\ 7 \end{pmatrix}, \begin{pmatrix} 4 \\ 3 \\ 1 \end{pmatrix}, \begin{pmatrix} 5 \\ 5 \\ -1 \end{pmatrix}.$$

How is the first equation related to the other two?

(*b*) Are the vectors $\begin{pmatrix} 1 \\ 4 \\ 5 \end{pmatrix}, \begin{pmatrix} -3 \\ 3 \\ 5 \end{pmatrix}, \begin{pmatrix} 7 \\ 1 \\ -1 \end{pmatrix}$ dependent? If so, find a dependence relation. Comment, with reference to (*a*).

**2.** Find *a* if the three equations

$$\left.\begin{aligned} x - y + z &= 0 \\ 3x - y + 2z &= 0 \\ ax + y + z &= 0 \end{aligned}\right\}$$

have a solution other than the trivial solution $x = y = z = 0$.

Show that in this case the vectors

$$\begin{pmatrix} 1 \\ -1 \\ 1 \end{pmatrix}, \begin{pmatrix} 3 \\ -1 \\ 2 \end{pmatrix}, \begin{pmatrix} a \\ 1 \\ 1 \end{pmatrix}$$

are linearly dependent, and exhibit the linear relation connecting them.

**3.** Show that the planes

$$x - 2y + 2z = 17, \quad 3x + 15y - z = -12, \quad 2x + 5y + z = 7$$

have a line in common, and find parametric equations for it. What does this tell you about the vectors

$$\begin{pmatrix} 1 \\ 3 \\ 2 \end{pmatrix}, \begin{pmatrix} -2 \\ 15 \\ 5 \end{pmatrix}, \begin{pmatrix} 2 \\ -1 \\ 1 \end{pmatrix}, \begin{pmatrix} 17 \\ -12 \\ 7 \end{pmatrix}?$$

What can you say about the space into which three-dimensional space is transformed by the matrix

$$\begin{pmatrix} 1 & -2 & 2 \\ 3 & 15 & -1 \\ 2 & 5 & 1 \end{pmatrix}?$$

Does the vector $\begin{pmatrix} 17 \\ -12 \\ 7 \end{pmatrix}$ lie in the transformed space?

**4.** (*a*) Are the three-dimensional Euclidean vectors

$$\begin{pmatrix} 4 \\ 2 \\ 1 \end{pmatrix}, \begin{pmatrix} 2 \\ 0 \\ 1 \end{pmatrix}, \begin{pmatrix} 3 \\ 1 \\ 1 \end{pmatrix}$$

linearly dependent or independent? Interpret your answer geometrically.
    (*b*) Discuss the solution of the equations

$$\left. \begin{aligned} x - y + z &= 1 \\ x + (\lambda^2 - \lambda - 1)y + (\lambda + 1)z &= 2 \\ 2x + (\lambda^2 - \lambda - 2)y + 2(\lambda + 1)z &= 3 \end{aligned} \right\}$$

for all real values of $\lambda$.   (OC)

# REVISION PAPERS

The questions in the following papers are selected from past SMP A-level Paper I examination papers or are of equivalent standard.

## C1

**1.** Sketch the curve which, in the $(x, y)$-plane, is given by $y(x^2 - 1) = x$.

**2.** State for each of the following functions whether it is odd, even, periodic, or none of these, justifying your answers:
    (a) $x \sin x$;    (b) $\sin x + \cos x$;    (c) $x + \cos x$.

**3.** Starting from the approximation $\sqrt{17} \approx 4$, apply Newton's method to the equation $x^2 = 17$ to obtain first the approximation $x \approx 4 \cdot 125$ and then the approximation $x \approx 4 \cdot 123$.

**4.** Prove that the maximum value of $(3 \cos \theta - \cos^2 \theta)$ is 2 if $\theta$ may take any real value.

Explain whether, by putting $\cos \theta = x$, it is correct to deduce that the maximum value of $(3x - x^2)$, for all $x$, is 2.

**5.** A man tosses a coin six times. Find the probability that he will throw two heads and four tails:
    (a) in any order;
    (b) the two heads being thrown consecutively.

**6.** A particle of mass 3 kg travelling at 40 m/s is deflected through 60° and has its speed halved. Calculate its change in momentum.

**7.** Solve the differential equation

$$\frac{ds}{dt} + s = 1,$$

given that $s = 2$ when $t = 1$.

**8.** The mean survival period of daisies after being sprayed with a certain make of weed killer is 24 days. If the probability of survival after 27 days is $\frac{1}{4}$, estimate the standard deviation of the survival period.

**9.** Draw a flow diagram for calculating, to a prescribed degree of accuracy, the real root of the equation $x^3 - x^2 + x + 1 = 0$.

**10.** Given that $x^3 - 2x^2 - 3x + 10 = 0$ has a zero which is an integer, find all its zeros.

## C2

**1.** Express in partial fractions:
    (a) $\dfrac{1}{(x+1)(x+2)}$;    (b) $\dfrac{x+7}{(x-1)(x+3)}$.

**2.** Evaluate $\displaystyle\int_{-2}^{2} \frac{2\,dt}{(4+t^2)}$ and $\displaystyle\int_{-2}^{2} \frac{2t\,dt}{(4+t^2)}$.

1082

**3.** Write a flow diagram to print a table of values of $n!$ from $n = 1$ to $n = 20$.

**4.** The position vector **r** of a particle can be expressed in terms of the constant orthogonal unit vectors **i**, **j** by means of the relation

$$\mathbf{r} = \mathbf{i} \cos nt + \mathbf{j} \sin nt.$$

Find the speed of the particle at time $t$. Show that its acceleration at time $t$ is the vector $-n^2 \mathbf{r}$.

**5.** Obtain a quadratic polynomial approximation to the function $\sec x$ in the neighbourhood of $x = 0$.

**6.** Express the complex number $2 + j\sqrt{3}$ in the form $r(\cos \theta + j \sin \theta)$. (Your value of $\theta$ may be given to the nearest degree.)

**7.** Solve the differential equations

(a) $\dfrac{dy}{dx} = x + 3;$     (b) $\dfrac{dy}{dx} = y + 3;$

given that $y = 2$ when $x = 0$ in both cases.

**8.** Prove that

$$1 + \frac{1}{2} + \frac{1}{4} + \ldots + \frac{1}{2^n} = 2 - \frac{1}{2^n}.$$

Use this finite summation to explain carefully what you mean when you say that 'the sum of the infinite series

$$1 + \frac{1}{2} + \frac{1}{4} + \ldots + \frac{1}{2^n} + \ldots$$

is 2'.

**9.** Estimate the probability of turning up exactly ten heads in twenty tosses of a coin.

**10.** If $O$ is the origin, and

$$\mathbf{OA} = \begin{pmatrix} 15 \\ -20 \\ 0 \end{pmatrix}, \qquad \mathbf{OB} = \begin{pmatrix} 12 \\ 9 \\ -20 \end{pmatrix}, \qquad \mathbf{OC} = \begin{pmatrix} 16 \\ 12 \\ 15 \end{pmatrix}$$

show that $O$, $A$, $B$, $C$ are four vertices of a cube, and find the other four.

## C3

**1.** Find the area enclosed between the $x$-axis and one hump of the following curves: (a) $y = \sin x$, (b) $y = x \sin x$.

**2.** The position vector **r** of a particle is given by

$$\mathbf{r} = t^3 \mathbf{i} - 3t\mathbf{j},$$

where **i** and **j** are constant orthogonal unit vectors. Show that its speed is never zero, and state the direction of its acceleration.

**3.** In a knock-out competition there are 32 competitors; half of the competitors remaining are eliminated in each round, so that in the fifth (final) round only two remain. Calculate, correct to 2 decimal places, the mean and variance of the numbers of rounds played by the individual competitors. (OC)

**4.** Show that the set of matrices of the form

$$\begin{pmatrix} \cos\theta & -\sin\theta \\ \sin\theta & \cos\theta \end{pmatrix}$$

is closed under the operation of matrix multiplication. (OC)

**5.** A skater $A$ of mass 50 kg who is travelling at 6 m/s crashes into a skater $B$ of mass 75 kg who is travelling at 4 m/s on a path at right-angles to $A$'s. Immediately after the impact, $A$ finds himself travelling at 2 m/s parallel to $B$'s original path.

Sketch a vector diagram showing clearly the momentum of each skater before and after the collision. By drawing a more accurate diagram, or otherwise, estimate the magnitude and direction of $B$'s velocity after the collision.

State briefly what assumption you make about forces between the skaters and the ice.

**6.** Two unequal electrical resistances combine in series to give a resistance $R_s$ and in parallel to give a resistance $R_p$. Prove that $R_s > R_p$. (OC)

**7.** Prove that

$$\int_0^4 \frac{x\,dx}{\sqrt{(x^2+1)}} = \sqrt{17} - 1.$$

Apply Simpson's rule, with ordinates at $x = 0, 2, 4$ to this integral to estimate the value of $\sqrt{17}$, given $\sqrt{5} \approx 2\cdot24$.

**8.** Calculate the inverse of the matrix

$$\begin{pmatrix} 1 & -1 & 1 \\ 3 & -9 & 5 \\ 1 & -3 & 3 \end{pmatrix}.$$

**9.** Write down vectors which are at right-angles to the planes $x - 2y + 2z = 5$ and $2x - y + 3z = 7$ respectively. Hence calculate the acute angle between the planes.

**10.** Five people taken at random are each asked to taste a sample of Brand A and a sample of Brand B margarine. Four of them prefer Brand A. Do you feel this provides conclusive evidence that 'people prefer Brand A to Brand B'? Give your reason. (OC)

## C4

**1.** Use the binomial theorem to evaluate $(1\cdot03)^{20}$ correct to 4 significant figures.

**2.** If $z = \frac{1}{2}(1+j)$, write down the modulus and argument of each of the numbers $z, z^2, z^3, z^4$. Hence or otherwise show, in a diagram of the complex plane drawn on squared paper to a scale of 8 cm to 1 unit, the point representing the number

$$1 + z + z^2 + z^3 + z^4.$$

On the same diagram show the point representing the number $1/(1-z)$. (OC)

**3.** Calculate the mean and the standard deviation of the number of letters in the words of this sentence.

**4.** $S$ denotes the set of matrices of the form

$$\begin{pmatrix} x & y \\ y & x \end{pmatrix}$$

where $x$ and $y$ are real numbers. Investigate whether, for the operation of matrix multiplication,

    (i) $S$ is closed;
    (ii) the identity belongs to $S$;
    (iii) every element of $S$ has an inverse. (OC)

**5.** The probability that a blue-eyed person is left-handed is $\frac{1}{7}$. The probability that a left-handed person is blue-eyed is $\frac{1}{3}$. The probability that a person has neither of these attributes is $\frac{4}{5}$. What is the probability that a person has both? (OC)

**6.** Functions $f_1, f_2, f_3$ have for domains the set of real numbers. Figure 1 shows the graph of each of these functions over the interval $0 \leqslant x \leqslant a$. You are given that

    (i) $f_1$ is an even function;
    (ii) $f_2$ is a periodic function with period $a$;
    (iii) $f_3$ is an odd periodic function with period $2a$.

Sketch as much of the graphs of these functions as this information allows. (OC)

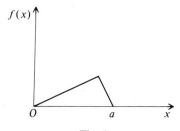

Fig. 1

**7.** Points $X, Y, Z$ have position vectors denoted by $\mathbf{x}, \mathbf{y}, \mathbf{z}$ relative to an origin $O$. Write the expression $\mathbf{p} = \frac{1}{2}\mathbf{x} + \frac{2}{5}\mathbf{y} + \frac{1}{10}\mathbf{z}$ in the form $a\mathbf{x} + b(c\mathbf{y} + d\mathbf{z})$, where $a + b = 1$. Hence describe how the point $P$, with position vector $\mathbf{p}$, is related to the points $X, Y, Z$. By writing $\mathbf{p}$ in terms of $\mathbf{x}, \mathbf{y}, \mathbf{z}$ in another way, give a different description of the relation of $P$ to $X, Y, Z$. (OC)

**8.** Using tables or a rough graph, find an approximation not more than $0 \cdot 1$ in error to the solution of the equation

$$x + 6 \ln x = 10.$$

Find a closer approximation to the solution of this equation, showing the details of your calculation and giving 3 decimal places in your answer. (OC)

**9.** The probability of a given light bulb failing in any one month is $0 \cdot 03$. What is the probability that none of the 15 bulbs in my house will fail during the next three months? (OC)

**10.** The expression $4 \sin 2t$ represents the vertical displacement $d$, at time $t$, of an oscillating weight on the end of an elastic string. Write down an expression for each of the following displacements:
    (i) that with double the amplitude of $d$ and the same frequency;
    (ii) that with half the amplitude and twice the frequency of $d$;
    (iii) that with the same amplitude and twice the periodic time of $d$.   (OC)

## C 5

**1.** Three distinct elements $a$, $b$, $c$ are subject to a law of combination $*$ for which

$$a * c = c * a = a, \tag{1}$$

$$b * c = c * b = b, \tag{2}$$

$$a * a = c. \tag{3}$$

Prove that they do not form a group. Keeping the relations (1) and (2), suggest an alternative value for $a * a$ under which the three elements do form a group.  (OC)

**2.** For the equations

$$\left. \begin{array}{l} x - 2y - 11z = 28 \\ 2x + 2y - z = 5 \\ 3x + 4y + 2z = -2 \end{array} \right\}$$

investigate the possibility of deriving the left side of the third equation by adding suitable multiples of the left sides of the first two equations. Explain the significance of your result in terms of the solution set of the equations.  (OC)

**3.** Estimate the value of

$$\int_1^{49} \frac{dx}{1 + \sqrt{x}}$$

by applying Simpson's rule with three ordinates. Show by an appropriate substitution that this integral is equal to

$$\int_1^7 \frac{2u}{1 + u} \, du.$$

Hence, using the fact that $u = (1 + u) - 1$ or otherwise, deduce an exact expression for the integral.  (OC)

**4.** Express

$$f(x) = \frac{4x - 1}{(2x - 3)(x + 1)}$$

in partial fractions and hence find $f'(x)$.
   Show that $f(\frac{1}{2} - x) = -f(x)$. What does this imply about the symmetry of the graph of $f$?  (OC)

**5.** (i) Given that $2 + j$ is a zero of $2x^6 - 9x^4 + 32x^2 + 75$, write down three other zeros.
   (ii) The graphs of two polynomials, each with real coefficients, are plotted with the same perpendicular axes and scales. If one polynomial is of degree five and the other of degree four, state the greatest and the least numbers of points in which the graphs could meet.  (OC)

1086

**6.** Over a number of years an average of 40 out of every 100 patients who underwent a difficult operation survived. Last year new medical techniques were introduced and 73 out of 150 patients survived the operation. Explain whether or not the maintaining of these techniques is statistically justified. (OC)

**7.** Show, with sketches, the stages by which the graph of $f: x \rightarrow 3 - \cos 2x$ may be obtained by linear transformations from the graph of $g: x \rightarrow \cos x$. (OC)

**8.** A sequence of numbers $x_1, x_2, x_3, \ldots$ is defined as follows:

$$x_1 = 0, \ x_{n+1} = 3x_n + 2 \quad \text{for } n \geqslant 1.$$

Write down the values of $1 + x_n$ for $n = 1, 2, 3, 4$ and so guess a formula for $x_n$. Prove by induction that your guess is correct. (OC)

**9.** An aircraft of mass $10^5$ kg is climbing along a straight flight path at $30°$ to the horizontal with an acceleration of 2 m/s$^2$. The engines exert a thrust of $8 \times 10^5$ N along the flight path. Show in one clearly labelled vector polygon the weight, the thrust and the total aerodynamic force, together with the mass-acceleration vector. (OC)

**10.** Sketch some typical members of the families of solution curves corresponding to each of the two differential equations:

(i) $\dfrac{dy}{dx} = \dfrac{y}{x}$;

(ii) $\dfrac{dy}{dx} = \dfrac{y+2}{x-1}$. (OC)

# MISCELLANEOUS REVISION EXERCISES

These are arranged by topics. Most questions are of the standard of SMP A-level Paper II questions and many are taken from past papers.

## 1. POLYNOMIALS AND COMPLEX NUMBERS

**1.** Draw a triangle in the complex plane with sides representing the complex numbers $z_1$, $z_2$, and $z_3$, where $z_1 = z_2 + z_3$. Explain why $|z_1| \leqslant |z_2| + |z_3|$ and state a condition on the arguments of $z_2$ and $z_3$ if the equality sign holds.

If $z = x + yj$, show that

$$\arg(z-1) = \arg(2j-z) \Rightarrow 2x + y = 2$$

and explain why the converse is not true.

Describe the locus of the point representing $z$ in the complex plane if $\arg(z-1) - \arg(2j-z) = \frac{1}{2}\pi$.   (OC)

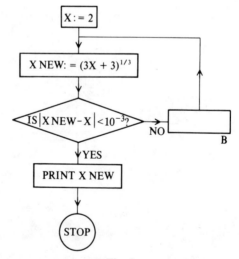

Fig. 1

**2.** The flow diagram is intended to represent an iterative process for finding an approximation to the root of

$$x^3 - 3x - 3 = 0$$

that lies near $x = 2$.

   (i) What should be inserted in the blank box B?

   (ii) Use the iteration to find the root of $x^3 - 3x - 3 = 0$ correct to 3 significant figures.

1088

(iii) Sketch the graphs $y = 3x + 3$ and $y = x^3$ and show geometrically how the iteration converges.   (OC)

**3.** (a) Express $P(x) = 6x^4 - 13x^3 + 60x^2 - 6x - 20$ as the product of irreducible polynomials over the complex numbers, given that $P(1 + 3j) = 0$.

(b) Find, correct to 3 significant figures, the zeros of

$$Q(x) = x^4 + 5x^3 + 4x^2 - 3x - 3.$$

Sketch the graph of $y = Q(x)$.

**4.** Find the four solutions of the equation

$$z^4 = \sqrt{3} + j,$$

and mark them on a sketch of the complex plane. If these solutions are $z_1$, $z_2$, $z_3$, $z_4$, prove that

$$z_2 + z_4 = z_3 + z_1 = 0.$$

**5.** Find $a$, $b$, $c$ and $R$ if $4x^3 - 7x^2 + 2x - 5 \equiv (x - 3)(ax^2 + bx + c) + R$.

Divide twice more by $(x - 3)$ and hence or otherwise find $p$, $q$, $r$ and $s$ if

$$4x^3 - 7x^2 + 2x - 5 \equiv p(x - 3)^3 + q(x - 3)^2 + r(x - 3) + s.$$

# 2. SEQUENCES, SERIES AND INDUCTION

**1.** (a) Construct a flow chart to generate the first ten terms of the geometric progression $2$, $0\cdot4$, $0\cdot08$, ...

(b) If the terms of the geometric progression in (a) are $u_1$, $u_2$, $u_3$, ..., $u_{10}$, modify your flow chart to print out $s_1$, $s_2$, $s_3$, ..., $s_{10}$ where $s_1 = u_1$, $s_2 = u_1 + u_2$, $s_3 = u_1 + u_2 + u_3$, etc. To what value does $s_n$ tend when $n$ is large?

**2.** A sequence of numbers $u_1$, $u_2$, $u_3$, ... is defined by the relation

$$u_{n+1} = 1 + \frac{2}{u_n} \quad \text{and} \quad u_1 = 1.$$

Calculate $u_6$ as a rational number, and guess the value of the limit $p$ of the sequence as $n$ tends to infinity. With this value of $p$, prove that

$$\frac{u_{n+2} - p}{u_n - p} = \frac{1}{u_n + p}.$$

Construct a flow diagram to find the smallest value of $n$ for which

$$|u_n - p| < 10^{-10}.$$

**3.** A sequence is defined inductively as follows:

$$x_1 = 1, \qquad x_{k+1} = \tfrac{1}{3}(2x_k + p/x_k^2)$$

for all $k \in \mathbb{N}$ where $p$ is a positive real number.

(a) Construct a flow chart to print the first ten terms of the sequence. Take $p = 8$ and find the values of the first five terms. To what limit do you think $x_n$ tends?

1089

(*b*) Use the Newton-Raphson method applied to the equation $x^3 - p = 0$ to show that if $x_k$ and $x_{k+1}$ are successive approximations, then they are connected by the above inductive relation.

**4.** A sequence is defined by $a_1 = k$, $a_{n+1} = 1 + 1/a_n$, $k > 0$. Construct a flow chart to calculate the values of $a_2, \ldots, a_5$ and calculate these terms in the case when $k = 1$.

Explain why the sequence $a_n$ converges to a *positive* limit, $a$, and find the value of $a$, showing that it is the same for all values of $k$. Calculate $1/a$ and comment on its value. Can you find an inductive definition for a sequence $b_n$ which will converge to $1/a$?

**5.** (i) Show that, if $y = e^{3x} \cos 4x$, $dy/dx = 5\,e^{3x} \cos(4x + \lambda)$, stating the values of $\cos \lambda$ and $\sin \lambda$. Express $d^2y/dx^2$ in the form $A\,e^{3x} \cos(4x + \mu)$, suggest a formula for $d^n y/dx^n$ and prove your result by induction.

(ii) Use the formula for $\sum_1^n r^2$ to write down $\sum_1^{2n} r^2$ and hence, or otherwise, find a formula for $\sum_1^n (2r - 1)^2$; check your result by induction.

# 3. FUNCTIONS AND GRAPHS

**1.** Find $A$ and $B$ such that

$$\frac{1}{x(2-x)} = \frac{A}{x} + \frac{B}{2-x}.$$

Sketch the graphs of the functions

$$x \to \frac{1}{x} \quad \text{and} \quad x \to \frac{1}{2-x}$$

and use them to sketch the graph of the function

$$x \to \frac{1}{x(2-x)},$$

indicating clearly on your sketch the relationship between the three graphs. Use your graph to estimate for what values of $k$ the equation

$$\frac{1}{x(2-x)} = k$$

has (i) two distinct real roots, (ii) no real roots. Explain also, with reference to your graph, why

$$\int_{-2}^{-1} \frac{dx}{x(2-x)} = \int_3^4 \frac{dx}{x(2-x)}. \tag{OC}$$

**2.** What are the periods of the functions
  (i) $x \to \cos x$;    (ii) $x \to \sin 2x$;    (ii) $x \to \tan x$?

If $f$ and $g$ are the two of these three functions which have the same period, show that $f.g$ also has the same period. Sketch the graphs of $f(x)$, $g(x)$ and $f(x).g(x)$ on the same diagram for a domain of

$$\{x: 0 \leqslant x \leqslant 2\pi, x \neq \tfrac{1}{2}\pi, \tfrac{3}{2}\pi\}.$$

What are the limiting values of $f(x).g(x)$ as $x$ tends to $\tfrac{1}{2}\pi$ and $x$ tends to $\tfrac{3}{2}\pi$?

Show, by constructing a counter-example, that if $p$ and $q$ are two functions with period $2\pi$ the function $p.q$ does not necessarily have period $2\pi$. (OC)

**3.** Sketch the graph of the function $f$ given by

$$f(x) = x^2 \quad (0 \leqslant x \leqslant 1),$$
$$f(x) = 1 - (x-1)^2 \quad (1 < x \leqslant 2).$$

A square is to be constructed with one vertex at $(u, 0)$, where $u < 1$, two vertices on the graph of $f$ and the fourth vertex also on $y = 0$. Prove that

$$u^2 + u - 1 = \sqrt{(1-u^2)}.$$

Show that this equation has a solution for $u$ between $0.8$ and $0.9$. (OC)

**4.** Discuss the existence of the derivative at $x = 0$ of the function

$$f: x \to x|x|,$$

showing that you have considered both positive and negative values as $x$ tends to 0.

State with reasons which of the following are true and which are false:
   (i) $f$ is an even function;
   (ii) $f$ is continuous at $x = 0$;
   (iii) $f$ is differentiable at $x = 0$.

Sketch a graph of the function $f$ and find the derived function $f'$. Is $f'$ differentiable at $x = 0$? (OC)

**5.** For the function $f$, where $f(x) = x^3 - 6x^2 + 9x + 7$, find the maximum and minimum values and the values of $x$ for which they occur. Draw the graph of $f$ for $-1 \leqslant x \leqslant 5$ and use it to discuss and distinguish the terms 'maximum', 'minimum', 'greatest value', 'least value' of $f$ in the interval $-1 \leqslant x \leqslant 5$.

Discuss these terms also in relation to the function $g$, which is defined by

$$g(x) = \frac{(2x-1)(x-5)}{(x-1)(x-4)}$$ for the interval $-3 \leqslant x \leqslant 5$. (For $g$ you need only sketch the graph; there is no need to use calculus unless you wish to do so).

## 4. STRUCTURE

**1.** Given that elements $e$, $a$, $b$ form a group under a law of combination $*$, complete the table

| $*$ | $e$ | $a$ | $b$ |
|---|---|---|---|
| $e$ | $e$ | $a$ | $b$ |
| $a$ | $a$ | | |
| $b$ | $b$ | | |

Hence explain why groups consisting of three elements are (i) all isomorphic to each other, (ii) cyclic. (OC)

**2.** Complete the table (for multiplication *modulo* 8)

|   | 1 | 2 | 3 | 4 | 5 | 6 | 7 |
|---|---|---|---|---|---|---|---|
| 1 | 1 | 2 | 3 | 4 |   |   |   |
| 2 | 2 | 4 | 6 | 0 |   |   |   |
| 3 | 3 | 6 | 1 |   |   |   |   |
| 4 | 4 | 0 | 4 |   |   |   |   |
| 5 | 5 | 2 |   |   |   |   |   |
| 6 | 6 | 4 |   |   |   |   |   |
| 7 | 7 |   |   |   |   |   |   |

where the entry in the $r$th row and the $s$th column is the remainder on dividing the ordinary arithmetical product $rs$ by 8.

Find the largest subset of the numbers 1, 2, 3, ... , 7 which forms a group under this rule of combination. Prove that, if $a$, $b$, $x$ are elements of this subset and

$$ax \equiv b \text{ (mod 8)},$$

then
$$x \equiv ab \text{ (mod 8)}. \qquad \text{(OC)}$$

**3.** Three indistinguishable coins are placed in a line on a table and the following operations defined on them.

        $P$: turn the left-hand one over and interchange the other two;
        $Q$: turn the right-hand one over and interchange the other two.

If $I$ is the identity operation, show that $P^2 = I$ and $Q^2 = I$. Show also that, if $PQ$ means '$Q$ and then $P$', then $PQ \neq QP$ and prove that $PQP = QPQ$.

Prove that only six possible operations are generated by $P$ and $Q$, and state one isomorphism between the group so formed and the group of symmetries of an equilateral triangle. (OC)

**4.** In the group $G$ of symmetry transformations of the square, let $R$ denote a 90° rotation about $O$, $I$ the identity transformation, and $X$ and $Y$ reflections in the axes indicated in Figure 2.

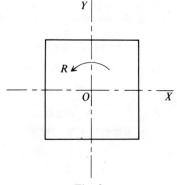

Fig. 2

Show that $\{I, X, Y, R^2\}$ is a subgroup of $G$ of order 4. Name another subgroup of order 4 which is not isomorphic to this subgroup, giving a simple reason for the lack of isomorphism.

Prove that if $A$ and $B$ are two subgroups of any group $H$, then $A \cap B$ is also a subgroup of $H$. Deduce a subgroup of $G$ of order 2. (OC)

**5.** Show that the set of ordered pairs of real numbers $(a, b)$ form a group under the operation $*$, where $(a, b) * (c, d) = (ac, bc + d)$. Find a set of $2 \times 2$ matrices isomorphic to this group under matrix multiplication.

# 5. VECTOR GEOMETRY AND LINEAR ALGEBRA

**1.** Find the equation of the plane through $A = (2, 2, -1)$ perpendicular to $OA$. Which point on this plane is closest to the point $(2, -1, 2)$?  (OC)

**2.** Solve the equations

$$
\left.
\begin{aligned}
x + y + 3z &= a \\
-2x + 5y + 3z &= b \\
-x + 3y + 2z &= c
\end{aligned}
\right\}
$$

for $x$, $y$ and $z$. Use your solution to write down the inverse of

$$
\begin{pmatrix}
1 & 1 & 3 \\
-2 & 5 & 3 \\
-1 & 3 & 2
\end{pmatrix}
$$

and check that it is the inverse matrix.

Find $k$ such that the three equations

$$
\left.
\begin{aligned}
x + y + 3z &= 1 \\
-2x + 5y + 3z &= b \\
3x + 7y + kz &= 4
\end{aligned}
\right\}
$$

are satisfied by the same values of $x$, $y$, $z$ as the original three equations, with $a = 1$, $c = 0$ and $b \neq -\frac{1}{4}$.  (OC)

**3.** A transformation is defined by

$$
\begin{pmatrix} x' \\ y' \\ z' \end{pmatrix} = \begin{pmatrix} -2 & 1 & 4 \\ 1 & 0 & -2 \\ 3 & 4 & -6 \end{pmatrix} \begin{pmatrix} x \\ y \\ z \end{pmatrix}.
$$

Show that the set of planes perpendicular to the $y$-axis maps onto a set of parallel lines. What is the direction of these lines? Which of these planes is mapped onto a line through the origin?

**4.** Lines $l$, $m$ have respectively the parametric equations

$$
\begin{pmatrix} x \\ y \\ z \end{pmatrix} = t \begin{pmatrix} 2 \\ 1 \\ -1 \end{pmatrix} + \begin{pmatrix} 0 \\ 1 \\ 3 \end{pmatrix}, \quad \begin{pmatrix} x \\ y \\ z \end{pmatrix} = u \begin{pmatrix} -2 \\ 1 \\ 1 \end{pmatrix} + \begin{pmatrix} 1 \\ 1 \\ -1 \end{pmatrix}.
$$

$A$ is the point on $l$ with parameter $t_1$, $B$ the point on $m$ with parameter $u_1$. Write down an expression for the vector $\mathbf{AB}$.

Given that the line $AB$ is perpendicular to both $l$ and $m$, find the values of $t_1$ and $u_1$ and show that the length of $AB$ is $7/\sqrt{5}$ units.  (OC)

1093

**5.** Show that the three planes

$$x + 2y + z = 7, \qquad 2x + 3y - z = 0, \qquad 3x - y + 2z = 3$$

meet at a point $X$, and find its coordinates.

If $3x - y + 2z = 3$ and $x + 2y + z = 7$ meet in the line $l$, explain why the vector

$$\lambda \begin{pmatrix} 3 \\ -1 \\ 2 \end{pmatrix} + \mu \begin{pmatrix} 1 \\ 2 \\ 1 \end{pmatrix} \qquad \text{(where } \lambda, \mu \text{ are scalars)}$$

is in a direction perpendicular to $l$.

Hence, or otherwise, find in parametric form the equation of the line through $X$ in the plane $2x + 3y - z = 0$ and perpendicular to $l$.   (OC)

# 6. PROBABILITY AND STATISTICS

**1.** A man leaves home at 8 a.m. every morning in order to arrive at work at 9 a.m. He finds that over a long period he is late once in forty times. He then tries leaving home at 7.55 a.m. and finds that over a similar period he is late once in one hundred times. Assuming that the time of his journey has a Normal distribution, before what time should he leave home in order not to be late more than once in two hundred times?   (OC)

**2.** The probability that a light bulb lasts longer than $t$ hours is $e^{-t/\mu}$. Find the probability density function for the lifetime of a bulb.

Show that the mean lifetime is $\mu$.

If the mean lifetime is 1500 hours, how unlikely is it that a bulb will last more than 3000 hours?

If the manufacturer wants to ensure that less than 1 in 1000 bulbs fail before 5 hours what is the lowest mean lifetime he can allow his bulbs to have?   (OC)

**3.** In a particular school, 1460 pupils were present on a particular day. By 8.40 a.m. 80 pupils had already arrived, and at 9.00 a.m. 12 pupils had not arrived but were on their way to school. By assuming that the frequency function of arrival times approximates to Normal form, use tables to estimate (i) the time by which half of those eventually present had arrived, and (ii) the standard deviation of the times of arrival. If registration occurred at 8.55 a.m. how many would not have arrived by then?

If each school entrance permitted a maximum of 30 pupils per minute to enter, find the minimum number of entrances required to cope with the 'peak' minute of arrival.   (OC)

**4.** A boy and girl play a game of 'spotting' approaching red cars when travelling along a road on which 25% of the cars are red. If a car is red, the first one to 'claim' it gains one point (a claim is always made by either the boy or the girl for a red car, but never by both simultaneously). If a car is not red, it is found that on half the occasions either the boy or girl (but not both) makes a claim, for which there is a penalty of two points. The first to be five or more points ahead is the winner.

The events 'a claim by the boy' and 'the car is red' are independent and the probability that he makes a claim on a car is $\frac{2}{5}$. (i) Draw a tree diagram in which the first two branches lead to the events 'red' and 'not red', and mark on the secondary branches the probabilities of claims by the children. (ii) If it is known that a claim has been made for a car which is not red, what is the probability it was made by the girl? (iii) If the score is 8–5 in favour of the girl, show that the probability that she will have won by the time two more cars have passed is 0·48. (OC)

**5.** In a joint honours degree, two departments $A$ and $B$ grade 32 candidates on a 7 point scale. The number of candidates in each grade is given by the frequency functions $f$ and $g$ as follows:

| Grade | $x_i$ | 1 | 2 | 3 | 4 | 5 | 6 | 7 |
|---|---|---|---|---|---|---|---|---|
| Subject $A$ | $f(x_i)$ | 0 | 1 | 2 | 13 | 12 | 4 | 0 |
| Subject $B$ | $g(x_i)$ | 1 | 2 | 9 | 8 | 8 | 4 | 0 |

Find the mean and variance of $x_i$ in both cases. It is required that the variance of the two frequency functions should be approximately the same. Calculate a possible redistribution of the candidates in subject $A$ between the grades in such a way that the new variance is approximately that of subject $B$ but the mean grade is the same as before. (Assume that the frequency function approximates to Normal form.)

Why would this kind of procedure be likely to be adopted? (OC)

**6.** A particular large batch of sweet-pea seeds is known to contain 25% that will not germinate. Samples of six seeds each are sown in pots. What is:
 (a) the expected number of seedlings to appear in a pot?
 (b) the most likely number of seedlings to appear in a pot?
 (c) the probability of precisely this number appearing?
 (d) the percentage of pots in which less than half the seeds germinate? (OC)

**7.** Approximate counts of flocks of oyster-catchers in two estuaries on ten occasions produced the following results:

| Size of flock | 251–750 | 751–1250 | 1251–1750 |
|---|---|---|---|
| Estuary $A$ | 0 | 0 | 2 |
| Estuary $B$˙ | 1 | 1 | 1 |

| Size of flock | 1751–2250 | 2251–2750 | 2751–4250 |
|---|---|---|---|
| Estuary $A$ | 4 | 3 | 1 |
| Estuary $B$ | 3 | 2 | 2 |

Draw histograms of the two populations. Calculate the means and indicate their positions clearly on your diagrams. Suggest, giving reasons, on which estuary a count exceeding 5000 is more likely to be recorded. (You can refer to assumed Normal frequency functions but no *calculations* of the standard deviations need be made.) (OC)

# 7. ELECTRICITY

**1.** In the circuit shown in Figure 3, with resistances $P, Q, R, S$ and e.m.f.s $E$ and $F$, no current passes through the resistance $S$. Prove that

$$PE = (P+Q)F.$$

(OC)

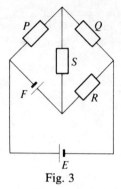

Fig. 3

**2.** The network on the left is part of an electrical circuit and is to be replaced by the network on the right in such a way that the currents and potentials at $A$, $B$

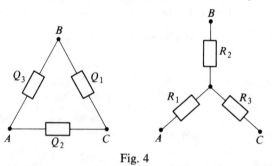

Fig. 4

and $C$ are unchanged. If $Q_1 = 50$, $Q_2 = 60$, $Q_3 = 90$, find a possible value for $R_1 + R_2$ by equating the total resistance between $A$ and $B$ in each of the two networks. Derive two other similar linear equations and hence find possible values of $R_1$, $R_2$ and $R_3$.

Show that if $Q_1 = Q_2 = Q_3 = Q$ then possible values of $R_1$, $R_2$, $R_3$ are given by

$$R_1 = R_2 = R_3 = \tfrac{1}{3}Q. \tag{OC}$$

**3.** A pair of resistors with resistances $r$, $s$ are connected across a battery of negligible resistance, first in series and then in parallel. In which case will the power output from the battery be greater?

Find the expression, in as simple an algebraic form as possible, for the ratio of the power output in the second case to that in the first.    (OC)

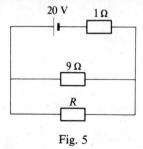

Fig. 5

**4.** In the circuit shown in Figure 5, find the value of $R$ for which the power consumed in it is a maximum. What then is the power:

(*a*) consumed in $R$;

(*b*) consumed in the $9\,\Omega$ resistor;

(*c*) wasted in the $1\,\Omega$ resistor (which represents the internal resistance of the battery)?

## 8. CALCULUS

**1.** The number $n$ of customers per day at a hot-dog stall is given approximately by $n = 100 \exp (9/x)$, where $x$ is the price of a hot-dog in pence. Using a linear approximation (or otherwise), estimate the percentage increase in $n$ if $x$ is reduced from $7\frac{1}{2}$ to 7. (OC)

**2.** Use a step-by-step method, with $0\cdot2$ as the step length, to estimate the value of $y(1)$, given that

$$\frac{dy}{dx} = 1 + y^2 \quad \text{and} \quad y(0) = 0.$$

Lay your work out in tabular form after the pattern:

| $x$ | $y$ | $y^2$ | $1+y^2$ | $\delta y$ |
|-----|-----|-------|---------|------------|
| 0   | 0   | 0     | 1       | $0\cdot2$  |
| $0\cdot2$ |     |       |         |            |

Compare your value of $y(1)$ with the exact value. (OC)

**3.** Tabulate a numerical solution of the differential equation $dx/dt = \sin x$ with initial conditions $x = 1$ when $t = 0$, taking intervals of 1 for $t$ from 0 to 4. (Work to two places of decimals throughout.)

Suggest the limit of $x$ as $t$ tends to infinity. Justify your answer by reference to the differential equation. What values other than 1 could we assign to $x$ at $t = 0$ without affecting this limit? Determine a family of parallel lines which are solutions of the equation. (OC)

**4.** Solve the differential equations:

(i) $2x\dfrac{dy}{dx} + y^2 = 1$, given that $y = 0$ when $x = 1$;

(ii) $\dfrac{dy}{dx} + 3y = x$, given that $y = 0$ when $x = 0$. (OC)

**5.** A function $F$ is such that $F'(x) > 0$ for all $x > 0$. In what two essentially different ways can $F(x)$ behave as $x$ tends to infinity? State two particular functions which exhibit these characteristics (one for each).

Sketch the graph of the function $f: x \to e^x/x$ for positive and negative values of $x$. By expressing $f'(x)$ in terms of $f(x)$, or otherwise, justify the shape of your graph as $x$ tends to infinity.

The numbers of birds $n$ of an island colony decreased and increased with time $t$ years according to the approximate formula $n = a\,e^{kt}/t$ over some interval of years, where $t$ is measured from 1900, and $a, k$ are constants. If during this period the population was the same in 1965 as it was in 1930, when was it least? (OC)

**6.** A solution contains substances $A$, $B$ and $C$. A chemical reaction changes substance $B$ into substance $C$ at a rate $kp$, where $p$ is the mass of substance $C$ present at time $t$ and $k$ is a constant; simultaneously, a second reaction changes substance $A$ into substance $B$ at a rate $2kq$, where $q$ is the *combined* mass of substances $B$ and $C$ present. Write down equations for $dp/dt$ and $dq/dt$.

Initially 48 grams of $A$, 1 gram of $B$ and 1 gram of $C$ are present. By solving your equations, show that substance $A$ is exhausted at time $t_1$, where $kt_1 = \ln 5$, and that the two reactions are completed at time $t_2$, where $kt_2 = \ln 50$.

Find the maximum amount of substance $B$ present during the reaction. (OC)

**7.** Water is flowing in one direction along a horizontal rectangular channel $l$ metres wide in such a way that the velocity at a point $x$ metres from a side and $h$ metres from the horizontal base is horizontal and of magnitude $hk \sin (\pi x/l)\,\mathrm{m\,s^{-1}}$, where $k$ is a constant.

Show that the amount of water flowing per second through a horizontal layer of thickness $\delta h$ metres at height $h$ metres from the base, where $\delta h$ is small, is approximately

$$2hkl(\delta h/\pi)\,\mathrm{m^3\,s^{-1}}.$$

If the depth of the flow is $0\cdot 5$ m find $k$, in terms of $l$, if the total flow along the channel is $0\cdot 1\,\mathrm{m^3\,s^{-1}}$. (OC)

**8.** (*a*) Using partial fractions, evaluate

$$\int_0^1 \frac{dx}{(x-3)(x+1)}.$$

(*b*) By means of a suitable substitution, show that

$$\int_a^{2a} f(x)\,dx = \int_0^a f(2a-x)\,dx.$$

Deduce that

$$\int_0^{2a} f(x)\,dx = \int_0^a f(x)\,dx + \int_0^a f(2a-x)\,dx.$$

Hence evaluate the integrals

$$\int_0^{2\pi} \sin^5 \theta\,d\theta \quad \text{and} \quad \int_0^{\pi} \cos^3 \theta\,d\theta. \tag{OC}$$

**9.** Figure 6 shows a horizontal semicircle $YXY'$ of radius $a$. On the semicircle stands a solid, the height of which is proportional to the horizontal distance from the diameter $YY'$. If at distance $x$ from $YY'$ the height is $kx$, explain briefly why the mass $M$ of the solid is given by

$$M = 2k\rho \int_0^a x\sqrt{(a^2 - x^2)}\,dx, \tag{1}$$

where $\rho$ is the density (assumed uniform).

A woodcutter makes a horizontal cut half-way through the trunk of a tree (which may be taken to be a circular cylinder of radius $a$ with axis vertical), finishing the cut along a diameter $YY'$. Then, from higher up on the same side,

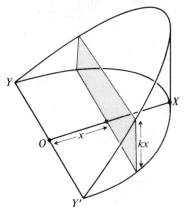

Fig. 6

he makes a cut downwards in a plane inclined at an angle $\alpha$ to the horizontal, meeting the first cut on the diameter $YY'$.

(a) Use (1) above to find the mass of the wedge cut free.

(b) By using the substitution $x = a \sin \theta$, or otherwise, evaluate

$$\int_0^a x^2 \sqrt{(a^2 - x^2)}\, dx.$$

Hence find the perpendicular distance of the centre of mass of the wedge from the axis of the trunk. (OC)

## 9. KINEMATICS AND MECHANICS

**1.** An aircraft takes off from the end of a runway in a southerly direction and climbs at an angle of $\tan^{-1}\left(\frac{1}{2}\right)$ to the horizontal at a speed of $225\sqrt{5}$ km h$^{-1}$. Show that $t$ seconds after take-off the position vector $\mathbf{r}$ of the aircraft with respect to the end of the runway is given by $\mathbf{r} = \frac{1}{16}t(2\mathbf{i}+\mathbf{k})$, where $\mathbf{i}, \mathbf{j}, \mathbf{k}$ represent vectors of length 1 km in directions south, east and vertically upwards.

At time $t = 0$, a second aircraft flying horizontally southwest at $720\sqrt{2}$ km h$^{-1}$ has position vector $-1\cdot2\mathbf{i}+3\cdot2\mathbf{j}+\mathbf{k}$. Find its position vector at time $t$ in terms of $\mathbf{i}, \mathbf{j}, \mathbf{k}$ and $t$. Show that there will be a collision unless courses are changed and state at what time it would occur. (OC)

**2.** The thrust $T$ in a spring when it is compressed a distance $x$ from its natural length is given by $T = kx$ (where $k$ is the 'stiffness' of the spring). Show that in this position the energy stored is $\frac{1}{2}kx^2$.

A man of mass 70 kg throws himself off platform $A$ so that his initial vertical velocity is zero. He lands on a trampoline surface at $B$, 4 m below $A$.

If we take as a simplified model for the action of the trampoline a light spring (initially uncompressed) with $k = 700g$ newton/metre (see Figure 7), find:

(a) how far below $B$ he will descend;

(b) to what height he will rise before he is next at rest;

(c) how much extra energy (by flexing his muscles on impact) he must impart to rise a further 2 m above his starting point.

1099

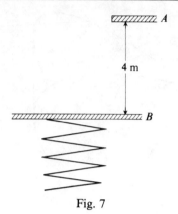

Fig. 7

State clearly which, if any, of $(a)$, $(b)$, $(c)$ would be altered if: (i) the same actions were formed by a boy of mass 45 kg; (ii) the same actions were performed by the man but on a trampoline of half the stiffness.   (OC)

**3.** In a 'golf driving practice kit', a ball of mass $0\cdot05$ kg is attached by a length of light elastic to the tee, so that, when the ball is $r$ metres from the tee, the tension in the elastic is $0\cdot2r$ newtons. The ball is struck with velocity $\mathbf{u}$ m/s at time $t = 0$. If $\mathbf{r}$ metres denotes the position vector at a subsequent time $t$ seconds (before it strikes the ground again), and if $\mathbf{j}$ denotes a unit vector vertically upwards and the acceleration of gravity is taken as $10$ m/s$^2$, obtain the differential equation

$$\ddot{\mathbf{r}} + 4\mathbf{r} + 10\mathbf{j} = \mathbf{0}.$$

Verify that all the conditions of the problem are satisfied by the solution

$$\mathbf{r} = \tfrac{1}{2}\mathbf{u}\sin 2t + \tfrac{5}{2}(\cos 2t - 1)\mathbf{j}.$$   (OC)

**4.** Two stones, each of mass $5m$, are moving across a sheet of smooth ice at equal speeds of $10v$ in opposite directions on parallel paths, so that no collision is involved. A frog of mass $m$, travelling on one of the stones, leaps across to the other one, and in so doing deflects the stone he leaves through $30°$ and changes its speed to $8v$.

Find, by drawing and measurement or by calculation, (i) through what angle the other stone is deflected and its subsequent speed; (ii) the (vector) impulse the frog exerts on the stone on which he lands.   (OC)

**5.** A particle of mass $m$ is set in motion along a straight path from point $O$ with initial speed $u$. It is subject to a variable resistive force $mkv^2$ (where $v$ is the speed of the particle) when its displacement from $O$ is $x$. Show that the equation of motion may be expressed in the form

$$\frac{1}{v}\frac{dv}{dx} = -k.$$

Solve this differential equation and deduce that the kinetic energy of the particle will have dropped to one half of the initial value when it has gone a distance $(1/2k)\ln 2$.

At this instant the particle collides and coalesces with a stationary particle of equal mass $m$. Show that immediately after the collision the joint particle will have speed $u/(2\sqrt{2})$. If the resistive force is now $2mkv^2$, find the kinetic energy of the joint particle when it also has travelled a distance $(1/2k)\ln 2$.   (OC)

# PROJECT EXERCISES

## 1. SYMMETRIES OF A CUBE

This exercise links together, in a simple and familiar geometrical context, various ideas about vectors, matrices and groups.

A model of a cube with its faces painted different colours (or distinguished in some other conspicuous way) may be found useful.

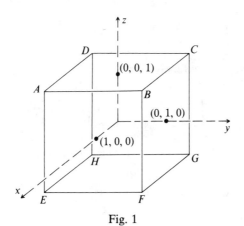

Fig. 1

**1.** Name an axis of rotational symmetry of the cube of order 4 (i.e. of 90° rotational symmetry). How many such axes has the cube?

**2.** Name an axis of rotational symmetry of order 3. How many of these axes are there?

**3.** How many axes of rotational symmetry has the cube apart from those already considered? What are the orders of these axes?

**4.** How many rotational symmetries has a cube altogether, including the identity? Show that they form a group and name some of the subgroups.

**5.** A quarter-turn $Q$ about the $z$-axis maps $A$ onto $B$. A 120° rotation $T$ about $FD$ maps $A$ onto $C$. Identify the single rotation equivalent to (a) $Q$ followed by $T$, (b) $T$ followed by $Q$.

(The rotations in this and the following questions are clockwise when viewed in the directions of the axes.)

**6.** What is the single rotation equivalent to a 90° rotation about $Oz$ followed by a 90° rotation about $Oy$?

**7.** Write down the images under $T$ (see Question 5) of the unit vectors $\begin{pmatrix} 1 \\ 0 \\ 0 \end{pmatrix}$,

$\begin{pmatrix}0\\1\\0\end{pmatrix}$, $\begin{pmatrix}0\\0\\1\end{pmatrix}$, and hence the matrix of $T$. What is the determinant of this matrix?

**8.** By considering the images of the unit vectors, find the transformations represented by

(a) $\begin{pmatrix} 0 & 1 & 0 \\ 0 & 0 & 1 \\ 1 & 0 & 0 \end{pmatrix}$,　　(b) $\begin{pmatrix} 0 & -1 & 0 \\ 0 & 0 & 1 \\ -1 & 0 & 0 \end{pmatrix}$,

(c) $\begin{pmatrix} -1 & 0 & 0 \\ 0 & 0 & 1 \\ 0 & 1 & 0 \end{pmatrix}$,　　(d) $\begin{pmatrix} -1 & 0 & 0 \\ 0 & 0 & -1 \\ 0 & -1 & 0 \end{pmatrix}$.

**9.** What can you say about the vector

$$\begin{pmatrix} p \\ q \\ r \end{pmatrix} \quad \text{if} \quad \begin{pmatrix} 0 & 0 & 1 \\ 0 & -1 & 0 \\ 1 & 0 & 0 \end{pmatrix} \begin{pmatrix} p \\ q \\ r \end{pmatrix} = \begin{pmatrix} p \\ q \\ r \end{pmatrix} ?$$

Find vectors invariant under the transformations represented by

(a) $\begin{pmatrix} 0 & -1 & 0 \\ 1 & 0 & 0 \\ 0 & 0 & 1 \end{pmatrix}$,　　(b) $\begin{pmatrix} 0 & 0 & -1 \\ -1 & 0 & 0 \\ 0 & 1 & 0 \end{pmatrix}$,

(c) $\begin{pmatrix} -1 & 0 & 0 \\ 0 & 1 & 0 \\ 0 & 0 & -1 \end{pmatrix}$,　　(d) $\begin{pmatrix} 0 & -1 & 0 \\ -1 & 0 & 0 \\ 0 & 0 & -1 \end{pmatrix}$.

**10.** Write down the matrix of $Q$ and form the matrix products $QT$ and $TQ$. Find invariant vectors of these matrices.

**11.** How many $3 \times 3$ matrices have six zeros and three 1s or $-1$s arranged so that the determinant is $+1$? How can you tell at a glance which of these represents (a) a 90° rotation, (b) a 120° or 240° rotation?

**12.** Investigate the subgroup generated by

$$\mathbf{M} = \begin{pmatrix} 0 & 1 & 0 \\ 0 & 0 & 1 \\ 1 & 0 & 0 \end{pmatrix} \quad \text{and} \quad \mathbf{N} = \begin{pmatrix} -1 & 0 & 0 \\ 0 & 0 & 1 \\ 0 & 1 & 0 \end{pmatrix}.$$

**13.** Form two left cosets (see Chapter 27, pp. 673–6) of the subgroup

$$\left\{ \begin{pmatrix} 1 & 0 & 0 \\ 0 & 1 & 0 \\ 0 & 0 & 1 \end{pmatrix}, \begin{pmatrix} 0 & 0 & -1 \\ 0 & 1 & 0 \\ 1 & 0 & 0 \end{pmatrix}, \begin{pmatrix} -1 & 0 & 0 \\ 0 & 1 & 0 \\ 0 & 0 & -1 \end{pmatrix}, \begin{pmatrix} 0 & 0 & 1 \\ 0 & 1 & 0 \\ -1 & 0 & 0 \end{pmatrix} \right\}.$$

Are these also right cosets?

**14.** How many $3 \times 3$ matrices have six zeros and three 1s or $-1$s arranged so that the determinant is $-1$? How many of these represent plane reflections of the cube? Identify the invariant planes of

$$(a) \begin{pmatrix} -1 & 0 & 0 \\ 0 & 1 & 0 \\ 0 & 0 & 1 \end{pmatrix}, \quad (b) \begin{pmatrix} 0 & 0 & 1 \\ 0 & 1 & 0 \\ 1 & 0 & 0 \end{pmatrix}, \quad (c) \begin{pmatrix} 0 & -1 & 0 \\ -1 & 0 & 0 \\ 0 & 0 & 1 \end{pmatrix}.$$

**15.** Describe the transformation represented by $\begin{pmatrix} -1 & 0 & 0 \\ 0 & -1 & 0 \\ 0 & 0 & -1 \end{pmatrix}$.

**16.** An *isometry* is a transformation that preserves lengths and angles (i.e. that maps any figure onto a congruent figure). Explain why the combination of any two isometries is an isometry and hence or otherwise show that $\mathbf{L} = \begin{pmatrix} 0 & 1 & 0 \\ 0 & 0 & 1 \\ -1 & 0 & 0 \end{pmatrix}$

represents an isometry. This is a new type called a *rotary reflection*. How many symmetry transformations of this kind does a cube have?

**17.** Find the period of the rotary reflection matrix in Question 16, i.e. the smallest natural number $n$ such that $\mathbf{L}^n = \mathbf{I}$.

**18.** The complete symmetry group of the cube is of order 48, i.e. it has 48 elements. Can you find subgroups of order $(a)$ 6, $(b)$ 8, $(c)$ 10, $(d)$ 12?

## 2. PI

When you first met $\pi$, you probably found its value roughly by measuring the diameter of a cylinder and the length of thread that would wind exactly 10 times, say, round the cylinder. Later we learnt that $\pi$ is an irrational number whose decimal representation, starting $3 \cdot 141\,592\,653$, continues infinitely without recurring. Moreover it is a transcendental number, meaning that no polynomial equation exists with integer coefficients for which $\pi$ is a root. In this it differs from irrational numbers composed of square roots, cube roots, etc.; $x = \sqrt[3]{2} + \sqrt{3}$, for example, is a root of $x^6 - 9x^4 - 4x^3 + 27x^2 - 36x - 23 = 0$ and can be found to any desired accuracy by the Newton–Raphson method.

The number $\pi$ crops up again and again, often in contexts apparently having no connection with circumferences and areas of circles from which $\pi$ was originally defined. How can $\pi$ be calculated to 100 decimal places?

This exercise starts with a block of five questions with variations on one simple method of evaluating $\pi$. The next four questions are all independent of each other, and introduce contrasting ways of writing $\pi$ as the limit of a sequence. The last four questions together lead in an unexpected way to the intriguing result

$$\int_{-\infty}^{\infty} \exp\left(-\tfrac{1}{2}x^2\right) dx = \sqrt{(2\pi)},$$

which is so vital to probability theory.

1103

**1.** Prove that

$$\frac{1}{1+x^2}=1-x^2+x^4-\ldots+x^{4n}-\frac{x^{4n+2}}{1+x^2}.$$

Deduce that

$$x-\frac{x^3}{3}+\frac{x^5}{5}-\ldots+\frac{x^{4n+1}}{4n+1}$$

is a good approximation for $\tan^{-1} x$ for small $x$.

**2.** If $S_n$ is the sum of the first $n$ terms of the series $1-\frac{1}{3}+\frac{1}{5}-\frac{1}{7}+\ldots$, plot the values of $S_n$ for $n = 1, 2, \ldots, 6$. Show that $S_n$ tends to $\frac{1}{4}\pi$ as $n$ tends to infinity. Is this of any use for calculating $\pi$?

**3.** If $\theta+\phi=\frac{1}{4}\pi$ and $\tan\theta=\frac{3}{5}$, find $\tan\phi$. Use the series of Question 1 to find $\theta$ and $\phi$ to 6 decimal places and hence deduce a value for $\pi$.

**4.** If $\alpha+\beta=\frac{1}{4}\pi$ and $\tan\alpha=\frac{1}{2}$, find $\tan\beta$. Use this to calculate $\pi$ with as great accuracy as your calculator can provide. Compare the amounts of work involved in this question and Question 3.

**5.** Prove that if $\tan\theta=\frac{1}{5}$, then $\tan 4\theta=\frac{120}{119}$, and $\tan(4\theta-\frac{1}{4}\pi)=\frac{1}{239}$. Evaluate $\pi$ to 6 decimal places using $\frac{1}{4}\pi=4\tan^{-1}\frac{1}{5}-\tan^{-1}\frac{1}{239}$.

**6.** Show, geometrically or otherwise, that $\int_0^{\frac{1}{2}}\sqrt{(1-x^2)}\,dx=\frac{1}{12}\pi+\frac{1}{8}\sqrt{3}$. Evaluate the integral (a) by Simpson's rule with 10 strips, (b) using a polynomial approximation for $\sqrt{(1-x^2)}$. What values do these give for $\pi$?

**7.** Using $\sin 2\theta=2\sin\theta\cos\theta=2\sin\theta\sqrt{(1-\sin^2\theta)}$, show that if $s=\sin\theta$ and $S=\sin 2\theta$, $2s^2=1-\sqrt{(1-S^2)}$. Deduce that $\sin 22\frac{1}{2}°=\frac{1}{2}\sqrt{(2-\sqrt{2})}$ and that a regular octagon inscribed in a circle of unit radius has perimeter $8\sqrt{(2-\sqrt{2})}$. Show further that a regular 16-gon inscribed in a unit circle has perimeter $16\sqrt{(2-\sqrt{(2+\sqrt{2})})}$ and a regular 32-gon has perimeter $32\sqrt{(2-\sqrt{(2+\sqrt{(2+\sqrt{2})})})}$.

Compare the circumference $2\pi$ of a unit circle with the values given by these expressions and the next few members of the sequence.

**8.** Show that $2\cos\frac{1}{2}\theta=\sqrt{(2+2\cos\theta)}=\dfrac{\sin\theta}{\sin\frac{1}{2}\theta}$, and hence that if $u_1=0$ ($=2\cos\frac{1}{2}\pi$) and $u_{i+1}=\sqrt{(2+u_i)}$, then $u_n=2\cos(\pi/2^n)$. Deduce that the sequence $v_n=\cos(\pi/2^n)$ is generated by $v_1=0$, $v_{i+1}=\sqrt{(\frac{1}{2}(1+v_i))}$.

Now show that $v_2 v_3 \ldots v_n=\dfrac{\sin\frac{1}{2}\pi}{2^{n-1}\sin(\pi/2^n)}$ and that this tends to $2/\pi$ as $n$ tends to infinity.

Use this method to compute $\pi$ on your calculator or on a computer.

**9.** If

$$s_n=1+\frac{1}{2^2}+\frac{1}{3^2}+\ldots+\frac{1}{n^2}$$

and

$$t_n=1+\frac{1}{2^4}+\frac{1}{3^4}+\ldots+\frac{1}{n^4},$$

it can be shown that $s_n \to \frac{1}{6}\pi^2$, $t_n \to \frac{1}{90}\pi^4$ as $n \to \infty$. Use each of these series to compute values of $\pi$.

**10.** It can be proved (see Chapter 20, p. 521) that if $I_n = \int_0^{\frac{1}{2}\pi} \sin^n \theta \, d\theta$, then

$$I_n = \frac{n-1}{n} I_{n-2}.$$

Show that $I_0 = \frac{1}{2}\pi$, $I_1 = 1$; find also the values (in factors) of $I_6$ and $I_7$.

If we write $V_n = \dfrac{I_{2n+1}}{I_{2n}}$, show that $1 > V_n > \dfrac{2n}{2n+1}$, so that $V_n \to 1$ as $n \to \infty$.

Show that $\dfrac{V_n}{V_{n-1}} = \dfrac{(2n)(2n)}{(2n+1)(2n-1)}$ and, using this, that

$$\tfrac{1}{2}\pi \times V_n = \frac{2\times2}{1\times3} \times \frac{4\times4}{3\times5} \times \ldots \times \frac{(2n)(2n)}{(2n-1)(2n+1)}.$$

**11.** Show that the final result of Question 10 can be written in the form

$$\tfrac{1}{2}\pi \times V_n = \frac{2^{4n}(n!)^4}{(2n+1)(2n!)^2}.$$

**12.** Show, using Question 11, that for large $n$ the probability of tossing exactly $n$ heads and $n$ tails in $2n$ tosses of a coin is approximately $1/\sqrt{(\pi n)}$.

**13.** We have shown in Chapter 39 that the Normal probability function can be derived as the limit of the binomial. The general Normal model is

$$\phi(x) = (k/\sigma) \exp\left[-(x-\mu)^2/2\sigma^2\right]$$

where $k$ is the reciprocal of $\displaystyle\int_{-\infty}^{\infty} \exp\left(-\tfrac{1}{2}x^2\right) dx$. Use Question 12 to show that

$$k = 1/\sqrt{(2\pi)}.$$

## 3. HYPERBOLIC FUNCTIONS

The *hyperbolic functions* $x \to \cosh x$ and $x \to \sinh x$ are defined by

$$\cosh x = \tfrac{1}{2}(e^x + e^{-x}), \qquad \sinh x = \tfrac{1}{2}(e^x - e^{-x}).$$

The reason for the notation is that these functions have properties which are similar to those of the circular functions $x \to \cos x$ and $x \to \sin x$. We shall investigate some of these properties, as well as the functions themselves, in the following exercise.

**1.** Show that $x \to \cosh x$ is an even function and $x \to \sinh x$ is odd.

**2.** Show that $\cosh x + \sinh x = e^x$ and $\cosh x - \sinh x = e^{-x}$. Hence deduce that $\cosh^2 x - \sinh^2 x = 1$.

**3.** (a) Sketch the graphs of $y = e^x$ and $y = e^{-x}$ on the same diagram. Use the above definition to add the graph of $y = \cosh x$ to your diagram.
   (b) In a similar manner, sketch the graph of $y = \sinh x$.
   (c) What restrictions must be placed on the domain of $x \to \cosh x$ so that the inverse function $x \to \cosh^{-1} x$ can exist?

(d) Sketch the graph of $y = \cosh^{-1} x$.

(e) Sketch the graph of $y = \sinh^{-1} x$.

**4.** Show that $y = \cosh^{-1} x \Rightarrow (e^y)^2 - 2xe^y + 1 = 0$. Solve this quadratic in $e^y$ and show that

$$y = \ln (x \pm \sqrt{(x^2 - 1)}).$$

Explain why your answer to Question 3(c) makes the negative root inadmissible, giving

$$\cosh^{-1} x = \ln (x + \sqrt{(x^2 - 1)}).$$

**5.** Find $\dfrac{d}{dx} (\sinh x)$ and $\dfrac{d}{dx} (\cosh x)$ from the definitions. Compare with $\dfrac{d}{dx} (\sin x)$ and $\dfrac{d}{dx} (\cos x)$.

**6.** Find $\displaystyle\int \dfrac{1}{\sqrt{(1 + x^2)}} \, dx$ by making the substitution $x = \sinh u$.

**7.** Find $\displaystyle\int \dfrac{1}{\sqrt{(x^2 - 1)}} \, dx$ by making the substitution $x = \cosh u$ (where $u > 0$).

**8.** Verify your results to Questions 6 and 7 by finding $\dfrac{d}{dx} (\sinh^{-1} x)$ and $\dfrac{d}{dx} (\cosh^{-1} x)$, paying careful attention to signs where necessary.

**9.** Use tables of $\sinh^{-1} x$ and $\cosh^{-1} x$ (see SMP *Advanced Tables*) or natural logarithm tables to find:

(a) $\displaystyle\int_1^3 \dfrac{1}{\sqrt{(1 + x^2)}} \, dx$;     (b) $\displaystyle\int_2^5 \dfrac{1}{\sqrt{(x^2 - 1)}} \, dx$;

(c) $\displaystyle\int_0^6 \dfrac{1}{\sqrt{(9 + x^2)}} \, dx$;     (d) $\displaystyle\int_{-1}^1 \dfrac{1}{\sqrt{(x^2 + 6x + 8)}} \, dx$.

**10.** Show that:

(a) $\cosh (a + b) = \cosh a \cosh b + \sinh a \sinh b$;

(b) $\sinh (a + b) = \sinh a \cosh b + \cosh a \sinh b$.

Find results for the hyperbolic functions analogous to:

(c) $\cos 2x = 2 \cos^2 x - 1 = 1 - 2 \sin^2 x$;

(d) $y = A \sin nx + B \cos nx \Rightarrow \dfrac{d^2 y}{dx^2} = -n^2 y$.

**11.** Use a hyperbolic substitution and the formulae of Question 10 to find:

(a) $\displaystyle\int_4^6 \sqrt{(x^2 - 9)} \, dx$;     (b) $\displaystyle\int_{-2}^2 \sqrt{(x^2 + 9)} \, dx$.

**12.** Prove that $(\cosh x + \sinh x)^n = \cosh nx + \sinh nx$. To what result in the circular functions is this analogous?

**13.** Prove that, for all values of $t$, the point $P$ with coordinates $(a \cosh t, a \sinh t)$ lies on the *rectangular hyperbola* $x^2 - y^2 = a^2$. Describe how $P$ moves on the hyperbola as $t$ increases through the real numbers. Are all points of the hyperbola expressible in this form?

What curve is traced out by $Q$, with coordinates $(a \cos t, a \sin t)$, as $t$ varies?

# 4. CONICS

Figure 2 shows the intersection of a plane with a (double) cone. The set of points in the intersection make up a curve called a *conic*.

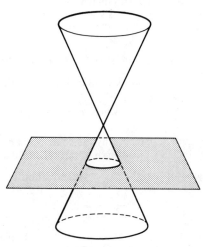

Fig. 2

**1.** Show that, after a rotation given by the matrix

$$\begin{pmatrix} \cos \varepsilon & 0 & -\sin \varepsilon \\ 0 & 1 & 0 \\ \sin \varepsilon & 0 & \cos \varepsilon \end{pmatrix},$$

the equation of the cone $z^2 = x^2 + y^2$ becomes

$$(x^2 - z^2) \cos 2\varepsilon + 2xz \sin 2\varepsilon + y^2 = 0$$

(see Chapter 3, p. 57).

**2.** Show that the intersection of the surface obtained in Question 1 with the plane $z = k$ is a curve with equation

$$x^2 + 2kx \tan 2\varepsilon + y^2 \sec 2\varepsilon = k^2 \qquad (\varepsilon \neq \tfrac{1}{4}\pi).$$

**3.** The equation obtained in Question 2 will be that of a conic in the $(x, y)$ plane. By a suitable change of origin (a translation parallel to the $x$-axis), obtain the equation

$$x^2 + y^2 \sec 2\varepsilon = k^2 \sec^2 2\varepsilon \qquad (\varepsilon \neq \tfrac{1}{4}\pi).$$

**4.** In the case where $\varepsilon = \tfrac{1}{4}\pi$, show that the conic is a parabola. Illustrate with a sketch, similar to Figure 2.

1107

**5.** If $\varepsilon < \frac{1}{4}\pi$, prove that the equation of Question 3 may be written

$$\frac{x^2}{a^2} + \frac{y^2}{b^2} = 1, \quad \text{where } b^2 = a^2(1-e^2).$$

With reference to Figure 2, explain why the conic is a *closed* curve in this case. What is the significance of $e$? ($e$ is known as the *eccentricity* of the conic.) Sketch a typical curve of this type (called an ellipse). Between what values may $e$ lie?

**6.** Show that a two-way stretch with matrix

$$\begin{pmatrix} 1/a & 0 \\ 0 & 1/b \end{pmatrix}$$

maps the ellipse of Question 5 onto a circle. Hence find the area of the ellipse.

**7.** If $\varepsilon > \frac{1}{4}\pi$, prove the equation of Question 3 may be written

$$\frac{x^2}{a^2} - \frac{y^2}{b^2} = 1, \quad \text{where } b^2 = a^2(e^2-1).$$

With reference to Figure 2, explain why the conic is not closed in this case, and has two branches. Sketch a typical curve of this type (called a *hyperbola*).

**8.** What are the asymptotes of the curve with equation

$$\frac{x^2}{a^2} - \frac{y^2}{b^2} = 1?$$

Sketch a curve having this equation, for which $b > a$. Explain why such a curve cannot be obtained from the cone of Question 1.

**9.** Taking $\varepsilon = \frac{1}{2}\pi$, show how the curve of Question 8 may be obtained from the cone

$$x^2 + y^2 = \frac{b^2}{a^2} z^2.$$

**10.** If $\varepsilon \neq \frac{1}{4}\pi$, show that each of the equations of Questions 5, 7 and 8 is that of the locus of a point whose distance from a fixed point $S$ with coordinates $(ae, 0)$ is $e$ times its distance from the fixed line $m$, whose equation is $x = a/e$. $S$ is called the *focus*, and $m$ the *directrix* of the conic.

**11.** Show that the equation of the parabola of Question 4 may (after a suitable change of origin) be written $y^2 = 4ax$. What are its focus and directrix?

**12.** Obtain the polar equation for each of the three types of conic in the form $l/r = 1 + e\cos\theta$. (Take $S$ as origin, and the line of symmetry through $S$ as central direction.)

# 5. FOURIER SERIES

In Chapter 25 we saw that when we combine several wave functions, even of differing amplitudes and periods, the resultant function is still periodic. Conversely, any 'reasonable' periodic function can be represented by a suitable combination of sine and cosine functions.

**1.** Draw the graphs of (a) $\sin t$, (b) $\sin t + \frac{1}{3}\sin 3t$, (c) $\sin t + \frac{1}{3}\sin 3t + \frac{1}{5}\sin 5t$. What do you think the graph would look like if several more terms of the same kind were added?

**2.** (a) Draw the graph of the square wave function

$$\left.\begin{array}{l} f(x) = -1 \quad (-\pi \leqslant x < 0) \\ f(x) = 1 \quad (0 \leqslant x < \pi) \\ f(x + 2\pi) = f(x) \end{array}\right\} \tag{1}$$

(b) Suppose that $f(x)$ can be represented by a function of the form

$$f(x) = a_1 \sin x + a_2 \sin 2x + a_3 \sin 3x + \ldots \tag{2}$$

To find the values of $a_1$, $a_2$, $a_3$, etc. we perform a series of integrals:
  (i) Establish the result that

$$\int_{-\pi}^{\pi} \sin mx \sin x \, dx = 0 \quad \text{for} \quad m \neq 1. \tag{3}$$

[Hint: use the formula $2 \sin P \sin Q = \cos(P-Q) - \cos(P+Q)$.] Show that

$$\int_{-\pi}^{\pi} f(x) \sin x \, dx = \int_{-\pi}^{0} -\sin x \, dx + \int_{0}^{\pi} \sin x \, dx \quad \text{(from (1))}.$$

Multiply both sides of equation (2) by $\sin x$ and show also that

$$\int_{-\pi}^{\pi} f(x) \sin x \, dx = \int_{-\pi}^{\pi} a_1 \sin^2 x \, dx \quad \text{(using (3))}.$$

By evaluating and equating these integrals, find $a_1$.

  (ii) Establish the result that $\int_{-\pi}^{\pi} \sin mx \, \sin 2x \, dx = 0$ for $m \neq 2$. Hence, by multiplying both sides of equation (2) by $\sin 2x$, show that

$$\int_{-\pi}^{0} -\sin 2x \, dx + \int_{0}^{\pi} \sin 2x \, dx = \int_{-\pi}^{\pi} a_2 \sin^2 2x \, dx$$

and find $a_2$.

  (iii) Find $a_3$ from the similar result

$$\int_{-\pi}^{0} -\sin 3x \, dx + \int_{0}^{\pi} \sin 3x \, dx = \int_{-\pi}^{\pi} a_3 \sin^2 3x \, dx.$$

**3.** Show that $\int_{-\pi}^{\pi} \sin mx \sin nx \, dx = \begin{cases} 0 & (m \neq n) \\ \pi & (m = n) \end{cases}$. Deduce that if a function $f(x)$ whose domain is $\{x: -\pi \leqslant x < \pi\}$ can be represented by a series of the form

$$f(x) = a_1 \sin x + a_2 \sin 2x + a_3 \sin 3x + \ldots.$$

then

$$a_m = \frac{1}{\pi} \int_{-\pi}^{\pi} f(x) \sin mx \, dx \quad (m \geqslant 1).$$

**4.** Use the result of Question 3 to find a series

$$a_1 \sin x + a_2 \sin 2x + a_3 \sin 3x + \ldots$$

for the periodic function

$$f(x) = x \quad (-\pi \leqslant x < \pi) \atop f(x + 2\pi) = f(x) \quad \text{for all } x \Big\}.$$

Sketch the graphs of $y = f(x)$ and $y = a_1 \sin x + a_2 \sin 2x + a_3 \sin 3x$ and compare.

**5.** Show that $\displaystyle\int_{-\pi}^{\pi} \cos mx \cos nx \, dx = \begin{cases} 0 & (m \neq n) \\ \pi & (m = n) \end{cases}$. Deduce that if a function $g(x)$ whose domain is $\{x: -\pi \leqslant x < \pi\}$ can be represented by a series of the form

$$g(x) = \tfrac{1}{2}b_0 + b_1 \cos x + b_2 \cos 2x + b_3 \cos 3x + \ldots$$

then

$$b_m = \frac{1}{\pi} \int_{-\pi}^{\pi} g(x) \cos mx \, dx \quad (m \geqslant 0).$$

**6.** Use the result of Question 5 to find an expansion of the form $\tfrac{1}{2}b_0 + b_1 \cos x + b_2 \cos 2x + \ldots$ for

$$g(x) = |x| \quad (-\pi \leqslant x < \pi) \atop g(x + 2\pi) = g(x) \quad \text{for all } x \Big\}.$$

**7.** The trigonometrical series we have been deriving for given functions are called *Fourier series* (developed by the French mathematician Joseph Fourier in 1822). Under certain (mild) conditions, any finite function $f(x)$ can be expanded over the domain $\{x: -\pi \leqslant x < \pi\}$ to give a series of the form

$$f(x) = a_1 \sin x + a_2 \sin 2x + a_3 \sin 3x + \ldots + \tfrac{1}{2}b_0 + b_1 \cos x + b_2 \cos 2x + \ldots$$

(which has period $2\pi$).

    (*a*) Show that if $f(x)$ is odd then the Fourier series consists only of sine terms.

    (*b*) Show that if $f(x)$ is even then the coefficients of all the sine terms in the Fourier series are zero.

**8.** Show that the Fourier series for

$$f(x) = 0 \quad (-\pi \leqslant x < 0) \atop f(x) = 1 \quad (0 \leqslant x < \pi) \Big\}$$

is $f(x) = \tfrac{1}{2} + (2/\pi) \{\sin x + \tfrac{1}{3} \sin 3x + \tfrac{1}{5} \sin 5x + \ldots\}$. By choosing a suitable value for $x$, deduce that

$$1 - \tfrac{1}{3} + \tfrac{1}{5} - \tfrac{1}{7} + \ldots = \tfrac{1}{4}\pi.$$

# 6. DIFFERENTIAL AND DIFFERENCE EQUATIONS

In Chapter 33 we saw how to use a step-by-step method to produce approximate solutions to differential equations. On each occasion we produce a sequence of points, which we might call $(x_0, y_0)$, $(x_1, y_1)$, $(x_2, y_2), \ldots$, and so we have a *discrete solution sequence* in place of the *continuous solution curve*. We usually take a constant step length $h$ for $x$. The sequence of $y$s is defined inductively and the defining relation is often called a *difference equation*.

For the differential equation $\dfrac{dy}{dx} = 5x - 3y$ with starting values $x_0 = 1$, $y_0 = 4$,

$$x_{i+1} - x_i = h \quad \text{and} \quad x_n = 1 + nh.$$

Also $\dfrac{y_3 - y_2}{h} = \text{gradient of } P_2P_3 = \text{value of } \dfrac{dy}{dx} \text{ at } P_2 = 5x_2 - 3y_2.$

More generally, $\dfrac{y_{i+1} - y_i}{h} = 5x_i - 3y_i.$

That is, $\qquad\qquad y_{i+1} - (1 - 3h)y_i = 5hx_i$

or $\qquad\qquad y_{i+1} - (1 - 3h)y_i = 5h(1 + ih).$

**1.** (a) Set out the first five stages of a step-by-step solution of $\dfrac{dy}{dx} = 5x - 3y$ in the usual way, starting with $x = 1$, $y = 4$ and taking a step length $h = 0 \cdot 2$ for $x$.

(b) Work out $y_1$, $y_2$, $y_3$, $y_4$, $y_5$ from the difference equation

$$y_{i+1} - 0 \cdot 4 y_i = 1 + 0 \cdot 2i, \text{ given } y_0 = 4.$$

**2.** Consider $\dfrac{dy}{dx} = 2x$ with initial values $x = 0$, $y = 0$, for which the exact solution is $y = x^2$.

(a) Show that the step-by-step method with $h = 1$ gives $y_{i+1} = y_i + 2i$, $y_0 = 0$. Write down $y_1$, $y_2$, $y_3$, $y_4$, $y_5$, and give a formula for $y_n$. Deduce that the solution points satisfy $y_n = x_n(x_n - 1)$.

(b) Now take shorter steps with $h = \frac{1}{2}$. Show that this time we have $y_{i+1} = y_i + \frac{1}{2}i$. 'Solve' this difference equation with $y_0 = 0$ and hence show that the step-by-step method gives points for which $y_n = x_n(x_n - \frac{1}{2})$.

(c) Draw together the graphs of $y = x^2$, $y = x(x - 1)$ and $y = x(x - \frac{1}{2})$ for values of $x$ up to 4.

**3.** The 'solution' of a difference equation consists of an explicit formula for $u_n$ in terms of $n$. Solve the following:

(a) $u_{i+1} - 2u_i = 0, \qquad u_0 = 3;$      (e) $u_{i+1} - 2u_i = -3, \qquad u_0 = 5;$
(b) $u_{i+1} - 2u_i = 1, \qquad u_0 = 2;$      (f) $u_{i+1} - 5u_i = 8, \qquad u_0 = -2;$
(c) $u_{i+1} - 2u_i = 1, \qquad u_0 = 4;$      (g) $u_{i+1} - 5u_i = 8, \qquad u_0 = -1;$
(d) $u_{i+1} - 2u_i = 1, \qquad u_0 = -1;$      (h) $u_{i+1} + 3u_i = 8, \qquad u_0 = 2.$

**4.** The particular integral, complementary function method for differential equations has a counterpart in the solution of difference equations. Thus all solutions of $u_{i+1} - 5u_i = 8$ are of the form $u_n = -2 + A \times 5^n$, the value of $A$ depending upon the initial value. Find $K$ and $L$ if:

(a) $u_n = K$ is a solution of $u_{i+1} - 7u_i = 4$;
(b) $u_n = K$ is a solution of $u_{i+1} + 7u_i = 4$;
(c) $u_n = Kn + L$ is a solution of $u_{i+1} - 3u_i = i$;
(d) $u_n = Kn + L$ is a solution of $u_{i+1} + 3u_i = i + 4$.

**5.** Show that for all values of $A$:

(a) $u_n = 5 + A \times 3^n$ is a solution of $u_{i+1} - 3u_i = -10$;

(b) $u_n = -n - 1 + A \times 2^n$ is a solution of $u_{i+1} - 2u_i = i$;

(c) $u_n = -\frac{1}{3} \times 2^n + A \times 5^n$ is a solution of $u_{i+1} - 5u_i = 2^i$.

Reconsider Question 3 in the light of this question and Question 4.

**6.** Obtain the general solution of

(a) $\dfrac{dy}{dx} + 2y = 12$,    (b) $\dfrac{dy}{dx} + 2y = 12x + 5$,    (c) $\dfrac{dy}{dx} - 6y = e^{3x}$.

**7.** Obtain the general solution of

(a) $u_{i+1} + 2u_i = 12$,      (b) $u_{i+1} + 2u_i = 12i + 5$,

(c) $u_{i+1} - 6u_i = 3^i$,      (d) $u_{i+1} - u_i = 3^i$.

**8.** (a) Show that the simple step-by-step method with $\dfrac{dy}{dx} = y$ and step length 1

gives $y_{i+1} = 2y_i$ and hence $y_n = 2^n$ if we start at $(0, 1)$, whereas the solution of the differential equation is $y = e^x$.

(b) Show that, with step length $h$, $y_n = \left(1 + \dfrac{x_n}{n}\right)^n$.

(c) Using a calculator, find $\left(1 + \dfrac{1}{n}\right)^n$ when $n = 4, 10, 20, 100$.

(d) Write down the first five terms of the binomial expansion of $\left(1 + \dfrac{x}{n}\right)^n$ and

explain why, for large $n$, these are approximately equal to the first five terms of a Taylor approximation for $e^x$.

(e) Show, as in the earlier parts of this question, that the step-by-step method

applied to $\dfrac{dy}{dx} = 3y$ with initial values $x = 0$, $y = 2$, gives a solution which tends to

the correct solution of the differential equation as the step length $h$ is made smaller and smaller.

**9.** For the simple step-by-step solution of $\dfrac{dy}{dx} = y + 2x$ starting at $(0, 1)$, show

that $y_{i+1} - (1 + h)y_i = 2h^2 i$ and $x_i = ih$. Obtain a formula for $y_n$ in terms of $x_n$ and show that this solution tends to the correct solution of the differential equation as the step length tends to zero.

**10.** Translate these equations into difference equations:

(a) $\dfrac{dy}{dx} = x - y$;      (b) $\dfrac{dy}{dx} = xy$;

(c) $\dfrac{dy}{dx} = y - x^2$;      (d) $\dfrac{dy}{dx} = \dfrac{y^2}{1 + x^2}$.

**11.** (a) Obtain general solutions of any of the difference equations from Question 10 that you can solve, and show (as in Question 9) that the solutions have the correct limit as $h \to 0$.

(b) Set up a computer program, or calculator routine, to solve each of the other difference equations from Question 10, with suitable starting points of your own choice, and compare your approximation after five steps of $0 \cdot 1$ with the exact solution.

## 7. EXPECTATION ALGEBRA

The expected value is the theoretical mean. If value $x_i$ occurs with probability $p(x_i)$, then $E[x] = \mu = \sum x_i p(x_i)$ and variance $V[x] = \sum (x_i - E[x])^2 p(x_i)$.

### *Single variable*

A card is drawn from a pack. You win an amount $x$ as follows: 2 for a spade, 3 for a red card, 4 for a club.

**1.** Show that $E[x] = 3$.

**2.** Calculate $E[2x]$; that is, the expected value if all amounts received were doubled.

**3.** Write down $E[kx]$; make a general statement about how $E[kx]$ is related to $E[x]$ and prove it for the limited case where $x_1, x_2, x_3$ occur with probabilities $p_1, p_2, p_3$.

**4.** Generalize your proof for $n$ values of $x$.

**5.** Show that the variance $V[x] = 0\cdot5$.

**6.** Calculate $V[2x]$.

**7.** Write down $V[kx]$; make a general statement about how $V[kx]$ is related to $V[x]$ and prove it for the limited case as in Question 3.

**8.** Generalize your proof for $n$ values of $x$.

**9.** Calculate $E[x^2]$; that is, the expected value if all amounts received were squared.

**10.** Verify that $V[x] = E[x^2] - (E[x])^2$.

**11.** Prove this result for the limited case as in Question 3.

**12.** Generalize your proof for $n$ values of $x$.

**13.** Use the results of Questions 10 and 3 to give an alternative proof of the result in Question 7.

**14.** Investigate the truth of $V[x] = E[(E[x] - x)^2]$.

### *Two variables*

A spinner can show one of ten pictures of a fruit. One is an apple, two are bananas, three are cherries, four plums. You win an amount $y$ as follows: 8 for an apple, 7 for a banana, 6 for a cherry, 5 for a plum.

**15.** Calculate $E[y]$ and $V[y]$.

**16.** A card is drawn *and* the spinner is rotated. Make a 3 by 4 table to show the twelve possible combinations of $x + y$; and another table to show the corresponding probabilities. Hence verify that $E[x + y] = 9$.

**17.** Make a statement about the relation between $E[x + y]$ and $E[x] + E[y]$.

1113

**18.** Prove your statement in a limited 3 by 4 case and generalize your proof to $m$ values of $x$ and $n$ values of $y$.

**19.** Make a 3 by 4 table to show the twelve possible combinations of $xy$. Use your corresponding probability table to verify that $E[xy] = 18$.

**20.** Make a statement about the relation between $E[xy]$ and $E[x]E[y]$.

**21.** Prove your statement in a limited 3 by 4 case and generalize your proof to $m$ values of $x$ with $n$ values of $y$.

**22.** Calculate $V[x+y]$.

**23.** Make a statement about the relation between $V[x+y]$ and $V[x]+V[y]$.

**24.** Prove your statement by using the result of Question 10, together with those of Questions 17 and 20.

### Dependence

The card originally drawn is re-examined and you win an amount $z$ as follows: 3 for a spade, 1 for any other card.

**25.** Calculate $E[z]$, $V[z]$, $E[x+z]$, $E[xz]$, $V[x+z]$. State which of the relations of Questions 17, 20, 23 are no longer true. Re-examine your proofs to find where they break down. State a sufficient condition for these relations to be true.

## 8. MARKOV CHAINS

320 people use a works canteen every day. Tea and coffee are supplied as alternatives with lunch. Of those who have tea on any one day, 10% decide next day to have coffee. Regrettably the coffee is worse. Of those who take it on any day, 40% change to tea for the next day.

**1.** If 160 people have tea and 160 people have coffee on Monday, check that 208 people have tea and 112 have coffee on Tuesday. Calculate how many have coffee and tea on Wednesday, Thursday and Friday.

**2.** Does the proportion of tea and coffee drinkers seem to be settling down? Can you guess what the 'steady-state' situation might be? Suggest the number of teas that should be provided.

**3.** If $\begin{pmatrix} 160 \\ 160 \end{pmatrix}$ represents the $\begin{pmatrix} \text{tea} \\ \text{coffee} \end{pmatrix}$ drinkers vector for Monday, show that

$$\begin{pmatrix} 0 \cdot 9 & 0 \cdot 4 \\ 0 \cdot 1 & 0 \cdot 6 \end{pmatrix}\begin{pmatrix} 160 \\ 160 \end{pmatrix}$$

gives the vector for Tuesday. Explain the significance of the entries in the matrix

$$\mathbf{P} = \begin{pmatrix} 0 \cdot 9 & 0 \cdot 4 \\ 0 \cdot 1 & 0 \cdot 6 \end{pmatrix}.$$

**4.** Find $\mathbf{P}^2$, $\mathbf{P}^3$ and $\mathbf{P}^4(=\mathbf{Q})$. Check that $\mathbf{Q}\begin{pmatrix} 160 \\ 160 \end{pmatrix}$ gives the vector for Friday. Do you think $\mathbf{P}^n$ will tend to a limit? (See Question 2.)

1114

**5.** Show that if $\mathbf{U} = \begin{pmatrix} 4 & 1 \\ 1 & -1 \end{pmatrix}$, then $\mathbf{PU} = \mathbf{U}\begin{pmatrix} 1 & 0 \\ 0 & 0{\cdot}5 \end{pmatrix} = \mathbf{UD}$, say.

**6.** Writing $\mathbf{P}$ as $\mathbf{UDU}^{-1}$, what is $\mathbf{P}^n$? What is the limit of $\mathbf{D}^n$ as $n \to \infty$? What then is the limit of $\mathbf{P}^n$ as $n \to \infty$? Does this agree with your answers to Questions 2 and 4?

**7.** If the situation reaches a steady state given by $\begin{pmatrix} T \\ C \end{pmatrix}$, then $\mathbf{P}\begin{pmatrix} T \\ C \end{pmatrix} = \begin{pmatrix} T \\ C \end{pmatrix}$. Use this equation to find $\begin{pmatrix} T \\ C \end{pmatrix}$, and compare with the result of Question 6.

**8.** In general, consider the matrix

$$\mathbf{Q} = \begin{pmatrix} 1-a & b \\ a & 1-b \end{pmatrix} \quad \text{where } 0 < a+b < 1.$$

(a) Find vectors $\mathbf{v}_1$, $\mathbf{v}_2$ for which $\mathbf{Q}\mathbf{v} = \lambda\mathbf{v}$, where $\lambda$ is a scalar.
(b) Show that $\mathbf{Q}(\mathbf{v}_1\ \mathbf{v}_2) = (\mathbf{v}_1\ \mathbf{v}_2)\mathbf{D}$, where $\mathbf{D}$ is a diagonal matrix.
(c) Show that $\mathbf{Q}^n\mathbf{v}$ tends to a limit for all vectors $\mathbf{v}$ as $n \to \infty$, and find this limit.

Suppose a system has two states (call them $L$ and $R$) and can switch from one to the other at definite moments of time. Suppose also that the probability of a switch from $L$ to $R$ or from $R$ to $L$ depends only on the state the system is in and not on the time (i.e. not on previous history). The process is called a *Markov process* and the chain of successive states a *Markov chain*. If $a$ is the probability of a switch from $L$ to $R$, and $b$ that of a switch from $R$ to $L$, then if $p_n$, $q_n$ are the probabilities of the system's being in states $L$, $R$ after $n$ time-pulses, it is clear that

$$\begin{pmatrix} p_{n+1} \\ q_{n+1} \end{pmatrix} = \mathbf{Q}\begin{pmatrix} p_n \\ q_n \end{pmatrix}.$$

So long as $a$, $b \neq 0$, 1, we have shown that $\begin{pmatrix} p_n \\ q_n \end{pmatrix}$ tends to a limit, and a sufficiently large number of similar systems will reach a numerically steady state.

**9.** Take a die and operate as follows:
(i) States $L$, $R$ are having the die in the left, right hands respectively.
(ii) Start with the die in the left hand.
(iii) Throw the die and determine the transitions as follows:

(A) If in state $L$ and a *one* is thrown, change to state $R$. If in state $R$ and a *one* or *two* is thrown, change to state $L$.

(iv) Record the states, the initial one being called the state at instant $t = 0$.
(v) Determine the state at $t = 50$.
Repeat with the following transition rules:

(B) $L$ to $R$: if *one* or *two* is thrown;
$R$ to $L$: if *one*, *two*, *three* or *four* is thrown.

(C) $L$ to $R$: if *one*, *two* or *three* is thrown;
$R$ to $L$: if anything at all is thrown.

(Note that with ingenuity the same series of 50 throws of a die can be used in all cases provided the throws are recorded. The states and changes can be interpreted afterwards by examining the sequence.)

Suggest a physical situation for which method $(C)$ is a suitable mathematical model.

The Markov chains set up suggest various problems such as:

($a$) At the start of the experiment, what is the probability that at the $n$th instant the state will be $L$? will be $R$? How are these probabilities affected if the chain starts at state $R$? Take $n$ to be large.

($b$) What are the probabilities of various lengths of run in each state?

($c$) What is the mean length of run in each state?

($d$) What is the mean number of changes of state occurring in a unit interval of time?

($e$) How are the results affected by changing the transition probabilities? (Note that in cases $(A)$, $(B)$, $(C)$ the ratios of the transition probabilities are equal.)

You may find connections between the problems but most of them are too hard to solve here. Experimental results can be obtained to suggest likely sizes for the answers. Random number tables are preferable to dice for long runs.

## 9. ROCKETS AND SATELLITES

In earlier chapters we used Newton's second law in the form $\mathbf{F} = m\dfrac{d\mathbf{v}}{dt}$. This was applied to particles with constant mass. In situations where mass may be ejected from or added to a body we must use the second law in the form originally postulated by Newton:

If a force $\mathbf{F}$ is applied to a particle, the rate of change of momentum is proportional to $\mathbf{F}$. If the units of $\mathbf{F}$ are newtons, mass is measured in kilograms and speed in metres per second we have

$$\mathbf{F} = \frac{d}{dt}(m\mathbf{v}).$$

**1.** A space vehicle in force-free space speeds up by ejecting propellant gases (formed by burning liquid fuels) backwards at a speed $u$ relative to the vehicle. The mass of the vehicle including fuel is $m_0$ initially and fuel is burned at a constant rate $\alpha$ so that the total mass $m$ at time $t$ is such that $\dfrac{dm}{dt} = -\alpha$.

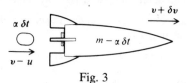

Fig. 3

(i) If the speed of the vehicle is $v$ at time $t$, by considering the conservation of linear momentum of the system, show that in a small interval of time $\delta t$ the vehicle increases its speed by $\delta v$ where

$$(m - \alpha\delta t)(v + \delta v) + \alpha\delta t(v - u) \approx mv.$$

1116

(ii) By rearranging the equation of (i) and allowing $\delta t$ to tend to zero, show that

$$\frac{dv}{dt} = \frac{\alpha u}{m}.$$

(iii) Show that $m = m_0 - \alpha t$ and hence that

$$v = v_0 - u \ln \left( 1 - \frac{\alpha t}{m_0} \right)$$

where $v = v_0$ when $t = 0$.

**2.** The *mass ratio* $\rho$ of a rocket is the ratio of its initial mass $m_0$ (including fuel) to its final mass $m_1$ (with all fuel used). If the rocket is fired in force-free space, show that the maximum increase of speed is $u \ln \rho$, where $u$ is the speed of the ejected fuel gases relative to the rocket.

Evaluate this expression for a rocket with a mass ratio of 6 and an exhaust gas speed of 3·3 km/s. (These figures are approximately correct for an efficiently designed rocket using a mixture of liquid oxygen and hydrogen.)

**3.** A rocket is accelerated from rest by ejecting burnt fuel gases at velocity $\mathbf{u}$ relative to the rocket.

(i) If the rocket is acted upon by an external force $\mathbf{F}$, show that its velocity $\mathbf{v}$ is given by the equation of motion

$$\mathbf{F} + \mathbf{u}\frac{dm}{dt} = m\frac{d\mathbf{v}}{dt},$$

where $m$ is the mass of the rocket at time $t$.

(ii) If $\mathbf{F} = m\mathbf{g}$ and the mass ratio of the rocket is $\rho$ (see Question 2), show that the velocity attained by the rocket at burn-out (i.e. when the fuel is exhausted) is $\mathbf{u} \ln \rho + \mathbf{g}T$, where $T$ is the time taken for burn-out to be achieved.

**4.** (i) Newton's law of gravitation implies that the acceleration due to gravity at a distance $x$ above the earth's surface is given by $\dfrac{gR^2}{(R+x)^2}$, where $R$ is the radius of the earth and $g$ is the acceleration due to gravity at the surface of the earth (see Chapter 12). Find the value of the acceleration due to gravity at a point 300 km above the earth. (Take $R \approx 6400$ km and $g \approx 9\cdot8$ m/s$^2$.)

(ii) A satellite is moving in a circular orbit 300 km above the earth. Find the orbital speed. Why does the air resistance on a satellite tend to *increase* the orbital speed?

(iii) Show that a rocket with mass ratio 6 and fuel exit speed of 3·3 km/s could not put the satellite of (ii) into orbit.

**5.** (*a*) A rocket consists of a 10 kg payload attached to a structure of mass 1000 kg together with 5000 kg of fuel. (See Figure 4.) If the exit velocity of the fuel is 3·3 km/s, find the maximum speed that could be imparted to the payload in force-free space.

(*b*) (i) A two-stage rocket consists of a first-stage structure of mass 900 kg, fuel of mass 4510 kg, attached to a second-stage rocket of total mass 600 kg. (See Figure 5.) Find the speed of the combined rocket at burn-out of the first stage in force-free space.

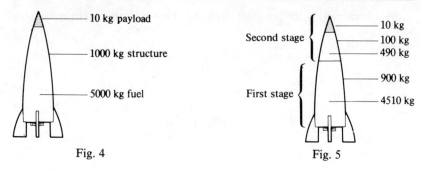

Fig. 4                                                 Fig. 5

(ii) The second stage, consisting of 10 kg payload, structure of 100 kg, and 490 kg of fuel, separates from the first after burn-out of stage one. The second-stage fuel is then burned. Find the final speed imparted to the payload. Compare your answer with (*a*).

**6.** (*a*) Discuss whether the two-stage rocket of Question 5(*b*) could be used to send a 10 kg payload from the earth to the moon. (You may ignore air resistance.)

(*b*) List some modifications to the mathematical models discussed above which would be needed to investigate (i) putting a satellite into orbit near the earth, (ii) sending a rocket to the moon.

## 10. NETWORKS AND SQUARES

**1.** Find the currents in each arm of the network shown in Figure 6, if the resistance in each arm is 1 $\Omega$.

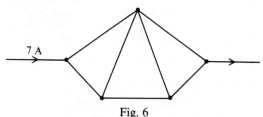

Fig. 6

**2.** Represent a wire carrying a current of *x* amperes through a potential difference of *y* volts by a rectangle *x* units wide and *y* units long. (See Figure 7.)

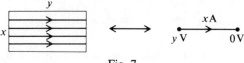

Fig. 7

Show that, for each link in the network of Figure 6, the corresponding rectangle is a square.

**3.** Explain why the network corresponds to the dissection of a rectangle into squares shown in Figure 8, and give the number of units in the side of each square.

1118

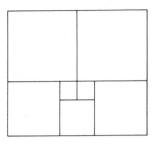

Fig. 8

**4.** What is the equivalent resistance of the network?

**5.** Now consider the network of Figure 9, each link again having resistance 1 $\Omega$. Find the currents and draw the corresponding rectangle dissected into squares. Show that this solves the problem of dissecting a rectangle into a set of *different* integral-sided squares. (It is the smallest such rectangle.)

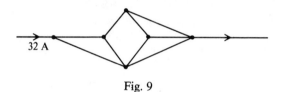

Fig. 9

**6.** Complete the dimensions of the pattern of squares in Figure 10, and draw the corresponding network.

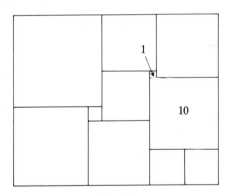

Fig. 10

What corresponds to the area of each square, and of the whole rectangle? What is the equivalent resistance of the network?

**7.** Now consider links of different resistances. Show that we now have a dissection of a rectangle into rectangles, and explain the connection between the resistance of each link and the rectangle that represents it. What do Figures 11(*a*) and (*b*) represent, in general?

1119

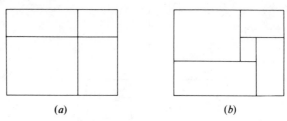

(a)                           (b)

Fig. 11

**8.** Investigate:
    (a) the possible uses of such diagrams in the solution of network problems;
    (b) the use of networks in the solution of dissection problems.
Find out how the problem of dividing a square into unequal squares was solved.
(See, for example, Martin Gardner's *More Mathematical Puzzles and Diversions*; Penguin, 1969.)

## 11. COIN TOSSING

**1.** Here are the results of tossing a coin twenty times. Underneath the results is the running count of whether we have more heads ($+$) or more tails ($-$). (For convenience, when the score is *level* we count it $+$ or $-$ depending on whether heads or tails were ahead the toss before.)

    T  T H T H H H H T H T H H T T T H T T T
    $-$  $-$ $-$ $-$ $-$ $-$ $+$ $+$ $+$ $+$ $+$ $+$ $+$ $+$ $+$ $+$ $+$ $-$ $-$

Record the total number of $+$s and $-$s. Are the totals equal? Is this what you would expect?

**2.** (i) Write out the list of $+/-$s for the running count in these twenty tosses:

    H  H T  T H T H T H T H H H T H T H T T H H

(ii) Toss a coin twenty times and record the $+/-$ running count.
In (i) and (ii) record the totals of $+/-$s.

**3.** Is it more likely that the count of heads usually exceeds that of tails, or vice versa? Do some more experiments and record the fraction of tosses for which heads are ahead $\left(\text{i.e. } \dfrac{\text{total no. of } +\text{s}}{\text{total tosses}}\right)$.

**4.** It can be proved that for a long run the probability of heads being ahead for a total fraction $x$ of the time is given approximately by the probability density function

$$\phi(x) = \frac{1}{\pi\sqrt{(x-x^2)}}.$$

Plot the graph of $\phi(x)$ for $0 < x < 1$ and comment on it. Is it consistent with your results in Questions 1, 2 and 3?

**5.** Calculate $\displaystyle\int_0^1 \phi(x)\,dx.$

**6.** What is the probability (in terms of $t$) of heads being ahead for less than a fraction $t$ of the time?

**7.** Show that, under the rule about zero excess, in an even number of tosses the number of occasions when heads are in excess must always be even. What would you use as an estimate of the probability of this number being zero in a total of twenty tosses?

**8.** Using $\int_{9/20}^{11/20} \phi(x)\, dx$ as an estimate, evaluate the probability of heads being in excess on just ten occasions out of twenty tosses. (The actual probabilities are: for zero excess, 0·176; for half-time excess, 0·061.)

**9.** In a number of trials, each of 100 tosses, what is the number of occasions when heads are in excess which will not be exceeded on about one trial in every five?

# ANSWERS

## CHAPTER 29

**Ex. A 1.** (a) 0·950; (b) 1·283; (c) 1·117. **3.** (a) 1·812;
(b) 0·697; (c) 1·103. **7.** 1·622.

**Ex. B 1.** (a) 2·485; (b) 2·99(6); (c) 4·60(6); (d) 4·15(8);
(e) 0·916. **7.** $-0·693, -1·386, -2·303.$

**Ex. C 1.** (a) $1/x$; (b) $1/x$; (c) $3/x$; (d) $-1/x$; (e) $3/x$;
(f) $1/(2x)$. **3.** (a) $1+\ln x$; (c) $x+2x\ln 3x$; (e) $\ln x$.
**5.** (a) $1/(1+x)$; (c) $2x/(3+x^2)$; (e) $\cot x$; (f) $\ln|1+x|+k$;
(h) $\ln|3+x^2|+k$; (j) $\ln|\sin x|+k$. **7.** (a) $0·2231$; (b) $0·6931$;
(c) $1·7918$; (d) $0·6931$; (e) $-0·9163$; (f) $1·0986$.

**Ex. D 1.** $y=-\ln x$; domain real positive $x$; range all real $y$.
**3.** (a) 7·389; (b) 0·3679; (c) 22 030; (d) 1·105;
(e) 0·006 738. **5.** (a) $-e^{-x}+k$; (c) $e^{x+1}+k$. **7.** (i) $y$;
(iii) stretch by 5 parallel to $y$-axis, or translation to left by $\ln 5$.
**9.** $e^{-x}(1-x)$; $e^{-x}(x-2)$; maximum at $(1, 1/e)$;
inflexion at $(2, 2/e^2)$. **11.** $-x\exp(-\tfrac{1}{2}x^2)$;
inflexions at $(\pm 1, \exp(-\tfrac{1}{2}))$. **13.** (a) 2; (c) $x^2$; (e) $\ln(2+e^x)$;
(g) $ex$. **15.** (a) $1e^{0·6931x}$; (b) $1000e^{1·5041x}$; (c) $2968e^x$;
(d) $1e^{0·2376x}$.

**Ex. E 3.** 20·0. **5.** (a) 181·4 g; (b) 3·47 h; (c) (i) 6·93 h,
(ii) 13·9 h; (d) $dm/dt=-0·2m$. **7.** $dP/dt=0·02P$; 1000;
(a) 1350; (b) 1650; 1980.

**Ex. F 1.** (a) $\tfrac{1}{4}\ln|4x+7|+k$; (c) $x+\ln|x^2-3x+3|+k$;
(d) $\ln|\sec x|+k$; (e) $\ln|\sin x-\cos x|+k$.
**5.** (a) $7\ln|x-3|+2\ln|x+1|+k$; (c) $x+9\ln|x-2|+6\ln|x-3|+k$;
(e) $2\ln|x-3|-\ln|x+3|+k$. **7.** 0·8219 **9.** (a) $\tfrac{1}{2}\ln|(x-1)/(x+1)|+k$;
(c) $\ln|x/(x+1)|+k$; (e) $\ln|(x-2)^3/(x-1)^2|+k$. **11.** $\tfrac{7}{9}, -\tfrac{7}{9}, -\tfrac{4}{3}$.
**13.** (a) $2, -1, 1$; (b) $\tfrac{1}{3}, -\tfrac{1}{3}, -\tfrac{2}{3}$.

**Ex. G 1.** 2·718 28. **9.** 0·405; $-0·693$; (a) 1·098;
(b) $-0·288$; (c) 0·693. **11.** (b) 0·6931; (c) (i) 1·3862, (ii) 2·0793.

**Misc. 1.** Turning points when $x=n\pi+\tfrac{1}{4}\pi$; (a) $y=e^{-x}/\sqrt{2}$;
(b) $y=-e^{-x}/\sqrt{2}$. **3.** $x\ln x-x$.
**5.** $\ln x=\ln 10\times\log_{10}x\approx 2·3\log_{10}x$; stretch parallel to $y$-axis.
**7.** $(n/x)-1$; turns where $x=n$. **9.** Turns at $(2, -1)$ and $(-2, -\tfrac{1}{9})$.
**11.** Writing $e^{-1}=a$, $(a, a^a)\approx(0·368, 0·692)$. **13.** $(e, 1/e)$.
**15.** $a=-0·041, b=0·408$.

## CHAPTER 30

**Ex. A 1.** 0·343, 0·441, 0·189, 0·027.
**3.** 0·0625, 0·25, 0·375, 0·25, 0·0625. **5.** (a) 0·205; (b) 0·051.

**Ex. B 1.** 0·038. **3.** 0·194. **5.** 1. **7.** 0·820. **9.** 0·174.

**Ex. C** **1.** (*a*) 792; (*b*) 593 775, 19 600, 300, 252. **3.** (*a*) 2002; (*c*) 11 440; (*e*) 105. **7.** 0·032. **9.** (*a*) 0·145; (*b*) 0·046. **11.** (*a*) 0·092; (*b*) 0·049; (*c*) 0·046. **13.** (*a*) 0·172; (*b*) 0·179; (*c*) 0·154.

**Ex. D** **1.** (*b*) 646 646, 705 432.

**Ex. E** **1.** (*a*) $1-3h+6h^2-10h^3$; (*c*) $1+\frac{1}{3}h-\frac{1}{9}h^2+\frac{5}{81}h^3$; (*e*) $1-\frac{1}{2}h-\frac{1}{8}h^2-\frac{1}{16}h^3$. **3.** 3·873.

**Misc.** **1.** (*a*) 81, 243. **5.** (*a*) 12, 9 or 10, 3, 0, 0; (*b*) 2 or 3. **7.** 24 040 016; (*a*) 0·088; (*b*) 0·207. **9.** $1·575 \times 10^{-12}$.

# CHAPTER 31

**Ex. A.** **1.** (*a*) 40 700 m³; (*b*) 21 200 m³. **3.** 159 m³; 134 m³. **5.** $5·58 \times 10^5$ cm³. **7.** 15·6 m³.

**Ex. B** **1.** 4500 cm³. **3.** $5·02 \times 10^5$ cm³. **7.** $1·7 \times 10^4$ m³. **9.** 25·1 cm³. **11.** (*a*) $2\pi$; (*b*) 19. **13.** $6·4\pi$. **15.** (*a*) (i) $\frac{1}{2}\pi^2$, (ii) 45·6, (iii) 17·4; (*b*) (i) 50·3, (ii) 1·21. (iii) $\frac{1}{4}\pi^2$.

**Ex. C** **1.** $125\pi$ cm³. **3.** 3·59. **5.** $\pi[1-\exp(-b^2)]$; approaches $\pi$. **7.** 74 600.

**Ex. D** **1.** $1440\pi \approx 4520$ g. **3.** 2560 kg. **5.** $192\pi \approx 603$ g. **7.** $\frac{2}{3}\pi ka^3$. **9.** $\frac{1}{2}\pi kr^4$. **11.** $5600/\pi \approx 1780$.

**Ex. E** **1.** (*a*) 37·5; (*b*) 12·5; (*c*) $16\frac{2}{3}$; (*d*) 26·5; (*e*) 22·4. **3.** (*a*) $2/\pi$; (*b*) $\frac{1}{4}\pi$; (*c*) $\frac{1}{4}\pi$; (*d*) 3·63. **5.** 0·360. **7.** 0·02; 0; 169·7.

**Ex. F** **1.** $3\frac{1}{3}$ cm up axis of symmetry. **3.** $4\sqrt{2}\,a/3\pi$ from centre, on axis of symmetry. **5.** (7·5, 0).

**Misc.** **1.** $0·8\pi \approx 2·51$ m³. **5.** $(\pi \ln 2)/k$. **7.** $7\frac{1}{2}$ cm.

# CHAPTER 32

**Ex. A** **1.** (*a*) $(x+3)(x+4)$; (*c*) $(x-1)^2$; (*e*) $x(x-1)(x+1)$; (*g*) $(x-1)^2(x-2)(x+2)$. **3.** (*a*) 4·73, 1·27; (*c*) none; (*e*) $-3$.

**Ex. B** **1.** $-9, -7, -16, -12$. **3.** (*a*) $-1\pm3j$; (*c*) $-2, 3$; (*e*) $2, \frac{1}{3}$. **5.** (*a*) $x^2-4x+5=0$; (*b*) $x^2-6x+25=0$; (*c*) $x^2-2x+3=0$; (*d*) $x^2-x+1=0$. **7.** (*a*) (i) 0, (ii) $2-2j$, (iii) $4-18j, x=1+2j$ or $-1-j$; (*b*) (i) $-2$, (ii) 0, (iii) 0, (iv) $-3-j$, (v) 0, $x=3$ or $1\pm j$. **9.** $-j, -2$. **11.** No; $(x+j)(x-j)(x+2j)(x-2j)$.

**Ex. C** **5.** Rotation through $\frac{1}{2}\pi$, enlargement $\times 2$. **7.** (i) $4+2j$, (ii) 4.

**Ex. D** **1.** (*a*) [5, 0·93]; (*c*) $[\sqrt{5}, 5·82]$; (*e*) $[\sqrt{5}, 0·46]$; (*g*) [5, 3·79]; (i) $[\sqrt{13}, 4·12]$. **3.** (*a*) $[1, \frac{1}{6}\pi]$; (*b*) $[1, \frac{1}{4}\pi]$; (*c*) $[1, \frac{2}{3}\pi]$. **5.** (*a*) $14-3j$; (*b*) $10-5j$. **7.** (*a*) $[2, \frac{1}{6}\pi]$; (*c*) $[\frac{1}{2}, \frac{2}{3}\pi]$; (*e*) $[r_2/r_1, \theta_2-\theta_1]$. **9.** (*a*) $[1, \frac{2}{3}\pi], [1, \pi], [1, \frac{4}{3}\pi], [1, \frac{1}{3}n\pi]$; (*c*) $[4, \frac{1}{2}\pi], [8, \frac{3}{4}\pi], [16, \pi], [2^n, \frac{1}{4}n\pi]$.

**Ex. E 1.** $(z-1)(z+\frac{1}{2}-j\frac{1}{2}\sqrt{3})(z+\frac{1}{2}+j\frac{1}{2}\sqrt{3})$. **3.** $[3,\frac{1}{3}\pi],[3,\frac{5}{3}\pi]$; $(z+3)(z-\frac{3}{2}-j\frac{3}{2}\sqrt{3})(z-\frac{3}{2}+j\frac{3}{2}\sqrt{3})$. **5.** $[1,\frac{1}{4}\pi],[1,\frac{3}{4}\pi],[1,\frac{5}{4}\pi],[1,\frac{7}{4}\pi]$.
**7.** $(z-1\cdot059-0\cdot168j)(z-0\cdot168-1\cdot059j)(z+0\cdot955-0\cdot487j)(z-0\cdot487+0\cdot955j)(z+0\cdot758+0\cdot758j)$.

**Ex. F 1.** (a) $5-2j$; (c) $3+4j$; (e) $-3$. **3.** (i) $2a$; (ii) $2bj$; (iii) $a^2+b^2$.
**5.** (a) $\pm2+j$; (b) $\pm\frac{1}{2}\sqrt{3}-\frac{1}{2}j$; $(z-2-j)(z+2-j)$; $(z-\frac{1}{2}\sqrt{3}+\frac{1}{2}j)(z+\frac{1}{2}\sqrt{3}+\frac{1}{2}j)$.

**Ex. G 1.** $\frac{1}{2}-j\frac{1}{2}\sqrt{3}$; $(z^2-z+1)(z^2+4z+1)$; $-2\pm\sqrt{3}$.
**3.** $-2$; $-j,1\pm2j$; $(z+2)(z+j)(z-j)(z-1+2j)(z-1-2j)$; $(z+2)(z^2+1)(z^2-2z+5)$. **5.** $2+j,-2$.

**Misc. 1.** $z^2+(1-j)z+(5+j),-1+6j$.
**3.** $[1,\frac{2}{3}\pi]$; $[2,\frac{5}{6}\pi],[2,\frac{3}{2}\pi]$. **7.** $\frac{1}{2}(-1-j\sqrt{3})$; $[1,\frac{2}{3}\pi],[1,\frac{4}{3}\pi]$.

# REVISION EXERCISES

**Rev. 29 1.** (a) $0\cdot916$; (c) $3\cdot916$; (e) $-\frac{1}{2}\ln2\approx-0\cdot347$.
**2.** (a) $1/x$; (c) $3/(3x-2)$; (e) $2\cot x$. **3.** (a) $\frac{1}{2}\ln(4+x^2)$;
(c) $\frac{1}{2}\ln(x^2-1)-\ln x$; (e) $1\cdot6$. **5.** $4e^{-2}$; $2$. **7.** (a) $x>2\cdot63$;
(c) $t>69\cdot1$.

**Rev. 30 1.** $\frac{11}{32}$. **3.** (a) $(\frac{2}{3})^7\approx0\cdot059$; (c) $0\cdot993$.

**Rev. 31 2.** $7\cdot1\,\mathrm{m}^3$. **4.** (a) $(0,0),(2,4)$; (b) $\frac{16}{3}\pi$. **6.** $k\approx6500$.

**Rev. 32 1.** (a) $3+2j,-1$; (b) (i) $(x+1)(x^2-6x+13)$,
(ii) $(x+1)(x-3+2j)(x-3-2j)$. **4.** $[r,-\theta]$; (i) $\frac{4}{3}\pi$, (ii) $\frac{2}{3}\pi$.
**5.** $[30,-0\cdot395]$.

# CHAPTER 33

**Ex. A 1.** $80\,\mathrm{m/s}$. **3.** $-12\cdot5\,\mathrm{m/s}^2$; $0\,\mathrm{m/s}^2$, $10\,\mathrm{m/s}$.

**Ex. B 1.** $0,20,28,31\cdot2,32\cdot4,33$.
**3.** $15,12\cdot5,11\cdot4,10\cdot8,10\cdot5,10\cdot3$. **5.** $10^7,1\cdot08\times10^7,1\cdot17\times10^7$, $1\cdot26\times10^7,1\cdot36\times10^7,1\cdot47\times10^7$.

**Ex. C 1.** $60\cdot5\,°\mathrm{C}$; too low. **3.** $0\cdot86$; $0\cdot828$. **5.** $1\cdot38$.
**7.** $3500$.

**Ex. E 1.** $1\cdot05$; $1\cdot28,1\cdot099$.

**Misc. 5.** $y=-1\cdot74$ when $t=2$.

# CHAPTER 34

**Ex. A 1.** (a) $0\cdot04\,\mathrm{s}$; (b) $0\cdot067\,\mathrm{s}$. **3.** $t=m(v-u)/F$.
**5.** $60\,\mathrm{kN}$; $24\,\mathrm{kN}$.

**Ex. B 1.** (a) $1\cdot8\times10^7\,\mathrm{Ns}$; (b) $20\,\mathrm{Ns}$; (c) $700\,\mathrm{Ns}$;
(d) $6\times10^5\,\mathrm{Ns}$; (e) $2\cdot7\times10^{-23}\,\mathrm{Ns}$. **3.** $4\cdot17\,\mathrm{m/s}$. **5.** $0\cdot175\,\mathrm{Ns}$.
**7.** $18\cdot3\,\mathrm{m/s}$ at $19\cdot1°$ to wall.

**9.** 18·75 Ns at 36·9° to reversed original direction. **11.** $10^{-10}$ s;

(a) $1·15 \times 10^8$ m/s; (b) $5·20 \times 10^{-13}$ N. **13.** (a) $\begin{pmatrix} -30 \\ 40 \\ 20 \end{pmatrix}$ N;

(b) $\begin{pmatrix} 1 \\ 4 \\ 1 \end{pmatrix}$ m/s. **15.** 39·8 N. **16.** 47·7 N. **18.** (a) 0·707 N;

(b) 0·565 N.

**Ex. C** **1.** $\frac{2}{3}$ m/s. **3.** 0·141 kg. **5.** (a) $\begin{pmatrix} 1 \\ 0 \end{pmatrix}$; (b) $\begin{pmatrix} 3 \\ 0 \end{pmatrix}$;

(c) 4. **9.** 1·97 m/s, 1·18 m/s. **11.** 1·04 m/s, 1·76 m/s.
**13.** 2 m/s. **15.** 1·72 m/s.

**Ex. D** **1.** $1·72 \times 10^4$ Ns; 14·3 m/s.
**3.** Simpson's rule: $2·20 \times 10^4$ Ns, 22 m/s; trapezium rule:
$2·255 \times 10^4$ Ns, 22·6 m/s. **5.** $1·34 \times 10^4$ Ns, 17·4 m/s at 3·8° to barrier.

**Ex. E** **1.** 0·7. **3.** $-i$ m/s, 3 kg. **5.** 0·85. **7.** $\begin{pmatrix} -1 \\ 3 \end{pmatrix}, \begin{pmatrix} 0 \\ 1 \end{pmatrix}$.

**9.** $\frac{1}{5}v(1+e)\sqrt{3}$ at 30° either side of common tangent.

**Misc.** **5.** $mv/(m+M)$, $mMv/P(m+M)$.

# CHAPTER 35

**Ex. A** **1.** $\frac{1}{8}, \frac{3}{8}, \frac{3}{8}, \frac{1}{8}$; 12p, $1\frac{1}{2}$p. **3.** $\frac{1}{100}, \frac{6}{100}, \frac{30}{100}$.

**Ex. B** **1.** 1·95p, 2p. **3.** £2·44$\frac{1}{2}$. **5.** 18p. **7.** (a) $\frac{11}{18}$p loss;
(b) $\frac{1}{2}$p loss. **9.** $3\frac{2}{3}$. **11.** 3·4.

**Ex. C** **1.** 4·98p. **3.** $19\frac{1}{2}$p. **5.** (a) 2·05; (b) 2·05.
**7.** (a) 8·22p; (b) 1·12p. **9.** 2·21. **11.** $2\frac{1}{2}, 1\frac{1}{4}$; (a) 0·5, 0·45;
(b) 2, 1·2; (c) 3·5, 1·05; $\mu = na, \sigma^2 = nab$.

**Ex. D** **1.** (a) 5, 1·58; (b) 50, 5;
(c) 500, 15·8; the second is more surprising. **3.** $10/N$.
**5.** $\mu = 180, \sigma = 8·49$, yes. **7.** Yes.

**Ex. E** **1.** 0·04; (a) 0·08; (b) 0·18. **3.** (a) 0·259;
(b) 0·0259. **5.** (a) 0·098; (b) 67 years. **7.** $1/\pi$; 0·554.
**9.** (a) 2·25; (b) 4·75.

**Ex. F** **1.** 1200 hours, 1200 hours. **3.** (a) 1·8, 0·6; (b) 1·2, 0·6;
(c) 2, 0·53; (d) 1·5, 0·57. **5.** 12 kg.
**7.** (a) $k = 3/(4a^3), a/\sqrt{5}, 0·984$; (b) $k = 15/(16a^5), a/\sqrt{7}, 0·970$.

**Ex. G** **1.** (b) 0·548, $k = 0·954$. **3.** $k = 3/(4a^3)$; $k = 3/(160\sqrt{5})$,
$a/ = 2\sqrt{5}$. **5.** $8\frac{1}{3}, 16\frac{2}{3}$.

**Ex. H** **1.** 1·94p, 1·43; 0·056p loss, 1·43. **3.** $\mu - r, \sigma^2$.
**5.** 1·67, 1·05. **7.** $(6-5t)^{-2}$. **11.** (a) 5 units; (b) no fair fee;
(c) 2, 2; (d) $(\frac{1}{2})^{14}$; (e) 0·984; (f) 0·368.

# CHAPTER 36

**Ex. A** **1.** (a) 60 m;   (b) 45 m/s.   **3.** (a) 10 m/s;
(b) 2·81 m, 12·5 m/s;   (c) 12·5 m/s.   **5.** (a) 70 g sin θ, g sin θ;
(b) h/sin θ, $v^2 = u^2 + 2gh$;   (c) no, no;   (d) yes.

**Ex. B** **1.** (a) −2 J;   (b) 13 J;   (c) −3 J;   (d) 353 J.
**3.** (a) 6·32 m/s;   (b) 66·6 m/s.   **5.** 60 kN.   **7.** (a) $3·86 \times 10^8$ J;
(b) $1·93 \times 10^6$ N.   **9.** $4·48 \times 10^{10}$ J.   **11.** 5·04 N.
**13.** (a) (i) 28·8 J, 6·69 m/s,   (ii) 5·92 J, −2·43 m/s,   (iii) 9·11 J, 5 m/s,
(iv) 3·92 J, −4·46 m/s;   (b) (ii) 2·19 m,   (iii) 1·03 m.
**15.** 2500 N, 1125 m.   **17.** 1·39 N s;   (i) 6960 N;   (ii) 139 N.

**Ex. C** **1.** 14 m/s.   **3.** 12·5 m/s, 10·8 m/s.
**5.** 2g, 4g, 6g;   9800 N, 12 700 N, 15 700 N;   $v^2 = 2g (10 \cos θ − 7)$,
$T = 200g (15 \cos θ − 7)$;   no.
**7.** 0·885 m/s, 1·25 m/s, 1·53 m/s, 1·77 m/s, 1·98 m/s; 0·0078 N, −0·0039 N,
all others negative; **R** could be negative.
**9.** $v^2 = 1 + 6g(1 − \cos θ)$;   $R = m(3g \cos θ − 2g − \frac{1}{3})$;   θ = 47·3°.
**11.** (a) Thrust 665 N, tension 3450 N;
(b) thrust 602 N, tension 3510 N;   2·86 radians/sec., 4120 N.
**13.** (a) $\cos θ = \frac{2}{3} − u^2/3gl$;   (b) $2\sqrt{(gl)}$.

**Ex. D** **1.** (a) $\frac{5}{3}$;   (b) 2·01;   (c) 6·5;   (d) 0, 4 m/s;
(e) $\frac{1}{2}$, x = 8·2 m.   **3.** 33·1 cm.   **5.** 19 m/s.   **9.** $\frac{1}{2}λl$.
**11.** 1·52 m/s, 0·5 m and 0·99 m below support.   **13.** 16 J.

**15.** 14 800 N/m.   **17.** $\mathbf{v} = \begin{pmatrix} u \\ 0 \end{pmatrix} + gt \begin{pmatrix} λ\sqrt{3} \\ λ − 1 \end{pmatrix}, \mathbf{r} = \begin{pmatrix} ut + \frac{1}{2}gt^2 λ\sqrt{3} \\ h + \frac{1}{2}gt^2(λ − 1) \end{pmatrix}.$

**Ex. E** **1.** 1·96 W.   **5.** 0·753 kW.   **7.** 245 N/tonne, 7100 kW.
**9.** 1800 N, 94·3 km/h.   **11.** 660 kW, 530 kW.
**13.** −32 kW, −42 kW;   1·83 m/s², 0·349 m/s².

**Misc.** **1.** 2·6 m/s, 600 J.
**3.** (a) 4·93 m/s, 74·7 J, 913 N;   (b) 1870 J, 4 cm.   **5.** 1198 m/s.
**7.** 240 J.   **9.** (a) 12·6 kN;   (b) 37 cm.   **13.** 15·1 W.

# REVISION EXERCISES

**Rev. 33** **1.** (a) (0, 8);   (b) −16·4;   (c) −10;   (d) 6·36, 4·96, 3·71;
(e) 0·65.   **3.** (a) 3·75;   (b) 6·875;   (c) 8·39.

**Rev. 34** **1.** Taking **i** in original direction of the ball,   (a) −5**i** Ns;
(b) 127° to **i**;   (c) 1·39 N s.

**3.** $v_A = 9000$ at $\tan^{-1} \frac{4}{3}$, $v_B = 4110$ at 114°.   **5.** $\begin{pmatrix} 1·25 \\ 1 \end{pmatrix}$ m/s;   $\frac{3}{4}$.

**Rev. 35** **1.** (a) (i) $\frac{21}{6} = 3·5$;   (ii) $\frac{252}{36} = 7$;   (b) (i) $\sqrt{(\frac{35}{12})} \approx 1·71$;
(ii) $\sqrt{(\frac{35}{6})} \approx 2·42$.   **3.** $μ = \frac{4}{3}, σ^2 = \frac{7}{18}$;   0·033.
**6.** More than 190 or less than 144.

**Rev. 36** **1.** $4·9 \times 10^4$ J;   4·4 m/s.   **3.** 36 km.

# CHAPTER 37

**Ex. A 1.** (a) (i) 2 A, (ii) 6 A, (iii) 1 A; (b) (i) 20 V, (ii) 100 V, (iii) 10 V. **3.** (a) $1\frac{1}{2}$ A; (b) $1\frac{1}{9}$ A.

**Ex. B 1.** 5 A, 3 A, 8 A. **3.** (a) 13 A; (b) $\frac{12}{13}\,\Omega$. **7.** 6 A.

**Ex. C 1.** 2 A, 3 A, −1 A. **3.** $\frac{8}{15}$ A, $\frac{4}{15}$ A, $\frac{1}{5}$ A.
**5.** 4 A, 6 A, 2 A; 14 V, 1·4 $\Omega$. **7.** $\frac{2}{7}$ A, $\frac{1}{14}$ A; 0 V; no change.
**9.** $\frac{100}{39}$ A, $\frac{5}{39}$ A, $\frac{15}{13}$ A.

**Ex. D 1.** 2 A, 10 V. **3.** 1·5 V, $\frac{1}{2}\,\Omega$.
**5.** 52·9 $\Omega$; 804 W. **9.** 12.

**Ex. E 3.** $r\cos\varepsilon + jr\sin\varepsilon, r$.

**Ex. F 1.** (a) $\dfrac{500}{102\cdot 6}\sin 40t + \dfrac{80}{102\cdot 6}\cos 40t$.

# CHAPTER 38

**Ex. A 1.** $y = x^2 + c$. **3.** $y = Ae^x$. **5.** $y = \frac{1}{3}x^3 + c$.
**7.** $xy = c$. **9.** $y = 2\tan^{-1} x + c$.

**Ex. B 1.** (a) $y = \sin x + c$; (b) $y = \frac{1}{3}(x^2 + 7)^{\frac{3}{2}} + c$;
(c) $y = \frac{1}{3}\tan^{-1}(\frac{1}{3}x) + c$; (d) $y = \frac{1}{15}(x^3 + 5)^5 + c$; (e) $x = 2\sqrt{t} + c$;
(f) $v = \tan t + c$. **3.** (a) $y = Ae^x$; (b) $y = 1/x + c$; (c) $y = \ln Ax$.
**5.** $y = \frac{1}{5}(\ln t + 19 - 4/t)$. **7.** $53\frac{1}{3}$. **9.** (a) $y = \ln Ax$;
(b) $y = c - \frac{1}{2}x^2$; 90°.

**Ex. C 1.** (a) $y = Ae^{5x}$; (b) $y = Ae^{-3x}$; (c) $\frac{1}{2}y^2 + 2y = x + c$;
(d) $y = 8 - Ae^{-x}$; (e) $v^3 = 12t + c$; (f) $1/x = 10t + c$.
**3.** $y = \tan(x + c)$. **5.** (a) $y = (3 + Ae^{4x})/(1 - Ae^{4x})$;
(b) $p = (50 - 60Ae^{t/25})/(1 - 2Ae^{t/25})$; (c) $y = -\frac{1}{2}\ln A|1 - t^2|$;
(d) $x = 3\ln|y| - 5/y + c$. **7.** (a) 39·9 m/s; (b) 10 m/s.

**Ex. D 1.** 14 800 **3.** (a) $m = \frac{1}{50}e^{-t/20}$; (b) 13·9 days;
(c) 27·7 days; (d) $6·07\times 10^{-4}$ g/day. **5.** $dV/dt = -3A$; (a) 5 days;
(b) 2·1 days. **7.** −0·0223; 12·9 minutes. **9.** 36 s.
**11.** (a) Impossible; (b) $2b/\lambda$, likely. **13.** 4.54 a.m.

**Ex. E 1.** (a) $3x^2/2y$; (b) $2x/\cos y$; (c) $-1/(3x^2y^2)$; (d) $3x^2y$;
(e) $\cos x/3(y - 1)^2$.

**Ex. F 1.** (a) $s = kt$; (b) $2y^3 = 3x^2 + c$; (c) $1/x = c - \frac{1}{2}t^2$;
(d) $2(v + 1)^{\frac{1}{2}} = \ln t + c$; (e) $\ln y = x + \cos x + c$; (f) $\frac{1}{3}y^3 = x^{\frac{1}{2}} + c$.
**3.** (a) −; (b) $\ln(7 - 5y) = c - 5x$; (c) $y = \tan(\frac{1}{2}x^2 + c)$;
(e) $y^2 = 20x - x^2 + c$. **7.** $1·03\times 10^7 N_0$.

**Ex. G 1.** (a) 3; (b) 1, 2; (c) 4. **3.** (a) $y = Ae^{-3x} + 8$,
$y = 8 - 8e^{-3x}$; (b) $y = Ae^{-2x} + x - 4$, $y = 4e^{-2x} + x - 4$.
**5.** (a) $y = Ae^{-5x} + \frac{3}{5}$; (b) $y = Ae^{-5x/2} - 4e^{-3x}$;
(c) $y = Ae^{-x} + \frac{1}{10}(\sin 3x - 3\cos 3x)$; (d) $y = Ae^{-2x} + \frac{1}{2}x^2 - \frac{1}{2}x + \frac{1}{4}$;
(e) $y = Ae^{-x/2} + \frac{1}{5}$. **7.** $y = (3x + c)e^{4x}$. **9.** 241 000.
**11.** (b) $v = 10(1 - e^{-3t})$, $x = 10t - \frac{10}{3}(1 - e^{-3t})$; (c) 10 cm/s, no.

ANSWERS

**Ex. H**   **1.** $1 \cdot 15 \times 10^{-2}$ s.    **3.** (a) 10 V;   (b) $5 \times 10^{-6}$ A;
(c) $2 \cdot 23 \times 10^{-7}$ coulombs.    **5.** $(L \ln 2)/R$.    **7.** $1 \cdot 66 \times 10^{-3}$.

  **Misc.**   **1.** (a) $x = Ae^{-3t} + 5$;   (c) $x = Ae^{-4t} + \frac{5}{4}t^2 - \frac{5}{8}t + \frac{5}{32}$;
(e) $x = Ae^{-5t} + \frac{5}{29}\cos 2t + \frac{2}{29}\sin 2t$;   (g) $\ln(1-x^2) = c - 2t$;
(i) $x = Ae^t + \frac{1}{2}t^2 e^t$;   (k) $x = Ae^t + t - 3$.    **7.** (a) $x = (ct+k)e^{-at}$;
(b) $x = (A\cos bt + B\sin bt)e^{-at}$;   (c) $x = (Ae^{bt} + Be^{-bt})e^{-at}$.
**9.** $y = Ae^{-x}$; $(1, 3 \cdot 46)$, $(2, 1 \cdot 74)$.

# CHAPTER 39

**Ex. A**   **3.** (a) $\pm 0 \cdot 577$;   (b) $\pm 0 \cdot 880$;   (c) $\pm 0 \cdot 707$;   (d) $\pm \frac{1}{2}\pi$.

**Ex. B**   **1.** $2 \cdot 494, 2 \cdot 507$.

**Ex. C**   **3.** $0 \cdot 155$.    **7.** $0 \cdot 933$.    **9.** $0 \cdot 03$.    **11.** $4 \cdot 5$ days.
**13.** $0 \cdot 78$ months, 99.    **15.** (a) 49;   (b) 52;   (c) 9.
**17.** About 1580, 85.

**Ex. D**   **1.** $0 \cdot 184$;   (a) $0 \cdot 005$;   (c) negligible.    **3.** (a) $0 \cdot 081$;
(b) $0 \cdot 095$;   9 or 10.    **5.** $0 \cdot 053$.    **7.** (a) $0 \cdot 006$;   (b) $0 \cdot 013$.
**9.** (a) $0 \cdot 06$;   (b) $0 \cdot 096$.

**Ex. E**   **1.** $0 \cdot 164$, no.    **3.** Just reasonable at 5% level.
**5.** 5% level: at least 61;   1%: 65.    **7.** 270 at 1% level.

**Ex. F**   **1.** 56%–74%.    **3.** 24%–37%.    **7.** 24%–36%.
**9.** Quadruple.

**Ex. G**   **1.** 750 g, 625.    **5.** $0 \cdot 038$.    **7.** $0 \cdot 136$.    **9.** $0 \cdot 04$.

# CHAPTER 40

**Ex. A**   **1.** $\begin{pmatrix} 1 & 0 \\ -2 & 1 \end{pmatrix}$;   $\mathbf{i} + 2\mathbf{j}$;   2;   2.    **3.** (i) 18;   (ii) $|ad - bc|$.
**5.** $bc$.

**Ex. B**   **1.** (i) $-2$;   (ii) 0.    **3.** 4.

**Ex. C**   **1.** (a) $x = -2\lambda, y = -\lambda, z = \lambda$;   (b) $\begin{pmatrix} x \\ y \\ z \end{pmatrix} = \begin{pmatrix} 1 \\ -3 \\ 0 \end{pmatrix} + \lambda \begin{pmatrix} -2 \\ -1 \\ 1 \end{pmatrix}$;

(c) $\begin{pmatrix} p-q+r \\ 2p+q+5r \\ p+2r \end{pmatrix}$.    **3.** (a) (i) $x + 2y - z = 7$,

(ii) $\begin{pmatrix} x \\ y \\ z \end{pmatrix} = \begin{pmatrix} 7 \\ 0 \\ 0 \end{pmatrix} + \lambda \begin{pmatrix} 1 \\ 0 \\ 1 \end{pmatrix} + \mu \begin{pmatrix} -2 \\ 1 \\ 0 \end{pmatrix}$;   (b) $\begin{pmatrix} x \\ y \\ z \end{pmatrix} = k \begin{pmatrix} 1 \\ 2 \\ 5 \end{pmatrix}$.

**5.** All;   line of points; $\begin{pmatrix} x \\ y \\ z \end{pmatrix} = \begin{pmatrix} 1 \\ 1 \\ 0 \end{pmatrix} + \lambda \begin{pmatrix} 1 \\ 1 \\ 2 \end{pmatrix}$;   $7E_1 + 3E_2 - 4E_3 = 0$.

1128

**Ex. D** **1.** (a) $\begin{pmatrix} x \\ y \\ z \end{pmatrix} = \begin{pmatrix} 1 \\ 1 \\ 0 \end{pmatrix} + \lambda \begin{pmatrix} -2 \\ -1 \\ 1 \end{pmatrix}$. **3.** Prism. **5.** (a) Prism;

(b) $2x - z = 0$.

**Misc.** **1.** No; no. **3.** $\begin{pmatrix} \lambda \\ \lambda \\ -\lambda \end{pmatrix}, \begin{pmatrix} x \\ y \\ z \end{pmatrix} = \begin{pmatrix} 3 \\ 0 \\ 0 \end{pmatrix} + \lambda \begin{pmatrix} 1 \\ 1 \\ -1 \end{pmatrix}$. **7.** $1, 2, -3$.

**9.** 2 or 4; $\lambda \begin{pmatrix} 1 \\ -1 \end{pmatrix}$ or $\mu \begin{pmatrix} 1 \\ 1 \end{pmatrix}$.

## REVISION EXERCISES

**Rev. 37.** **1.** 4 V. **5.** $\frac{6}{7} \Omega$; 13·2 W.

**Rev. 38** **1.** (a) $y = \frac{5}{2}x^2 + k$; (c) $v = 1/3(k - t)$;
(e) $Q = Ae^{-t/10} + 20$. **3.** $y = \exp(-x^2)$. **5.** $q = 2e^{-t}(1 - e^{-t})$.

**Rev. 39** **1.** (a) 2·3%; (b) 0·34. **3.** (i) $2 \times 10^{-10}$; (ii) 0·0044;
$x = 73$. **5.** 0·0009, 0·063.

**Rev. 40** **1.** $(x, y, z) = (-1 - 8\lambda, 2 + 9\lambda, 5\lambda)$. **3.** $x = 4\lambda - 1$,
$y = -\lambda, z = 9 - 3\lambda$.

# INDEX